DISCARD

THE ENCYCLOPEDIA OF
GLOBAL POPULATION
AND DEMOGRAPHICS

VOLUME 1   Afghanistan ∎ Italy

THE ENCYCLOPEDIA OF
GLOBAL POPULATION
AND DEMOGRAPHICS

VOLUME 1   Afghanistan ▪ Italy

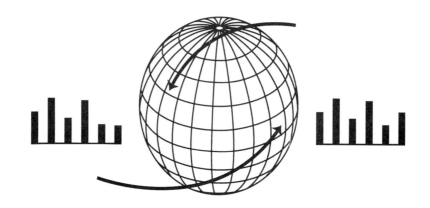

IMMANUEL NESS

Brooklyn College, City University of New York

JAMES CIMENT

New School University

SHARPE REFERENCE

an imprint of M.E. Sharpe, Inc.

SHARPE REFERENCE

Sharpe Reference is an imprint of M.E. Sharpe INC.

M.E. Sharpe INC.
80 Business Park Drive
Armonk, NY 10504

Library of Congress Cataloging-in-Publication Data

Ness, Immanuel.
The encyclopedia of global population and demographics / Immanuel Ness, James Ciment.
p. cm.
Includes bibliographical references.
ISBN 1-56324-710-0 (set: alk. paper)
1. Demography—Encyclopedias. 2. Population—Statistics—Encyclopedias.
I. Ciment, James. II. Title.
HB871.N43 1999
304.6'03—dc21
98-46436
CIP

Printed and bound in the United States of America

The paper used in this publication meets the minimum requirements of American National Standard for Information Sciences—Permanence of Paper for Printed Library Materials,
ANSI Z 39.48-1984.

(BM) 10 9 8 7 6 5 4 3 2 1

Evelyn M. Fazio
VP & Publisher

Carmen Chetti
VP & Production Director

Angela Piliouras
Senior Production Editor

Aud Thiessen
Editorial Coordinator

Elizabeth Granda
Editorial Assistant for Graphics

Esther Clark
Patricia Loo
Editorial Assistants

Debra Soled
Technical Advisor

Wilford Bryan Lammers
Yolanda Gavaghan
In-house Typesetters

Lee Goldstein
Cover Design

Monique Widyono
Fact Checker

Contents

Volume Two

Acknowledgments

The authors are grateful to the many individuals who made this project a success. In particular, we received valuable guidance and help from officials, librarians, and researchers at the United Nations and its member agencies, who provided valuable material, assistance, and direction for the gathering of our reference and data sources. In researching and writing this encyclopedia, we received invaluable help from Clare Newman, who helped us with the enormous task of organizing the tables and assembling the data. We would like to thank Evelyn Fazio, who saw the need for such an immense work on the state of humanity at the turn of the century, for advising us on the content of these volumes. On the production side, we would like to thank Angela Piliouras for managing this project by coordinating the copy editors, graphic artists, printers, and the authors. We also thank Aud Thiessen for her suggestions, and Esther Clark for helping to organize and prepare the manuscript for production.

Immanuel Ness
James D. Ciment

Part One

Essays

Introduction to Demography

THE NUMBERS TELL THE STORY

The numbers in this reference tell a story or, more accurately, two stories. The very title of this resource, *The Encyclopedia of Global Population and Demographics*, offers a clue to these narratives. The term *demography* come from two Greek words: *demo* (people) and *graph* (written record). This book, then, offers a written record of humanity—specifically, of human population.

The stories are alarming. The first concerns a species that has increasingly overcome the causes of death, and is paying the price for its selective achievement of growth. It is no secret that the population of planet Earth is increasing at an awesome and, perhaps, even unsustainable pace for one very simple reason. Death increasingly has been delayed, especially among the young, the vulnerable, and the potentially fertile, because of improved diet, better awareness of personal and public hygiene, and advances in medicine. At the same time, births continue to increase, particularly in the less economically developed and less-educated societies.

The consequences of this dichotomy are already evident, as seen most concisely in the timeline graph on page 4. In the ten thousand years from the discovery of agriculture to the beginnings of the industrial revolution, the human population increased from about 15 million to 800 million, that is, roughly doubling every fifteen hundred years.

Between 1750 and 1945—when World War II ended, and the great medical and farming advances of the postwar era began—the world's population doubled every 122 years. By the end

of that period, the total had swelled to some 2.5 billion. In the fifty-five years since then, it has doubled, totaling nearly 6 billion people

For anyone concerned about the future of the planet and the future of humanity, the upward line shown in the graph appears as frightening as a nuclear mushroom cloud, and potentially as destructive. Not surprisingly, the best book ever written on the subject of demography was entitled *The Population Bomb*.

The second story told by the essays and tables in this book relates less to the quantity of human beings on Earth and more to the quality of their lives. Specifically, the enormous amount of resources consumed by the so-called first, or developed, world has an inordinately heavy impact on the planet's environment as well as on humanity's ability to nourish itself, since part of the high-consumption life-style of developed-world residents includes the consumption of meat—cultivation of which requires far more land than does a vegetarian diet—and excessive use of water.

Equally troubling is the fact that most developing world inhabitants and governments are busily striving to move toward developed world standards of living; a goal that is understandable—given the misery in which much of the world's population lives and the ubiquity of developed world–controlled mass media, with its high-consumption messages and imagery—albeit destructive.

In *The Population Explosion*—Paul and Anne Ehrlich's sequel to Paul Ehrlich's *The Population Bomb*—the authors offer a simple equation to calculate the effects of the high-consumption standard of living currently enjoyed by the developed world and aspired to by the developing world: (Environmental) impact = population × affluence × technology, or I = PAT. (Although the definition of "affluence" is relatively straightforward in the equation—referring, roughly, to level of consumption—defining technology is a bit trickier. The authors are referring not to the amount but to the type of technology: Heating bath water with an oil burner has a greater impact on the environment and depletion of resources than doing it with solar panels.)

Thus, while this equation can be used to calculate hundreds of permutations of the environmental impact of the various elements, the equation inherently yields two basic messages. Small rises in population in high-consumption societies—such as the United States—have disproportionately large impacts on the environment, as do relatively small hikes in the level of consumption in high-population societies such as China.

As awareness of environmental stress and wealth disparities between developed and developing nations have increased in the past thirty years, theorists have tended to cast the central villain in the demographic narrative as either the prolific developing world or the overconsuming developed world.

In fact, there are more than enough "villains" to go around because of the many subplots in the demographic narrative. Deforestation—a particularly urgent environmental problem—illustrates this point. The well-publicized fires in Indonesia in 1997 are now widely believed to have been caused by the burning of rain forests by Indonesian and multinational corporations seeking cheap timber and land (largely to supply products to developed world countries—in this case, Japan). The denuding of forests in the Himalayan foothills—which is less publicized because it is less immediately catastrophic—has been caused by the astronomical population growth among small farmers in India and Nepal.

Of course, environment degradation is just one—albeit perhaps the most important—effect of rapid population growth and unsustainable

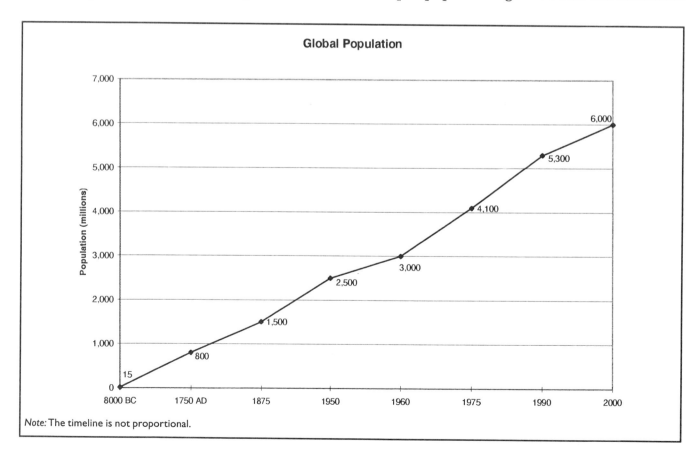

Note: The timeline is not proportional.

levels of consumption. Other issues include public health and hunger. As is true of so much else concerning the demographic narrative of recent decades, the story of public health and hunger is full of multiple ironies, the most obvious of which is the fact that the very gains made in recent years in medicine and agronomy have come to backfire on themselves. That is to say, these public health and agronomic advances have contributed to explosive population growth, which, in turn, undermines the gains already made. The overcrowding caused by the drop in birth rates often leads to public health problems and hunger.

Heavy consumption in the developed world offers the same implicit ironies, as the case of air conditioning makes clear. Because it emits (until recently) large amounts of freon and requires the burning of huge amounts of fossil fuels, air conditioning contributes to both global warming (and thus to hunger, in that global warming is widely believed to increase the likelihood and severity of drought) and ozone depletion (a documented public health problem in the form of increased cases of skin cancer)—two reasons to remain indoors and use even more air conditioning.

Political instability is yet another, even less understood effect of overpopulation and overconsumption. The struggle between the Palestinians and the Israelis offers a relevant case. One of the most important, but least-publicized, disputes between the two sides to this conflict concerns water—specifically, the large aquifer beneath the West Bank that is tapped by both Israelis and Palestinians. Each blames the other for its gradual depletion. The Israeli government argues that explosive population growth among the Palestinians is to blame; Palestinian authorities claim the problem lies in the heavy water-consumption patterns of Israelis.

Finally, as with any tale, the demographic narrative can be understood only if we take several steps back from it to examine the model within which it exists and the terms by which it is conveyed. In other words, the demographic narrative exists within a dominant model that says population growth is bad and economic growth is good. Now that communism has been vanquished on the world stage, the dominant model remains an essentially capitalist one, shaped by experts from the developed world and its dominant institutions like the World Bank: Endless growth is both positive and essential. (Of course, that is not to say that the socialist bloc did not develop its own model also stating that expanding economic output was always good.)

But this model is increasingly being challenged on two fronts. First, the environmental movement has forced people and governments to reconsider humanity's relationship to its planetary home. If endless population growth is unsustainable, how can endless growth in consumption be any different? In other words, can we have limitless growth of any kind on a planet with finite resources?

The second and more nuanced challenge to the existing model comes from the more radical population experts of the developing world: It is not so much economic growth per se that is unsustainable as its unequal distribution among the world's peoples. By means of the exploitative economic order, dominated by developed world–based multinational corporations and enforced by the various international lending and aid agencies, developing-world societies have no choice but to pursue economic agendas that further impoverish their own people.

In Colombia, for example, highly productive farmland has been taken from peasants and given over to plantations that supply cheap flowers for developed world countries, especially those in North America. In other words, various parts of Colombia are experiencing a shortage of land for growing food that has little to do with the country's growing population. Moreover, the displaced peasantry inevitably flocks to urban areas, causing public health problems in the areas to which they migrate. Thus, in many poorer countries (except in certain selective and obvious cases like overcrowded Bangladesh), it is not overpopulation alone that is destroying environments and leading to the degradation of human life, but rather the exploitation of the resources and labor of those societies to support developed world consumption patterns.

At the same time, both developed-world environmentalists and developing-world demographers have been challenging the terms in which the dominant demographic and economic narrative of recent decades is conveyed. Take, they say, the most important conventional measure of economic progress—gross domestic product, or the total value of goods and services created by a nation-state. Environmentalists say it masks the true costs of economic growth by ignoring or devaluing that growth's impact on the environment and human health. For example, if a country burns more petroleum for transport, heating, or industry, this is measured as economic progress, while the health problems (rising rates of respiratory disease, for instance) and environmental costs are dismissed or underestimated.

Developing-world demographics add an additional spin by pointing out that much of the cost of economic "progress" is borne by the more poverty-stricken societies on Earth or by the poorest and least-represented elements within a given nation-state. Because they have inadequate access to health care, they are more likely to suffer from the effects of increased air pollution. Moreover, they suffer the consequences without gaining the benefits. While the tiny middle and upper classes of developing-world societies gain increased mobility from the burning of hydrocarbons for transportation via automobiles, the poor do not. The same pattern operates on a global scale, as countries that are low consumers of hydrocarbon suffer from the effects of increased consumption of petroleum worldwide—in the form of global warming—while gaining few if any of the benefits of burning those hydrocarbons.

Finally, both developed-world environmentalists and developing-world demographers point out that the very category of measurement—the nation-state—offers a flawed statistical view of reality. As the former point out, exploitation of the natural environment creates effects that do not respect borders and thus must be considered in a global context. Regionwide droughts, partly caused by global warming, are felt in the American Midwest and the African Sahel alike (though, of course, the human costs to the latter—where inhabitants exist much closer to the margins of life—are far greater).

For developing-world critics of the dominant model, or paradigm, the nation-state as a standard of measurement is flawed for two reasons. First, this conception often lays the blame in the wrong place for the human degradation caused by overpopulation and environmental destruction and does so in several ways. It fails to recognize the powerlessness of developing-world governments in the face of pressure from pro-export multinational corporations and international lending institutions. It ignores the fact that many unpopular developing-world governments—which fail to serve their own people's needs—are essentially kept in power by the same multinational institutions that are exploiting their societies (or have been trained to think in terms conducive to those institutions by being educated at developed-world universities and business schools). Finally, the use of the nation-state as the standard of measurement masks critical internal differences within that country. What does it mean when a country like Chile, for example, boasts rising income levels at a time of increasing polarization of wealth?

This encyclopedia both succumbs to these shortcomings and attempts to overcome them. Like any compendium of statistics, this work includes tables that rely on existing sources of data, which both emphasize standard measurements of economic progress and catalog them by nation-state. At the same time, the nine essays in Part One analyze those numbers based on the critique offered by both developed-world environmental leaders and developing-world demographic experts.

Before turning to these contemporary debates, let us, then, begin with a history of demographic ideas or theories.

A HISTORY OF DEMOGRAPHIC DOCTRINE AND THOUGHT

Pre-Malthusian Thinkers

Since ancient times, philosophers have considered the two basic questions of demography:

What causes population growth or decline, and what are the consequences? Their thinking clearly emphasized the latter. The Western tradition, at least, has usually attributed population growth or decline to forces beyond human control and comprehension—an act of the gods pleased or displeased by human individual and group behavior.

Because of the isolated nature of early civilization and the vast open spaces in the world, until modern times those considering the consequences of population change obviously lacked a global perspective. Thus various societies examined the question only in light of their own immediate circumstances. In his work *The Laws*, Plato wrote that a healthy society should place a greater importance on the quality of life than on the quantity of lives. Given the lack of space and fertile land in ancient Greece, this perspective should not be surprising nor should the more expansive Roman government's emphasis on population growth policies.

In the early Middle Ages, the prevalent philosophy was the opposite of that of pro-growth Roman doctrine. The collapse of ancient civilization and the barbarity of life in the Dark Ages led early Christian thinkers to emphasize the relative unimportance of life in this world. If God and the afterlife were the ultimate reasons for life in this world, then removing oneself from the needs and desires of this world was a human duty. Thus, St. Augustine argued, procreation was a less godly path than abstinence.

As in so much else, the late medieval thinker Thomas Aquinas contradicted early Christian thought, contending that marriage and procreation were as godly a path as celibacy. Aquinas's thinking on the subject prefigured Protestant thinkers who believed that the individual's achievements in this world foretold his or her existence in the next. Procreation, like hard work, was a means of achieving a more godly order on this Earth as well as a place in heaven, two objectives that were no longer seen as mutually exclusive.

As one might expect in such a religious age, secular thinkers reflected sacred ones. The first great school of political economic thought in modern times—mercantilism—emphasized the importance of expansion. Since a given political entity increased its power and wealth by capturing more resources—including human resources—population growth was only to the good. Mercantile thinking arose at a time when Europe was undergoing great physical expansion not only by expanding outward but by newly exploiting lands from marshes and forests through the power of commercial endeavor and as a consequence of growing population.

By the mid-eighteenth century, it was becoming clear that population growth often led to more human misery, especially as the movement to incorporate common land into commercial holdings spread—beginning in England in the seventeenth century and accelerating in the eighteenth century. The mercantilist notion that all growth—territorial, human, or otherwise—was good came into increasing disrepute among a group of thinkers known as the physiocrats.

The antimercantilist English economist Adam Smith came to the conclusion in the late eighteenth century that land—not people—was the source of wealth and power. Economic growth—through the better commercial exploitation of land and other natural resources—was a prerequisite for population growth. In fact, he argued, the two were always in natural harmony since population size was determined by demand for labor, which was, in turn, determined by the productivity of land. This was, of course, part of his overall assault on mercantilist political doctrine promoting economic direction by the state. Governments, he implied, should not have a doctrine of limiting population.

This was essentially a positive doctrine since it offered a conceptual path out of the dilemma that increasing population would necessarily lead to increasing misery. Taking this even further, scholars like the Marquis de Condorcet and William Godwin added technology to the equation. Scientific understanding, they claimed, would increase the productivity of land and thereby create increased wealth, which would lead to better education. As people became more aware of their situation, they would come to understand that limiting fertility promised them a way of ensuring that population growth never outstripped increased productivity. Indeed, Godwin believed that the first part of this equation—increasing productivity—was already occuring, but was masked from view by social inequities in which the few consumed more than the many.

Malthus and the Neo-Malthusians

All these thinkers were less concerned about how population grew or shrank—at least, in the real world—than about the consequences of that change. The Reverend Thomas Malthus, an English college professor, offered the first theoretical inquiry into the first basic question of demography. According to Malthus's theory—first published in 1798—humanity has two basic needs: to feed itself and to reproduce. Both, he said, were incontrovertible and unchanging.

Thus, as long as there was sufficient food, population would grow at a geometric pace, that is, it would constantly double. Food production, however, can grow only in arithmetic fashion since nature has been somewhat stingy in the availability of fertile land. "A slight acquaintance with the first," he laconically noted, "will shew [show] the immensity of the first power in comparison with the second." Given an unlimited source of food and unlimited space, he concluded, humanity "would fill millions of worlds in the course of a few thousand years." That it obviously doesn't, he said, was due to "positive checks"—those measures "whether of a moral or physical nature, which tend prematurely to weaken and destroy the human frame." Disease, war, starvation, accidents—what modern demographers refer to as "causes of mortality."

Seemingly fatalistic about increasing human population and the immiseration of life, Malthus offered a way out: "preventive checks," or limits on birth. Although current Malthusian believers condone various kinds of checks—such as contraception and abortion (infanticide is largely shunned in Western society, though it has been practiced in certain island cultures where land

limitations are most apparent)—Malthus advocated but one: "moral restraint," or abstinence.

Indeed, the willingness to accept contraception and abortion is the main difference between Malthus and his intellectual successors, for example, the Ehrlichs. In a chapter of *The Population Explosion* entitled "The Bang, the Whimper, and the Alternative," they argue that if humanity does not voluntarily employ such Malthusian "preventive checks," human nature or the natural world will impose "positive" ones. These include "the bang," a nuclear war caused by the tensions inherent in an overpopulated world (less likely with the demise of the Cold War or perhaps more likely with the current arms race on the Indian subcontinent) or "the whimper," a gradual collapse of our ecosystem.

Malthus was not very optimistic, citing the natural propensity to reproduce as almost impossible to overcome. Neither are today's neo-Malthusians, who offer a more sophisticated gloss on this idea. Human beings, they say, evolved brains and intellect best able to cope with immediate and proximate dangers, since they comprised the majority of the threats to continued existence during most of our prehistory. Long-term, less-immediate problems (most obviously, overpopulation), which are less discernible on a daily basis, are usually ignored.

To be fair, most thoughtful neo-Malthusians argue—as Malthus himself did, though it is rarely mentioned in discussions of his theory—that a redistribution of wealth and more social equity are prerequisites for implementing preventive checks on growth. The poverty caused by an unequal social order, Malthus argued, kept the masses ignorant of their own good—that is, of the necessity for "moral restraint."

Neo-Malthusians, with their eyes on the nuclear and environmental clock, note that continued high levels of consumption by developed world societies allow neither the time nor the motivation for "preventive" measures to take effect. Using the $I = PAT$ equation, they note that overconsumption may overwhelm the planet before the current demographic momentum (that is, population continuing to increase for a time after effective preventive measures take effect) can be stopped. In addition, they rhetorically ask, why should developing-world societies limit population growth at the behest of overconsuming developed-world countries?

Marxist and Neo-Marxist Perspectives

Both Karl Marx and Friedrich Engels essentially rejected many of the implications of Malthusian population theory, even if they did not discount the theory itself. In short, they had little quarrel with his idea that humanity grew geometrically through the constant impulse to procreate (though they saw no harm in birth control). Where Marx and Engels disagreed with Malthus was in the universality of his theory. Overpopulation, they argued, was a problem only where the social structure was incapable of handling it—specifically, in capitalist societies.

Marx and Engels believed that each society had its own population law. In capitalist societies, unchecked population growth led to poverty and want because the ruling class needed a surplus labor force in which to whip the working class into line. It was not that there were too many people in capitalist societies but that there were too many poor, a direct consequence of stripping land and control over the means of production away from workers. In fact, the very basis of the Marxist theory of surplus value bolstered their point since, in a capitalist system, workers always produced more value than they received in wages. If that was so, how could overpopulation be the cause of poverty?

Conversely, they argued, in socialist societies, overpopulation would not be a problem because its application of a "scientific" approach to humanity, new technologies, and the use of natural resources would guarantee that both population growth and production would grow in sync with each other and not at odds, as Malthus had argued. Philosophically, Marx and Engels dismissed Malthus's "vile and infamous doctrine" as placing blame on the poor for their own troubles, rather than on the exploitative owners of capital, where it belonged.

The leaders of communist revolutions in the twentieth century instituted policies that reflected these Marxist assumptions. This was the case in underpopulated Russia, as well as in densely populated China. As Mao Zedong argued in the 1950s, "a large population in China is a good thing. With a population increase of several fold we still have an adequate solution. The solution lies in production."

By the 1960s, the increasingly obvious need for birth control in many parts of the world led to a revision of Marxist theory concerning overpopulation. By the 1970s, Chinese officials were arguing that a rational socialist order required planning for population as well as for production. Other Marxist theorists returned to an old physiocratic idea, but with a twist. Condorcet, for one, believed that scientific reasoning would teach people to limit their reproduction for their own good, but socialist education would convince people to do the same for the good of society.

Two neo-Marxist schools of thought have reconsidered the idea of capitalism—not overpopulation—as the cause of human misery in a global context. Both Immanuel Wallerstein in his world system theory and the dependency theorists among Latin American scholars (considering things at a national and regional level) maintain that the inequities of the global economy—specifically, the exploitation of developing world populations by the developed world—are the cause of problems like hunger, war, and public health deterioration, which at first glance appear to be the direct outgrowth of overpopulation.

Indeed, these neo-Marxists argue that just as national capitalist economies maintain a surplus labor force—in order to hold down wages—global capitalism ensures that the developing world remains underdeveloped and therefore a source of both cheap labor and cheap resources. In short, then, overpopulation is not the cause of the continuing impoverishment of much of the world, but rather the result. Lower levels of education and health care induce couples to have more children to assure that some survive.

Table 1.1

Governments and Migration Policy

| Country | Limitations | | Groups | Political factors | Economic factors |
	Immigration	Emigration			
United States	Discourage		Poor persons	Vote-getting issue	Loss of jobs
Israel	Encourage		Jews	Ethnic composition of state	
Brazil	Encourage		Skilled and moneyed		Develop country
East Germany		Discourage	All	Politically embarrassing	Loss of skilled workers
Philippines		Encourage	Young workers		Bring in revenue
Saudi Arabia	Encourage		Skilled		Necessary for running economy
Mexico		Encourage	Poor		Ease economic stress

Interestingly, on this last point, neo-Marxist thinkers share an outlook with certain secular and religious conservatives who argue that the world does not suffer from overpopulation. While the Catholic Church includes a strong critique of the inequitable global economic situation in its attacks on birth control policies, secular conservatives leave the economic question unchallenged, maintaining that increasing the number of human beings increases the number of human minds and thereby the possibility that new ideas will emerge to cope with the problems introduced by increased population.

SETTING POLICY: THE USES OF DEMOGRAPHY

Demography proves useful in many important fields, of which three of the most critical are business, politics, and social and infrastructure planning. For businesses, demography can be used to determine marketing and investment strategies, as well as better use of human resources within a given corporate structure. Politicians can use demographics to help design their campaigns, as well as project the likelihood of support for given legislative programs. These two uses of demography—though important—are not pertinent here. Social planning is, however. Obviously, it would be foolhardy for any institution or government to embark on any kind of

social and infrastructure planning without a consideration of the targeted population. To fail to do so is to guarantee one or both of the following outcomes: a program that fails to have the desired effect, or one that has a harmful effect. Social programs intended to provide health care, education, social services, transportation and communications facilities, and the like require a demographic analysis. Finally, there is the overall question of population growth and fertility itself.

International organizations like the United Nations and its agencies, such as the United Nations Population Fund, and international financial institutions, such as the World Bank, as well as many national governments, recognize the need for population policies. In most cases, this recognition leads to attempts at limiting growth, though, in some European countries with zero or negative population growth, population policies are often directed at increasing population growth or maintaining it at its current level.

Governments and institutions can implement population policies in one of three ways: by influencing mortality (or death), by influencing fertility, or by influencing migration.

Of the three, the first is the least acceptable politically, socially, and morally. No institution could openly advocate increasing mortality levels to produce drops in population. Still, this approach is not entirely taboo. Nongovernmental organizations and international agencies are often forced to make critical decisions about where to utilize scarce funds and resources. Like doctors in war or after natural disasters, they are forced to apply their skills, time, and energy on those cases that show the best chances of survival. This is known as triage and can lead to charges of covert racism when, for example, the world community chooses to send peacekeepers to a European country like Bosnia but not to an African one such as Rwanda, thereby condoning higher mortality rates in the latter.

Migration is a more palatable way of dealing with population problems, though one that often creates geopolitical problems. As a direct or even indirect social policy, migration is multifaceted. A government might want to limit its country's population growth by encouraging emigration or by discouraging immigration. Conversely, a government might encourage population growth by opening the country's gates to immigrants or by limiting emigration. Usually, but not always, limitations on immigration or emigration involve factors other than population growth and concern various population sectors. Table 1 offers some examples.

Ultimately, the most efficacious and widely used population programs involve efforts to limit—or, in rare cases, encourage—fertility. Fertility programs take three different forms: direct, indirect, and coercive. The most common—especially in developing countries where the population situation is most critical—are direct methods, such as spreading the use of contraceptives, educating the public in their use, promoting voluntary sterilization programs, or, in the case of some former members of the socialist bloc, providing cheap and easily obtained abortions. This latter policy was often an outgrowth of these planned economies' inability to produce and distribute enough contraceptive devices.

Indirect methods vary between those countries attempting to promote and those trying to discourage fertility. In some European countries suffering from low, zero, or negative population growth, governments actively encourage larger families by offering financial incentives, sometimes in the form of tax waivers and sometimes in the form of subsidies. In developing countries, indirect methods occasionally include economic incentives as well, but usually involve expanding educational resources. In recent years, for example, the United Nations has stressed the education of women as the best means of limiting fertility since educated women—aside from being more aware of contraceptive options—are more likely to see the benefits of smaller families. An even less direct method, supported by some, is simply the promotion of economic growth or, more usefully, economic growth and equity, which help limit fertility because better-situated families often have fewer children.

Coercive methods have been employed in the most desperate situations or, at least, in those countries where the government both perceives the need and has the capacity to implement such policies. The governments of China and Singapore are prime examples: They both use negative economic incentives—including fines and higher taxes—to discourage fertility. In addition, some experts' reports—denied by the Chinese government—claim that the measures have become truly coercive, in the form of forced abortions and sterilizations, particularly in the countryside. At the same time, the coercive policies of the Chinese government have had an unintended and unfortunate side effect. Since the government's population goal was the extremely ambitious zero population growth by 2000, single-child families were promoted as the ideal. The result was the infanticide of first-born children if they turned out to be girls, since sons are more highly valued in Chinese culture.

In short, as this book makes clear, the world faces a dual problem of the highest order. Citizens of developed countries continue to consume resources at an unsustainable pace, while citizens in many, though not all, developing countries continue to reproduce at unsustainable rates. Because they are resentful of developed-country lecturing and bitter over past and current exploitation, neo-Marxist, developing world–influenced population experts remain focused on the inequities of the global economic order. Because they are fearful that the environment's ability to function will be overwhelmed and the planet's capacity to feed its increasing numbers will be compromised (in addition, say third worlders, to having racist fears of the "dark" races overwhelming the Caucasians), neo-Malthusian, developed world–influenced scholars emphasize the need for population control in the developing world. As this work makes clear, both sides may be right.

FURTHER READING

Abernathy, Virginia. *Population Politics: The Choices That Shape Our Future.* New York: Insight Books, 1993.

Appleman, Philip, ed. *Thomas Robert Malthus: An Essay on the Principle of Population.* New York. W.W. Norton, 1976.

Ehrlich, Paul. *The Population Bomb.* New York: Ballantine, 1968.

Ehrlich, Paul, and Anne Ehrlich. *The Population Explosion.* New York: Simon and Schuster, 1990.

Lancaster, Henry O. *Expectations of Life: A Study in the Demography, Statistics, and History of World Mortality.* New York: Springer-Verlag, 1990.

Menard, Scott W., and Elizabeth W. Moen. *Perspectives on Population: An Introduction to Concepts and Issues.* New York: Oxford University Press, 1987.

Neurath, Paul. *From Malthus to the Club of Rome and Back: Problems of Limits to Growth, Population Control, and Migrations.* Armonk, NY: M.E. Sharpe, 1994.

Sen, Armartya, and Martha Nussbaum, eds. *The Quality of Life.* New York: Oxford University Press, 1993.

Valentey, D.I., ed. *The Theory of Population: Essays in Marxist Research.* Moscow: Progress Publishers, 1978.

Weeks, John. *Population: An Introduction to Concepts and Issues.* 3d ed. Belmont, CA: Wadsworth, 1986.

Yaukey, David. *Demography: The Study of Human Population.* New York: St. Martin's Press, 1985.

Demography, Resources, and the Environment

Almost everyone has seen a version of the political cartoon showing a long-haired, scraggly-bearded, doom-saying eccentric standing on a street holding a sign that reads: "The End Is Near." This show of unreasoning pessimism—this doomsday man—is usually an object of ridicule.

Yet, as we all know, there is a good deal of truth in his dark prediction. At the heart of the demographic problem facing modern humanity is a simple two-horned dilemma: how to ensure unending economic growth for an ever-increasing population on a planet with finite resources, and how to avoid burying ourselves in the endless waste that is an inevitable byproduct of this growth. This section examines both problems.

RESOURCE EXPLOITATION AND ENVIRONMENTAL POLLUTION

Through most of human history, it has been assumed that the Earth offered an inexhaustible supply of resources and, given the limited human population during most of that period, this was a reasonable assumption to make. But the commercial and industrial revolutions that began in Western Europe in the 1600s and 1700s, and spread to much of the rest of the world by the 1800s and 1900s, changed all that—the first by establishing an economic system requiring perpetual growth, and the second by developing the technology to sustain that growth through the ever-increasing exploitation of natural resources.

In their book *The Population Explosion*, Paul and Anne Ehrlich refer to what they call "the one-time bonanza," the fact that billions of years of geological history and hundreds of millions of years of biological history have deposited a vast treasure trove of resources for humanity to use, much like a balance in a savings account. The problem is that humanity, instead of living off the interest—that is, through the sustainable use of resources—is dipping deeply into the principal. Through overexploitation—caused by economic growth, consumption and rapidly increasing population levels—humanity is using up in decades what it took the planet hundreds of millions of years to create.

Two examples of these resources are petroleum and arable land. Humanity first began significantly to exploit the former of these about a century ago. Even the most optimistic estimate for existing and potentially recoverable reserves gives us no more than a hundred more years of exploitation, at currently expanding rates of use. That is, a resource that took nature hundreds of millions of years to accumulate will most likely be used up in two hundred years, a blink of an eye in geological time.

As for soil, it has been estimated by Lester Brown, an agricultural and environmental economist at the Worldwatch Institute, that every year some 25 billion more tons of topsoil are lost globally because of harmful agricultural methods than are being created naturally. The primacy of land to almost any discussion of resource depletion makes that a good place to start.

Land

Of the roughly 200 million square miles that make up planet Earth, approximately a third, or 60 million square miles, are land. Of this, about 33 percent is forest and woodland, 25 percent is meadow and pastureland, and 10 percent is arable (that is, land suited for intensive agriculture). The other 30 percent or so is icecap, tundra, high mountains, desert, and other lands incapable of sustaining more than minimal permanent human settlements.

It is estimated that at least 400 square miles of arable land are required to feed a population of 1 million, assuming that this population consumes a basic, vegetarian diet. Multiplying this figure by the roughly 6 billion people alive today, it can be roughly calculated that humanity requires 2.4 million square miles or approximately 40 percent of all arable land. At first glance, this would seem to imply that humanity could grow another 150 percent—to some 15 billion—before reaching the limits of arable land. Indeed, the 1988 anti–birth control Catholic encyclical, *Humanae Vitae*, argued that the world's arable land was capable of supporting 40 billion people.

True or not, this is based on several questionable assumptions, the first of which was the underlying insistence that all lands currently or potentially suitable for agriculture would stay that way. But approximately 2 percent of all land—much of it arable—is already paved over or used in some way to house or otherwise service humanity. Multiplying the population by a factor of twenty would obviously increase significantly the amount of land devoted to villages, cities, and other areas of human habitation.

In addition, there is the problem of desertification, a process by which arable land is rendered into unusable desert through climate change (greenhouse gas production, or carbon dioxide that traps the sun's heat in the atmosphere), overgrazing and soil compaction (too many animals in too small an area), erosion (poor

land management), salinization (making soil saltier through overdrilling of wells), and land poisoning (runoffs of industrial and agricultural chemicals). All of these, of course, are the direct result of either too many people in a given area or unsustainable agricultural practices.

According to the United Nations, over the past half-century, approximately 13 million square miles of arable land (four times the entire area of the United States) have lost one-quarter of their productivity, another 6 million square miles have lost half their productivity, and some 80,000 square miles (half the size of California) have been rendered entirely useless by desertification. Overall, approximately 250 million people—largely in the developing world—have been affected. Nor is this problem entirely new. Historians—often using texts from ancient philosophers—believe that much of the territory of Greece was made into semidesert by the overgrazing of goats thousands of years ago.

But what of moving to new lands, such as the forests or pasturelands that constitute nearly 60 percent of the land mass of the planet? Surely, this would offer humanity a virtually inexhaustible source of new lands to farm. First, this assumes that these lands are suitable for farming. But much of the pastureland is far too arid for agriculture, unless suitable irrigation is employed, which presents a problem of overexploitation of water resources (see the following section on water).

As for forests, many of them—particularly in the tropics—are not suitable for sustained agriculture. Belying their luxuriousness, many of these forests actually exist on extremely poor and thin soils that quickly lose their nutrients after a few years of farming. Deforestation is caused both by corporate economic exploitation—driven by the insatiable appetite for wood and paper in the developed world—and by rapidly expanding populations of small farmers in the developing world.

Moreover, deforestation has other negative effects on the land. The loss of forests can lead to serious erosion downstream in the short term—as the loss of root structure leads to rapid runoff, especially during heavy tropical down-pours—and global warming in the long term. Global warming occurs when carbon dioxide builds up in the atmosphere, trapping sunlight and heat in a phenomenon scientists call the "greenhouse effect." And, forests absorb massive quantities of carbon dioxide and produce oxygen in its place. Thus, deforestation leads to a build-up of carbon dioxide and, hence, global warming.

Ultimately, global warming may have a catastrophic effect on low-lying areas around the globe since, as the average global temperature increases, more of the ice at the poles melts. While it is difficult to predict an exact correlation between temperature increases and rising ocean levels, we do know that sea level was nearly 300 feet lower during the last ice age, when global temperatures were roughly 5 to 10 degrees Fahrenheit colder than they are now. Meanwhile, it is commonly accepted among climate experts that average global temperatures have risen about 3 degrees farenheit in the past 100 or so years of the industrial age. Whether this is part of a natural cycle or caused by the burning of fossil fuels by humankind is debatable, though most scientists believe human activity plays an increasingly significant role in global warming.

Rising ocean levels will permanently flood such heavily populated and agriculturally rich areas as Bangladesh, Florida, Rio de la Plata (Argentina), the Netherlands, the Nile Delta, and others (see the section on climate). Deforestation also leads to the mass extinction of plant and animal life, since forests—especially in the tropics—tend to sustain the highest number of species. The trend toward more rapid extinction of species can be seen in both the developed and developing world. In the former, this is largely due to pollution and, in the latter, to loss of habitat, though both causes are evident everywhere. A sampling of countries gives a sense of the scale of the loss. In tropical Cameroon, it was estimated in 1994 that some 62 individual species of animals alone were threatened; in arid Tunisia, 15; Arctic Canada, 43; temperate Chile, 91; is-

land-based Madagascar, 99; highly industrialized France, 109; and largely undeveloped Haiti, 26. Nor is species destruction a mere sentimental loss, confined to those who love nature. The extinction of an animal or plant species reduces the genetic resources of the planet, depriving humanity of potential life-saving drugs and other critical items. While there have been massive species die-offs at various times over millions of years, the current one is the first since the appearance of the human species 3 million years ago. And whereas past die-offs are believed to have had specific causes like changes in the sun-spot cycle or asteroid impacts, the current die-off will go on and on until humanity changes its habit of spewing out ever greater quantities of carbon dioxide and destroying carbon dioxide-absorbing forests.

In short, to paraphrase President Franklin D. Roosevelt, in office during the Dust Bowl era of the 1930s, one of America's worst soil-based environmental catastrophes, a people that destroys its soil destroys itself.

Water

Although water covers about two-thirds of the planet's surface, most of it is unusable because of its salt content. Current desalinization techniques are both expensive and extremely energy-intensive. The costs in dollars and fuel make the process feasible only in countries where water is in very short supply and oil is plentiful—namely, the Persian Gulf countries. In short, humanity is—for the foreseeable future—restricted to existing freshwater sources.

In the United States, the world's largest agricultural country, water is being pumped out of the ground far more rapidly than it can be replenished. The Ogallala aquifer in the Midwest—the largest underground source in the country—is replenished at a rate of about 2 inches annually. But current pumping drops the level by as much as 4 to 6 feet a year. Because the Midwest is supplying much of the grain necessary both to feed many parts of the developing world and provide feed for cattle consumed in the developed world, aquifer depletion is expected to grow in coming years, especially if droughts, which many scientists believe are caused by global warming, continue.

Nor is the United States alone in the problem of aquifer depletion. China and India—the two most populous countries in the world—have reported major water shortage problems, despite recent flooding in the former. For example, the United Nations expects that by 2000 more than two-thirds of Chinese cities will face a water shortfall because of overpumping for agricultural purposes. (In general, roughly ten times the water is needed to irrigate crops in arid lands than is required for direct human use.) It is estimated by the U.N. that some 40,000 square miles of agricultural land in India are now suffering from water-poisoning and salinization, reducing its average productivity 20 percent.

The problem of depletion is thus accompanied by the danger of salinization. The pumping of aquifers—particularly those in low-lying areas—creates the risk that ocean water may seep in. Moreover, heavy irrigation tends to lead to salinization because, though required for many of the new high-yield crops developed in the "green revolution" of the 1960s and 1970s, it tends to waterlog land, causing natural salts in the soil to be leached out and carried into the aquifer.

In addition, chemical fertilizers—equally crucial to the new high-yield strains—have also entered many aquifers, along with industrial runoffs, poisoning them to the point that many may soon become unusable (see the section on food below). Deforestation also contributes to water shortages because the denuding of watersheds through timber operations or the clearing of lands for farming makes it more likely that rainfall will run off the land rather than sinking into it, thereby replenishing aquifers.

Energy

As anyone who has filled up a car's gas tank in recent years can attest, gasoline prices in the United States are low—the lowest, when adjusted for inflation, in the country's history. How can this be, just two decades after some of the worst peacetime shortfalls in recent memory?

There are several reasons: (1) conservation efforts and more efficient use of oil have helped keep demand from growing as rapidly as it might have; (2) high prices in the 1970s and early 1980s spurred oil companies to look for new sources, and they were very successful; (3) the price Americans pay at the pump does not reflect the true cost of the gasoline.

With regard to this last point, it is important to note that the price per gallon fails to factor in properly such related costs as defense (to protect overseas sources, primarily in the Persian Gulf); government subsidies to oil drillers, refiners, and shippers; or the environmental (global warning) and health (respiratory diseases) costs of burning gasoline. Thus, because oil and gas are so cheap, Americans have cut back on their conservation efforts and are consuming petroleum at an ever-increasing rate. In the single year from 1995 to 1996, sales at gasoline stations in the United States increased from $146 billion to $154 billion, or 5.5 percent. Lower gasoline prices lead to faster energy consumption in two ways: Drivers can maintain the total cost of their gas purchases, but consume more gas by using less-energy-efficient vehicles—such as the popular sport utility vehicles (SUVs)—and by driving more, car-pooling less, and not using mass transit.

Around the world, the story is the same. Between 1991 and 1994, in Africa, petroleum and coal imports increased from roughly 70 to 80 million coal-equivalent tons (that is, the amount of energy that can be obtained from a ton of coal); in North America imports increased from 761 to 916 million; in South America from 84 to 101 million; in Asia from 1.092 to 1.349 billion; in Europe (including Russia and former Soviet republics within Europe) from 1.528 to 1.727 billion; and in Oceania from 29 to 38 million tons. Yet, between 1990 and 1994, conservation policies and economic depression in many parts of the developing world helped maintain the per capita consumption of fossil fuels at roughly the same level (4,408 pounds per capita in 1990, compared with 4,385 pounds per capita in 1994). But because the world population grew some 500 million over that period, a billion more tons of fossil fuels were consumed in 1994 than in 1990.

A quick glance at the tables in this encyclopedia reveals one of the major reasons for this constantly increasing level of energy use. There is not a single major country—and virtually no minor ones—in which the number of private automobiles and commercial vehicles is not rising, often at a faster rate than population growth. (For a more detailed examination of these numbers, see Section 8: The Demography of Transportation and Communications.)

Nevertheless, energy prices continue to decline in much of the world because of newly discovered reserves of hydrocarbons. Indeed, every continent except Africa has seen increases in fossil fuel production. Between 1990 and 1994, production in North America increased from 2.999 to 3.236 billion tons; in South America from 493 to 561 million tons; in Asia from 3.270 to 4.017 billion tons; in Europe (including Russia and former Soviet republics within Europe) from 1.485 to 3.085 billion tons; and in Oceania from 240 to 261 million tons. (In Africa energy production fell slightly, from 739 to 732 million tons.) Overall, between 1990 and 1995, world energy output, including fossil fuel, wood, nuclear, solar, geothermal, wind, and other renewable sources, increased from 11.444 to 11.893 billion tons, or 3.9 percent, nearly equal to the rate of population growth. (The careful reader will note that the population growth rate outpaced the production growth rate by 1.6 percent in those five years. The majority of that population growth was in countries with low consumption of energy per capita, so while per capita use is going down, rapidly rising population means rapidly rising energy consumption, despite technology-created efficiency improvements and drops in energy use caused by economic downturns in the developing world.)

Ultimately, continued increases in energy production mean faster rates of fossil fuel depletion. Since the sources of these fuels, of course, are finite—indeed, expected to run dry before the end of the twenty-first century—the problem of overpopulation and overconsumption's impact on world energy sources is still with us, even if it does not seem as urgent as it did a couple of decades ago.

Food

The history of food production includes three great leaps in output. The first, of course, came with the agricultural revolution that began in the Neolithic era, about 10,000 years ago. Beginning in the Middle East and soon spreading to North Africa and South and East Asia—and later to Europe and the Americas—the agricultural revolution allowed humanity a much more predictable and bountiful supply of food than could be achieved by gathering natural food plants. Similarly, the domestication of livestock was a quantum leap over hunting in the supply of meat as well as in the introduction of dairy products.

The second great leap came with the commercial and industrial revolutions that began in Western Europe in the seventeenth century and had spread to much of the rest of the world by the twentieth century. By introducing the profit motive—first in the form of plantation slavery and later through free labor farms and eventually corporate food production—farmers had an economic incentive to continue increasing their output beyond immediate consumption. At roughly the same time, the industrial revolution led to urbanization and the growth of a nonagricultural workforce. The industrial revolution also had a more direct effect on food production, by introducing labor-saving devices for sowing, weeding, harvesting, shipping, and packaging foods in exponentially greater amounts than was possible before.

The third revolution—the so-called green revolution—occured in our own time. Beginning shortly after World War II ended, scientists in both developed and developing countries sought out particular strains of staple crops that seemed to prosper in certain climates. These crops were then scientifically bred to maximize output. Thus high-yield rice, wheat, corn, and other grains were developed to grow in the tropics and other regions where the population was growing rapidly. The spread of these crops was remarkably rapid. For example, in 1965 only 200 acres of high-yield variety (HYV) wheat was grown experimentally on a farm in the Philippines. By 1971, more than 50 million acres devoted to this hybrid were planted globally. The impact of new grain hybrids like HYV wheat cannot be overestimated. In India, for example, between 1965 and 1968 wheat production increased from 11 to 27 million tons.

Despite all these gains—critical to feeding burgeoning populations—both the industrial and the green revolutions have created problems. Both have made farmers far more reliant on nonsustainable energy sources, like fossil fuels, for their production. The new hybrids of the green revolution, in particular, require massive inputs of expensive and unsustainable petroleum-based fertilizers. In the Philippines, hybrid strains of wheat are estimated to require inputs costing fifty times more than those of normal strains. Not surprisingly, the cost of these inputs has made it more difficult for small farmers to compete and forced many to leave the land for urban areas, where they are transformed from food producers to consumers.

The use of green revolution crops also requires vast inputs of water and pesticides, since many of the hybrids are particularly vulnerable to drought and insect infestation. In addition to the enormous monetary costs involved, the heavy use of water and pesticides can destroy both soil and water supplies through salinization (see the earlier section on water) and poisoning. Moreover, the law of diminishing returns applies to fertilizer and pesticide inputs. It is estimated that a ton of additional fertilizer in 1950 increased grain output by 46 tons; by 1965, that figure had fallen to 23 tons; and by the 1980s, to just 13 tons.

Pesticides, of course, have their own built-in obsolescence. Insects quickly develop pesticide resistance since only the hardy survive the first years of a given pesticide's use. So, larger quantities are continually needed, especially with delicate hybrids. For example, in areas utilizing green revolution crops in the Philippines, the amount of pesticide use increased by a factor of

several dozen from the mid-1960s to the late 1970s.

Citing these problems, food experts are now placing their faith in what has the potential to become the fourth great leap in agricultural production: the "genetic revolution, " which involves the manipulation of the DNA in food crops. Genetic manipulation is nothing new. Throughout the ages, humanity has selected particulars strains of plants and animals for their productivity and other attributes. But the earlier attempts were based on what nature had already provided. By manipulating genes directly, scientists can now custom-design new breeds of plants and animals. For example, it is possible to create plants that are resistant to insects and drought.

The potential of genetic engineering is great, and so are the risks. Much work is being done on the manipulation of plants that consume nitrogen, a key nutrient in soil, to turn them into nitrogen producers. This involves rendering them less harmful to bacterias that live in nitrogen-producing plants. But the spread of such bacterias in formerly nitrogen-consuming plants is unknown and could lead to new strains of bacteria that could destroy crops.

In addition, genetically manipulated crops introduce some economic perils. Increasingly, the corporations developing the new seeds are patenting them. If these crops are patented, these companies—which, by the rules of economic behavior, must place profit-making first—will gain total control over new food supplies. Moreover, many chemical companies—which are heavily invested in genetic engineering—are developing strains that are more—not less—resistant to their herbicides and pesticides. Although this kind of genetic engineering increases profits, it also makes both producers and consumers of food ever more dependent on a few giant corporations. And because most of these corporations are based in the developed world, the developing world—with its rapidly growing population—will become ever more dependent for its food supply. (Even before this genetic engineering revolution, the world had become dependent on crops grown in the developed world. By 1980, just four countries—the United States, Canada, Australia, and Argentina, in that order—supplied virtually all of the world's grain exports.)

Finally, problems regarding the consumption of food exist in both the developing and the developed worlds. While rapid increases in population spell danger for food levels in the developing world, so does food waste and meat consumption in the developed world. It is estimated that Americans throw away approximately a quarter of the food they purchase or grow. At the same time, the enormous quantity of meat consumed by citizens of the developed world requires as much as ten times the grain, water, and other resources as a vegetarian diet. Worldwide about 40 percent of all grain is fed to animals.

Meanwhile, natural sources of foods are disappearing rapidly. Destroying rainforests for farmland may increase food production in the short term—though much of this is in the form of wasteful herding of cattle destined to be consumed in the developed world or by the elite of the developing world—but it limits the possibility of sustained harvests of natural forest foods. Similarly, world fisheries are being depleted by both overfishing and water pollution. According to the United Nations' Food and Agriculture Organization, 255 of the 280 major fisheries it monitored in the 1990s were considered heavily exploited or overexploited. As for pollution, China provides a frightening example. The discharge from industry, farms and cities of nearly 2 trillion gallons of domestic, agricultural, and industrial waste annually has destroyed most of the fisheries and shell-fisheries of the Yellow Sea, once a prime source of high-protein food. This destruction of fisheries is an inevitable outgrowth of China's race to industrialize, urbanize and increase its farm output through the more intensive use of pesticides.

Climate

The complex interaction of the different variables involved in economic production is most readily apparent in climate change. It is widely accepted in the scientific community that global temperatures have been increasing in the past several decades. The ten hottest years recorded in this century have all occurred in the past two decades. Global ocean temperatures have been rising on average about 0.2°F annually. Of course, because it is so volatile, climactic change does not occur evenly. Vast fluctuations, such as those caused in 1998 by El Niño—the shift of warm waters from the western to the eastern Pacific—occur from time to time, but the overall tendency has been toward a warmer world. Physically, warmer temperatures are more energy-intensive, producing greater disturbances in the atmosphere—largely in the form of devastating hurricanes, excessive flooding, or drought. The increasing severity of droughts both in the developing and developed world—notably in Africa and North America—in the past couple of decades may very well be a direct result of global warming.

In 1988, a Stanford University research team attempted to calculate the impact of global warming on world food production and supplies. The team set a base level of production in which average climatic conditions would allow food supplies to grow at a pace equal to population increases, roughly following the trend of the twenty-five years preceding the study.

But the report issued by the study team said that global warming would increase the number of major unfavorable climatic events—largely in the form of regional droughts—from one every 5 years to one every 3.3 years. With each event likely to cause a 10 percent drop in the upward trend of food production, it was estimated that future unfavorable climatic events in the coming century might cause the deaths of between 50 million and 400 million persons worldwide, though nearly all of these would occur in the developing world. This last prediction, they said, would be true regardless of whether or not the drought occurred there, since—as noted above—so much of the developing world has become dependent on grain exports from the developed world.

While the existence and effects of global warming are virtually beyond dispute, this is not quite the case when it comes to causes. Although a small minority of scientists insist that global warming is an entirely natural phenomenon, the vast majority agree that humanity's economic production and manipulation of the environment are factors. How large these factors are, however, is open to debate.

The most important contributor to global warming is the burning of hydrocarbon—oil, gas, coal—and other organic fuels—wood, peat, and manure. This burning causes the release of massive quantities of carbon dioxide, a naturally occurring element in the atmosphere. Indeed, carbon dioxide helps trap heat in the Earth's atmosphere by allowing sunlight to penetrate and then retain it, in the so-called greenhouse effect. Without carbon dioxide, the Earth's surface would be a lot colder than it is. But too much carbon dioxide means too much trapped heat, hence, global warming. Adding to the problem is deforestation. Plant life—through the process of photosynthesis—converts carbon dioxide into oxygen. Thus the destruction of the Earth's biomass (that is, the total mass of animal, bacteria, and plant life)—consisting largely of the clearing of temperate and tropical forests—means that the global environment is less able to absorb increases in carbon dioxide.

With regard to the production of carbon dioxide, the issue of developed world consumption patterns versus developing world population growth becomes especially acute. In 1992, the United States produced more carbon dioxide emissions (1.3 trillion tons) than the entire developing world combined, minus China. This fact has led many developing world environmentalists to cite overconsumption in the developed world as the main factor in global warming. That may be true at the moment, but slower economic growth and improving emission-control technology in the United States limited the increase in its carbon dioxide output to just 16 percent from 1983 to 1992. By contrast, in rapidly developing China—with its heavy emphasis on domestic but dirty coal supplies and

more primitive emission control technology—carbon dioxide output over the same period increased from 455,215 to 728,161 million tons annually, an increase of roughly 60 percent. Nor is China alone. Output has increased proportionately by the same amount or more over the same period in countries as geographically and economically diverse as Nigeria (16,343 to 26,341 million tons), Malaysia (10,359 to 19,239 million tons), and Turkey (25,985 to 39,708 million tons).

Meanwhile, the reduction in the absorption rate of carbon dioxide emissions caused by deforestation is growing rapidly. It is estimated that in Central and South America, there is a loss of some 10,000 square miles of rainforest annually, or more than 10 acres a minute. Moreover, much of the rainforest is cleared for farming by slash-and-burn methods, releasing enormous—albeit one-time—quantities of carbon dioxide. Although the burning of forests is largely a tropical phenomenon, the systematic destruction of forests continues at an unsustainable pace in such temperate areas as the Pacific Northwest of the United States and British Columbia in Canada.

POLITICAL IMPLICATIONS

The depletion of global resources due to the consumerism of the developed world and rapid population increases in the developing world has enormous implications for political and economic stability worldwide. Recent events illustrate the tensions and conflicts ignited by the struggle for sources of energy and food. The most obvious example is the 1991 Persian Gulf War fought between Iraq and a coalition of twenty-seven countries led by the United States (but under the official aegis of the United Nations).

The crisis began with Iraq's invasion of Kuwait in August 1990. Saddam Hussein, Iraq's leader, insisted that Kuwait was illegally pumping too much oil from a field the two countries shared. Iraq, determined to pump more oil to earn revenues lost during a long-standing war with Iran, first asked, then threatened, and finally invaded Kuwait to obtain the oil. The world responded with a massive army that not only drove Iraq out of Kuwait but destroyed much of the former's military establishment and infrastructure. In response, Hussein's army set off massive oil-well fires in Kuwait, leading to one of the most serious environmental crises in recent years. But the disputes over energy sources need not always be global in scope. Ecuador and Peru have been fighting border skirmishes for years over a remote but disputed section of the upper Amazon basin that is reputed to contain signficant petroleum reserves.

Food resources, both natural and cultivated, can be a source of international and civil instability. North Atlantic states—including Canada and Iceland—have seized fishing boats owned by European nationals who were allegedly poaching in their territorial waters. Meanwhile, in the northeastern Pacific, the United States and Canada remain in a tense standoff over salmon stocks.

At the same time, disputes over food prices in many developing countries have led to riots, coups, and near–civil wars. The scenario follows a similar pattern in many places. The government of a developing country, usually located in a large metropolis, lacks credibility and support among the urban masses, usually because its institutions are weak, its officials corrupt, and its leaders repressive. To maintain civil order in the vulnerable cities, its leaders often subsidize the price of food and fuel, or pay less than market prices for produce from less politicially explosive or influential farmers. When that is no longer economically feasible—and prices have to be raised—unrest and violence often break out, leading in some cases, such as most recently in Indonesia, to mass killings.

In several worst-case scenarios, food aid itself has become either a weapon or a hostage of war. In the Angolan and Sudanese civil wars of the 1980s and 1990s, rebels often forced military concessions from the government before allowing food aid to be brought into the famine-stricken areas under their control.

Many population experts say that in the future, political instability and civil and interna-

tional conflicts might be triggered by famine on a regional, rather than a national, scale. This might happen if leaders use international tensions to distract their hungry citizens from internal problems or if governments attempt to seize the resources of their neighbors.

In general, there is little debate among scientists that humanity is having a significant impact on the global environment, though the extent and consequences of that impact are the source of great controversy. Meanwhile, policymakers in the developed and developing world exchange charges about who is more responsible for the human-based environmental damage—the citizens of the former, who consume far more resources and produce far more trash per capita, or the inhabitants of the latter whose numbers are doubling every thirty-five years.

The question, then, is not whether humanity will survive, but how. As a species, humanity will survive almost any environmental catastrophe, short of an all-out nuclear war, a possibility which has declined significantly since the end of the Cold War. But the quality of that life for the vast majority of the planet's inhabitants may continue to decline as the environment deteriorates. In addition, there is the very real possibility that great numbers of people in the most vulnerable famine- or flood-prone areas may be wiped out unless current trends toward ever-greater consumption in the developed world, and ever-greater population levels in the developing world, are not stopped and are ultimately reversed.

FURTHER READING

Arizpe, Lourdes, M. Priscilla Stone, and David C. Major, eds. *Population and Environment: Rethinking the Debate*. Boulder, CO: Westview Press, 1994.

Brown, Lester. *State of the World, 1989*. New York: Worldwatch Institute, 1990.

Ehrlich, Paul, Anne Ehrlich, and Gretchen Daily. *The Stork and the Plow: The Equity Answer to the Human Dilemma*. New York: Putnam's, 1995.

Coward, Harold G., ed. *Population, Consumption and*

the Environment: Religious and Secular Response. Albany: State University of New York Press, 1995.

Lindahl-Kiessling, Kerstin, and Hans Landberg, eds. *Population, Economic Development, and the Environment.* New York: Oxford University Press, 1994.

Mazur, Laurie Ann, ed. *Beyond the Numbers: A Reader on Population, Consumption, and the Environment.* Washington DC: Island Press, 1994.

Myers, Norman. *Population, Resources, and the Environment: The Critical Challenges.* New York: United Nations Population Fund, 1991.

Piel, Gerard. *Only One World: Our Own to Make and to Keep.* New York: W.H. Freeman, 1992.

Salk, Jonas. *World Population and Human Values: A New Reality.* New York: Harper & Row, 1981.

Tobias, Michael. *World War III: Population and the Biosphere at the End of the Millenium.* New York: Continuum, 1998.

Section 3

General Population and Vital Statistics

There are several key demographic questions to be considered in this section: How many people is too many people? Have we reached that number yet? Are we going to reach it soon, or ever? Finally, is there such a number at all?

First, of course, there is a more neutral question to answer: How many of us are there ? According to the last population estimate—calculated by the United Nations through mid-1995—there were 5.716 billion human beings on planet Earth. Assuming that the 1.6 percent annual growth rate for the first half of the decade continues into the second half, the population will have reached 5.995 billion by mid-1998 and surpassed the 6 billion mark sometime in late July. By the year 2000, the world's population is expected to reach 6.14 billion.

Numbers like this can sometimes be overwhelming. What does 6 billion mean? And what does 6 billion mean in the context of a planet with a surface area of roughly 60 million square miles? What does 109 persons per square mile—the average global density—imply? A few examples show that visual aids can be as treacherous as numbers in conveying the sheer quantity of human beings on the planet. Take the meaning of 6 billion, for instance. Stretched end to end, humanity would stretch from the Earth to its moon and back again a dozen times. That sounds like a lot. But standing side by side—with 4 square feet each—every human being on Earth could fit inside Rhode Island, the smallest of the United States.

HISTORY OF HUMAN POPULATION

The Long Term

As noted in the Section 1 of this encyclopedia, the rate at which human population has grown in the more than 10,000 years since the development of agriculture has increased rapidly, with the time span required for doubling dropping from roughly 1,500 years (at around the time of the industrial revolution) to about 35 years today. Indeed, if we go back even further in time, the change in the rate of increase becomes even more dramatic. If, as archaeologists tell us, the human species has been in existence on the planet for roughly 3.5 million years, then it took humanity millions of years to reach the estimated 8 million people living at the time of the agricultural revolution. Today, the world's population grows by 8 million persons every month. In other words, if an extraterrestrial visitor came to Earth, say 100,000 years ago, human beings would have represented a relatively minor life form of life in terms of quantity—the equivalent of, say, the chimpanzee today.

Still, there is something a bit misleading about growth rates and doubling averages. They make it appear that demographic expansion is consistent, over both time and space. But that is not the case. In fact, there have been several periods in which human population was able to grow dramatically faster than in others. The first of these great expansions occurred with the previously mentioned agricultural revolution. Agriculture, of course, allowed human beings to grow exponentially greater amounts of food than could be obtained by hunting or gathering.

Moreover, the process reinforces itself on an ever-greater scale. A steadier and greater food supply allows populations to become geographically stable, leading to the growth of cities, the development of classes of nonagriculturalists, and the steady advance of toolmaking and weaponry. At the same time, the development of agriculture requires a more ordered social structure. People live closer to one another. They acquire property, both land and personal. More rules, rule makers and rule enforcers are needed. More complex forms of government arise that can both organize and command greater internal human and nonhuman resources. The need for more land and other resources—including slaves—leads to military expeditions and conquests, often of less-advanced peoples. These are then incorporated into the existing political, economic, and cultural system, thereby expanding the realm of stable, agriculturally based economies and hence the number of human beings.

This process, of course, can and has been reversed from time to time in human history. The barbarian invasions of Rome after the year A.D. 400 and the Mongol conquest of China in the thirteenth century witnessed the triumph of more thinly populated nomadic pastoralists over more densely populated settled agriculturalists. Ultimately, however, while this may have resulted in a short-term breakdown of order and hence a drop in production and population, the long-term trend of increasing numbers of agriculturalists was not altered. Pastoralist invaders have almost always been assimilated into the existing agricultural society, not vice versa.

The second great spurt in human population occurred as a result of the scientific, commercial, industrial, and agricultural revolutions. Combined, the experimentation method of the scientific revolution (beginning in the seventeenth century), the more sophisticated modes of economic organization inherent in the commercial revolution (seventeenth century), the vast in-

crease in productive capacity created by the industrial revolution (late eighteenth century), and the enormous food bounties produced by the agricultural revolution (mid-twentieth century) have allowed far more people to meet their basic needs with far less effort in a far shorter period of time than was ever possible before.

Of course, these "revolutions" began in Europe and places where European settlers came to predominate (during the centuries noted in parentheses above)—and, thus, had their initial demographic impact there—before spreading to the rest of the world in the late twentieth century, as the following numbers reveal. For example, death rates—an excellent measure of a population's relative development profile—fell from about 34 to 18 per 1,000 persons annually in the developed world between the late eighteenth century and the first half of the twentieth century. That downward trend continued in the late twentieth century, falling by about half again to just 10 deaths per 1,000 persons. In the developing world, however, a very different pattern emerged. In the eighteenth century, the death rate stood at 37 per 1,000 persons, reflecting the fact that, before the great "revolutions" in science and commerce, the health and development profile of the now-developed and -developing worlds were roughly equal. But while the above-noted "revolutions" began having their impact on the death rates of the developed world over the next two hundred years, there was but a modest drop in the developing world—from 37 to 32 deaths per 1,000 persons—until those "revolutions" began to be exported. Thus only in the late twentieth century has the developing world seen a drop in death rates from 32 to 14 per 1,000 persons, bringing the developing world once again close to the levels enjoyed by the developed world.

The Short Term

Although Europeans and people of European origin were the main beneficiaries of the various "revolutions" described above, the ultimate demographic effect has been on non-Europeans, especially since the end of World War II. This has come about largely through the dispersion of more and cheaper machine-made goods, new agricultural methods and supplies, public health policies, and new medicines and medical techniques. Making all of this possible was the great economic boom of the postwar years. From roughly the late 1940s until the mid-1970s, the capitalist and socialist economies of both the developed and developing worlds experienced enormous growth, making it possible for individuals to improve their own lives and for governments to better the conditions of life for their citizens.

Economic growth and the expansion of social services—whether provided by the public or the private sector—had a major effect on population growth, particularly in the developing world for several mutually reinforcing reasons. First, improved diets led to healthier and more fertile mothers, helping raise the birth rate. Second, advances in public health and new medicines and medical techniques gradually—and, in some cases, rapidly—lowered death rates. As people lived longer, populations inevitably increased. Third, economic growth meant that families could afford to raise more children.

The result of all this has been a rapidly increasing population worldwide, as well as a rapidly rising rate of population growth. Thus the world's population grew from 1.96 billion in 1925 to 2.505 billion in 1950, an increase of some 545 million persons, or 27.8 percent. Between 1950 and 1975, the population expanded to 3.988 billion, an increase of 1.483 billion, or 59.2 percent. Finally, by 2000, the population is expected to reach 6.140, an increase of 2.152 billion, or 54.0 percent.

The fact that the absolute number of persons has risen more in the past quarter century than in the quarter century before it, while the percentage of growth has declined somewhat, is more than just a mathematical anomaly or contradiction (that is, the same growth from a larger base in absolute number always means a lower growth rate). It reflects a contradictory trend in the demographic profile of the past half century. On the one hand, the same factors that have contributed to population growth in the short run

begin to undermine that process in the longer run. This occurs in a variety of ways, both direct and indirect. To take one of the more direct ways, the same health facilities that a government builds to help extend lives—including both schools that teach hygiene and clinics that dispense medicines—are often the same institutions that can be and are used to spread knowledge of birth control methods. To take a less direct example, if better health care and diet increases the chances of a child reaching adulthood, parents who hope to have their surviving children provide for them in old age—a common practice in much of the developing world—will gradually realize that they do not need to have so many children. Moreover, economic globalization—the process by which manufacturing and commercial agriculture spreads to the developing world—tends to push people off the land. In cities, it is less advantageous to have large families. Economic modernization, too, plays a role. As economies become more sophisticated, education becomes more critical to success. Keeping children in school—as opposed to putting them to work—represents a financial drag on a family. So, parents make the decision to have fewer children. These developments have tended to occur in developed nations first, though they are increasingly spreading to the developing world.

Why, then, does the absolute number of persons continue to grow more rapidly even if the pace of growth is slowing? The answer relates to the above-mentioned mathematical anomaly and to something population experts call demographic lag. Demographic lag means that if a given population has a large number of births in one time period, a chain reaction is set off that takes several more time periods to work out. If, for example, country X has a massive increase in births during time period A, then its population of young persons of reproductive age is likely to swell in time period A plus fifteen to twenty years or so (depending on the age at which women tend to start having babies), even if the overall number of children born to each couple has decreased. This has been very typical of the past twenty-five years and is likely to continue at ever-diminishing rates for the next seventy-five years or so, as the bubble of children born during the 1950-1975 period begins to work its way up the age ladder.

Indeed, the slowing growth of the bubble is already noticeable. Between 1980 and 1995, the number of persons worldwide under the age of 15—that is, persons whose reproductive years are ahead of them—increased in absolute terms from 1.551 billion to 1.829 billion, implying a future growth in births; at the same time, however, the percentage of persons under age 15 worldwide dropped from 35 to 32 percent. In short, the bubble in the number of reproductive age persons is expanding, but at a slower pace, implying that at some point in the future, it will disappear.

There is also something that might be called the "cultural" demographic time lag. It was hinted at above in the statement concerning parental choice in the number of children. As noted above, when parents realize that their children are more likely to survive—or that fewer children mean a greater chance of economic success for both offspring and parent—they will have fewer of them. But it may take a generation for this result to become apparent to people. Hence, there is a lag between falling death rates and rising birth rates, resulting in accelerated population growth.

It is important to note here the differences between the developed and developing worlds. As noted above, a more modernized economy and society rewards families with fewer children, though it often takes a generation or two for parents to realize this. In the case of the developed nations of the world, however, it took more than a hundred years. That is, between the late eighteenth and the late nineteenth centuries—the height of the industrial revolution in Western Europe and North America—birth rates stood unchanged at 38 per 1,000 persons. In the developing world, on the other hand, there has already been a drop from 41 to 37 births per 1,000 in just the fifty years since the end of World War II, years roughly corresponding to the period in which the effects of the European-initiated "revolutions" have begun to spread to much of the rest of the world. Why the difference?

First, the first century of "revolutions" in Europe coincided with a period of mass European migration. The opening up of new territories meant that almost as many agriculturalists were being created in European-settled overseas territories as were being destroyed in industrializing and urbanizing Europe. This opening up of new territories has no counterpart in the developing world. Second, the processes of industrialization and especially urbanization have occurred much more rapidly in the developing world. Finally, declining birth rates in the developing world have been affected not just by economic modernization but through the conscious efforts of national governments and international institutions, through the power of universal education and mass media. None of this occurred during the early period of economic modernization in the developed world.

REGIONS OF THE WORLD

An assessment of humanity's numbers would depend very much on where one looked. If it one looked in Bangladesh—which has a density of 2,165 persons per square mile—Earth might seem like a very crowded place. Looking at Australia—which has about 5 persons per square mile—would lead one to the opposite conclusion. Similarly, if someone stayed for a while, he might notice that people tended to have fewer children who lived longer in the temperate zones of the planet than was the case in the tropical parts of the world.

Indeed, in the previous sections much has been made of the differences between the developed and developing worlds. But this division of the world into two neat camps presents some problems. First, of course, is the definition of the terms themselves. What does it mean to call a country "developed" or "developing"? That question is clarified, in Section 6, The Demography of Labor and the Economy.

A second problem involves the categories or

designations themselves. If developed countries can range from relatively impoverished Portugal to extremely wealthy Switzerland, the gap among developing nations renders the term *developing* nearly meaningless. Developing countries can include relatively prosperous and industrialized South Korea, oil-rich Kuwait, struggling Mexico, and destitute Mozambique. Categories such as "newly industrialized countries" (NICs), for places like Singapore, and "fourth world," for many of the economically stagnant and undeveloped countries of sub-Saharan Africa, have been used to differentiate among the states of the so-called developing world.

More helpful than the general categories of developed and developing nations are regions and subregions. Regions roughly constitute the major continents: Africa, Asia, North America, Latin America (South and Central Americas, plus the Caribbean), Europe (including Russia), and Oceania (Australia, New Zealand, and the Pacific islands). Subregions are more precise yet, for these differentiate among such culturally, politically, and economically distinct zones as Eastern and Western Europe or the relatively prosperous countries of South America's "southern cone" (Argentina, Chile, and Uruguay) and the impoverished Andean countries (Bolivia, Peru, and Ecuador).

Africa

In many ways, Africa lags behind the rest of the world demographically. That is not to say that the rate of its population growth is slower. Quite the contrary: Africa represents the region with the fastest-growing population in the world. Between 1965 and 1995, its population expanded from 311 million to 728 million, an increase of 134 percent. This rapid increase—and its status as the region with the fastest-growing population—is relatively new. Between 1925 and 1950, the population in Africa grew from 153 to 219 million, an increase of 43 percent. During that same period, the population of Latin America grew 67 percent. But from 1965 to 1995, the rate of population growth in Latin America fell sig-

nificantly behind Africa's, though the population in Latin America was growing at the still-rapid rate of 69 percent. Other regions of the developing world provide an even greater contrast with Africa.

Indeed, Africa is the only major region of the world in which the rate of growth is still rising. In 1965, the population of the continent was increasing at the rate of 2.3 percent annually. Thirty years later that figure was 3.0 percent. Thus, it is expected that Africa—which had roughly the same population as North America in 1875 or Europe (minus the former Soviet Union) in 1975—will have almost eight times the population of the former and four times that of the latter by 2075.

Of course, Africa is not a monolith. There is the great divide of the Sahara Desert separating North Africa—which, culturally and economically, is more akin to the Middle East—from the rest of the continent, so-called sub-Saharan Africa. In North Africa, growth rates peaked in 1980 at 2.9 percent annually and have since fallen to 2.3 percent, a rate that is still higher than that of virtually any other region outside Africa. On the rest of the continent, growth rates continue to climb.

Several factors are causing this enormous growth. First, birth rates continue to be quite high at some 42 per 1,000 persons. Although this is a decline from the 46 per 1,000 of 1980, the drop is insignificant when compared to rates in most other regions of the developing world. Second, death rates have fallen dramatically in recent years, from 23 per 1,000 persons in 1965 to 14 per 1,000 in 1995. In effect, Africa has experienced the impact of the "revolutions" in science and commerce long after the rest of the world. Finally, there is the matter of population density. Despite its enormous growth rates, Africa is relatively underpopulated at just 62 persons per square mile, compared with roughly 280 in Eurasia. Indeed, Africa is both the second largest land mass and, next to Europe and Latin America, the continent with the highest proportion of land capable of sustaining large human populations. This has led many demographers—particularly African ones—to assert that Africa's problem is not too many people but too little development.

Latin America

Although much of Latin America shares linguistic and, to a limited degree, cultural roots in the Iberian countries (Spain and Portugal) that conquered the region in the sixteenth century, there are nevertheless dramatic differences of race, economics, and society (see Section 5, Demography and Cultural Identity and Section 6, The Demography of Labor and the Economy). Although the peoples of the southern part of the region are largely of European descent and the area among the most prosperous subregions of the developing world, the rest of the region is more ethnically and racially heterogeneous and is generally far less economically developed.

Still, there are some significant overall patterns in the demography of the region. Like North America and Africa, Latin America is relatively thinly populated, with just 60 persons per square mile. As in Europe, most of the continent is quite habitable. Even the high valleys of the Andean chain—located as they are largely in the tropics—support large populations. Overall, Latin America has seen its annual population growth rate drop significantly in the past thirty years from 2.8 percent to 1.8 percent, the most dramatic decrease of any major world region.

At the same time, Latin America's birth rate has declined from 41 to 26 per 1,000 and the number of persons under age 15 has fallen from 40 to 34 percent, a decrease attributable, say demographers, to more education and a reduction in the influence of the Catholic Church's anti–birth-control doctrine. Yet, despite all this, Latin America's population continues to grow rapidly in absolute numbers, a classic example of demographic lag. Thus, it is expected that Latin America's population will double to roughly 1.3 billion by 2075 before leveling off.

North America

After Europe, North America has the slowest rate of population growth of any major region of the world. Between 1965 and 1995, its population grew just 37 percent, from 214 million to 293 million. At the same time, its growth rate fell from an already low 1.5 percent annually in 1965 to just 1 percent thirty years later. Yet even this modest growth is misleading. Host to the second-largest number of immigrants annually—after Europe—its natural increase is barely above zero. (For more information on immigration, see Section 7, The Demography of Migration).

The region's slow growth rate is due primarily to low birth rates. In 1995, there were just 16 births per 1,000 persons, down nearly a third from 22 per 1,000 in 1965. At the same time, the death rate has stayed even at 9 persons per 1,000, reflecting the region's well-established health care system and nutritious diets. A second contributing factor is the age profile. With just 22 percent of the population under age 15, North America has the oldest population of any region in the world outside Europe. Unlike Europe, however, the region is thinly populated, with just 36 persons per square mile, though this low density rate is somewhat misleading since some 50 percent of the region consists of northern Canada and Alaska, where only a few million people live.

Because the rate of immigration is projected to slow due to stricter laws, the population of North America is expected to grow to only about 350 million by 2075, an increase of about 10 percent from 1999.

Asia

It is virtually impossible to speak of Asia as a unified region in any meaningful way. By far the most heavily populated continent, Asia is home to well over half of humanity. The largest continent in area, Asia can be divided into roughly four geographic and cultural zones: East Asia, Southeast Asia, South Asia, and Southwest Asia. (This does not include Siberia, the vast but sparsely populated northern third of the continent. Politically part of Russia, it was once included in statistics for the Soviet Union and is now lumped together with Europe.)

East Asia is the most populous of the subregions; its population in 1995 was 1.424 billion, up from 864 million in 1965, an increase of 65 percent. Although vast in area, at some 4.54 million square miles, it is quite crowded, with 313 persons per square mile. This, of course, varies from place to place within the subregion. Eastern China, the two Koreas, and Japan are intensely crowded, while western China is relatively underpopulated. East Asia's annual growth rate was already low in 1965 at 1.4 percent, and it has since dropped to 1 percent, largely as a result of China's strict one-child family policy. Thus the birth rate in the subregion has declined from 33 to 18 per 1,000 persons, roughly equivalent to the rate in highly developed North America. This is reflected in the rising age of East Asia's population, with the number of children under the age of 15 declining from 33 to 25 percent over the past thirty years.

South Asia, the second most populous subregion, presents an entirely different profile from East Asia's. Dominated by India and its relatively lax birth control efforts, South Asia has witnessed an increase in its population from 681 million in 1965 to 1.381 billion in 1995. At the same time, its annual population growth rate fell only slightly, from 2.4 percent in 1965 to 2.1 percent thirty years later. Even more densely populated than East Asia, with virtually no major part of the subregion uninhabitable, South Asia has a density of 332 persons per square mile, the highest of any major continental region in the world.

Like East Asia and South Asia, the subregion of Southeast Asia is dominated by a single state: Indonesia. With its population of roughly 200 million, Indonesia is nearly three times the size of its next largest neighbor, Vietnam. Southeast Asia, with some wealthy states and some rather impoverished ones, shows a wide range of economic conditions. Vietnam remains one of the poorest countries in Asia; Singapore is among the richest. Overall, however, the subregion has seen enormous economic growth in the past thirty years, which is reflected in its demographic profile. As a region, its annual population growth rate declined from 2.6 percent in 1965 to 1.8 per-

cent in 1995, while birth and death rates fell from 43 to 27 per 1,000 and 17 to 8 per 1,000, respectively, in the same period.

Southwest Asia largely overlaps the Middle East and is mostly made up of the Central Asian republics of the former Soviet Union. Southwest Asia has no single dominant state and has extremes of poverty and wealth, ranging from war-devastated Afghanistan to the oil-rich United Arab Emirates. Overall, Southwest Asia is an extremely rapidly growing region, where the population has increased 147 percent between 1965 and 1995, the fastest of any major subregion of the world. Indeed, as in Africa, the annual population growth rate is bucking international trends, although whereas in Africa this statistic has risen, in Southwest Asia it has remained the same. Ironically, the rapid increase in population has been evident in both the wealthy Persian Gulf countries and the poorer states to the north. Demographers believe that this is because the high income levels in the former derive from a rise in oil prices, which occurred rapidly and did not lead to a cultural shift toward smaller families.

It is expected that, while East Asia's population will increase by about a third over the next seventy-five years, the rest of Asia's population will more than double to exceed 5 billion by 2075.

Europe

If any region of the world can be said to lead the way in demographic change, it is Europe. From roughly 1700 to 1900, it remained the fastest-growing region of the world, if its emigrant population is included. But in the years since World War II, it has become the slowest- growing region of the world. Moreover, the population in many parts of the region is expected to remain stable or even decline in the coming century. This is especially true of Eastern Europe, where, in the wake of communism's collapse, health care and diets have deteriorated. These demographic problems are compounded by the fact that hundreds of thousands of Eastern Europeans have been emigrating to Western Europe, the United States, and Israel in recent years. Indeed, Eastern Europe had an annual growth rate of –0.1 percent in 1995, the only major region in the world whose population has declined. Birth and death rates reveal why this is happening. Whereas death rates increased from 9 per 1,000 persons in 1965 to 12 per 1,000 in 1995, birth rates fell from 17 per 1,000 to 12 per 1,000. So, although the natural increase is flat, outmigration produces a slight decline.

Western Europe presents a profile that is both similar and dissimilar to that of Eastern Europe. In Western Europe, the annual growth rate hovers just above zero, even though birth and death rates have nearly converged. Of course, this convergence did not occur because death rates are rising but because birth rates have fallen so dramatically. The population increase owes to in-migration, largely from the former colonies of West European powers or from Eastern Europe.

Thus it is expected that Europe's population will probably stabilize at about 800 million (including Russia) by the middle of the next century, up from about 727 million today.

Oceania

The world's smallest major region by both size and population, Oceania consists of three subregions: the tiny islands of Micronesia and Polynesia, scattered over millions of square miles of the Pacific Ocean; the medium-size islands of Melanesia off Asia and Australia; and the continent of Australia itself, along with the major islands of New Zealand. This difference is always noticeable first in the population densities of the various subregions. While the islands of Micronesia and Polynesia have some of the world's highest densities, Australia has perhaps the lowest of any major country in the world. Culturally, the three regions are quite distinct as well, with the former two among the middle rank of developing nations and the latter subregion a part of the developed world.

In Oceania the population rose from 17.5 million in 1965 to 28.5 million in 1995, an increase of 63 percent. The growth rate fell from 2.1 per-

cent annually in 1965 to 1.5 in 1995. The reasons for this growth vary in the different subregions. In the islands of Melanesia, Polynesia, and Micronesia, the growth pattern comes from high birth rates and falling death rates. In Australia, it derives from immigration, especially from Asia. Indeed, this rise in immigration to Australia and New Zealand was responsible for increases in the annual growth rates there from 1.2 to 1.4 percent between 1980 and 1995. It is expected that the population of Oceania will climb to about 52 million by 2075, an increase of roughly 85 percent.

PROJECTIONS

Population projections are tricky affairs. They must take into consideration such factors as improved health care and diet, which leads to lower death rates. At the same time, they must include factors—including higher educational rates, better economic conditions, and the implementation of family-planning policies—that tend to lower birth rates. Moreover, they must weigh which of these trends is most likely to prevail and to what degree. Finally, they have to account for all these factors and trends for the different regions of the world and then arrive at a global profile. As the recent history of U.N. demographic projections makes clear, it is easy to miscalculate.

Recognizing the hazards inherent in such a complex set of calculations—based as they are on projecting past trends into the future—most of the studies conducted by the United Nations have attempted to chart population changes along several variants. Known as low, medium, and high, these variants assume different weights for different variables. Will economic growth and urbanization have a greater impact on reducing the birth rate than improved access to health care will have on reducing death rates? And if this so, when will this shift occur? Simply put, low variants imply a slower rate of growth, high variants a rapid rate, and medium variants a rate somewhere in between.

During the great takeoff in developing world

population growth in the mid-1960s, for example, the United Nations predicted that the world's population would reach 7 billion by 2000. This high-variant projection was based on continued declines in death rates and a stable but high birth rate. The 7 billion figure was predicated on annual growth rates continuing their climb upward, reaching about 2.6 percent annually around 1990, then remaining stable. The medium variant, which predicted a global population of 6.5 billion in 2000, assumed that the rate of growth in 1965—roughly 2 percent annually—would continue through 1985, then fall to 1.7 percent by 2000. The low variant regarded 1965 as the peak, with the growth rate falling continually to about 1.3 percent annually in 2000, increasing the population of the world to about 5.9 billion by the end of the century.

By 1983, when another major U.N. population projection was done, population experts had the chance to reconsider the weight of the variables. Their most important changes concerned Asia. By the early 1980s, it had become clear that the heavily populated eastern half of the continent was undergoing rapid and sustained economic and urban growth—trends that were bound to lower birth rates substantially. At the same time, it became increasingly clear that the Chinese government had changed its position on population growth, reversing its earlier position favoring high birth rates. With its complex bureaucracy down to local and even neighborhood levels, Beijing could effectively implement family planning, particularly in urban areas. A final factor in the new projection calculations was the surprisingly sharp decline in European and Soviet birth rates.

Together these new variables led the United Nations to offer several new variants on population growth. In the new study, the high, medium, and low variants predicted a 2000 population of 6.36, 6.12, and 5.90 billion, respectively. As noted above, the world's population is now expected to reach 6.14 billion in 2000, very close to the median variant calculated in the 1983 study but significantly below the same variant in the mid-1960s projection.

More significantly, the 1983 study took the projections well into the future, calculating the population through the end of the twenty-first century. Here, the differences in the variants were remarkable, with the high, medium, and low predictions being 14.20, 10.19, and 7.52 billion, respectively. As in the calculations for 2000, the different variants assumed that virtually all the population growth would occur in the developing world. Indeed, even the high variant projected that population in the developed world would increase only about 70 percent, from roughly 1.10 billion in 1975 to 1.73 billion in 2100. At the same time, the high variant saw the developing world's population grow from 2.98 to 12.47 billion over the same period, an increase of 318 percent.

At its 1994 population conference held in Cairo, the United Nations offered its latest projections, using 1992 as the base year and projecting as far forward as 2025. According to the medium variant, the world's population would reach 8.472 billion in the latter year; again, most of the population growth would come in the developing world. While population in the developed world would grow from 1.225 to 1.403 billion—an increase of 14.5 percent—the developing world's population would increase from 4.254 to 7.069 billion, a jump of 66.2 percent.

Overall, population growth rates are declining throughout the developed and developing world, pushed downward by rising levels of education, income and urbanization. Over the past decade, the UN has gradually lowered its expectation for global population in 2000 from 7 to 6 billion, a 14 percent difference. The discrepancy reveals the difficulty in making population predictions, a difficulty that becomes more acute the further into the future the projection is made. In its most recent long-term prediction, the UN offered a high-variant prediction for the year 2150 of some 27 billion people worldwide and a low-variant of 3.6 billion. This immense difference reveals not only the difficulty in making such population projections, but the importance of individual decisions multiplied by billions. Indeed, the difference between the two figures comes down to every couple deciding to have just one extra child over the next 150 years.

FURTHER READINGS

Department of Economic and Social Information and Policy Analysis. *Population and Policies and Programmes: Proceedings of the United Nations Expert Group Meeting on Population Policies and Programmes, Cairo, Egypt, 12-16 April 1992.* New York: United Nations, 1993.

Johnson, Stanley. *World Population: Turning the Tide, Three Decades of Progress.* Boston: Graham and Trotman, Martinius Nijhoff, 1994.

Johnson, Stanley, ed. *The Earth Summit: The United Nations Conference on Environment and Development.* Boston: Graham and Trotman, Martinius Nijhoff, 1993.

Jones, Gawin, ed. *The Continuing Demographic Transition.* New York: Oxford University Press, 1997.

Lutz, Wolfgang, ed. *The Future Population of the World: What Can We Assume Today?* London: Earthscan, 1996.

———. *Distributional Aspects of Human Fertility: A Global Comparative Study.* San Diego: Academic Press, 1989.

Piel, Gerard. *Only One World: Our Own to Make and to Keep.* New York: W.H. Freeman, 1992.

Preston, Samuel, ed. "World Population: Approaching the Year 2000." *Annals of the American Academy of Political and Social Science* 510 (July 1990): 8-177.

Section 4

The Demography of Families and Households

A BRIEF HISTORY OF THE MODERN FAMILY/HOUSEHOLD

Throughout history, the structure of the family has almost always been in transition. Sociologists believe that there is no one definition of the family that has been accurate across all time. To scholars of modern history, the great transition in family structure came with industrialization and urbanization, which began in England in the late eighteenth century. It then spread to parts of Western Europe and the northeastern United States in the early nineteenth century, enveloping most of the United States and Europe by the late nineteenth and early twentieth centuries. Finally it moved to many parts of the developing world—most notably East Asia and parts of the Middle East and Latin America—by the end of the twentieth century.

Industrialization and urbanization's impact on the family were extremely complex, making any summary of these developments an oversimplification. Nevertheless, it can be safely noted that these economic and geographic phenomena tended to shrink family size in two ways. First, these factors motivated parents to have fewer children. Second, they tended to replace extended families with nuclear ones—that is, families consisting of parents and children only.

Preindustrial families tended to be large and extended. They were large because they were centers of production and social welfare, that is, most families were farm families, which grew their own food, made most of the goods they used, and provided education, health care services, and charity for their members. Given these requirements, large and extended families made sense economically. Different members performed different tasks and resources were shared, which made for greater productivity and efficiency. Thus many families working as a single economic unit contained relatives of all generations as well as servants.

Moreover, death was a nearly constant companion of preindustrial families. Babies and young children often died of illness, making it essential for parents to have many children so that a few would survive to contribute to family production in the short term and provide for aging parents in the long term. Young and middle-aged adults were not immune to death either. It was quite common for parents—in particular, mothers in childbirth—to die before some or all of their children were fully grown. The presence of aunts, uncles, in-laws, and even grandparents within a single family unit helped guarantee the survival of children specifically and the family generally.

The advent of industrialization and mass urbanization changed. First, industrialization made it possible to buy cheaply many of the goods that were once produced in the home. Gradually, the family ceased to be a unit of production and became one of nurturing and comsumption. In an increasingly industrialized world, it made more sense to have fewer children, since the requirements of modern urban life put a premium on education. A child in school cannot work and thus becomes a financial burden—rather than an asset—for the family. Moreover, industrialization paid off in rising levels of health care and improved medicines, allowing more children to mature to adulthood. Similarly, the rise of the modern bureaucratic state—a by-product of industrialization and urbanization—led to social programs that took care of people in their later years of life, reducing the need for children to care for their aging parents.

Of course, this process was not evenly distributed across societies or even across classes within a single society. As noted above, the impact of industrialization and urbanization is only now affecting most parts of the world. Similarly, the modern family structure was first seen in middle-class families. Long after industrialization and urbanization had taken hold in America, for instance, many urban and rural poorer families continued to need children as contributors to family income and so could not send them to school. The uneven impact of industrialization and urbanization on the family is also seen in the developing world.

Before proceeding to a discussion of families in the modern world, we should define the terms used here. Demographers prefer the term *household* over *family* for several reasons. Households—that is, the community of people living under the same roof and sharing financial and other resources—are easier to measure statistically simply because they are concentrated in one place and usually have one (or sometimes more) householder(s) who is (are) legally responsible for the other members. Thus most censuses measure households and not families, since families are often dispersed geographically. And because families are dispersed—and so do not always share resources—family members living in different households may have radically different economic profiles. Therefore the term *householder* is used here.

Fertility measures the number of children born to each woman in a given society. One way of gauging fertility is to measure it for given time periods—usually a year—or for age cohorts, that is, over the course of a woman's reproductive life. These numbers can be arrived at three different ways. First, the crude birth rate can be analyzed. The crude birth rate is reached by dividing the total number of live births in a given year by the total population and then multiplying by 1,000. Another method, the general fertility rate, is found by dividing the total number of live births in a given year by the total number of women of reproductive age (usually 15-44), and then multiplying by 1,000. Finally, if actual birth statistics are unavailable or inadequate, there is the child–women ratio, in which the total number of young children (usually up to age 4) are divided by the total number of women of reproductive age plus 4 (usually 15-49) and multiplied by 1,000. The plus four is meant to factor in the possibility that a woman had a baby at age 44, who is now as much as five years old.

Because the crude birth rate is the most widely used by demographers and data-collecting institutions worldwide, this reference uses the crude birth rate as the standard of measurement.

FERTILITY AND CHILDBIRTH

As noted earlier, the term *fertility* is used to define the number of children born to each woman. There are two determinants of the level of fertility in a given society. The first is biological, that is, the physical ability to bear children, or fecundity. Since few women—especially in the developing world—are ever tested for their fecundity, demographers tend to use fertility—the actual bearing of children—as the prime measurement of a society's natural rate of increase. Nevertheless, some general guesses about the relationship between fecundity and fertility can be made. It is estimated that approximately 10 percent of all couples in the United States are infertile or sterile, that is, incapable of having children, whether the infertility lies with the man or the woman. Sterility varies by age, affecting about 2 percent of teenagers, and nearly 20 percent of those over age 40. Estimates in other developed countries indicate that the American rate is about average.

How can these figures be extrapolated to the developing world, where few estimates of fecundity exist? Two factors need to be considered. On the one hand, the generally younger age profile of developing countries means that there are more fecund women and men. On the other, however, poorer diets and health care may raise infertility rates. To what extent these two factors cancel each other out is impossible to say, but it does not matter much, since most reproductive decisions are made for social, not biological reasons.

The second determinant of fertility levels is social, chief among which is the use of contraceptives. Are the participants informed about contraceptives? Natural methods of birth control are, of course, almost as ancient as the family itself. They include natural abortifacients (natural medicines that cause women to abort fetuses), coitus interruptus (in which the man withdraws before ejaculating), and the "rhythm method," in which couples restrict their sexual intercourse to the less-fertile portion of a woman's menstrual cycle. These methods have been practiced by virtually all human societies.

Awareness of Western methods—including barrier methods (condoms, intrauterine devices, and diaphragms), surgical techiques (such as vasectomies for men or the tying of the fallopian tubes in women), birth-control pills, and, most recently, pharmaceutical abortifacients like the French drug RU-486—is prevalent in both developed and developing countries, albeit at different rates, though the majority of women in the developed countries are informed about most birth-control options.

In much of the developing world—as in the developed world before it—the idea that birth control is an option has been slow in coming, although it has become more widespread in recent years. Several conceptual obstacles had to be overcome first, prime of which was acceptance of the idea of planning or limiting families. Much of the developing world remains at an early phase in the transition toward industrialization and urbanization, so a large portion of the population works on the land, where every child is a potential source of labor.

A second key obstacle to introducing birth control has often been the fact that women in developing countries have little decision-making power in the family. Because they have greater responsibility for the children and their well-being, women are usually more acutely aware of the changing economics of child-rearing and the need to have fewer children in an urban and industrial setting. Decision-making power is often tied to education and income, which are mutually reinforcing. Higher income usually means more education, and more education brings a greater awareness of the needs for a small family, a stronger commitment to limit births, and an awareness of birth-control options.

Even when their income does not rise, women often show lower fertility levels when their status changes as a result of urbanization. For example, they gain better access to education and an independent income, which often give women the confidence and the power to demand a say in marriage and family-planning decisions. They either postpone marriage, thereby limiting fertility by reducing the number of years in which the woman is likely to have children, or, after marriage, they insist on longer delays between children. The ability to earn an independent income also allows some women to forgo marriage—or remarriage after the death or divorce of a husband. Although the proportion of women in the developing world who forgo marriage remains small, it does have an impact on overall fertility rates by removing some women from child-bearing status.

Moreover, when urbanization removes them from traditional village society, where there is family and communal pressure to have many children, women can more readily assess the desired number of children on their own terms. Moreover, in cities, women are less likely to be as influenced by the church. Since most religions emphasize the benefits of large families, their absence in women's lives often leads to lower fertility rates. Finally, a newly urbanized woman often finds that she has more options in terms of education and income if she forgoes early or repeated childbirth.

It should now be clear that women are the key to fertility rates and that raising their social status—through access to education and, to a smaller extent, higher household income levels or independent sources of income for women—is the key to lowering those rates. Not surprisingly, given this dynamic, fertility levels in the developed and developing world differ dramatically. In the former, some industrialized countries are actually experiencing flat or even negative growth rates, while in most developing countries, fertility levels are only beginning to fall or level off. Thus, to understand the impact of economic modernization on fertility, it is important to examine both low- and high-fertility countries, beginning with the latter.

Theories of Fertility Reduction

Most developing countries have developed birth control and family planning policies, outlined in Section 1 of this book. The following discussion covers the two general theories of falling fertility rates.

The first such theory is based largely on economic criteria. Using the rational decision maker of classical economic theory—in this case, the parent who makes rational decisions based on complete information about the pluses and minuses involved in that decision—the economic approach to understanding fertility rates states that people will make the logical tradeoff of preferring higher living standards over large families. Knowing that having fewer children means that they and their child will lead better-quality lives, they will logically choose this option. Thus, as economies modernize and make smaller families the more rational choice, fertility levels drop accordingly.

The second general theory deals with the sociocultural bases of the decision to have children. The economic explanation for fertility levels, while logical by itself, fails to include this sociocultural aspect. The decision to have children can also be viewed as a rational one in social terms, motivated by ego gratification, the need to maintain a lineage, or obligations to extended family, community, nation, or religion. Thus fertility levels will drop only after such sociocultural needs are satisfied.

High-Fertility Countries

High fertility has both general social and immediate family causes. The social causes include the need for a given society to survive, as is the case for many indigenous tribal peoples. The survival imperative has been employed by some modern cultures as well. Both the Nazi regime in Europe and the communist government in North Korea incessantly propagandized about the need for and virtues of high fertility, and rewarded couples for having many children. Both believed that high fertility was necessary for their society to survive and ultimately triumph in struggles with other societies—Slavic Europe in Germany's case, South Korea in North Korea's case. Similarly, Palestinian leaders have advocated high levels of fertility in order to overwhelm the Jewish population of Israel and force the Israeli government to allow the Palestinians to form their own state. Indeed, for many years, the government of Israel has faced a demographic and political dilemma concerning the occupied territories. On the one hand, Israel considers itself a democracy. Absorption of the territories would require offering the vote to Palestinians. Their rapidly growing numbers would soon turn a Jewish state into a multicultural one. In other words, Israel appeared to be faced with a choice between its democratic and Jewish identities when it came to dealing with territories, a dilemma that has been partially eliminated by the move toward increased Palestinian autonomy in Gaza and the West Bank. While Israel has a low birth rate of 20.3 live births per 1,000—typical of an industrialized society—the occupied territories have some of the highest birth rates in the world—38.8 per 1,000 in the West Bank and 50.7 per 1,000 in Gaza in 1995.

As noted above, the need for children as laborers and for future security is an important factor in high-fertility societies, particularly where most people remain on the land. Thus it is not surprising to find that such largely rural African countries as Kenya (72 percent rural) and Tanzania (80 percent rural) have some of the highest fertility rates in the world: Kenya had 33.4 live births per 1,000 persons and Tanzania 41.3 per 1,000 in 1995. Moreover, as these societies have begun to urbanize, their birth rates have dropped.

For example, in Kenya, the percentage of people living in rural areas was nearly 85 percent in 1965. That same year, the birth rate was more than 55 live births per 1,000 persons. In other words, the percentage of people living in rural areas dropped by some 11.8 percent, while birth rates fell 39.3 percent. This indicates that the move from rural to urban areas provides only part of the explanation for falling birth rates. Much of the difference can be explained by the increasingly aggressive efforts by the government and by national and international non-governmnental organizations to expand birth-control use in the country. The prevalence of condom use, for instance, climbed from barely 8 percent of the population in 1975 to about 30 percent in 1990.

Other factors in high-fertility societies include rising social expectations and falling infant mortality levels. If parents can be convinced that their children are likely to live to adulthood, they become willing to reduce the number of children they have. Again, using Kenya as an example, life expectancy climbed from 40.5 years in 1965 to 55.6 years in 1995. From 1980 to 1985, the infant mortality rate fell from 80 per 1,000 live births to 55.3. Yet, as many demographers point out, there is a lag between rising life expectancy rates and lower birth rates because it can take as much as a generation before the realization sinks in that parents can expect more of their children to survive to adulthood.

This is especially true in places where women's status remains low. When infants' and children's mortality rates fall, it is often the women who are burdened with the problems of rearing a large family, including cooking, cleaning, and other household tasks. In poverty-stricken households, the man may be forced to recognize that he cannot support a large family. But in families where income is rising or already high enough to support many children, the traditional prestige attached to a man with many offspring is not offset by the difficulties of managing a large household since this burden falls primarily on the woman.

Another consideration in explaining high fertility rates in many developing societies is the widespread cultural preference for sons. Despite gains made in women's status in recent years, the preference for male offspring remains strong in many societies. This cultural bias is particularly strong in Asian societies, such as China and India. The desire for sons has contributed to female infanticide rates. Under China's strict one-child policy, some parents abandoned female infants if they were the firstborn, leading to a slightly higher number of boys than girls over the past two decades. In India, where there are no such restrictions on single families, the desire for sons leads parents to conceive until they have a boy, and then stop. This helps explain the fact that the country has one of the world's highest ratios of men to women: 1.08 men for every woman. (It should be noted that preference for male children permeates Western societies as well. When asked in a 1980s-era survey, five out of six potential American parents responded that if they could choose the sex of an only child, they would prefer a boy.)

Low-Fertility Countries

Much of the developed world falls into the category of low-fertility countries. As noted above, this drop in fertility rates has resulted from industrialization and urbanization, which have been taking place in Europe, the United States, and other developed nations for about a century. Indeed, aside from a brief rise in fertility after the end of World War II—an exceptional period known as the baby boom, in which a combination of cultural and economic factors led to a brief increase in the number of children born in the developed world—the size of the Western family has been shrinking steadily since the industrial revolution.

There are several key reasons for this, primarily the economic factors noted above. The modern requirement of a long educational period for children dictates smaller families for all but the small minority who have the means to support them. But economic factors do not suffice as an explanation; cultural factors are also critical. Greater prestige and higher status—not to mention a higher standard of living—accrue to those who are able to amass wealth. And by the time some aspiring couples have reached a higher income and wealth plateau, they may very well have passed their prime reproductive years. A variation on this theme existed in the communist bloc countries of Eastern Europe and the western parts of the Soviet Union as well. There, a perennial shortage of consumer goods and housing dictated smaller families.

The continuing drop in fertility rates—especially in the post–baby boom years of the 1960s through the 1990s—can be explained in terms of income and prestige. Because wages were stagnant in much of the Western world during this period, two incomes became necessary to attain higher incomes, usually by having both spouses work in paid employment. Women who work outside the home are more likely to have fewer children and to wait longer to have them, compared with those who do not work outside the household. Indeed, the expanding opportunities for women have introduced life options other than marriage and child-bearing and so have further dampened the fertility rates.

At the same time, the economic environment of the developed world has shifted jobs away from basic manufacturing in recent decades, just as employment has shifted away from the agricultural sector over the past century or two. The so-called postindustrial economies place a higher value on education and make postsecondary and even postgraduate degrees necessary for attaining higher income. To earn these degrees, both men and women must stay in school until well into their reproductive years, often delaying marriage and child-bearing.

HOUSEHOLDS

Urbanization and industrialization have transformed the modern household, first by making it smaller. Over the past century, households gradually shrank from large extended families to smaller nuclear families, beginning in what is now the developed world. In addition, the number of children living in each household has shrunk from an average of four or more in much of Europe in 1900 to fewer than two, and sometimes one, at the end of the century. As noted above, these trends are largely—though not entirely—the result of rational decisions made by citizens living in industrialized urban societies, where education is preferred over early childbearing; higher standards of living are enjoyed by smaller families; and, more recently, two incomes are needed to sustain a single household.

Sociocultural influences—including the increase in single-person households—have also affected the size of households in the developing world. As cultural pressures toward marriage have been removed in much of the developed world, many people now have the option to remain single throughout their reproductive years and, indeed, throughout their lives. Similarly, the easing of social pressures to bear children has led to the rise of childless families. Finally, the increasing acceptance of divorce as a legitimate cultural decision—and an easier legal choice—has caused many households to split into two, thereby reducing the average size of each household. The size of households in Europe, the United States, Japan, and elsewhere in the developed world has fallen significantly. Whereas, at the turn of the century, the average household in the developed world consisted of five or six persons, at century's end the average is closer to three.

All these factors, of course, are becoming increasingly evident in the developing world, though to varying degrees in different countries. The industrialization and urbanization of much of East and Southeast Asia have clearly led to a significant decline in the size of households there. In South Korea, for example, the average household size has decreased from 5.6 to 3.7 in just the past thirty years, reflecting that country's rapid shift to an economy dominated by the middle-class. But even where that shift to a middle-class society has not occurred, rising urbanization—which affects both economically vibrant and economically stagnant countries—has an impact, since urban families tend to be smaller than their rural counterparts. Thus, in Turkey, the average size of a rural household is 6 persons, while that of an urban household is 4.6, some 23 percent smaller.

The recent cultural changes in the Western world—the shift toward more single-person households and the rise in divorce rates—have been less apparent in the developing world, largely because cultural shifts usually follow economic change. Industrialization and urbanization often reduce traditional influences of family, community, and religion on the first generation to arrive in the city less than on their offspring, who are fully socialized to urban life.

So, while the number of children per household and the number of households with extended families have been shrinking in the developing world since the end of World War II, the number of single households and divorce rates have not risen to the same extent. For example, whereas both a developed country like Italy and a developing country like Jordan had comparable marriage rates in 1965—7.4 and 7.8 per 1,000 persons, respectively—Italy's has fallen to 5 per 1,000 persons, while Jordan's has risen slightly to 8 per 1,000 persons. Similarly, while a developed country like Canada has seen its divorce rate climb from 0.5 to 2.7 persons per 1,000 between 1965 and 1995—an increase of 440 percent—the divorce rate in Jamaica—equal to Canada's in the 1960s—remained roughly the same as that of 1995.

There has also been a marked trend toward more female heads of households. In this, unlike in divorce and marriage rates, the developed and the developing worlds are changing simultaneously. In countries as diverse economically and culturally as Namibia and New Zealand, the number of households headed by females—which almost always means there is no male adult in the household—now stands above 35 per-

cent. At the same time, in Iran, where Islamic culture holds sway, the rate is below 6 percent. Clearly, both cultural and economic factors are at play.

In the developed world, the explanation is largely cultural: the rising acceptance of divorce and the increased number of out-of-wedlock births. In Iran, the cultural pressure against—as well as the lack of economic options for—single women is critical. But what of Namibia? The high rate of female-headed households is related to high mortality rates among males, the large number of illegitimate births, and the widespread use of migrant labor in the country, which usually draws the men away from their families for extended periods and leaves the women to head the household. In short, then, the rise in the number of female-headed households has no single cause in Namibia. The reasons for female-headed households vary widely by society, though the number of such households is rising in most parts of the world.

AGE AND SEX STRUCTURES

Age

Changes in household size and composition are following a similar trend in both the developed and developing worlds, despite a difference in the pace of the changes, but the same cannot be said for age structures. An age structure is a snapshot of the number of persons in each age group, or cohort, of a society at a particular moment. Although these cohorts are sometimes distributed into segments as small as five years, demographers generally prefer to use three large segments: children or dependents (0-14); adults of working age (15-64), and older adults generally beyond working age (65 and up). (Readers in developed countries may find that the age when actual adulthood commences here seems early, but in many developing countries—even with the rise in educational opportunities—15 is the age at which many children begin to work.)

With respect to age structure, population experts generally distinguish three kinds of societies. A "young" society is one in which at least

35 percent of the population is under the age of 15 and less than 5 percent is over age 65; a "balanced" age structure refers to a society where 25 to 35 percent of the population is under age 15 and 5 to 10 percent of the population is over 65; an "old" society is one in which less than 25 percent of the population is under age 15 and more than 10 percent is over age 65. Most of the developing world falls into the first two categories, while virtually all of the developed world falls into the third.

Age structures are often pictured as pyramids, though this is not always the best way to describe the shape of age structures. A pyramid consists of bars representing each age cohort placed one on top of another. In "young" societies, the bulk of the people are represented in broader lower bars, which quickly taper off, forming a kind of pyramid. In "balanced" societies, the best description of the age cohorts might be a cone, in which a slightly larger base tapers off gradually. An "old" society might best be depicted as a column, in which the elderly and the young are roughly even.

The oldest societies are those of Europe, especially Western Europe, where modern medical techniques that extend life, combined with rapidly declining birth rates, produce populations in which the percentages of persons under age 15 and over age 65 are nearly equal. Italy, for example, has one of the lowest birth rates in the world—9.9 per 1,000 persons—and one of the oldest age structures—just 15 percent of the population is under age 15 and 17 percent is over age 65. East European countries, though also experiencing low birth rates, do not have quite as old an age structure because of rising death rates, in the wake of the collapse of communism and the social welfare network the communist governments provided. Russia has a low birth rate of 10.2 per 1,000 persons, but the declining life expectancy—now down to 63 years—means that the age structure, while still "old," is younger than that of Italy. In Russia, 21 percent of the population is under age 15, while some 12 percent is over age 65.

Countries with a moderate rate of population growth, such as the United States, offer what at first appears to be an age structure similar to Russia's. In the United States, some 22 percent of the population is under the age of 15, while 13 percent is over 65. The causes for this convergence of age structures, however, are very different in the two countries. Whereas in Russia declining life expectancy and falling birth rates explain the moderately old age structure, in the United States the causes lie in families with more children, especially among immigrants.

The "balanced countries" (a technical term, not meant to imply the ideal) include many of the newly industrialized and urbanized countries of East and Southeast Asia. In these regions, traditionally high birth rates are slowly being reduced by family planning programs, the economic decision making of parents, and changing cultural attitudes about families and children. At the same time, high death rates are being brought down through a combination of better diet and health care. Thailand, for example, has an age structure in which 25 percent of the population is under age 15 and 6 percent is over age 65. Other "balanced" countries include the more developed Latin American countries like Argentina, where 28 percent of the population is under age 15 and 9 percent is over age 65. A final group of "balanced" countries includes those that are less developed industrially but have advanced family planning programs. The most significant example of this group is China, where 26 percent of the population is under the age of 15, while 7 percent is over 65.

The "young" societies include virtually all of Africa, Southwest Asia, and tropical Latin America, though this last group has begun to slip into the younger end of the "balanced" group. To take three key examples: in Brazil 31 percent of the population is under the age 15 and 4 percent over 65, while in Nigeria and Iran 45 percent of the population is under age 15 and just 3 percent is over age 65. The key factor in "young" societies is continued high birth rates, since in many of these countries improved diet and health care mean longer life expectancy.

Both "old" and "young" populations present

problems for governments and social planners. In the case of the former, large segments of the population have moved beyond working age. Since this age structure is typical of societies—such as those in Europe or North America—in which social programs have replaced children and families as providers of care for the elderly, a political and economic dilemma arises: how to provide funds for the retired without draining the resources of those who are working through excessively high taxation. Young societies have the same problem, but in reverse: Large numbers of children tax the abilities of working-age people to support them.

Demographers measure the extent of these problems with what they call the "dependency ratio," the ratio of people of nonworking or dependent ages (under 15 and over 65) to those of working age. The ratio is calculated as follows: Japan, where 31 percent of the population is under 15 or over 65 and 69 percent is of working age, has a dependency ratio of 31/69, or .45. By comparison, in the Philippines, where 42 percent of the population is of nonworking age and 58 percent is of working age, the dependency ratio is 42/58, or .72. This means that an average working-age person in the Philippines has to support nearly three-quarters of a person more than his or her counterpart in Japan.

Of course, both societies face greater problems in the future. As Japan's population continues to age, its dependency ratio will rise. In developing countries like the Philippines, the future holds quite different and potentially more explosive political and economic problems. The increasing number of young persons means that jobs, housing, and other facilities must be created for the society to maintain current standards of living. And as these youths move into their reproductive years, they will flood the society with new children—even if they have fewer per family than their parents did.

Sex

Sex structures, like age structures, offer a snapshot of a society at a particular moment. The extreme differences among countries evident in age structures do not appear regarding sex structures, simply because, statistically speaking, there are only two "cohorts," male and female, which are normally evenly distributed. However, an evenly balanced sex structure can be skewed for several reasons. The first relates to women's status. If male children are valued more highly than female children, then human intervention may lead to a higher male to female ratio. As discussed above, India, which has 1.08 males for every female, illustrates this sex structure phenomenon.

The second is out- and in-migration. In general, males tend to migrate more often than do females. So, countries with high levels of out-migration have a higher ratio of females to males. El Salvador is a typical example, with a female-to-male ratio of 1.08. Conversely, countries that have high in-migration rates have higher male-to-female ratios among the younger age cohorts in which most immigrants lie.

Of course, one has to be extremely careful with these statistics, since most countries with high out-migration rates tend to be in the developing world, where life expectancy is shorter, while countries with high in-migration rates tend to be in the developed world where life expectancies are longer. This is important to keep in mind because women tend to live longer than men in all developed societies and in all but the poorest developing societies (exceptions being places where health care is so inadequate and birth rates are so high that many women die in childbirth). Indeed, the fact that women tend to live longer is the main reason women tend to outnumber men in the vast majority of countries.

Households have indeed changed dramatically over the course of the past 200 years, a period roughly corresponding to the birth of industrialization in England and its spread to much of the rest of the globe. Households have become smaller and more nuclear. But now a new phenomenon is occurring in the developed world and, to a lesser extent, in the more Westernized, urban sections of the developing world. With the rise of women's economic independence and the acceptance of alternative lifestyles—including lifelong single status and single parenthood—the household appears to be changing again, though the trend toward ever-smaller families continues.

FURTHER READINGS

Adepoju, Aderanti, ed. *Family, Population and Development in Africa.* Atlantic Highlands, NJ: Zed Books, 1997.

Bandarage, Asoka. *Women, Population and Global Crisis: A Political-Economic Analysis.* Atlantic Highlands, NJ: Zed Books, 1997.

Corson, Stephen, Richard Derman, and Louise B. Tyrer, eds. *Fertility Control.* London, Ontario: Goldin, 1994.

Donaldson, Loraine. *Fertility Transition: The Social Dynamics of Population Change.* Cambridge, MA: B. Blackwell, 1991.

Finkle, Jason, and Alison C. McIntosh, eds. *The New Politics of Population: Conflict and Consensus in Family Planning.* New York: Population Council, 1994.

Goldscheider, Calvin, ed. *Fertility Transitions, Family Structure, and Population Policy.* Boulder, CO: Westview Press, 1992.

Hartmann, Betsy. *Reproductive Rights and Wrongs: The Global Politics of Population Control.* Boston: South End Press, 1995.

Moffett, George D. *Critical Masses: The Global Population Challenge.* New York: Viking, 1994.

Niven, Catherine, and Anne Walker, eds. *Reproductive Potential and Fertility Control.* Boston: Butterworth-Heinemann, 1996.

Quale, G. Robina. *Families in Context: A World History of Population.* New York: Greenwood, 1992.

Section 5

Demography and Cultural Identity

HISTORY OF STATES AND ETHNICITY

Nearly six billion in all, the human community often seems as if it were divided into 6 billion different subgroups. There are differences of race, ethnicity, language, religion, and culture, along with biological distinctions like sex and economic differences such as class. Laid over these differences is the nation-state. A relatively new phenomenon in human history, the nation-state has become the dominant political entity in the world today. But the nation-state and the various identities outlined above do not always correspond. And therein lies the problem of ethnic and cultural identity and ethnic and cultural conflict, two phenomena that have become especially acute in recent years as the basic global ideological division—Western capitalism versus Eastern communism— has largely faded away.

Julius Nyerere, the former president of Tanzania, well understood the dilemma as it pertained to Africa. He remarked that because Africa's borders were so absurdly drawn, they must remain unchanging. Nyerere's paradoxical statement revealed much about Africa's past and its present predicament. More than in other parts of the developing world, the national borders in Africa were drawn up in the late nineteenth century by European colonialists who took little notice of existing ethnic, religious, and linguistic settlement patterns. This ignorance is hardly surprising given the fact that the colonial borders—many of which became national borders after the wave of independence that

swept Africa in the 1960s—were drawn solely by Europeans, without consultation with Africans. The result of this practice was a collection of nations in which numerous ethnicities, religions, and language groups coexisted—often uneasily—within a single sovereign state. Despite these shortcomings, Nyerere believed, to disturb these borders might unleash endless wars in Africa.

The Middle East, another arena where Europeans did the border drawing—this time in the wake of World War I—found itself with a problem exactly the opposite of Africa's. Here, the Europeans—acting under the authority of the League of Nations, the predecessor of the United Nations—divided a single cultural, religious, and ethnic group—the Arabs—among many states. Arab historians believe this was done to ensure that no great post-independent pan-Arab state would challenge European hegemony. Of course, it should also be noted that some of the same problems of several ethnicities or religious groups in one state plagued the Middle East as it did Africa. In Iraq, for example, Shi'a Muslim Arabs represent more than 50 percent of the population, with Sunni Muslim Arabs and Sunni Muslim, non-Arab Kurds constituting the rest.

More than in other places in the world, in Africa and the Middle East, borders reflect an almost complete disregard for cultural divisions and unities. These regions are unique only in the degree that each state represents an artificial unit or place. Indeed, many of the states of the world—especially among the former communist

Table 5.1

Nation-States and Minorities (minority = at least 10 percent of the population)

Region	Total no. of countries*	Ethnic/racial minority	Language minority	Religious minority	No majority	No minority
Africa	52	16	4	8	29	4
Latin America/ Caribbean	34	15	2	6	4	12
North America	2	2	1	2	0	0
Asia	42	18	13	15	8	13
Europe	46	15	14	19	2	18
Oceania	14	3	0	7	2	5
World	190	69	34	57	45	52

*The number of different minorities does not correspond to total countries because many countries have more than one minority.

states of Eastern Europe and the Soviet Union—are home to multiple ethnic, religious, and linguistic groups, or, conversely, have larger groups broken up into different states. Even Western Europe, where the idea of nationalism first took shape, contains states with culturally divided polities. The very birthplace of nationalism—France—includes indigenous, geographically contained cultural minorities that believe they have a right to cultural autonomy.

South and East Asia and the Americas also consist largely of states with significant ethnic, religious, and linguistic minorities. In Asia, those states with large minorities include some of the biggest (India, Indonesia, and Iran), as well as smaller states such as Malaysia and Sri Lanka.

In the Americas, the mix of cultural, religious, and ethnic groups is the result largely of immigration or slavery. While the latter's legacy of racism leaves a heritage of ethnic bitterness in the United States, Brazil, and several smaller countries, immigration has blurred differences through what used to be called the "melting pot." Even with today's emphasis on cultural roots and identity politics, the power of assimilation—along with the fact that minorities in immigrant countries tend to be dispersed geographically—has helped eliminate the worst of irredentist, or separatist, impulses. The major exception to this is Canada, where a significant

French minority in Quebec seems to have opted for independence, even if the English speakers there continue to prevent a majority of Québécois from voting for separation from Canada.

Religions and Ethnic Edentity

A review of the world's religions reveals that a majority of countries today either have significant ethnic, linguistic, or religious minorities or are so divided that they lack a single cultural majority. Table 5.1 shows how many countries either have significant minorities (meaning at least 10 percent of the population) or so many minorities that there is no majority culture.

Of the 190 countries surveyed, only 52 had no significant ethnic, linguistic, or religious minorities. The regions with the highest rate of nonminority countries were Latin America and Europe. This should not be surprising, since Europe and Latin American represent regions where nationalism and the modern nation-state have existed for the longest time. At the other extreme—countries with no clear ethnic, religious, or linguistic majority—the largest number by far was in Africa. Some 56 percent of African countries do not have a single cultural majority and, of all the countries without a single cultural majority, 64 percent were in Africa. As for specific types of minorities, the most common worldwide was ethnic/racial. Some 36 percent of the countries in the world have significant racial or ethnic minorities, followed by 30 percent with religious minorities, and about 18 percent with linguistic minorities.

Ethnic, linguistic, and religious minorities can contribute greatly to the economic and cultural life of a country. Imagine American music without the influence of African-Americans or American food without the input of Asian-Americans. At the same time, the presence of minorities—as well as the lack of a majority culture—can create enormous political, economic, and social problems. Because ethnic identity is so heavily determined by history, it is difficult to generalize about the significance of ethnic minorities from one state to another and one society to another. Instead, a national and regional approach is required. The following section discusses the ethnic, religious, and linguistic composition of the various regions of the world, as well as selecting several representative or significant states from those regions for closer examination. The emphasis is on demography rather than culture; that is, on how demography shapes cultural minorities and majorities, and how cultural minorities and majorities, affect demography.

Africa

As noted above, African borders were determined largely by European colonialists, with little regard to existing settlement patterns. Almost all African states have minorities. These states can be divided into two rough groups: those in which there is no absolute majority, and those in which there are one or more significant minority groups. This represents a key difference in the histories of those countries since independence, as the following various country examples will show.

Nigeria

A British colony until 1960 and the most populous state in Africa, Nigeria consists of dozens of minor ethnic groups, as well as four major ones: the Hausa, the Fulani, the Yoruba, and the Ibo. The main division in the country falls along religious and geographic lines, however. The northern part of the country is dominated by the Muslim Hausa and Fulani; the southern half of the nation is mainly Christian or practices the tratitional faiths of the Ibo and Yoruba. The population is roughly 50 percent Muslim and 50 percent non-Muslim.

Rapid population growth in all parts of the country has meant that this ratio of Muslims to non-Muslims has not changed. However, the urban migration of the past thirty years has allowed the south's population to grow considerably at the expense of the north, since the country's major cities—including Lagos, its largest metropolis—are located in the south, as are the crucial gas and oil fields that generate the vast bulk of the country's revenues. This fact has only increased northerners' anxieties of southerners dominating the state.

In the first years after Nigeria's independence, the southern Christians governed the country. The northern Muslims felt excluded from the political and economic centers of power, although, under the British, the Muslims had been used largely as the colony's soldiers and police. This military tradition continued after independence, eventually leading in the mid-1960s to a coup by northern officers. This was followed by a secession by the Ibos in 1967 and the horrific Biafra secession war in which up to a million Nigerians died, most of them Ibo civilians. Fearing southern dominance ever since, the northern Muslim military elite has maintained an iron grip on political power to this day.

Rwanda

Rwanda, a former Belgian colony in the Great Lakes region of East Africa, has long been one of the most agriculturally fertile and densely populated parts of Africa. As of 1995, there were more than 670 persons living on every square mile of land. Because of the historically high density rates, the country developed a highly bureaucratic, monarchical system long before the arrival of European colonizers at the end of the nineteenth century.

Ethnically, the country has been divided into two main ethnic groups: the Tutsis and the Hutus. Although the origins of the former, a pastoral people composing 10 percent of the population, are unclear, they eventually came to dominate and subjugate the majority Hutus. But there has been much intermarriage and comingling of the two peoples, and in time they came to speak the same language.

When the Belgians came, they tended to favor the Tutsis. With their more angular features and warlike tradition, the Tutsis were seen as racially superior. Tutsis were made the local administrators and police of the colony. Upon independence, the Belgians handed power over to them. The Tutsis were quickly overthrown and subjected to nearly constant harassment from the government for thirty years, leading eventually to the infamous genocide of 1994, when Hutus murdered as many as 500,000 or nearly 80 percent of the Rwandan Tutsi population, until forced to stop by an invading Tutsi army from Uganda. These Tutsis from Uganda continue to rule the country.

Sudan

The largest country in Africa by area—nearly a million square miles—Sudan was ruled jointly by Great Britain and Egypt until 1956, when it gained its independence. Because of its huge size, Sudan straddled the line dividing Arab-dominated North Africa from black-dominated Central Africa. This division corresponded roughly to the country's religious and linguistic split between the Muslim, Arabic-speaking north and the Christian and animist south, where a variety of African languages were spoken.

Although Arabs composed only 40 percent of the population, they dominated the country's politics, since both the British and Egyptian administrators established more schools in the north. After Sudan's independence, the northern Arabs largely ignored the needs of the southern blacks. By the 1960s, this neglect had sparked a bitter civil war that has persisted to this day.

Latin America

Latin America has one of the most racially mixed populations in the world. Different races have intermarried and had children together to a much greater degree than in North America and Asia. Out of this Latin American mixing came two distinctive populations: the Spanish-speaking mestizo of mainland Latin America, who are mixed Indian and European, and the mulatto, who are mixed European and African. The mulatto are prevalent in Brazil and in the Spanish-speaking Caribbean islands. The descendents of European settlers have largely dominated the politics and business of Latin America.

Brazil

The largest country in South America in both geographic area and population, Brazil is the largest Portuguese-speaking country in the world. First settled by Amer-Indians tens of thousands of years ago, Brazil was colonized by the Portuguese beginning in the sixteenth century, and achieved full independence near the end of the nineteenth century. Outside the remote and barely settled Amazon region, most Amer-Indians quickly died out from diseases like smallpox and the measles because they had no immunities to the new illnesses introduced by Europeans.

During those three hundred years of Portuguese rule, millions of Africans were transported to Brazil as slaves, mostly to labor on the plantations in the central and northeastern parts of the country. Slavery was abolished near the end of the nineteenth century. Both during and after the time of slavery, however, there were few white females in these regions. The male white settlers often took African women as wives or had children by them without marriage. Meanwhile, by the late nineteenth and early twentieth centuries, the more temperate regions of southern Brazil were attracting European immigrants by the millions.

This dual influx of Africans in the north and Europeans in the south gives Brazil its complex racial makeup, in which 55 percent of the population is labeled white, 39 percent mulatto, and 6 percent African. Because of their tradition of racial intermixing, Brazilians claim that their society is much more racially tolerant than that of the United States, which has a somewhat similar racial profile. But Brazil has the most unequal distribution of wealth of any country in the world, and this inequality breaks down largely along racial lines, with whites far richer than mulattos and blacks.

Guatemala

The most populous country in Central America, Guatemala was part of Spain's American empire until the early part of the nineteenth century. As in other parts of Latin America, Spanish colonizers—most of whom were male—intermarried and interbred with the native population, creating a large group of mestizos. Yet in Guatemala, unlike other Latin American countries, a significant Indian population—many of them descendents of the Maya—survived in the Guatemalan highlands, where they maintained their own culture and language, even if they adopted Roman Catholicism. So, today, 60 percent of Guatemalans speak Spanish, while 40 percent continue to speak Mayan and other Indian languages. At the same time, virtually all Guatemalans, mestizo or Indian, practice Christianity, usually as Roman Catholics but increasingly as evangelical Protestants.

Despite their numbers, the Indians of Guatemala remained politically and economically powerless. Many of them were forcibly recruited to work the plantations of the lowlands—plantations owned by North American corporations and administered by Spanish-speaking mestizos or whites. When the Indians began to resist with a guerrilla movement in the 1970s, the army cracked down, conducting a brutal—some say genocidal—campaign against the Indians of the highlands. It is estimated that some 100,000 Indians, mostly civilians, were killed at the hands of the Guatemalan army in the 1980s.

Trinidad and Tobago

Trinidad and Tobago, twin islands at the southern end of the Lesser Antilles, has one of the most peculiar ethnic and religious profiles of any country in Latin America. First a Spanish, then a French,

and finally a British colonial possession, Trinidad relied heavily on the population of African slaves who worked the commercial plantations. In 1833, Britain outlawed slavery and the plantation system collapsed. To revive it, planters came up with a plan to bring in tens of thousands of indentured servants from India, another British colony.

In 1962, Trinidad won its independence from Britain. Since then, the country's racial relations have exhibited a remarkable tolerance, largely due to the unofficial power-sharing arrangements in the country, in which the descendents of Asian Indians run the business sector and the descendents of African slaves administer the government. Although generally tolerant of each other, the two groups rarely intermarry or interbreed. Trinidad's racial profile reflects this complex history, with 43 percent of the population black, 40 percent Asian Indian, and just 14 percent mixed. The remaining 3 percent consists of whites and Chinese. Religious affiliation follows a similar division: Most blacks are Christian, and most Asian Indians are Hindu or Muslim. Tobago is almost entirely black and Christian, as there were few imported Asian workers because of limited plantation agriculture.

North America

The continent of North America consists of two countries: Canada and the United States. In many ways, these countries have similar ethnic profiles. Both were originally inhabited by indigenous populations; colonized by Britain; and eventually settled by waves of immigration from Europe and, more recently, Asia. But these similarities mask key differences. Canada never condoned slavery and so has few people of African descent. Moreover, its greater land area and smaller European population allowed native American Indian nations to maintain more cohesion. But, most important, Canada and the United States differ linguistically—the former being bilingual and the latter generally only English-speaking.

Canada

France was the first European country to settle Canada. But unlike the English colonists to the south, the French did not emigrate to the country in tremendous numbers. By the mid-eighteenth century, English colonists in North America outnumbered the French by more than ten to one. In the French and Indian Wars from 1756 to 1763, the English used their numerical superiority to conquer French Canada. Over the years, the English came to dominate the colony as a whole, both politically and economically. This was also true of the first hundred years of independent Canadian history, from the 1860s to the 1960s. Moreover, the waves of European immigrants who came to the country in the late nineteenth and early twentieth centuries adopted English as their primary language.

So, today, while only 40 percent of Canadians trace their origins to Great Britain, 70 percent speak English as their first language. Meanwhile, only 27 percent of Canadians trace their origins to France and roughly a similar percentage speak French as their first language. (A small percentage of Canadians speak native Indian languages.) But the French speakers are geographically concentrated in the province of Quebec. Beginning in the 1960s, they have agitated for independence. In recent referenda on the subject, the majority of French-speaking Québécois have voted for separation from Canada, but they have been unable to win an absolute majority because of the near-total opposition of English speakers in the province, including many of the newest immigrants from the Caribbean and Asia.

United States

America's current ethnic composition—and ethnic tensions—can be traced through its history. During the 1600s and 1700s, settlers poured in largely from Great Britain and Northern Europe, pushed back the native Americans to west of the Appalachian mountains, and imported hundreds of thousands of African slaves, primarily to the southern part of the country. At the same time, these so-called White Anglo-Saxon Protestants (WASPs) dominated government and business until the twentieth century.

In the nineteenth century, the country expanded westward to the Pacific Ocean, annexing nearly half of Mexico and confining the surviving native Americans to reservations. Meanwhile, slavery ended, but racist oppression continued against African-Americans. The nineteenth and early twentieth centuries also saw a massive influx of immigrants from Eastern and Southern Europe, China, and Mexico.

During the middle third of the twentieth century, immigration was reduced by legislation. But, at the same time, a massive migration of African-Americans from the southern to the northern portion of the United States occurred. Since the passage of new, more open immigration laws in the 1960s, a new wave of arrivals, this time largely from Asia and Latin America, has come to America's shores.

America's current ethnic profile reflects this history. African-Americans—two-thirds of whom are now in the northern United States and one-third in the southern part of the country—remain the largest minority group, composing about 12 percent of the population. But it is expected that they will be outnumbered by Hispanics early in the twenty-first century. As of 1997, Hispanics made up about 11 percent of the U.S. population, and Asians comprised another 4 percent. If current trends continue, people of European descent will make up less than half the population by the middle of the next century.

Asia

It is, of course, difficult to generalize about such a vast and heavily populated region as Asia, but several overall points can be made. Like Africa, Asia was heavily colonized or dominated by European imperialists in the late nineteenth and early twentieth centuries. But, unlike African states, most Asian states were further along on the road to nationhood upon the arrival of the Europeans, so colonial borders could roughly follow ethnic lines. In addition, many Asian states were empires of their own. Countries like China, India, and Iran housed numerous minority peoples within their borders.

Malaysia

Until the economic meltdown of 1997, Malaysia had one of the fastest-growing economies in the world, growing at an annual rate of 8 percent for more than a decade. Its per capita income in 1995 was $9,800, placing it in the top tier of developing countries.

This economic success has helped offset the ethnic tensions that once plagued the country. Malaysia's population for most of this century has been divided into roughly three groups. The native Muslim Malays make up roughly 60 percent of the population. Ethnic Chinese, who for hundreds of years have been settling in this country, which sits astride key trading routes in East Asia, compose about a third of the population. The remainder consists largely of Indians, brought by the British to work on plantations in what was called Malaya in the late nineteenth and early twentieth centuries.

Because the Chinese controlled much of the state's business, ethnic tensions built up between them and the more rural and impoverished Malays. Some of this tension took on religious overtones, as the Malays tried to legislate Muslim precepts into law. Gradually, a compromise has been reached between the two groups, giving Malays control of the government and, through affirmative action–type programs, better educational opportunities. Thus Malaysia has been able to avoid the anti-Chinese violence that recently erupted in neighboring Indonesia.

India

The second largest country in population in the world, India was born in a fire of ethnic violence. A largely Hindu region of the world through the early modern age, India began to come under the control of Muslim emperors by the 1500s. Particularly in the northern part of the country, millions of Hindus—largely from low castes, or inherited classes—converted to Islam over the next several centuries. By 1900—by which time the British had thoroughly colonized the region—roughly 30 percent of the subcontinent

(including modern-day Pakistan and Bangladesh) was Muslim.

The British generally recruited Muslims to serve in the military and the police force. At the same time, the early independence movement was dominated by Hindus—a fact of some concern to Muslim nationalists, who demanded a separate state of their own. At the time of India's independence in 1947, Britain was forced by Muslim militants and politicians to divide the subcontinent into two countries, India and Pakistan. With this partition came violence. More than a million people of Hindu or Muslim descent were massacred simply for being in the sector predominantly populated by the other group. Some 15 million people were forced to migrate: Muslims to Pakistan, Hindus (and other non-Muslims) to India. Because of this mass migration, India's Muslim population shrank to about 15 percent, where it remains today. Meanwhile, tensions persist both between Pakistan and India, and between India's Hindu majority and Muslim minority, especially since the electoral victory of a Hindu nationalist party in 1997.

Israel

Unique among the countries of the world, Israel is not only a state of its citizens, but also a homeland for Jews around the world, who are granted immediate and automatic citizenship upon their arrival in Israel and their declaration of an intention to remain there. The Palestinians who left—or were forced out—during Israel's independence war in 1948–1949 are not permitted to return.

Israel is also one of the most ethnically heterogenous countries in the world. Twenty percent of its citizens are Arab (who are mostly Muslim, though a minority are Christian or Druze), and the 80 percent who are Jewish are racially and ethnically diverse, owing to the history of Jews in the twentieth century. There are four major groups of Jews worldwide, only one of which—those living in the Middle East—moved to the country early on. Most European Jews were killed in the Holocaust; most American Jews preferred to stay in the United States; and most Jews in the former Soviet Union were not permitted to emigrate (until the collapse of the Soviet Union. Since that time, however, many have left).

Not surprisingly, this complex mix of religion and ethnicity has dominated the country's history for all of its fifty years as a modern state. The conflict between Palestinian Arabs and Israeli Jews is well known. But there has also been the struggle for political and economic power between Sephardic Jews, who come from the Middle East, and Ashkenazi Jews, who come from Europe and the Americas. In only one area has Israel proved successful at dissolving differences: linguistically. It has been able to revive and disseminate the use of Hebrew as the language of all its people.

Turkey

Once at the core of the great Ottoman empire—which ruled the Middle East and southeastern Europe—Turkey's power ebbed in the face of the more aggressive British and Russian empires in the nineteenth century. The Ottomans, who sided with Germany in World War I, were utterly defeated and had their empire stripped from them at the conclusion of the war in 1918. Even the Anatolian heartland of Turkey seemed threatened with dismemberment.

But out of this disaster emerged Kemal Ataturk, a Turkish military officer, who was able to salvage the country by driving out the British and Greek invaders. Rather than opting for a multiethnic state, Ataturk and his successors—who rule the country to this day—brutally imposed a Turkish identity on all inhabitants. This was particularly galling for the Kurdish minority in the southeastern part of the country. The Kurds, who are heirs to one of the most ancient cultures in the world, compose about 20 percent of the population and are currently engaged in a guerrilla struggle for independence or cultural autonomy. But the military and political elite are unwilling to accept any further division of the country. Thus, the war in Turkish Kurdistan grinds on.

Europe

Europe is where both the modern nation-state and modern nationalism were born—the former as early as the fifteenth century in Western Europe, the latter a by-product of the French Revolution of the late eighteenth century. In the nineteenth century, the concept of the nation-state spread to Central Europe, and in the early twentieth century it moved on to the eastern half of the continent. But only with the collapse of the last great European empire—the Soviet Union in 1991—did nationalism finally triumph in Eastern Europe. Many European states are home to significant ethnic minorities—several of which have agitated politically or militarily for their independence.

Bosnia and Herzegovina

Until 1992—when its citizens voted for independence—Bosnia and Herzegovina constituted one of six provinces of the Yugoslav Federation. This federation and the territory in which it existed had a checkered history. Conquered by the Muslim Ottomans in the sixteenth and seventeenth centuries, portions of it were gradually annexed to the Austro-Hungarian empire or won their independence until, by the eve of World War I, the Ottomans had been completely driven out—not, however, before hundreds of thousands of Muslims from other parts of the Ottoman Empire had settled in the region, alongside thousands of local inhabitants who had converted to Islam. The effect of these conversions and settlements was a patchwork of Christian (both Eastern Orthodox and Roman Catholic) and Muslim communities in what would first become Yugoslavia and then Bosnia and Herzegovina.

Following World War I, the various parts of what would become Yugoslavia were united under Serbian King Peter to form the Kingdom of Serbs, Croats, and Slovenes. In 1929, the name was changed to the more inclusive Yugoslavia, which, in Serbo-Croatian, means Land of the Southern Slavs. During World War II, the territory was occupied by the Nazis and was liberated in large part by the communist partisans under Marshal Tito (Josef Broz), who used strong-arm tactics and economic stimuli to dampen the religious and ethnolinguistic rivalries. But after his death in 1980, the situation slowly began to unravel, and after the fall of communism in Eastern Europe in 1989, it finally collapsed.

Of all the former Yugoslav republics, Bosnia was the most divided religiously and ethnically. Eastern Orthodox Serbs and Bosnian Muslims each composed about 40 percent of the population, while Roman Catholic Croatians constituted 20 percent. The country was plunged into war as the local Serbs—backed by Serbia itself—tried to carve out an independent state. Only with the intervention of the North Atlantic Treaty Organization (NATO) in the mid-1990s was the war stopped. Tensions remain high however, and Bosnia is still provisionally divided into Serbian and Bosnian/Croatian sectors.

Northern Ireland (United Kingdom)

Often called the world's first modern European colony, Ireland was conquered by England in the late Middle Ages. Beginning in the 1500s and 1600s, the English government began to recruit Scottish people to settle in Ireland, as a kind of settler militia society, to maintain English control there. Most settled in what would become the northern six counties that now make up Northern Ireland, or Ulster. The settlers were Protestant; the indigenous inhabitants of Ireland were Catholic.

In 1916, the southern part of Ireland won its independence, but the north remained part of the United Kingdom. London argued that since 60 percent of Northern Ireland was Protestant—and preferred to remain British—Northern Ireland should remain part of the United Kingdom. Over the centuries, the English conquest and the Protestant presence led to a two-tiered society in Northern Ireland, with Protestants ruling over the Catholics. This led to bitterness, violence, and the outbreak of a civil war that has lasted from 1969 to the present.

Many observers believe that, given enough time, the Catholics—who tend to have larger families than the Protestants—will become the majority and

vote peacefully for amalgation with Ireland. But because of the poor economy, out-migration rates in the region remain high, and the majority of those who leave are poor and Catholic.

Spain

Ironically, although it was among the first states to form in Europe—the monarchies of Castille and Aragon merged in the late 1400s—Spain has also been home to some of the most vociferous ethnic minorities in modern European history. Two groups among these stand out: the Basques in the north and the Catalans in the northeast.

Brutally suppressed under the dictatorship of Francisco Franco from the late 1930s until his death in 1975, the movements for Basque and Catalan autonomy and independence have become quite potent since Spain's return to republican rule in the late 1970s. Both the Catalans and the Basques (who speak one of the most ancient languages in the world, one unrelated to any other in Europe) are culturally distinctive. But it may be their economic position that spurs on their ethnic and linguistic demands. Two of the most prosperous areas of Spain, the Basque region and Catalonia, do not want to be burdened by supporting the central government in Madrid or the poorer regions in the south.

Oceania

The smallest of the world's major regions in both population and land area, Oceania consists of two major Western-style countries—Australia and New Zealand—and several tiny island republics inhabited by Melanesian, Micronesian, and Polynesian peoples. In addition, several islands remain colonies of France (French Polynesia) and territories of the United States (American Samoa and Guam). All were once colonized by European or American governments, but only Australia and New Zealand became states settled largely by Europeans.

Australia

Initially settled by convicts from England, Australia continued to be largely a colony of Britain, even after independence in 1910. Most of its people—aside from the tiny minority of native Aborigines—came from the Great Britain, which dominated the country's culture. This began to change in the 1960s. First, there was Australia's involvement in the Vietnam War. Then came the rise of the Asian economies, which forged closer financial links between the two regions. And, finally, there has been a wave of Asian immigrants to Australia, who now outnumber the Aborigines four to one and make up almost 5 percent of the country's population. While this has produced a racist backlash among a minority of Australia's whites, most accept that the country must break its old but geographically strained ties with England and become more culturally and economically integrated with nearby Asia.

Fiji

Once an independent Melanesian kingdom, Fiji came under British rule as a protectorate in the late nineteenth century. Shortly thereafter, Britain began to import Indian laborers to work the commercial plantations of the islands. Gradually, the population of the two groups—the native Melanesians and the immigrant Indians—grew to be about even. During the first years of independence during the 1970s and early 1980s, the country was ruled by a consortium of Fijians and Indians. But, in 1987, Fijian nationalists in the army, angry about Indian control of the country's economy, overthrew the government and instituted programs aimed at improving the educational and economic opportunities of Fijians.

GLOBAL ISSUES

The demographic implications of ethnic, linguistic, and religious divisions are not confined to nation-states, as the previous survey of countries might imply. Demography and cultural issues can also be global. Since the fall of communism in the late 1980s and the subsequent end of the Cold War, cultural divisions seem to have taken precedence over ideological ones. Three of these cultural issues—(1) ethnic and racial, (2) linguistic and cultural, and (3) religious—appear to be especially crucial.

Ethnic and Racial

Near the beginning of the century, the African-American sociologist W.E.B. Dubois pronounced that "the problem of the twentieth century is the problem of the color-line—the relation of the darker to the lighter races of men in Asia and Africa, in America and the islands of the sea." Despite the diversion of the Cold War—which pitted two white superpowers against each other—and the rapid decolonization of the developing world in the two decades after World War II ended, Dubois's remarks remain prescient. Euphemisms like "developed" and "developing worlds" or "first" and "third worlds" only partly hide the reality: With few exceptions, most of the wealthier countries of the world remain predominantly white.

This was not always so. Until the industrial revolution and the vast spread of European colonialism to Africa and Asia (the Americas, of course, were colonized and won their independence much earlier), the differences in wealth between what we now call the developed and developing worlds were minimal, as is reflected in birth and death rates. In the latter half of the eighteenth century, what are now the developed nations of the world had birth and death rates of 38 and 34 per 1,000 persons, respectively; what are now the developing nations had rates of 41 and 37 per 1,000, respectively. But the industrial revolution and the conquest of much of the world by Europe changed that. By the first decade of this century, the developed world had birth and death rates of 34 and 21 per 1,000, respectively, while the developing world had rates of 41 and 34 per 1,000.

The income and wealth ratios were even more sharply divergent. In the 1700s, it is estimated that the ratio of incomes in what are now developed countries to what are now developing countries was just three to two. Today, it is roughly ten to one. A 1998 United Nations Development Program study found that the world's richest 20 percent consumed 86 percent of all goods and services, half the energy, and nearly half the animal protein in the world. And despite the recent collapse of former white Soviet bloc countries and the rise of a few Asian economies and petroleum-rich, underpopulated countries in the Middle East, the divide between rich and poor remains largely a divide between whites and nonwhites.

Linguistic and Cultural

Classically defined, imperialism implies the political and economic control of one country by another. In so effecting this conquest, the imperialist power exploits the colony for cheap natural resources or labor and as a market for manufactured goods of the mother country. This was the model the British used in their global empire. And, arguably, this is the model—aside from outright annexation—that the United States has used to maintain its economic control over much of Latin America. Whether the United States is an imperialist power is more widely debated. Those who argue in the affirmative say that the only difference between the British Empire and U.S. economic hegemony in Latin America for instance is that, in the latter case, the region has not been annexed politically. Still, proponents of the so-called neo-colonialist argument insist that, through U.S.-based multinational corporations and U.S.-dominated international lending institutions like the World Bank and the International Monetary Fund, the United States is able to exploit natural and human resources, while dominating local markets for manufactured goods. Opponents of the neo-colonialist argument insist trade in the region is open and free, and that various other developed nations play as important a role as the United States does in the development of Latin American economies. Moreover, they insist that local elites—not foreign interests—have control over the political and economic decision-making process. More controversial is the definition of imperialism as a cultural offensive. Can it be called imperialism if one nation aggressively exports its cultural products—and, by implication, its language—to the rest of the world, especially if

the rest of the world can be said to accept it voluntarily? Clearly, one such country is the United States, which exports its film, fashion, TV shows, advertising, sports, music, and, most recently, its Internet to the rest of the world.

To critics of American cultural and linguistic hegemony, or dominance (though the basis for the linguistic hegemony of English was laid by British imperialists), the threat is to indigenous cultures and languages around the world. Nor is this division one between the developed and the developing worlds. Indeed, it could be argued that wealthier countries are more threatened by American cultural and consumer dominance because these are the countries with the higher disposable incomes to spend on cultural and consumer products. The most vociferous critics of American cultural dominance are high-income countries like France and Canada.

Moreover, linguistic issues continue to be interwoven with political ones in Africa. There, France—which once controlled a vast empire and still yearns for cultural dominance—has made the preservation of the French language on that continent a major pillar of its foreign policy. For example, in Rwanda, it has been argued by critics of French foreign policy, that France deliberately supported the genocidal Hutu regime because its leaders were francophones (or French speakers), while the Tutsi rebels—who were attempting to overthrow the government and stop the genocide—were English-speaking exiles from Uganda, a former British colony.

Religion

The collapse of communism and the great ideological struggle between East and West has led many political scientists to believe that the globe is being divided into great ethnocultural blocs, whose different values and interests place them at odds with one another. The most famous of these theorists is Samuel Huntington, who says that one of the sharpest differences between these cultural blocs is religion and the cultures influenced by religion.

Of course, this so-called clash of civilizations is nothing new. It was the basis for the millenium-long struggle between Christianity and Islam in the Mediterranean region, and for the conquest of the Americas by Roman Catholic and Protestant settlers from Europe. Nevertheless, the rise to political power of religious fundamentalists in India and Iran—as well as their increasing power in America, Israel, and some Arab and Asian states—is noteworthy and seems to bear out Huntington's argument. Critics, however, point out that religion remains a largely symbolic issue, a convenient political handle for struggles over old-fashioned economic privilege and political power.

CONCLUSION

It is often said that, with the end of the Cold War, humanity has entered the post-ideological age. No longer is the globe divided between capitalist West, communist East, and a developing world caught in the middle. The positive effects of this cannot be overstated. The simple fact that the threat of global thermo-nuclear war no longer hangs over humanity's collective head is enough for anyone to appreciate the demise of the old order.

But the fall of communism and the lifting of the ideological straitjacket has permitted ethnic and cultural minorities to voice and sometimes act upon their grievances against the dominant majority in nation-state after nation-state. Indeed, there has been a tendency to subdivide larger states into smaller and more ethnically homogenous mini-states. Sometimes this has occurred nonviolently—as in the case of Czechoslovakia—and sometimes it has led to war, as in the tragic case of the former Yugoslavia.

But there is a great irony in all of this. While these new culturally homogenous mini-states may provide a more politically stable and ethnically agreeable climate for their peoples, they may also be more economically vulnerable. That is because the trend toward mini-states has been occurring alongside a trend toward economic bigness. Multinational corporations, the global communications web, and the increasing power of international lending institutions are rendering the nation-state less important, with national governments facing decreased powers over their own economies. Ultimately, the struggle for cultural independence may be won even as the struggle for economic independence is surrendered without a fight.

FURTHER READINGS

Clarke, Angus, and Evelyn Parsons, eds. *Culture, Kinship and Genes: Toward Cross-Cultural Genetics.* New York: St. Martin's Press, 1997.

Driedger, Leo, and Neena L. Chappell. *Aging and Ethnicity: Toward an Interface.* Boston: Butterworth's, 1987.

Goldscheider, Calvin, ed. *Population, Ethnicity, and Nation-Building.* Boulder, CO: Westview Press, 1995.

Herzfeld, Michael. *Cultural Intimacy: Social Poetics in the Nation-State.* New York: Routledge, 1997.

Huntington, Samuel P. *The Clash of Civilizations and the Remaking of World Order.* New York: Simon & Schuster, 1996.

Jurgensmeyer, Mark. *The New Cold War: Religious Nationalism Confronts the Secular State.* Berkeley: University of California Press, 1993.

Samarasinghe, S.W.R. de A., and Reed Coughlan, eds. *Economic Dimensions of Ethnic Conflict: International Perspectives.* New York: St. Martin's Press, 1991.

Szporluk, Roman, ed. *National Identity and Ethnicity in Russia and the New States of Eurasia.* Armonk, NY: M.E. Sharpe, 1994.

Van Horne, Winston A., ed. *Global Convulsions: Race, Ethnicity, and Nationalism at the End of the Twentieth Century.* Albany: State University of New York Press, 1997.

Wallerstein, Immanuel, and E. Balibar, eds. *Race, Nation, Class: Ambiguous Identities.* New York: Verso, 1991.

The Demography of Labor and the Economy

LABOR AND THE ECONOMY

The world economy at the close of the twentieth century would be unrecognizable to observers of the world economy in the 1950s and 1960s. At mid-century, the United States, Western Europe, Japan, and the Soviet Union were the leading industrial countries. Today the United States, Western Europe, and Japan are the leading economies of the world and the engines of global economic expansion. However, in these three regions, manufacturing employment has significantly declined as a share of their respective labor forces. There are two major causes for this decline: (1) technological advancements that have sharply reduced the demand for manufacturing workers; and (2) the relocation of manufacturing industry to developing countries where workers are paid significantly lower wages and environmental and workplace regulations are less extensive. Although these developed countries maintain high relative standards of living, they have lost much of their manufacturing industry to developing countries of the third world. In these developed economies, the vast majority of all workers are employed in the service, government, and trade sectors. Factories that once dotted the urban landscapes have been torn down. By 1996, the service sector contributed almost two-thirds of global gross domestic product (GDP). Although concentrated in the developed countries, the service sector is expanding to become a growing share of GDP in developing countries as well.

As developed countries have shifted from manufacturing to services, leading countries in Asia and Latin America have transformed their economies into industrial powerhouses. At the century's close, Brazil, China, Indonesia, Korea, and Mexico have larger shares of their labor force employed in the industrial sector than either the United States or Western Europe. In the past half-century, the Soviet Union, once considered one of the world's leading industrial powers, has declined and shriveled. By the end of the century, many factories of Russia and the Soviet Union's successor states and former socialist economies in Eastern Europe have closed. Although people have greater freedom to make their own economic decisions, the cradle-to-grave economic security provided by the planned economies has largely been eliminated by new leaders embracing neoliberal economic reform.

What accounts for this shift? The major force in this change is private industry's drive for greater productivity and profitability. The typical manufacturing facility at mid-century was the large centralized factory that produced and assembled every component of the final product sold on the consumer market. For example, the typical automobile producer was responsible for fabricating the steel, glass, and rubber materials into engines, transmissions, windshields, dashboards, radios, door handles, and all the other parts that went into the car that rolled off the assembly line. Today, automobile companies do not make most of the parts that go into the final product but contract out (or outsource) production to parts makers that typically pay their workers lower wages. Economists call this change in industrial product a shift from large centralized manufacturing to smaller-scale production facilities. Changes in the structure of industrial production—from centralized production to decentralized production and global competition from low-wage producers—have, in turn, lowered inflation-adjusted industrial wages in the developed economies of North America and Western Europe.

From Keynesianism to Neoliberalism

Keynesianism is an economic theory developed and elaborated by John Maynard Keynes (1883-1945), an English economist who argued that free markets are subject to periodic downturns and crises known as recessions and depressions. To curb the effect of these downturns, Keynes argued that it was necessary for governments to play a leading role in the economy by regulating the money supply and by spending public funds to create jobs and promote economic growth. In the 1950s and 1960s, most of the world's developed economies embraced this Keynesian economic strategy. While Keynesianism has many variations, from state ownership of key sectors of the economy to tinkering with the money supply, the model was put to use in virtually every country of the capitalist and socialist world.

However, in the 1970s and 1980s, Keynesianism was gradually superseded by what is commonly known as neoliberalism, an economic theory that advocates free capitalist markets with limited government intervention. Free marketers in academia and business leaders endorsed the neoliberal model, contending that government intervention was counterproductive because it artificially propped up weak economies. Increasingly, the neoliberal economic model was applied to developing countries in the third world.

By the early 1990s, after the collapse of the Soviet Union, the neoliberal model had virtually replaced the Keynesian model throughout the world. In country after country, national leaders were curtailing state ownership and participation in economic activities and opening their economies to greater global economic activity. Under the new economic regime, countries that want to attract foreign capital and investment are required to reduce and eliminate trade barriers that inhibit foreign competition. Moreover, national governments are required to reverse tariffs, regulations, and laws restricting money transfers from their countries. The formation of trade unions, which help prop up the wages of workers, is also discouraged because they are seen by national economic leaders as raising production costs and reducing economic competitiveness. For the last two decades of the twentieth century, national governments, with few exceptions, have sold off failing state-owned enterprises to domestic and foreign-owned investors. Many other countries have established stock markets that trade shares in private companies to investors throughout the world. Even China, which still calls itself communist, actively promotes private investment and ownership in its productive factories and resources.

What is neoliberalism's record thus far? Clearly freer global markets have produced tremendous profits for the powerful, the affluent, and the educated. Unleashing the free market throughout the world has made markets more responsive to the needs of consumers who can afford to purchase goods and services. However, as the twenty-first century approaches, the record of neoliberal reform seems to have raised more questions than answers for the economic future of all of humanity. In industrialized countries of the developed world, between the mid-1970s and the late 1990s, inflation-adjusted wages have fallen and basic social protections provided by governments have been withdrawn. Moreover, poverty has continued to grow throughout much of the world. Although many countries of the developing world would like to take advantage of increased foreign trade, their economies remain vulnerable to shifting raw material and commodity prices, as well as the vicissitudes of financial and capital markets.

Moreover, many developing countries pay significant shares of their national income to repay foreign debt, preventing them from dedicating economic resources to growth and development. Some poorer countries of Africa and Asia with a per capita GDP well below $750 a year use a majority of their national income to repay foreign debt. Thus, the economic record of developing countries over the past two decades is mixed. While some developing countries (notably Malaysia, Korea, and Indonesia) have experienced strong growth rates that have improved living standards, others (including those in sub-Saharan Africa, the Caribbean basin, Latin America, Oceania, and South Asia) have remained mired in poverty, with poor economic performance and declining living standards.

Although neoliberalism may rationalize markets and improve living standards for those who are already better off, much of humankind remains in abject poverty. In addition, the Asian and Russian economic crises of the late 1990s demonstrate that unregulated financial and capital markets may promote investment, but are more likely to aggravate the weaknesses of national economies and lead to severe economic slowdowns and even depressions. Indonesia, Malaysia, and other Southeast Asian countries that were celebrated as models of neoliberalism in 1997 were facing bankruptcy and economic collapse one year later. South Korea, which rapidly developed into one of the world's leading industrial powers through government-sponsored planning and investment in the 1980s and 1990s, was negotiating with international lenders for debt relief as the economy stumbled into a long recession.

The Decline of Organized Labor

How has the neoliberal model affected labor? In recent decades, governments have rolled back their regulations over labor markets. Deregulation and increasingly lax enforcement of statutory and administrative laws have permitted the entry, in both developed and developing countries, of new business competitors that are not complying with long-standing policies and rules

built up over the past century. The consequences for workers have been detrimental. Competition is leading firms to reduce production costs by ignoring laws and regulations governing wages, benefits, and working conditions. In previous decades, labor regulations protected most workers. However, in the deregulated economy, business profitability in general is enhanced by casting off government policies that provide standardized wage scales, government benefits, and safe working conditions. Today, calls for deregulation in developing countries are a customary response to globalization and capital flight. Until recently, deregulated labor markets were characteristic of underdeveloped countries. However, low wages, marginal labor, and informal economic activity have become primary features of urban centers in North America and Western Europe. Economists call labor deregulation "informalization"—meaning economic activities that are carried on outside the system of national regulations. By 1989, scholars were identifying the growth of informal labor markets in the United States and in Western Europe. In many cases, even large multinational corporations were depending on informal labor to produce garments, food, electronic goods, and other products for sale. Frequently workers were employed in sweatshops in both advanced and developing countries.

Many other workers who relied on stable jobs in manufacturing and service industries have seen their wages erode and working conditions decline. This decline is due in part to the weakening of labor unions, which have been a major force responsible for the improvement of wages and working conditions throughout the world.

Since the global economic decline in the 1970s, the number of low-paying jobs in the United States has grown, as has mass unemployment in Western Europe. Trade unions, which were first organized in the late nineteenth century in industrializing countries to protect worker rights, could not significantly curb the decline in wages. In the industrialized world, unions' weakness stems in part from labor's failure to organize marginal economic groups that are at the greatest risk of economic dislocation, including minorities, women, and immigrants. In Latin America (Guatemala, Mexico), East and Southeast Asia (China, Indonesia, Vietnam), and other countries of the developing world, independent trade unions have often been banned by national governments and labor leaders have often been arrested and imprisoned.

Despite these challenges to labor power, workers are organizing into unions in many countries throughout the world to fight for wage gains and improved working conditions. Major strike waves have challenged efforts by government and corporate leaders to initiate wage and benefit cuts. In the winter of 1995, French transportation workers waged a general strike that crippled the country and eventually led to the collapse of that country's conservative government. The following year, in South Korea, as the national legislature attempted to implement an austerity plan and to change laws so as to weaken labor, Korean workers in many industries went on strike to force the government to rescind the plan. In the United States, a revitalized labor movement is seeking to focus on organizing among minorities, the poor, and the working class.

From the mid-1980s to the mid-1990s, trade union density, or the share of nonagricultural workers who are members of trade unions, declined in most countries throughout the world (see Table 6.1). Trade union density has declined in sixteen of the twenty-one countries shown in Table 6.1, ranging from a 71.9 percent decline in union density in Bangladesh to a 56.2 percent increase in union density in Spain. Aside from Spain, the only countries to experience union density growth were South Africa (40.7 percent), the Philippines (24.1 percent), South Korea (4.7 percent), and Denmark (1.2 percent).

Economic Expansion and Poverty

The unprecedented expansion of the free market on a global scale in the 1980s and 1990s may have expanded international trade, but this growth has not reduced the human need and deprivation that stem from poverty. At the end

Table 6.1

Changes in Trade Union Density
(in ascending order)

Country	Year	Density	% Change
Bangladesh	1985-1995	4.3	-71.9
Kenya	1985-1995	16.9	-59.6
Portugal	1986-1995	18.8	-53.7
Argentina	1986-1995	25.4	-47.9
Mexico	1989-1991	31.0	-42.7
Austria	1985-1995	51.7	-29.2
United Kingdom	1985-1995	36.0	-27.2
Australia	1985-1995	28.6	-26.9
Egypt	1985-1995	29.6	-23.9
United States	1985-1995	12.7	-15.2
China	1985-1995	54.7	-7.8
Thailand	1985-1995	3.3	-7.4
Italy	1985-1994	32.9	-7.0
Japan	1985-1995	18.6	-4.0
Germany	1991-1995	29.6	-3.5
Canada	1985-1993	31.0	-0.6
Denmark	1985-1994	67.4	1.2
Republic of Korea	1985-1995	9.0	4.7
Philippines	1985-1995	18.4	24.1
South Africa	1985-1995	21.8	40.7
Spain	1985-1994	11.4	56.2

Source: International Labor Office, *World Labour Report: Industrial Relations, Democracy and Social Stability 1997-98.* Geneva: International Labor Organization, 1997.

of the twentieth century, about a third of the world's population is unable to afford everyday necessitities—food, shelter, and access to basic health care. Although economic wealth varies from one country to another, according to the World Bank, it is possible to calculate the percentage of a country's population that is living on less than $1 a day and $2 a day at 1985 international prices, adjusted for purchasing parity. These calculations produce a very disturbing picture (see Figure 6.1). Most states in Africa remain mired in abject poverty, with large portions of the population surviving on less than $2 a day. Of the twenty most poverty-stricken countries in the world, as measured by the percentage of the population surviving on the equivalent of $1 or less a day, fourteen are in Africa. Africa is home to the six at the top of that list: Guinea-Bissau (88.2 percent of the population defined as poor), Zambia (84.6 percent), Madagascar

(69.3 percent), Uganda (69.3 percent), Niger (61.5 percent), and Senegal (54 percent).

Abject poverty is not limited to Africa, but extends to every continent of the world. According to World Bank statistics, poverty remains high even in countries that have robust economies. About 43.5 percent of Brazil's population and 57.8 percent of China's population, among the most rapidly growing industrial powers in the world, survive on less than $2 a day. About 50.2 percent of all residents in India, the world's second most populous country, subsist on $1 a day or less, and 88.8 percent on less than $2 a day. In Latin America, about 40 percent of Mexico's population live on less than $2 a day, and in Guatemala, about 76.8 percent live on less than $2 a day and 53.3 percent live on less than $1 a day.

Although the causes of poverty are complicated, difficult to quantify, and varied, economic inequality and underdevelopment are the two factors that can be identified throughout the world. The distribution of income and wealth is critical in understanding poverty. Even in countries with a high per capita GDP, high poverty rates persist because of the unequal distribution and investment of income and wealth. Poverty is increasing because when a few people own and control most of a nation's wealth, many people have little access to economic resources. Thus, while the number of multimillionaires in China, Mexico, and Brazil has grown over the past two decades, the number of homeless, unemployed, and hungry has also grown. Moreover, populations in many poorer countries in Africa, Asia, and Latin America have become even more destitute as a result of their inability to gain access to capital to use in developing health care, housing, sanitation, educational institutions, and transportation.

An analysis of the twenty countries with the highest poverty rates shows that most of them also have low life expectancies, high infant mortality rates, low literacy rates, and high national unemployment rates. A clear distinction should be made between low per capita GDP and poverty. Although countries with the highest pov-

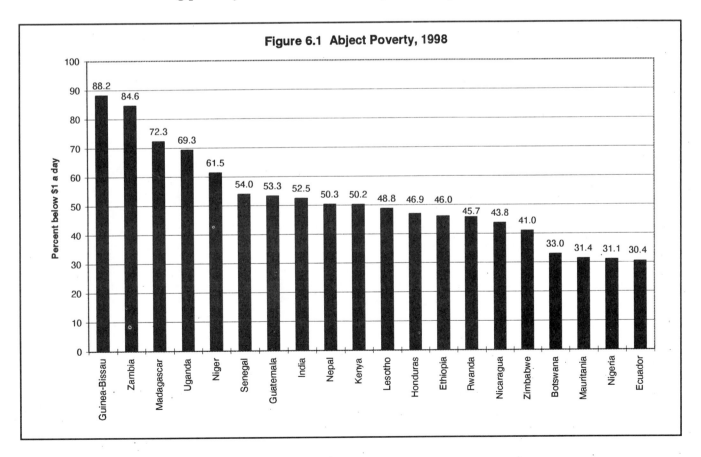

Figure 6.1 Abject Poverty, 1998

erty rates also tend to have low per capita GDP, certain countries have reduced poverty by redirecting resources to those in greatest need. Cuba, for example, which has weathered an American economic embargo for forty years since the 1959 revolution, ranks fairly high on most social indicators because of its more egalitarian distribution of wealth and income. Although much of its population is poor and does not have access to many commodities, Cuba continues to have a high life expectancy, low infant mortality, and a high literacy rate because of the country's effort to reduce income and wealth inequality.

REGIONAL ECONOMIES AT THE END OF THE TWENTIETH CENTURY

The world is significantly more integrated and interdependent than it was even a decade ago. This newfound global integration can be seen in the growth of regional trade blocs, the decline of global trade barriers, and the expansion of capital markets throughout the world. The decline in regional and global trade barriers, known conventionally as globalization, has important consequences for the fate of humanity. The following is a regional analysis of important economic and labor trends throughout the world.

North America

A major economic shift occurred in North America between the 1960s and the 1990s. As the United States and Canada changed from primarily manufacturing-based to service-based economies, Mexico went from being an agricultural producer to being a leading global manufacturer. By the end of the twentieth century, a larger percentage of workers was employed in manufacturing industries in Mexico than in the United States and Canada. Since the early 1970s, average wages have declined in the United States and income inequality has widened. Mexican, Central American, and Caribbean industrial workers, on average, are employed at a fraction of the wages and benefits of U.S. and Canadian workers. The poorer countries of the Caribbean

basin—the Dominican Republic, Guatemala, Haiti, Honduras, Nicaragua, and Panama—continue to depend on the export of agricultural commodities and raw materials for foreign exchange; most of their rural poor and new urban dwellers are living in poverty. After the Soviet Union suspended economic support for Cuba in 1991, the Cuban economy descended into economic crisis. Until 1991, Cuba benefited from substantial Soviet aid. After a "special period" of economic austerity, the country's economy has rebounded. However, the partial market reforms introduced have created greater inequality and jeopardized the country's socialist economy.

South America

Latin America's leading economies (Brazil, Venezuela, and Argentina) are among the most industrialized in the world, with large segments of their workforces employed in manufacturing. In the early 1980s, the region shifted from industrialization based on domestic production of goods from local markets that are produced abroad even if the foreign goods can be produced at lower cost (a term known as import substitution), to export promotion, which aims to expand exports of manufactured goods. Now a large proportion of manufacturing in Latin America is produced for export markets in North America and Western Europe. The export-oriented economies improved the national balance of payments in regional economies and eased a debt crisis in the region, which resulted from earlier policies that focused on the expansion of domestic markets. A second major development in the region has been the reduction in the high inflation rates that plagued the region during the 1980s. In Argentina and Brazil, the substantial reduction of double-digit rates of annual inflation in the 1990s has encouraged increased domestic and foreign investment. The high inflation rates of the early 1990s have been reduced as neoliberal economic reforms were instituted in countries throughout the region, including currency devaluation, privatization of state-owned industry, and reduction in public spending. In the 1990s, although

South America experienced intensified economic growth, the region became heavily dependent on exports. Brazil, the largest country in the region, remains heavily in debt to foreign lenders. South America, as a whole, is enduring high and growing levels of poverty and income inequality that are not being addressed by the individual governments. Despite these trends, Chile remains an economic success story in the region. The country's market-oriented economy has grown dramatically since the 1970s, significantly improving living standards for large segments of the population. Critics, however, argue that this growth has come at the cost of political repression and growing inequality.

Africa

Africa is the least developed populated continent in the world. Although significant differences exist among African countries, most of the population in Africa is mired in persistent poverty and destitution. With the exception of South Africa and perhaps Algeria, the region's leading exports are agricultural commodities, minerals, and natural resources, which provide limited foreign exchange with which to develop the continent. A significant impediment to economic growth in Africa since the 1960s is the persistence of insurrections, civil wars, and border disputes throughout the continent. On important economic measures, Africa is home to the poorest populations in the world. The continent has the highest poverty rates, the lowest per capita GDP, and the lowest level of industrialization. Moreover, the countries are heavily in debt to foreign lenders and must pay substantial proportions of national income to service foreign debt. The market reforms in Ghana, Tanzania and other countries of the continent have improved the capacity to export agricultural commodities and natural resources to Western Europe and North America. Although South Africa's economy is more economically advanced, the country's wealth is unequally distributed between an affluent European population and a poorer African population.

Asia

Asia is a continent of tremendous contrasts between economic development and underdevelopment. East Asia has been the center of economic growth and development. Since the end of World War II, standards of living in East and Southeast Asia have improved dramatically. By the 1980s, Japan, the economic powerhouse of the region, had become the world's second largest economic power after the United States. Japan's economic growth was stimulated by significant government investment in the private sector, a high savings rate, and an export-oriented economy. In the 1970s and 1980s, the Republic of Korea, Singapore, Taiwan, and Hong Kong duplicated this economic growth model with tremendous success. However, as wages have increased, international investors have been attracted to even lower-cost producers throughout the region—to Indonesia, Malaysia, and Thailand and, more recently, to China, the Philippines, and Vietnam. In the late 1990s, however, the region was suffering from a major financial economic crisis stemming from overspeculation that depressed most of the region's economies. Korea, Indonesia, Malaysia, and Thailand, facing default, were forced to negotiate debt relief with international lending institutions. The economic crisis threatened political stability throughout the region, and caused the collapse of a thirty-year dictatorship in Indonesia. In the late 1990s, governments fell in Korea and Thailand while Malaysia was in the throes of political crisis.

Beginning in the late 1970s, the Chinese government instituted capitalist economic reforms that have stimulated industrial growth and development. Although the country still calls itself a communist state, the private sector has expanded and developed as the state and collective sectors have declined. In the process, China has become a major exporter of industrial goods to North American and West European markets. Much of China's economic growth is concentrated in major cities. The growth of the capitalist economy has contributed to a widening income gap between a new affluent class and urban workers and rural peasants. Since the 1970s, the rural countryside, where a majority of the country's population resides, has stagnated and declined. Many of the new workers are undocumented migrants from rural areas who come to the cities in search of work. Rural poverty has grown dramatically in China since the 1980s as the government emphasizes urban development and neglects the countryside.

South Asia is not as economically developed as East and Southeast Asia. Although India instituted neoliberal market reforms in the early 1990s aimed at promoting private foreign investment, the economy remains primarily agrarian and undeveloped. The poorest major power in the world, India has one of Asia's highest poverty rates and a low per capita GDP of $1,500 a year. Much of India's population depends on subsistence agriculture. The country's burgeoning cities are overcrowded and beset by poor health and sanitation services, malnutrition, homelessness, and unemployment. India's market reforms have not penetrated significantly beyond a burgeoning high-technology sector in urban areas, due in part to limited access to capital and restrictive government regulations.

Although relatively more advanced than South Asia, Southwest Asia (including the Middle East, Afghanistan and the former Soviet Republics) is significantly less developed economically than East and Southeast Asia. The region's economic lethargy and underperformance are linked in part to political instability and military conflict in the region, including civil wars in Afghanistan and Lebanon, the legacy of the Iranian revolution, past conflicts between Iraq and Iran, the Persian Gulf War, and the persisting Arab-Israel conflict. Much of the region's economic wealth is concentrated in the oil-producing states (Bahrain, Iran, Kuwait, Oman, Qatar, Saudi Arabia, and United Arab Emirates). Labor shortages in the oil-producing states have encouraged large numbers of foreigners from poorer countries in the region to migrate to the region in search of employment. The largest economies in the region are Iran, Saudi Arabia, and Turkey.

Europe

Western Europe has an advanced industrial economy and a highly skilled workforce. Although Western Europe has endured a long-term economic downturn since the 1970s, it continues to have one of the world's highest standards of living. The economic downturn combined with growing global competition presents significant challenges to the region. In the 1990s, Western Europe has experienced high and persistent unemployment, due in part to growing global competition from low-wage producers in the United States, Latin America, East Asia, and Southeast Asia.

However, unemployment is mitigated by comprehensive social welfare systems in most countries of the region. In France, Germany, Scandinavia, and elsewhere in Western Europe, social protections (universal health care, unemployment insurance, family support) are significantly broader than in the United States. Efforts by national leaders to reduce national budgetary deficits in the 1990s by paring down social welfare programs have come under popular resistance. The creation of a single monetary unit, known as the euro, is expected to put additional pressure on governments to reduce budget deficits. Significant differences in wealth in West European (e.g., northern and southern Italy, eastern and western Germany) have intensified political conflicts in countries in the region.

In their efforts to move from state control to private market economies, Russia and Eastern Europe are undergoing serious economic turmoil. Many inefficient factories that were once supported by the state have been closed. Moreover, currency devaluation has severely strained the ability of emerging capitalist economies in Eastern Europe to service foreign debt. Since the collapse of the Soviet Union, the economies of Russia and the successor states have contracted, as inefficient factories have closed. In 1998, the Russian government, unable to stem the decline of the Russian ruble, defaulted on foreign debt. The economic crisis intensified political conflict and renewed calls for greater state intervention to protect and stabilize the economy. The Polish economy has rebounded from a period of economic decline in the early 1990s as it reorients its market economy from an Eastern European focus to Western Europe and North American markets. Although the Czech Republic and Hungarian economies have prospered in the post-Soviet era, the region as a whole has suffered from growing unemployment and higher poverty rates.

CONCLUSION

At the end of the twentieth century, the global economy faces opportunity, challenge, and uncertainty. Many countries have initiated economic reforms designed to reduce government bureaucracy and to promote the growth of investment and the expansion of free markets. The globalization of the world's economy has created tremendous opportunity for investors and speculators seeking greater profits through the development of new markets in developed and developing countries. However, many of these market reforms have at least initially taken a significant toll on the stability of traditional capital, industrial, and labor markets. In the former Soviet bloc and the developing world, populations endured long periods of economic crisis with high unemployment and inflation. Moreover, although urban centers have received greater investment, rural areas, where large segments of the world's population live, have often been ignored and face growing poverty. A major question in the twenty-first century is the degree to which governments will participate in managing markets through economic planning and regulation. With an uncertain future, there are many outlooks and perspectives on the economic future, ranging from those advocating the expansion of global markets to those favoring the return of national government regulation and planning. Which policies will ultimately be implemented? The future of the global economy, and by extension, the status of humanity, will rest on the direction of continued market growth or renewed government planning.

FURTHER READINGS

Aronowitz, Stanley. *From the Ashes of the Old: American Labor and America's Future*. New York: Houghton Mifflin Company, 1998.

Block, Fred. "Postindustrial Development and the Obsolescence of Economic Categories." *Politics and Society*, 14, 1985.

Bluestone, Barry, and Bennett Harrison. *The Deindustrialization of America: Plant Closings, Community Abandonment, and the Dismantling of Basic Industry*. New York: Basic Books, 1982.

Brooks, David, and Jim Cason. "Mexican Unions: Will Turmoil Lead to Independence?" *Working USA*, March/April 1998.

Chomsky, Noam. "Power in the Global Arena." *New Left Review*, Number 230, 1998.

Davis, Mike. *Prisoners of the American Dream*. London: Verso, 1986.

Drucker, Peter F. "The Age of Social Transformation." *Atlantic Monthly*, November 1994.

Greider, William. *One World, Ready or Not: The Manic Logic of Global Capitalism*. New York: Simon & Schuster, 1997.

Hayek, F.A. *The Road to Serfdom*. Chicago: University of Chicago Press, 1994.

International Labor Office. *World Labor Report: Industrial Relations, Democracy, and Social Stability 1997-1998*. Geneva, Switzerland: International Labor Organization, 1997.

Kuttner, Robert. *Everything for Sale: The Virtues and Limits of Markets*. New York: Alfred A. Knopf, 1997.

Lindblom, Charles E. *Politics and Markets*. New York: Basic Books, 1977.

Miliband, Ralph. *Divided Societies: Class Struggles in Contemporary Capitalism*. Oxford: Oxford University Press, 1987.

Piore, Michael, and Charles Sabel. *The Second Industrial Divide*. New York: Basic Books, 1984.

Portes, Alejandro, Manuel Castells, and Lauren A. Benton. *The Informal Economy: Studies in Advanced and Less Developed Countries*. Baltimore, MD: The Johns Hopkins University Press, 1989.

Schumpeter, Joseph A. *Capitalism, Socialism, and Democracy*. New York: Harper & Brothers, 1943.

Sen, Amartya. *Inequality Reexamined*. New York: Russell Sage Foundation, 1992.

Wilson, William Julius. *When Work Disappears*. Cambridge, MA: Harvard University Press, 1996.

Section 7

The Demography of Migration

DEFINITION OF MIGRATION

Since the origins of humankind, population movement from one geographic location to another has always taken place. Throughout human civilization, people have adapted to adverse environmental changes (for example, drought and floods) or social and political conditions (economic depressions, war, foreign occupation) by migrating to new localities that offer the opportunity to survive and prosper. Therefore, almost no ethnic or national group can justifiably claim to be the descendants of the original inhabitants of a region or country.

There are two types of migration: internal and external. Internal migration is the movement of people within the geographic boundaries of a nation-state, including population movement from one region of a nation-state to another, from rural areas to cities, and from cities to suburbs and rural areas. External migration is the movement of people across international boundaries of nation-states.

PUSH-PULL AND MIGRATION

Why do people move from one city, region, or nation-state to another? No single explanation can account for all forms of migration. However, historically, most demographers have embraced the push-pull theory as the most persuasive explanation for the movement of people across geopolitical boundaries. The push-pull theory, which emerged in the late nineteenth century, consists of two opposing arguments that lead to disagreement about the causes of migration.

Demographers who emphasize the push factor contend that migrants are forced by economic hardship from their impoverished regions of origin to new regions that offer greater opportunity for economic survival. Thus, although most people would prefer to stay in their home regions, economic catastrophe and disaster compel them to migrate to new locations that offer greater economic opportunity. Demographers who emphasize the pull factor argue that migrants are drawn to new areas by the opportunity for improving standards of living.

Two historical examples of migration, one drawn from eighteenth-century Europe and the other from the contemporary developing world, illustrate the push-pull factors causing migration. Since the seventeenth century, technical advancements in farming have reduced the need for peasant labor in the countryside. At the end of the eighteenth century, the emergence of capitalism brought about new social relations between feudal lords and peasants in England and much of Western Europe. Peasant economic survival in the rural countryside, where the majority of the population lived, became more difficult because of the growth of the enclosure movement, an activity that forced peasants off the estates and into the cities. The emergence of manufacturing industries in the burgeoning cities of Birmingham, Liverpool, and Manchester in the mid-eighteenth century spurred a greater demand for workers. The mass wave of migration from the English countryside followed the growing need for workers by manufacturers in the industrialized cities.

Although the life and culture of cities were clearly more dynamic and offered greater opportunity than the rural countryside, they were also sites of extreme poverty and exploitation. Newcomers to cities were exposed to overcrowded housing conditions and poor sanitation, which contributed to plagues and epidemics. The former peasants who went to cities in the millions formed part of the urban working class, forced by economic necessity and opportunity to work in factories and mills where occupational and health conditions were usually extremely dangerous. There were no laws regulating child labor, minimum wages, or working hours. The improvement of wages and industrial conditions for the new working class occurred only after the growth of a militant and politically influential labor movement in the nineteenth and twentieth centuries that demanded better working conditions, housing, and health care.

Migrants from developing countries in the late twentieth century face challenging social and economic conditions similar to those faced by English migrants in the eighteenth and nineteenth centuries. Peasants of developing countries are compelled to migrate to the cities as a result of economic necessity. As conditions erode in the rural countryside of developing nations, urban areas offer the possibility of survival and greater economic opportunity. For example, the stagnation and decline in the quality of life in the countryside in late-twentieth-century China has pushed many displaced peasants to migrate to the growing cities. Since unauthorized migration from rural to urban areas is illegal in China, these newcomers have few legal rights and little protection from economic exploitation.

Rural migrants regularly end up working as low-wage industrial employees and day laborers in the homes of middle class and affluent urban residents. In developing countries, the growth of cities and the decline of economic opportunities in rural areas have encouraged urban migration. As in eighteenth- and nineteenth-century Europe, new migrants from rural regions of developing countries are youths and young adults who have little opportunity for a productive life in the countryside. Although cities offer greater potential for improving living standards, migrant newcomers ordinarily endure years of destitution before they improve their living and working conditions. Migrants often reside in improvised and haphazard squatter communities on the fringes of big cities that lack adequate housing, sanitation, or health care. Those migrant workers lucky enough to find employment in factories typically put in long hours under adverse conditions for low wages. In many countries of Latin America, South Asia, and Southeast Asia, migrants are often adolescent girls employed in factories, sweatshops, and households as low-wage workers. Migrants from the developing to the industrialized world also endure poor living conditions and low-wage jobs.

THE DECISION TO MIGRATE

Although humans frequently move from place to place in search of gainful employment, the decision to move is not easy and has significant consequences for those who migrate, those who remain behind, and those who live in the areas to which the migrants go. In many cases, those who migrate are making a resolute statement that they cannot comfortably survive in their place of origin. Often when they move, they uproot themselves over a long period of time or even permanently from family members, homes, jobs, and culture (language, religion, ethnicity), usually for a harsh, often uncertain nomadic lifestyle somewhere else. At the turn of the twenty-first century, as many industrial countries close their borders to legal population movement, migrants are increasingly enduring extremely difficult and dangerous conditions, and often risk their lives in their trek to a new home. Thousands of migrants die each year from drowning, heat exhaustion, starvation, falls, vehicular accidents, and other injuries. Although migrants from less developed regions are needed as low-wage workers in industrialized countries, they are often designated as undesirable and illegal by those countries.

Upon arrival in a new location, migrants are almost always considered outcasts and faced with exclusion from the dominant culture. They must therefore adapt to significant changes in life-style or risk continuous isolation and extreme poverty. Even if migrants can earn relatively higher wages in their new location than at home, they almost always occupy the lowest rungs of the economic hierarchy, typically working at low-wage jobs shunned by those in the new area. In North America and Western Europe, migrants are employed as farm workers, housekeepers, nannies, low-level food service workers, construction workers, garment workers, and day laborers. Many migrant workers are employed in sweatshops, where working conditions are arduous, hours are long, and pay is low. Resident low-wage and unemployed workers often argue that migrants reduce wage standards and compete for scarce jobs, and so should return to their country of origin. Frequently, disreputable employers seize on the opportunity to hire low-wage immigrants who are afraid to assert their rights as workers. These employers are attracted to the enlarged pool of low-wage labor provided by migrant workers. Conditions are even worse in countries and regions with high concentrations of migrant workers, where labor regulations are ignored, wages and benefits are low, and working conditions are oppressive.

Migration often has harmful consequences for people left behind in the less economically developed regions and countries of origin. Those who are most likely to leave are the young, single, better-educated, and able-bodied, who can sustain the hardships associated with migration. Often, migrants are forced by necessity to leave destitute areas where traditional economies have been undermined by new political and social forces. For example, the decline of subsistence agriculture, privatization, industrial closures, and currency devaluation have made life extremely difficult for the peasants and working class of Latin America and the Caribbean, prompting many to leave for the United States and Canada. The migration of the able-bodied further drains the local economy of the young and educated. Many who are left behind are older residents, young children, and the less educated, who tend to be less productive than those leaving for greater opportunity. Nevertheless, migrant workers often perform an important economic function for their kin in their country

of origin, as many send home a portion of their wages to help support their families.

ECONOMIC AND POLITICAL CAUSES OF MIGRATION

People migrate from one country to another for two basic reasons: (1) to seek economic opportunity, and (2) to cope with geopolitical change. Both forms of migration have important consequences for the countries migrants leave and the ones they go to. Economic migration typically includes population movement due to the inability to survive in one's country of origin and the possibility for gainful employment in the country to which one is relocating. Geopolitical migration results from changing government policies that restrict or encourage migration of segments of the population. It also flows from significant political change, including decolonization, independence, and the emergence of nationalist movements. Political migrants typically leave their country of origin because they feel unwelcome for reasons related to their identity. The four most important identity factors in migration, and thus the bases of potential discrimination in countries of origin, are nationality, religion, ethnicity, and political ideology.

Economic Factors: Disparity in Wealth Between North and South

Much of the cross-border migration since the end of World War II has been caused by inequality between the developed countries of North America, Western Europe, and East Asia and the developing countries of Africa, Asia, and Latin America. Economic inequality motivates migrants from the developing countries in search of employment to relocate in countries that have developed economies. In the 1960s and early 1970s, migration from the developing countries was encouraged by the developed world in response to the growing demand for foreign labor. However, in the aftermath of the economic decline in the industrialized economies since the mid-1970s, migration has been discouraged. In the 1980s and 1990s, restrictions and limits have been placed on legal immigration by developed countries. However, despite the legal and personal risks, and industrial government policies limiting the entry of foreign workers, migrants have continued voluntarily to leave their home countries.

Typically, migration is regional. Migrants from poorer regions in Africa and Southwest Asia travel to Western Europe for employment and send money to families in their country of origin. Migrants from less developed countries of the Arab world tend to travel to the oil-rich states of Kuwait, Saudi Arabia, and the United Arab Emirates in search of higher-wage employment. In Southeast Asia, Filipino and Indonesian migrants travel to the more affluent states of Brunei, Malaysia, and Singapore in search of work and economic opportunity. Immigrants from Latin America, the Caribbean, and East Asia form the majority of migrant workers to the United States. Figure 7.1 shows thirteen countries that experienced high rates of migration in 1995.

Although most jobs in countries receiving new migrants are low-wage positions that provide little opportunity for advancement (housekeepers, nannies, and fruit and vegetable pickers), migrants continue to come in large numbers, primarily because of the persistence and growth of poverty and income inequality in their countries of origin. Most migrants tend to be the young poor and working class, who have little opportunity for gainful opportunity at home. Figure 7.2 compares the out-migration levels of 1980 and 1995 in countries of the Caribbean basin. The growth in out-migration from Jamaica, Guyana, Grenada, Dominica, Cuba, Belize, Barbados, and the Bahamas was caused by increasing poverty.

Geopolitical Change and Realignment

A second cause of international migration is geopolitical change and realignment that leads to significant government policy shifts encouraging population movement. Typically, geopolitical change and realignment follow decolonization, independence, the emergence of nationalist governments, and the promulgation of policies that restrict or promote migration.

Status as a refugee is an important push factor in political migrations. Political refugees are typically forced to leave their country of origin to take refuge from danger or persecution. For example, during World War II, millions of Jews and other minorities fled Germany and Central European countries to escape Nazism, an ideology that advocated the extermination of Jews and other non-Aryan peoples. Although most of European Jewry was wiped out, many of those who survived migrated to North America, South America, and the Middle East. In the mid-1990s, the Bosnian civil war among Bosnian, Croatian, and Serbian ethnic minorities led to the extermination of hundreds of thousands of innocent civilians through a policy known as "ethnic cleansing." The war led to a mass exodus of refugees to safe havens in Europe. Also in the mid-1990s, in East Central Africa, the Tutsis, an ethnic minority in Burundi and Rwanda, fled to Zaïre, Tanzania, and Uganda to escape Hutu-led governments that persecuted them. Other refugees flee to escape military conflicts and wars that have spread to civilian areas. For example, during the 1990s, thousands of refugees from the Liberian civil war fled to nearby Sierra Leone. (See Figure 7.3.)

There are two types of refugees: those forced to leave under threat of persecution or death, and those who leave when military conflicts spill over into civilian regions. Refugees may be forced to leave because of their ethnic or religious identity (e.g., Armenians, Jews, Tutsis, Bosnian Muslims) or because of their political beliefs, which might be seen as threatening to the government. In the 1930s, communists and other opponents of Nazi Germany were forced to leave under threat of persecution. During the twentieth century, the number of refugees forced to leave their home under threat of persecution because of their identity has greatly increased and accelerated.

Independence and Decolonization

Geopolitical change and realignment has shaped the two leading waves of international migra-

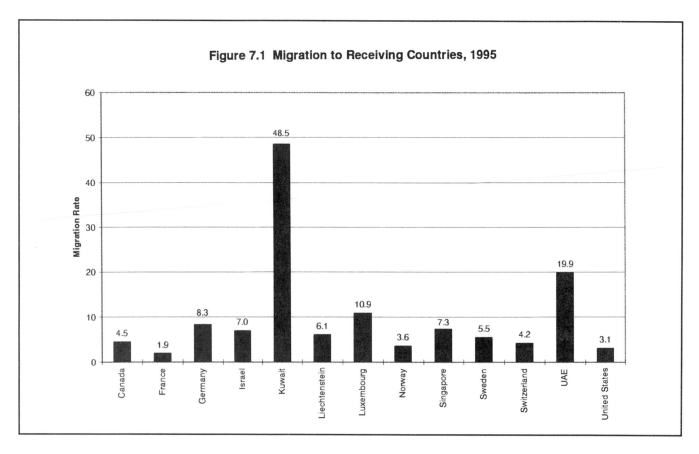

Figure 7.1 Migration to Receiving Countries, 1995

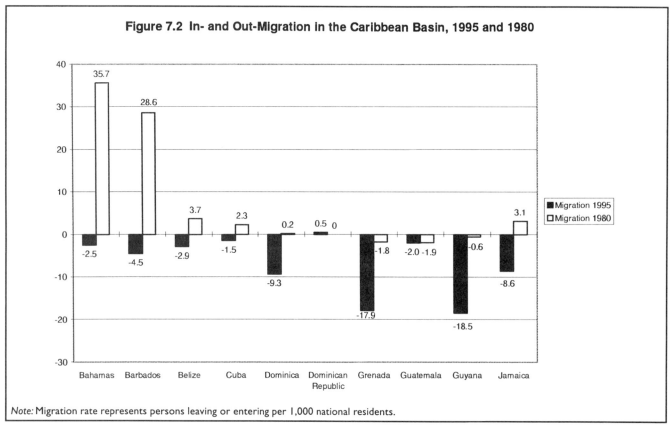

Figure 7.2 In- and Out-Migration in the Caribbean Basin, 1995 and 1980

Note: Migration rate represents persons leaving or entering per 1,000 national residents.

tion since the end of World War II. The first migratory wave, from the late 1940s to the early 1980s, followed the anticolonial movements in Africa and Asia that led to decolonization and independence. The independence movements forced European powers to relinquish control over colonial territories to national governments in Africa, Asia, the Caribbean, and the Pacific. After independence, settlers who had held political and economic power in the territory no longer felt welcome and many migrated to Europe. The three leading European powers that retained colonies in the developing world at the end of World War II were France, Portugal, and the United Kingdom. From the late 1950s to the early 1960s, hundreds of thousands of French nationals who had resided in Algeria and Vietnam for generations left for France. In the 1940s and 1950s, British citizens in India returned to England, as did British nationals in the 1960s and 1970s who had lived in Kenya and Zambia. In the 1970s, in the aftermath of the Portuguese revolution, expatriates living in Angola, Mozambique, and Portuguese Guinea returned to Portugal.

The second leading wave of migration since the end of World War II followed the collapse of the Soviet empire in 1991 and the formal independence of the former Soviet republics in Eastern Europe and Central Asia. Many Russian nationals have lost their economic and political power in the new states that have emerged, and, since the 1990s, millions of Russian nationals residing in the former Soviet republics (as well as the Baltic states) have returned to Russia. By the early 1990s, Russian émigrés from the former Soviet Union represented one of the world's largest migrant populations. (See Figure 7.4.)

Government Policies

Government policies restricting and promoting population movement strongly influence the ebb and flow of migration. During the Cold War, the Soviet Union restricted population movement between East and West. The Soviet Union's poli-

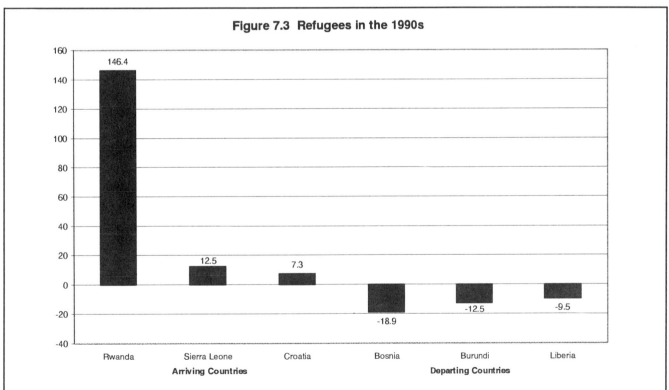

Figure 7.3 Refugees in the 1990s

	Arriving Countries			Departing Countries		
	Rwanda	Sierra Leone	Croatia	Bosnia	Burundi	Liberia
	146.4	12.5	7.3	-18.9	-12.5	-9.5

Note: Migration rate represents persons leaving or entering per 1,000 national residents. A negative number indicates that refugees are fleeing a country, and a positive number indicates that refugees are entering the country.

cies restricting emigration were symbolized by the construction of the Berlin Wall, which divided Germany into two parts, separating East Germany, the Soviet zone of occupation, from West Germany, originally occupied by the United States, Britain, and France. During the Cold War, restrictions on migration were reproduced in Eastern European countries in the Soviet bloc. The policies preventing migration were motivated in part by both political and economic considerations. Migration restrictions from East to West were gradually relaxed during the 1970s and 1980s. In Eastern Europe in the late 1980s, the inability of Soviet bloc countries to control mass waves of undocumented migration caused by economic stagnation and the lack of democracy spurred the fall of communist-dominated regimes throughout the region in 1989. Restrictions on emigration to the West were lifted after the Soviet-dominated governments fell.

Paradoxically, most migratory restrictions in the post–Cold War era have been enacted by governments in North America and Western Europe, in an effort to limit the flow of potential immigrants seeking to escape economic uncertainties throughout the world caused in part by the globalization of production and rising unemployment. The growing disparity in wealth and living standards between industrialized and developing countries has led many migrants from the developing world to move in search of gainful employment. However, in the receiving countries, public support for unrestricted migration is declining and support for closing the borders to foreigners is increasing. Consequently, in the industrialized world, immigration policies are under review and new policies have been passed to dissuade and prevent migrants from entering.

REGIONAL MIGRATORY TRENDS

What are the primary regional migratory patterns at the turn of the twentieth century? Although the key global causes of migration are

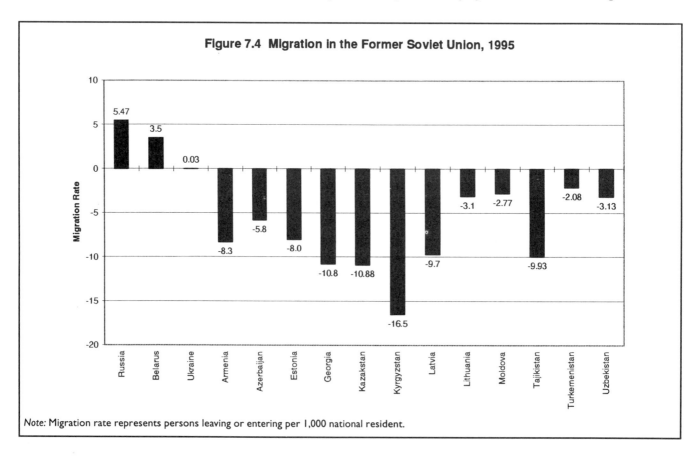

Figure 7.4 Migration in the Former Soviet Union, 1995

Note: Migration rate represents persons leaving or entering per 1,000 national resident.

economic need and geopolitical change, distinctive regional patterns of migration are themselves causing economic stress, political conflict, and policy shifts. The following is a summary of the key patterns in North America, Latin America, Africa, Asia, and Europe.

North America

During the 1980s and 1990s, migration to the United States and Canada continued to grow rapidly even as both governments reformed their immigration policies. During both decades, the United States enacted legislation curbing migration motivated by economic factors. By the early 1990s, the leading sources of migration to the United States, in descending order, were Mexico, Central America, the Caribbean, the Philippines, South America, China, Korea, India, the United Kingdom, Vietnam, Italy, and Germany. In addition, according to government estimates, in the early 1990s there were between 2 million and 3.5 million undocumented foreign nationals residing in the United States.

However, despite the passage of the 1986 Immigration and Reform Control Act, which sought to limit population movement to the United States, immigration from Latin America to the United States continued to grow. During the 1990s, immigration to the United States was restricted further by state and national governments, which instituted severe penalties for undocumented migration and narrowed the political and economic rights of immigrants who lacked either a green card (denoting their status as permanent residents) or citizenship. Government law discourages the immigration of those who require financial assistance and are too poor to survive without public support.

Canadian in-migration is determined by the Canadian government's estimates of the available government resources and financial capacity for absorbing immigrants. The three qualifications for legal migration are family reunification, refugee status, and financial status. Those immigrants that arrive with sufficient financial resources so they are not a burden on the state are more readily accepted. The primary sources of migration to Canada are Asia and the Pacific, Europe, the United States, and the Caribbean.

Latin America

Although Latin America was a major destination for immigrants from the late nineteenth century to the 1970s, in the past three decades the region has become primarily a source of emigration. After World War II ended, Argentina, Venezuela, and Uruguay were the leading destination countries in the region for migrants to and within Latin America. From 1970 to 1980, Latin America precipitously shifted from being a destination to being a source of migration: In 1970 the region gained a net 1.8 million migrants, but by 1980, the region lost a net 1.6 million residents because out-migration was greater than in-migration. Undocumented migration expanded rapidly in the 1980s and 1990s, in part due to legal restrictions placed on migration. The growth of rural and urban poverty in the region is a major reason migrants left for the more affluent United States and Canada. Moreover, migration has also increased in response to the rising cost of living and high unemployment throughout the region.

Asia

Asian countries are both sources and destinations of migration. The major reasons for the growth of migration are uneven economic standards and opportunities among countries in Asia. Moreover, as demand for skilled and semiskilled labor in Australia and North America has escalated, out-migration from Asia has increased steadily since the early 1960s. The Philippines, the Republic of Korea, China, and India are the leading source countries for immigration to Australia and North America. Although inter-Asian migration increased rapidly during the 1980s and 1990s to the newly industrialized countries (NICs) of East Asia and Southeast Asia, in the wake of the Asian financial crisis, the migratory flow has slowed and thousands of migrants have been sent back to their countries of origin. The economic misery may extend to Bangladesh, India, Nepal, and other countries that have depended on payments sent home by migrant laborers who have gone abroad for work.

In the last three decades of the twentieth century, political conflicts have produced major flows of refugees fleeing persecution and war. The two leading sources of refugees on the continent are in Southeast and Southwest Asia. Even though the war in Vietnam ended in the mid-1970s, large numbers of Cambodian, Laotian, and Vietnamese refugees still live in dire conditions throughout the region. The ongoing conflict in Afghanistan has produced nearly 6 million refugees, the vast majority of whom remain in Pakistan and Iran. Other sources of refugees in the region are China (Tibetans in India and Nepal), Sri Lanka (many now in India), Myanmar, or Burma (most now in Thailand), Israel (Palestinians in regional refugee camps and spread elsewhere throughout the Middle East), and Indonesia (refugees from the East Timorese and Irian Jayan regions now living in Papua New Guinea).

Africa

Africa has experienced two major waves of migration. The first wave of migration out of Africa followed World War II and the growth of the decolonization movement. Most migrants in this era were European expatriates who left the continent from the late 1950s to the 1970s, after the emergence of independent African states forced them out of positions of economic and social privilege under colonial regimes. The second major wave of migration in Africa has occurred in the postcolonial era, as a result of ethnic, political, and national conflicts and power struggles among countries in the region. Regional conflicts have produced millions of refugees throughout the African continent. Since the 1970s, ethnic conflicts, civil war, and political struggles have created mass migration and refugee crises in Angola, Burundi, the Democratic Republic of Congo (formerly Zaïre), Eritrea, Ethiopia, Liberia, Mozambique, Namibia,

Rwanda, Sierra Leone, Somalia, Sudan, Uganda, Western Sahara, and Zimbabwe. The growth of abject poverty throughout the continent increases pressure for migration to Western Europe and North America in search of improved economic conditions. In southern Africa, migrants from Mozambique, Zimbabwe, and other regional states have traveled to South Africa in search of work.

Europe

There were two major flows of international migration into Western Europe in the 1980s and 1990s—migrant workers and their families from southern Europe, Southwest Asia, and Africa who moved in search of greater economic opportunity, and East European emigrants from the former Soviet bloc. Since the economic downturn throughout Western Europe in the 1970s, government restrictions have been placed on legal immigration to the region. There is a growing sentiment against foreigners in West European countries, evinced by the growth of right-wing parties pushing for restrictions on the entry of migrants, particularly those from the Middle East and North Africa. But, as Europe's population ages, the region will need foreign workers, primarily to fill the menial jobs shunned by local workers. While foreign workers continue to migrate to the region, few have the opportunity eventually to become permanent residents or citizens. However, Germany and other governments are relaxing the most onerous of these restrictions.

CONCLUSION

In the coming decades, international migration is expected to continue to grow and become a major component of population growth and decline in nations throughout the world. Moreover, the causes of migration are increasingly more complex and more complicated than in previous periods. There is no such individual as a typical migrant. Some migrants leave their places of origin temporarily, others leave for longer periods, and still others leave permanently. Migration shapes and influences economic, political, and cultural conditions in both migrant regions of departure and arrival. Increasingly, global economic integration is contributing to greater interdependence between regions where migrants are leaving and regions where migrants are entering. Economic conditions in sending regions are often shaped by the ability of migrants living abroad to send money back home. Moreover, economic growth in countries where there are large numbers of migration are often dependent on the ability of employers to find low-wage or highly specialized workers who cannot be found locally. The growth of nationalism throughout the world at the end of the twentieth century also influences migratory patterns. As a result, migrants in large numbers are leaving countries where they no longer feel welcome and entering countries where they have a political and cultural affinity. Moreover, growing legal restrictions on official migration in many countries are limiting human rights of individuals who move for economic, political, or cultural reasons. Thus, although migrants continue to come and go throughout the world and to contribute to economic, political, and cultural vi-

tality, at the turn of the century nationalist leaders are increasingly abridging their rights.

FURTHER READINGS

Macura, Miroslav, and David Coleman, eds. *International Migration: Regional Processes and Responses.* New York and Geneva: United Nations, 1994.

Sassen, Saskia. *The Global City: New York, London, Tokyo.* Princeton: Princeton University Press, 1991.

United Nations. *Demographic Yearbook 1996.* New York: United Nations, 1997.

United Nations Centre for Human Settlements (HABITAT). *An Urbanizing World: Global Report on Human Settlements.* Oxford: Oxford University Press, 1996.

United Nations Development Program. *Human Development Report 1996.* New York and Oxford: Oxford University Press, 1996.

United Nations High Commission on Refugees. *The State of the World's Refugees 1993.* New York: Penguin Books, 1993.

World Bank. *Annual Report 1996.* Washington, DC, 1997.

———. *World Development Indicators 1998.* Washington, DC, 1998.

Zolberg, A.R. "The Next Waves: Migration Theory for a Changing World." *International Migration Review* 23, no. 3 (1989).

Section 8

The Demography of Transportation and Communications

In the late nineteenth century, the pioneering French science fiction writer Jules Verne published his classic travel novel *Around the World in Eighty Days*. This story was meant in part to highlight the enormous progress humanity had made in taming distances. After all, roughly three centuries earlier, it had taken Ferdinand Magellan's fleet some three years to circle the globe. But the achievement of Verne's hero pales next to the strides made in travel in the twentieth century. Soviet cosmonaut Yuri Gagarin, the first human being in space, circled the Earth in less than eighty minutes in 1961, only seventy-odd years later.

It is, of course, a cliché to say that modern development in transportation and communications technology have shrunk the planet beyond the imagination of previous generations, but it is astonishing nevertheless. In the 1700s, it took months to cross the Atlantic in sailing ships; in the 1800s, it took weeks in steamships; in the first half of the twentieth century, it took just days in diesel-powered ocean liners; and in the second half of the century, it takes only hours in a transcontinental jet.

The achievements in communications are no less remarkable, if a bit different in kind. Since the invention of the telegraph in the 1830s, humans have been able to transmit data near the speed of light, providing virtually instant communication across vast distances. Because it is governed by the laws of physics, this speed cannot be exceeded. What has increased is the quantity and type of information, as well as the depth and reach of the communications network. A single telegraph message consisting of perhaps 100 individual bits of information moves near the speed of light, but requires several minutes to be transcribed. In contrast, using the most up-to-date form of written messages, e-mail, up to 56,000 bits of information can be transmitted in a single minute.

The benefits of these achievements are well known: instant transmission and reception of information, ease of travel, and the ability to sustain relationships across great distances. But the revolution in transportation and communications also has negative consequences: the ability to misinform and brainwash on a mass scale, the relentless drive toward a single dominant mass global culture and the destruction of local cultures, clashes of culture between tourists and native peoples, and the enormous environmental hazards caused by the burning of fossil fuels necessary for modern transportation.

TRANSPORTATION

Nearly all the forms of transportation in use between 1965 and 1995 were invented long before 1965: the automobile and airplane were invented at the turn of the century; railroads and fossil fuel–powered ships appeared in the first half of the nineteenth century. What is notable about the post-1965 era, however, is the sudden growth in the quantity and geographic spread of these transportation systems, and the impact this spread has had on societies throughout the world.

Motor Vehicles

No form of transportation has done more to revolutionize the movement of people and goods in the post-1965 era than motor vehicles—in particular, the private passenger automobile, the passenger bus, and the freight truck. This is especially the case with metropolitan and regional transport. If anything can rival the fantastic growth in the world's population and cities over the past thirty years, it is the increase in the number of motor vehicles. There are several reasons for this. First, growth in the number of human beings leads to a need for more transportation. Second, the rapid expansion of cities means that more people live at greater distances from their families and the sources of agricultural production. Third, although motor vehicle transport is not as crucial in international trade as freight-carrying aircraft and cargo ships, it does play a role in the globalization of the world's economy, serving as an intermediate link between smaller cities, outlying areas, and the major ports and air traffic hubs of the world.

Finally, there is the matter of prosperity. Higher disposable income in many developed and upper-tier developing countries means greater consumption of goods, which entails more transportation. Moreover, one of the key large consumer products purchased by newly prosperous individuals and families is the passenger car. Economists refer to a takeoff point for automobile purchases in the developing world, when an annual family income climbs to about 50 percent of the total purchase price of an automobile. In addition, experts also note that there is a kind of doubling effect at work: for every 1 percent rise in a country's per capita income, the number of motor vehicles tends to rise 2 percent. In view of these circumstances, it is not surprising that the overall number of vehicles is rapidly increasing in the developing world. What is more surprising is the rapid rise in the number of vehicles in the developed world as well, because of increases in the number of both commercial vehicles and passenger cars. Transformations in the production process in the developed world over the past thirty years have emphasized efficiency, primarily through maintaining lower inventories and "just-in-time" deliveries. This obviously means more goods in motion at any given time, hence the demand for more commercial vehicles. The increase in the number of private cars is due to prosperity—more two-car families—and the shrinking size of the household. As the number of single-person households or households led by a single breadwinner increases, so does the number of vehicles, for each of these smaller households requires its own car.

Table 8.1 shows the dramatic rise in the number of vehicles in key countries in both the developed and the developing world between 1965 and 1995. Several trends in the number of private cars are immediately evident. First, the greatest expansion has occurred either in newly industrialized countries like South Korea or in the former communist countries, like Poland, where economic, political, and cultural restrictions on automobiles were gradually lifted in the waning days of the communist regimes and were eliminated after those regimes fell.

Second, rapid expansion in private car ownership is seen in oil-rich states like Indonesia, Iran, and Nigeria, where the sudden increase in oil prices in the 1970s produced new wealth. In absolute terms, the greatest increases in private car ownership occurred in the developed world. Thus the increase in France from 1980 to 1995, for example, was just 35.3 percent, or 6.5 million passenger cars. In the more populous Nigeria, the increase was 393.5 percent for the same period, but this represented only 181,000 passenger cars.

Finally, the figures for the United States should be considered in terms of world totals. Living in what was easily the richest country in the world in 1965, Americans owned 53.6 percent of all the world's automobiles. Increasing incomes and consumption patterns in other developed countries reduced that to 37.4 percent by 1980. By 1995, with the rise of the newly industrialized countries of Asia, and with the removal of restrictions on automobile ownership in the former communist world, the percentage of the world's

Table 8.1

Passenger Cars in Selected Countries, 1965-1995

Country	No. of passenger cars (per thousand persons)			Percent change	
	1965	1980	1995	1965-1980	1980-1995
Brazil	1,140.8	8,004.6	8,098.4	601.6	1.2
	(1.6)	(6.7)	(5.0)		
Fiji	7.3	23.4	47.7	220.5	103.8
	(1.8)	(3.9)	(6.1)		
France	9,600.0	18,400.0	24,900.0	91.7	35.3
	(17.8)	(34.5)	(42.7)		
India	415.7	1,054.4	3,205.0	153.6	204.0
	(0.1)	(0.2)	(0.3)		
Indonesia	151.0	639.5	1,890.3	323.5	195.6
	(0.2)	(0.4)	(0.9)		
Iran	105.9	958.0	1,557.0	804.6	62.5
	(0.4)	(2.8)	(2.4)		
Nigeria	n/a	46.0	227.0	n/a	393.5
		(0.1)	(0.2)		
Poland	245.5	2,383.0	7,153.1	870.7	200.2
	(0.8)	(6.8)	(20.4)		
South Korea	16.3	249.1	5,148.7	1,428.2	1,966.9
	(0.1)	(0.9)	(11.3)		
United States	74,904.3	118,458.7	147,710.0	58.1	24.7
	(38.1)	(52.3)	(55.4)		
World	139,730.0	316,400.0	458,488.7	126.4	44.9
	(4.2)	(7.1)	(8.0)		

cars owned by Americans had been reduced further, to 32.2 percent.

The implications of this expansion in the number of motor vehicles for both the global and the individual countries' environments are staggering. Table 8.2 compares carbon dioxide emissions in 1992 over the levels in 1983 for the same countries listed in Table 8.1. The rise in carbon dioxide emissions—produced largely by motor vehicles, but also a by-product of various manufacturing processes—is the main cause of global warming, according to many scientists.

As Table 8.2 indicates, the general trend in carbon dioxide emissions is upward, though the pace varies in different countries because of differing rates of economic growth and the adoption of new technologies. The greatest increases are generally in countries with the highest increase in passenger car ownership, such as Nigeria and South Korea. But more environmentally friendly technologies also can play a role. Although the number of cars in Poland increased some 200 percent between 1983 and 1992, its carbon dioxide emissions actually declined because of the shift from highly polluting cars made under the communist regime to the cleaner cars either imported or made in Polish factories which employ advanced Western car manufacturing technologies. In France, the decline is due to both cleaner cars and the general stagnation of the economy, which results in less driving, as unemployed people will no longer commute.

Air Transport

As in the case of automobiles, the expansion of air transport has dramatically transformed the nature of long-distance passenger travel and trade. Table 8.3 shows the increase in passenger traffic by air from 1980 to 1995. As demonstrated in the table, the world as a whole and most individual countries have seen dramatic increases in air travel because of an increase in

Table 8.2

Carbon Dioxide Emissions for Selected Countries, 1983-1992

Country	Carbon dioxide emissions (thousands of metric tons)		Percent change
	1983	1992	
Brazil	44,483	59,245	33.2
Fiji	196	194	-1.0
France	108,731	98,820	-9.1
India	118,457	210,000	77.3
Indonesia	30,981	50,378	62.6
Iran	36,904	64,268	74.1
Nigeria	16,343	26,341	61.2
Poland	114,445	93,311	-18.5
South Korea	38,517	79,103	105.4
United States	1,143,714	1,332,246	16.5

Table 8.3

Air Transport for Selected Countries, 1980-1995

Country	Passengers (thousands)		Percent change
	1980	1995	
Bahamas	345	862	149.9
China	2,568	37,498	1,360.2
Egypt	2,028	3,538	74.5
Ghana	279	182	-34.8
Hungary	874	1,325	51.6
India	6,603	11,518	74.4
Peru	1,980	1,895	-4.3
Saudi Arabia	9,241	11,922	29.0
Spain	15,089	21,992	45.7
Thailand	2,459	11,405	363.8
United Kingdom	25,551	55,475	117.1
United States	295,281	513,756	74.0
World	748,978	1,225,067	63.6

domestic travel, tourism, and higher levels of migration. Each of the countries listed in the table has individual reasons for its own trends. The expansion in air travel among the Chinese is linked to China's opening toward the rest of the world in the 1980s, as well as its rapid economic growth. The rise in U.S. air travel relates to airline deregulation and falling ticket prices. The decline in Peru is attributable to its depressed economy and the drop in tourism because of political instability. Air transport levels in Ghana have fallen because of the economic recession that followed a decline in international prices for Ghana's tropical food exports, due to increased competition from other tropical countries and changes in tastes in the developed world (such as decreased consumption of sugar). The increase in air transport in the United Kingdom results from the country's new status as a transportation hub for Europe.

The rapid growth in air travel has had two lasting impacts regarding passengers. With respect to immigrants, there has not been an increase in numbers per se, since ships and railroads once carried millions of migrants to their destinations. Instead, migration and immigration by air have allowed many immigrants to go back and forth between their homeland and their newly adopted country.

Consequences that follow from this include increased money brought to the homeland as well as investment there by those who have emigrated. The impact on assimilation, however, is complex. On the one hand, the ease of travel and the ubiquity of modern communications have given people around the world common cultural references, such as a fascination with Hollywood film stars and rock and roll music, and a taste for Western products like Coca-Cola and McDonald's hamburgers. On the other hand, the ability to travel back and forth between the old and new countries may delay immigrants' assimilation to their new home country. (For more on transportation and migration, see Section 7, The Demography of Migration.)

With regard to tourism and travel, the increased accessibility of air transport has led to increases in both the number of persons traveling for vacations and the number and distances of their destinations. Nearly every major tourist destination has experienced a major increase in the number of annual tourists. Interestingly, the largest increases have been in countries that are either distant from the developed world (where most tourists originate) or not traditionally tourist-oriented. For example, the Maldives in the Indian Ocean hosted roughly 25 percent more visitors in 1994 than in 1990, while more accessible and traditional tourist destinations like Jamaica experienced an increase of 15 percent. Tourism levels are also related to political stability in the destination country and to fashion and economics in the country of origination. The recent trend toward "eco-tourism"—that is, tourism that is environmentally friendly and does not require ecologically unsound developments like hotels and resorts—may lead to more remote areas being opened up to tourists, though with less harmful impact.

COMMUNICATIONS

Even more than transportation, the world of communications has undergone a revolution of far-reaching proportions. As noted above, this has less to do with the speed of communications than with the quantity of information and entertainment that can be transmitted, the geographic scope of the modern communications infrastructure, and the different types of communication this infrastructure can support. The communications revolution involves the spread of one-way media broadcasting from a single point and received at many points (radio and television), two-way forms sending information from one point to another (telephones and faxes), and multiple sender and receiver forms (the Internet).

But before turning to electronic forms of communications, it is important to examine the extent of print media, which remain a key method of transmitting information.

Newspapers and Literacy

Although, at first glance, it would appear that the diffusion of print media, unlike radio and television, would increase with literacy, that is not necessarily the case, as seen in Table 8.4. Why not?

Perhaps, the most important reason for the simultaneous rise in literacy rates in developing countries and the decline in newspaper readership—the latter a factor in developed countries as well—can be ascribed to the rise of electronic media. Unlike newspapers, television and radio can provide information and entertainment

Table 8.4

Adult Literacy Rates, 1965-1995

Country	Newspapers per 1,000 persons*/ Adult literacy rate		
	1965	1980	1995
Argentina	148	142	143
	n.a.	94.0%	96%
Canada	227	221	204
	95%	96%	98%
China	19	34	43
	n.a.	56%	81.5%
France	245	192	205
	96%	98%	98%
Ghana	29	47	18
	26.7%	53.4%	64.5%
Guatemala	31	29	18
	38%	55.3%	55.5%
Malaysia	57	59	117
	n.a.	73.5%	83.5%
Pakistan	n.a.	12	6
	n.a	25.6%	37%
Poland	167	236	159
	n.a.	98.8%	98%
Syria	21	13	22
	40%	59.7%	71%

* Among daily and weekly newspapers sold on a regular basis.

without a distribution network. At the same time, as television and radio become more widespread, people choose to obtain their news and entertainment from a medium that is both more visually engaging and, after the initial purchase of the television set or radio, free of charge. Moreover, the younger population in much of the developing world does not have a strong newspaper reading tradition because it has grown up with radio and television. Thus, as the youth population rises, there are fewer newspapers sold per person, a phenomenon also seen in the developing world, though at a slower pace.

Television and Radio

The explosion in the number of radios and televisions—in both the developing and the developed world—has reduced the cost of reception and transmission equipment. At the same time, the size of this equipment has shrunk greatly, even as its power has expanded, allowing more of the world's poor to afford at least a radio; those with minimal discretionary income can even afford a television set. Table 8.5 records the increase in radio and television ownership between 1965 and 1995 for selected countries.

As noted in the introduction to the section on communications, the rapid spread of radio and television availability has both positive and negative implications. On the one hand, widespread radio and television ownership allows critical information to be broadcast to wide sectors of the population at low cost to governments and international agencies. As the United Nations has found, the level of awareness of contraceptive methods and sources rises with the level of radio and television ownership, particularly in countries with high rates of female illiteracy.

On the other hand, the potential for Western, and in particular American, cultural influence also rises with the extent of radio and television ownership, a trend that is evident in both the developed and the developing world. In 1989, the United States was the largest broadcaster of external radio programs, at some 2,374 hours per week. At the same time, nonlocal broadcasts dominated many of the world's television airwaves. As of the mid-1980s, some 38 out of 53 countries surveyed in the developed and developing world broadcast programs originating from other countries at least a third of the time. The highest rate in the world was found in Uganda, some 83 percent of whose programming came from outside the country, mostly the United Kingdom and the United States.

Telephones and the Internet

Although the cost of telephone equipment has fallen, the telephone remains a relatively expensive means of communications since, until quite recently, it required wiring over great distances. The enormous cost of building such an infrastructure put the cost of telephone ownership beyond the means of all but the richest citizens of the developing world. Similarly, high infrastructure costs made it too expensive to hard-

Table 8.5

Radio and Television in Selected Countries 1965-1995 (per 1,000 persons)

| Country | Radios/televisions | | Percent change |
	1965	1995	
Argentina	310/80	672/220	116.8/175
Canada	502/267	992/618	97.6/31.5
China	14/0.2	184/38	1,214.3/18,400
France	330/138	890/412	169.7/198.6
Ghana	83/0.1	269/16	224.1/15,900
Guatemala	n.a./13	68/53	n.a./307.7
Malaysia	49/7	430/151	777.6/2,057
Pakistan	6/0.1	88/18	1,200/17,900
Poland	190/70	439/298	131.1/325.7
Syria	382/14	257/62	-32.7/342.9

wire regions with low populations densities, since the overall cost would be shared among too few telephone subscribers. Thus, in many developing countries, telephone ownership and even access have been confined to the larger towns and cities. At the same time, the inefficiency of many nationally owned telephone monopolies has created long waiting lists for connection. Many experts claim that privatization will shorten such lists, but it will also raise the cost of connection, thereby restricting telephones by other means. Mobile, or cellular, telephones might offer a way out of bottlenecks of cost, reach, and technology.

As of 1995, however, cellular phones had yet to penetrate much of the developed world and most of the developing world. Thus, telephone ownership remains far behind that of radio and television, especially in the developing world. Moreover, telephone ownership is much more closely tied to rising levels of economic prosperity. In countries like Malaysia and China, rapidly rising incomes mean higher telephone ownership. In countries with stagnant per capita incomes like Canada, telephone ownership has remained flat, while in economically depressed Ghana, it has dropped significantly. The upsurge in France—where the economy also remains flat—is related to increased competition and lower prices. Table 8.6 shows the growth in tele-

Table 8.6

Telephones in Selected Countries, 1975-1994
(per 100 persons)

	1975	1994	Percent change
Argentina	7.8	14.1	81
Canada	57.5	57.6	0.2
China	0.2	2.3	1.005
France	26.4	54.7	107
Ghana	0.6	0.3	-50
Guatemala	0.8	2.4	200
Malaysia	2.5	14.7	488
Pakistan	0.3	1.6	433
Poland	7.5	13.1	75
Syria	2.4	4.9	104

phone ownership in 1994 over the level in 1975.

The Internet offers a way out of the foreign content dilemma of one-way broadcasting systems like radio and television. But Internet access requires a computer, which, despite rapidly falling costs, remains outside the reach of a large minority of the developed world and the vast majority of the developing world. Moreover, most Internet access still requires telephone wiring, presenting the same access and cost problems as those associated with telephones. As of mid-1997, out of some 90 million people with Internet access worldwide, about 67 percent were in North America and another 20 percent in Europe, leaving just 13 percent in the rest of the world, including Japan.

CONCLUSION

The revolution in communications technologies and the further development of the local, national, and global transportation infrastructures promises to have a deep impact on demographic trends. On the one hand, the ever-expanding reach of telecommunications means closer contact between peoples around the globe. Similarly, the expanding transportation infrastructure—and the lower prices it brings to the movement of goods and peoples—promises more abundance, more travel, and more migration.

At the same time, however, there are poten-tial negatives to these developments as well. If, as current trends seem to indicate, the telecommunications infrastructure comes under the control of a few multinational firms and developed nations, the flow of information and communications may be restricted. Those who control the media can influence the opinions of the world. The flow of information can become one-way— that is, toward the developed world. The Internet, of course, offers an alternative since, by its very nature, it is controlled by all who have access to it. The question remains, however, how long that access will be free to all.

FURTHER READINGS

Andersson, Åke, Roland Hord, eds. *The Future of Transportation and Communication: Vision and Perspectives from Europe, Japan and the U.S.A.* New York: Springer Verlag, 1993.

Button, Kenneth, and David Pitfield, eds. *Transport Deregulation: An International Movement.* New York: St. Martin's Press, 1991.

International Energy Agency. *Transport, Energy and Climate Change.* Paris: International Energy Agency, 1997.

Lundberg, Donald, and Carolyn Lundberg. *International Travel and Tourism.* New York: John Wiley and Sons, 1993.

Makimoto, Tsugio, and David Manners. *Digital Nomad.* New York: John Wiley and Sons, 1997.

McLuhan, Marshall. *Understanding Media: The Extensions of Man.* Cambridge: MIT Press, 1994.

Nieuwenhuis, Paul, and Peter Wells, eds. *Motor Vehicles in the Environment: Principles and Practice.* New York: John Wiley and Sons, 1994.

Randall, Neil. *The Soul of the Internet: Net Gods, Netizens and the Wiring of the World.* Boston: International Thomson Computer Press, 1997.

Skovmand, Michael, ed. *Media Cultures: Reappraising Transnational Media.* New York: Routledge, 1992.

Theobald, William, ed. *Global Tourism: The Next Decade.* Boston: Butterworth-Heinemann, 1994.

Willis, William James. *The Age of Multimedia and Turbonews.* Westport, CT: Praeger, 1994.

Zacher, Mark W. *Governing Global Networks: International Regimes for Transportation and Communications.* New York: Cambridge University Press, 1996.

Section 9

The Demography of Health Care and Education

HEALTH AND HEALTH CARE

It takes little more than a quick glance at any statistical source, such as the tables in this book, to see the obvious global trend in health care and education. Simply put, humanity—with a few exceptions—is growing healthier and better educated with each passing decade. There are a variety of reasons for this trend. Growing economies mean greater tax revenues for governments to spend on health clinics and schools and higher incomes for families to use to pay for hospital and school fees. Growing urbanization means that people have more local access to education and health-care facilities. New medical and communication technologies have lowered the cost of health care and increased access to educational facilities through broadcasts and the Internet. Indeed, understanding the upward trend in global education and especially global health requires a multifaceted approach.

The demography of health care involves such related disciplines as medical sociology (the interaction of social institutions and forces on health), medical anthropology (non-Western health care and health care attitudes), medical geography (the spatial dimensions of disease and health care), medical economics (the financing of health care), and epidemiology (the course of diseases within a population).

Each of these components adds its own distinct contribution to the overall study of health care demography. Medical sociology—especially in recent decades—has helped establish the link between poverty and illiteracy, on the one hand, and the level of health, on the other. It also connects political institutions, political participation, and health. The field of medical anthropology has helped lead researchers to examine popular attitudes toward medicine—Western and non-Western—and a population's willingness and likelihood to avail itself of the two different medical traditions.

Medical geography examines a narrow but significant field: the spatial distribution of health care factors and health care provision. Medical economics, of course, looks into the links among economic development, class, and health care. How is health care financed? How is health care purchased? And which classes have access to it? Finally, epidemiology—a field that straddles the border between the health sciences and the social sciences—focuses on how various population measures of all kinds, from age cohorts to level of urbanization, explain the source, spread, and control of communicable and noncommunicable diseases.

Health Care Institutions and Influences

Health care institutions differ radically from one country to another, particularly between the developed and the developing worlds. In most developed countries, health care is provided by governmental or quasi-governmental agencies and financed through general government revenues. Most countries have small private health care sectors that provide elective procedures not covered by national insurance plans, as well as better conditions of health care, such as private hospital rooms. In the United States, unlike the other advanced industrial countries, health care is now provided largely through health maintenance organizations (HMOs), usually in the form of for-profit corporations financed jointly by employees and employers. In addition, the United States offers government health care for the elderly and, to a lesser extent, the poor. An estimated 40 million Americans are not covered by any private or government health insurance and are forced to rely on emergency rooms—which by law are required to treat all comers—for their primary care.

Developing countries almost always have less extensive and less well-financed health care infrastructures, with great variations in quality between rural and urban areas and among the different economic classes. Mexico's system provides a typical example. In major cities, modern, well-equipped clinics and hospitals with highly trained staff are available to the roughly 4 million members of the middle and upper classes with private health insurance. For employed urban workers, the government provides an adequate health care safety net through its Social Security program. But for casual laborers, the urban unemployed, and rural peasants, the Ministry of Health offers local clinics. Most of these clinics are underfinanced, and patients must wait long hours, provide their own supplies and food, and sometimes pay bribes to obtain treatment.

Other than the level of national economic development or an individual's finances, many factors—environmental, historical, geographic, demographic, cultural, political, and social—determine a person's health and the kind of health care he or she is likely to receive. Overcrowded housing, inaccessability of decent water and sanitation, and high levels of pollution are the chief environmental factors. Access to safe drinking water and adequate sanitation range from a low of 37 and 31 percent, respectively, in such sub-Saharan African countries as Mali; to 83 and 66 percent, respectively, in a midlevel

developing country such as Mexico; to 100 percent and 96 percent, respectively, in a developed country like the United Kingdom.

Historical factors include how long a health care program has been in effect. Germany, for example, has had a nationalized system of health care of one type or another for more than a hundred years; Singapore instituted one in the past few decades, and many developing countries have yet to create a coordinated system. Cultural influences on the health care system include attitudes about prevention versus healing (Japan emphasizes the former, the United States the latter), the role of the family as caregivers (especially important in cultures with large extended families), and the influence of traditional therapies, which are especially common in developing countries. In addition, there are social factors such as levels of smoking and nutrition.

Health Care and Economic Development

Clearly, however, the main ingredient in assessing the quality of health care in a given population is the level of economic development. With few exceptions, a country's health care program can be assessed best by taking account of its per capita income to measure overall wealth, and its level of poverty to determine the distribution of national wealth. Table 9.1 shows the levels of per capita income, poverty, and infant mortality for selected countries in 1995.

As the table clearly indicates, the lower the per capita income, the higher the infant mortality rate. Rwanda, which has a per capita income of $400 (the lowest of the countries listed in the table), has the highest infant mortality, 118.8 per 1,000 live births. But per capita income alone does not determine overall quality of health. For example, Brazil, which has a per capita income level of $6,100, has a relatively high infant mortality rate of 57.7 per 1,000. The enormous disparities in wealth—as reflected in the high poverty rate of 43.5 percent of the population living on less than $2 day—are clearly a factor there. Thailand, which has a similar per capita

Table 9.1

Income, Poverty Levels, and Infant Mortality in Selected Countries, 1995

Country	Per capita income ($)	Poverty (percent)*	Infant mortality per 1,000 live births
Algeria	3,800	17.6	48.7
Brazil	6,100	43.5	57.7
Bulgaria	4,920	23.5	15.8
China	2,900	57.8	44.5
Côte d'Ivoire	1,500	54.8	91.7
Germany	17,900	0.0	5.6
Hungary	7,000	10.7	12.3
India	1,500	88.8	71 .1
Jamaica	3,200	24.9	15.6
Kazakstan	2,700	12.1	63.2
Mexico	7,700	40.0	25.0
Rwanda	400	8 8.7	118.8
Thailand	6,900	23.5	33.4
United States	27,500	0.0	6.7

*Defined as living on $2 day or less.

income but roughly half the poverty rate, has an infant mortality rate of 33.4 per 1,000.

Political and institutional issues come into play as well. For example, the relatively extensive health care systems developed under communist regimes—now under pressure because of the financial chaos that has followed the transition to a market economy—have been able to keep infant mortality levels relatively low, despite falling per capita incomes and rising levels of poverty. Bulgaria—which has a per capita income just two-thirds that of Thailand and a similar poverty rate—has an infant mortality rate of just 15.8 per 1,000, well under the Thai level. At the high end of economic development, Germany and the United States provide a useful comparison. Although its per capita income is roughly two-thirds that of the United States, Germany has an infant mortality rate some 16 percent lower (6.7 per 1,000 live births), perhaps because Germany has an extensive national health care system and the United States does not.

This critical issue of health care provision becomes even more significant when health expenditures are considered. In 1994, the United States spent 13.6 percent of its gross domestic product

(GDP) on health care, or $3,086 per person. By comparison, Germany allocated just 8.7 percent of its GDP, or $1,775 per person. At the same time, a developing country like Mexico expended only 4.0 percent of its GDP on health care, roughly $300 per person. When we compare expenditures and infant mortality rates, it becomes clear that both Germany and Mexico allocated their health care dollars far more efficiently than did the United States: Germany had a lower rate of infant mortality despite spending two-thirds as much per person, while Mexico spent roughly one-tenth as much and had an infant mortality rate only four times as high. Although this is a crude comparison, it shows that health care expenditures alone do not determine the overall quality of health care in a given country. The market-driven system in the United States often duplicates facilities, and the fact that large segments of the population lack health care insurance results in the need for heavy expenditures in post-illness care rather than in preventive care. In Germany, where all citizens are automatically covered and all health care costs are assumed by the government, the emphasis is on preventive care, since this is more economically efficient. As for Mexico, its low-tech approach—along with its extensive and closely knit families, which often provide basic health care to their own family members—means that each health care dollar goes farther.

This relationship between health care and economic development can be examined in even finer detail. For instance, there is a direct relationship among per capita income, poverty rates, and death rates, as well as a connection between economic development and the causes of death. Taking Thailand—one of the newly industrialized countries (NICs) of Southeast Asia—as an example, it is possible to see how rising incomes lead to the prevalence of different diseases. In 1965, the number one cause of death in Thailand was diarrheal diseases—31 deaths per 100,000 persons, usually among infants and the children—caused by poor sanitation and inadequate supplies of safe drinking water. This was compounded by both the country's tropical climate and its primarily rural living conditions, making it difficult for many people to travel to basic health care clinics.

By 1985, the number of deaths caused by diarrheal diseases had fallen to just 3 per 100,000 and they had become the sixth most common cause of death in the country. During those same two decades, heart disease— a health condition primarily of the elderly—had climbed from the number five cause of death in the country to the leading cause. In 1965, some 12 persons per 100,000 died of heart disease; by 1985, that figure had risen to 37 per 100,000. The life expectancy at birth rose from 56.1 years in 1965 to roughly 63 years in 1985. In other words, as childhood diseases like diarrhea were conquered, people lived longer, leading to higher rates of other medical conditions that affect older people, such as heart disease.

Not all health care statistics—particularly in the developing world—have been this positive. Indeed, while Thailand, until quite recently, experienced one of the fastest rates of economic expansion in the world, much of the developing world was experiencing stagnant growth and high foreign debt. In order to revive their economies and alleviate their debt, many of them have

had to accept harsh financial measures from their creditors, the major international lending institutions like the World Bank and the International Monetary Fund. One of the key demands of these institutions has been a contraction in public spending, including that on health care.

In the early 1980s, at the height of the debt crisis in the developing world, many countries were forced to shrink their health care sectors. Zambia, for example, spent 22 percent less on health in 1985 than it did in 1982. Bolivia cut its spending in this sector by 30 percent between 1980 and 1984. Moreover, the deepest cuts have come in those areas where hard currencies, such as dollars, are needed—for instance, in the purchase of medical equipment and pharmaceuticals. While Zambia's overall health care spending fell 22 percent over three years, its purchases of medicines dropped 75 percent over roughly the same period. Not surprisingly, diseases that had seemed to be eliminated from much of the developing world by the 1970s were reappearing: for example, yellow fever in Ghana and typhoid in Chile.

Geography and Health Care

Geographic considerations must be included in assessing the health care situation in a given country. As seen in Table 9.1, Kazakstan and Jamaica have per capita incomes that are fairly close ($2,700 and $3,200 respectively), though Jamaica's poverty rate of 24.9 percent is more than double Kazakstan's 12.1 percent. But whereas Jamaica is a small, evenly populated island (with a population density of 596 persons per square mile) where nearly everyone lives close to health care facilities, Kazakstan (16 persons per square mile) is a vast, underpopulated land where many live hundreds of miles from a hospital.

Clearly, geography determines access to health care and urban populations are more likely to be served by nearby facilities than are those in rural areas. But even this basic difference masks the complexity of the problem of geography and access to health care. In large countries in particular, health care facilities are not evenly distributed, even within rural areas. In India, for example, the relatively prosperous state of Punjab has roughly four times more hospital beds per capita in rural areas than does the impoverished state of Bihar. Moreover, in Indian states where the government has made rural primary health care delivery a priority, the differences with lower-priority regions are even more marked. In Kerala, where the communist-led government has expended large amounts of money, there is roughly one rural hospital bed for every 1,000 persons. In Madhya Pradesh, where the government's effort to provide more health care facilities in rural areas has been more fitful and underfinanced, the rate is one hospital bed for every 33,000 persons.

Urbanization and industrialization are also critical in the provision of and access to health care facilities. In Zambia, for example, the difference is noticeable. In territories along the rail lines that knit the vast southern African country together and are more heavily urbanized, there are more than 50 doctors per every 100,000 persons. In the more remote areas of the north and west, the rate is just 2 to 3 physicians per 100,000 persons. This pattern is repeated throughout Africa. For example, in Mozambique in 1990, while 100 percent of urbanites had access to some Western-style free health care, just 30 percent of rural inhabitants did. In Uganda and Morocco, the rates were 90 percent for urban and 57 percent for rural, and 100 percent for urban and 50 percent for rural, respectively.

Although urbanization is accompanied by more health care providers and facilities, it also introduces more health problems. The proportion of the developing world's population living in urban areas has increased greatly in recent decades, a trend expected to continue into the foreseeable future. In 1965, roughly 1 in 7 people in the developing world lived in cities; by 1995, roughly 1 in 3 did; and by 2025, it is expected that half the population in the developing world will be city dwellers.

Most of these urbanites will be desperately poor, living in overcrowded slums or shantytowns, with little safe drinking water and inadequate sanitation. Although urban rates of health generally tend to be better, there remain vast discrepancies among different sectors of the urban population. It has been estimated by some health care researchers that infant mortality rates in the poorer parts of major urban areas of the developing world can be from 4 to 10 times higher than those in the wealthier parts. (Of course, this is also true in many cities of the developed world; in New York City, for example, it is estimated that infant mortality rates in Harlem are 4 times higher than those in the more affluent sections of the city.)

History and Health Care Demography

The discrepancies in health care provision and the sorry state of public health can be understood in part by examining the political and economic histories of countries in the developing world. By the turn of the twentieth century, outside Latin America, most of the developing world had been colonized by European states, Japan, or the United States. To differing degrees, these colonizers failed to create either an adequate health care infrastructure or one that largely met the needs of the local European population and the indigenous elite. For the most part, this meant an emphasis on hospitals in urban areas or in areas of critical economic importance to the colonizer.

After the wave of independence that swept most of the developing world in the two decades following World War II, local elites—particularly in countries that failed to develop democratic institutions—often picked up where the colonizers left off. Many lavished their few resources for health care on urban areas, particularly in the form of modern, Western-style "prestige" medical centers. These were meant to serve the urban elites as well as indicate that the country had achieved a certain level of modernity. There were significant variations, however. Some countries—in particular those undergoing social revolutions like Cuba or Mozambique, but also democratic countries like India—emphasized numerous small health clinics in poor urban and rural areas. But these were exceptions to the rule.

Thus, in much of the developing world, health care provision—poor to begin with—was devastated by the economic crisis that hit many poor countries in the 1980s, when international prices fell for the raw materials they exported. Moreover, because of corruption and mismanagement, many of these countries were heavily in debt, some of which was incurred to build the "prestige" medical centers. When banks and international lending agencies began to impose austerity plans and privatization programs, the already precarious health care facilities in poor urban and rural areas deteriorated. Moreover, many superior city hospitals were privatized, forcing them to raise prices or reduce services offered to the poor at no cost or at subsidized prices. Most of the gains in health and health care in the developing world came in the early period of independence, from 1965 to 1980, and less so in the later era from 1980 to 1995.

AIDS/HIV and the Cultural Dimension of Health

Since 1981, when it was first mentioned in the medical journals, acquired immune deficiency syndrome (AIDS) has grown to pandemic, or global epidemic, proportions. By 1992, the number of people afflicted with the disease had climbed to 1.5 million worldwide and, by 1998, to an estimated 10 million. The number of those infected with the human immunodeficiency virus (HIV) increased to an even greater extent, from about 10 million carriers in 1992 to roughly 100 million in 1998. (Of course, the huge jump is attributable in part to better detection techniques and efforts, as well as to the increasing willingness of governments to admit that their populations are affected.)

The global distribution of the disease was not even, however. As of 1992, the vast majority of cases—some two-thirds—were in sub-Saharan Africa. Southeast Asia had about 10 percent, as did Latin America. The remaining 15 percent of the cases were in the developed world, largely in the United States and Western Europe. More than just geography was involved.

In the developed world, the disease was con-

fined largely to male homosexuals and intravenous drug users, though more recently it has been spreading among African-American and Hispanic females. Extensive education campaigns among gay men in the developed world have lowered the rate of infection in that community, while the continued high use of intravenous drugs among blacks and Latinos has allowed the virus to cross over into the female population.

But it is in the developing world that the disease has taken the largest toll. In recent years, it has spread rapidly in Southeast Asia. There the problem has been caused by a lack of education, liberal sexual attitudes, and the prevalence of prostitution. In Africa, where many believe the disease originated, many experts blame urbanization for the massive spread of the disease. The breakdown of village culture—with its social restrictions and close-knit families—and the move to urban areas led many younger Africans to adopt the less restrictive ways associated with modern, Western-style life. Moreover, the disease tended to spread along lines of transport, as itinerant workers and truck drivers transmitted the disease from one urban area to another through sexual contacts with prostitutes.

Thus, today, the highest incidences of AIDS in Africa can be seen along the main transport routes of East Africa, from Uganda in the north to Zimbabwe in the south. In 1995, Uganda had roughly 48,000 official cases of AIDS out of a population of 20.2 million—a rate of 1 case for every 420 persons; Zimbabwe had 41,000 out of a population of 11.3 million—a rate of 1 case for every 275 persons. In West Africa, outside the main transmission route, the rate is much lower. In Cameroon, for example, there were just 5,375 cases out of a population of 14.3 million, a rate of 1 case for every 2,660 persons.

EDUCATION

The demographics of education involve three areas of inquiry. First is the impact of population and economic statistics—including age, sex, class, geographic distribution, and level of economic development—on various educational systems. Second are the demographics of the educational process itself: How many are enrolled in what kinds of educational institutions? Third is the impact of education on population statistics, including such key indicators as fertility, literacy, and employment.

Demographic and Economic Influences on Education

Educational levels have risen everywhere in the past thirty years, especially in the developing world. Along with the rise in health indicators, the increase in educational achievement is one of the more remarkable developments of the post–World War II era. The achievement is even more remarkable in light of the increase in the number of school-age children in most developing countries. In Brazil, for example, the population under the age of 15 climbed from 29 million in 1965 to more than 50 million in 1995; in Côte d'Ivoire, 1.4 million to 7.1 million; in India, 179 million to 324 million.

At the same time, these countries boasted substantial increases in the number of students attending school at various levels. In Brazil, where most children attended primary school, the advances were largely at the secondary level. In 1965, just 19 percent of the school-age population was attending secondary institutions; by 1995, that figure was 45 percent. In Côte d'Ivoire, substantial achievements were also made in secondary education, where the number of school-age children in such institutions rose from just 6 percent in 1965 to 23 percent in 1995. In India, the achievements have occurred at both the primary and secondary levels. In 1965, just 56 and 15 percent of all appropriate school-age children attended primary and secondary institutions, respectively; by 1995, those figures were 100 and 49 percent, respectively. (The rate at which school-age children attend a particular level of educational institution can be a misleading statistic since, in many developing countries, people outside that age group may also be attending. For example, the 100 percent figure for primary school enrollment in India in 1995 does not mean that 100 percent of all children between the ages

of 5 and 11 are attending primary school, since some of the students may be over the age of 11.)

What accounts for these achievements? First, there is the matter of expenditures. Throughout the developing world, governments have placed a great emphasis on education, since higher educational levels have been recognized as the key to economic development, better health, and slower population growth (see the section below on the influence of education on demographics). Of course, there is both a virtuous and a vicious cycle when it comes to education and economic development. On the positive side, in a country like Malaysia, rapid economic growth has meant more money for education and thus rapidly rising educational levels, which lead to better economic performance. On the negative side, declining economies have a direct impact on educational levels. In the case of Côte d'Ivoire, for example, rising international prices for Ivoirean exports like cocoa in the 1960s and 1970s allowed for more spending on education and thus for higher enrollment levels. Between 1965 and 1980, primary school enrollment increased from 60 to 75 percent of the school-age population. But the collapse of cocoa and other Ivoirean raw material prices in the 1980s had a direct impact on educational funding and, hence, on enrollment rates. By 1995, the enrollment rate at primary institutions in Côte d'Ivoire had fallen to 69 percent of the school-age population. This can only have a negative impact on the country's future economic development.

In addition to direct economic factors, there is the matter of urbanization. As in the case of health care, urbanites have a much better chance of receiving an education—even discounting for higher income levels—than those living in rural areas. Educational facilities are more geographically accessible in cities, and city schools in developing countries tend to be better financed than their rural counterparts.

Demographics of Education

As noted above, the level of enrollment in both primary and secondary schools around the world has increased greatly in the past thirty years, but the achievements represent a mixed bag. In the developed world (in both capitalist and communist countries), where primary and secondary education was nearly universal even in 1965, the real growth in enrollment has been at the tertiary level—that is, in colleges, universities, and professional schools. In France, for example, enrollment at tertiary institutions rose from 10.5 percent of university-age students in 1965 to 50 percent in 1995. Even in the lower tier of developed countries, the same held true. In Portugal, the rate climbed from about 4 percent to 34 percent over the same period. The same trend is noticeable in the former communist countries of Eastern Europe, despite the recent turmoil. In Romania, for instance, the rate of enrollment at tertiary institutions rose from roughly 7 percent of university-age students in 1965 to 18 percent in 1995.

In the developing world, the record is a bit less positive. At the primary and secondary levels, the biggest gains have come in countries with substantial economic growth. In Thailand, for example, the enrollment rate at secondary institutions increased from 12 percent of school-age children in 1965 to 55 percent in 1995. Economic growth was not the only criterion for expansion, however. Middle-tier developing countries that have not necessarily had rapid economic growth but have had relative political stability over the past thirty years have experienced improvement in their educational statistics. In Jamaica, for instance, the rate of school-age children attending secondary institutions climbed from 16 percent in 1965 to 67 percent in the 1980s. However, the declining economic fortunes of the island in the past couple of decades have led to stagnant growth in education. Between 1980 and 1995, the rate of school-age children attending secondary institutions remained roughly flat.

Even the poorest of countries have made substantial gains, although their low starting points mean that even substantial increases represent low enrollment. For example, in Guinea, where the per capita income is just $1,000 annually, the rate of school-age children attending primary institutions increased from 31 percent to 48 percent between 1965 and 1995, while the rate at the secondary level rose from just 1 percent to 24 percent in the same period. In war-torn or politically unstable countries, educational levels remain even more stunted. In Mozambique, for instance, where anticolonial and civil wars have been raging almost continuously since the early 1960s, the rate of school-age children attending primary institutions has fallen continuously from 99 percent in 1965 to just 60 percent in 1995.

One trend, however, is beyond dispute. The number of female children, young people, and adults attending various educational institutions has risen, in both relative and absolute numbers. This is true for primary and secondary institutions in the developing world and for tertiary institutions in the developed world. This trend has been most marked in those regions that previously denied education to most girls and women. In South Asia, for example, the enrollment rate of school-age girls attending primary and secondary institutions rose from 32 to 43 percent between 1980 and 1990; in primarily Islamic North Africa, the rates are 50 and 67 percent, respectively. Proportionally, too, the gains are impressive. Whereas girls represented just 40 percent of all students in primary and secondary students in North Africa in 1980, that proportion had risen to 45 percent by 1989. Similarly, in South Asia, the proportion rose from 38 to 42 percent.

Meanwhile, in the developed world, the number of women attending universities rose both proportionally and in absolute terms. In Western Europe, roughly 50 women attended tertiary educational institutions for every 100 men in 1980; by 1990, there were roughly 90 women for every 100 men. In Eastern Europe, the figure went from 78 to 102. In other words, slightly more women than men were attending tertiary institutions in Eastern Europe in 1990.

The Influence of Education on Demographics

As noted above, as educational levels in a given country rise (or fall), they have a direct impact on the economic and demographic profile of that society. The link with economic development has already been discussed, but rising levels of education also have an enormous impact on population growth. According to the United Nations, women's fertility is in inverse proportion to their educational levels. Areas where women's illiteracy rates are high have the highest fertility rates. The states of North Africa and Southwestern Asia (or the Middle East), for instance, have an average female illiteracy rate of 56 percent. Fertility rates there stand at roughly 4.8 children per woman. In the countries of East and Southeast Asia, where female illiteracy rates average 23 percent, the fertility level is 3.2 children per female.

In addition to illiteracy, various educational levels affect fertility. For example, women with no education in sub-Saharan Africa have a fertility rate of 7 children each; with six years of education (roughly primary school), the fertility rate drops to 6.5. But from there, it declines steeply. Women in sub-Saharan Africa with 10 years or more of education (that is, secondary or tertiary) have an average of just 4 children each. Sub-Saharan Africa is unique only in the small drop associated with primary school levels of education.

In Latin America and the Caribbean, the difference between no education and a primary school education is 6.4 children for those women with the former and just 4.1 for those with the latter. Asia presents a different scenario. There educational levels matter less. The difference between women with no education and women who have finished high school—in terms of their average number of children—is 3.4 and 2.4. In Asia, it appears, overall higher educational levels for the population as a whole have had the biggest impact on fertility, in that they have lowered it for all women of all educational levels.

CONCLUSION

Despite substantial gains in the areas of health care and education in the thirty years between 1965 and 1995, there are nevertheless dark clouds on the horizon. In the developed world, demo-graphic trends threaten to overwhelm health care facilities and undermine the political constituency for education. That is to say, as the population ages, it will require and demand increasing financial resources committed to health care. At the same time, an aging population means that there is a shrinking political consensus for adequately funding schools.

In the developing world, the problems are different, but even more acute. Here, rapidly expanding populations of young persons and steadily increasing populations of elderly threaten to overwhelm both health care and educational facilities. At the same time, the developing world remains mired in an economic slump that has affected even the best national performers in East and Southeast Asia. Ironically, the rapid economic gains made in these countries have been due in large part to expanded educational opportunities. Thus, the economic collapse in places like Indonesia and Thailand may be as self-perpetuating as the previous economic boom. That is, as economic resources dry up, so does educational funding. And with a less well-educated population, economies may suffer further.

FURTHER READINGS

Basch, Paul F. *Textbook of International Health.* New York: Oxford University Press, 1990.

Lassey, Marie, William Lassey, and Martin Jinks. *Health Care Systems Around the World: Characteristics, Issues, Reforms.* Englewood Cliffs, NJ: Prentice-Hall, 1997.

Phillips, David R., and Yola Verhasselt. *Health and Development.* New York: Routledge, 1994.

Pol, Louis G., and Richard K. Thomas. *The Demography of Health and Health Care.* New York: Plenum Press, 1992.

Roemer, Milton I. *National Health Care Systems of the World, Vol. 1, The Countries.* New York: Oxford University Press, 1991.

———. *National Health Care Systems of the World, Vol. 2, The Issues.* New York: Oxford University Press, 1993.

U.S. Department of Education, Office of Educational Research and Improvement. *Education in States and Nations: Indicators Comparing U.S. States with the OECD Countries in 1988.* Washington, DC, 1993.

United Nations Children's Education Fund. *The State of the World's Children,* 1993. New York: UNICEF, 1994.

United Nations Department for Economic and So-cial Information and Policy Analysis. Population Division. *Levels and Trends of Contraceptive Use as Assessed in 1994.* New York: United Nations, 1996.

———. Statistical Division. *The World's Women: 1995 Trends and Statistics.* New York: United Nations, 1995.

Part Two

Tables

How to Use the Tables

The tables in this encyclopedia offer a demographic profile of all the world's sovereign states (as well as Puerto Rico). The statistical information in the tables was gathered from various U.N. and other official publications. For a list of sources, see the bibliography immediately following this section. The authors have tried to simplify the presentation of statistical material as much as possible, through the use of consistent terms and comparable data. Still, the terms and data require some explanation. Below are explanations of some major categories, in the order in which they appear in the tables.

Note: Dates in parentheses correspond to data for years different from the ones listed at the top of the tables. For example, a datum in the 1995 column with a (91) after it means the datum actually refers to 1991. The term "rate" signifies the number per 1,000 residents.

GEOGRAPHY

AREA: Total area, including internal bodies of water.

LAND AREA: Total land area, excluding internal bodies of water.

COASTLINE: Total coastlines, including those on major internal seas.

CITIES: Population within city limits, *not* for entire metropolitan areas.

POPULATION

TOTAL: Total population at the end of the given year.

DENSITY: Number of persons living in a given geographical area.

ANNUAL GROWTH: Percentage growth of the population in a given year.

AGE COHORTS: Percentage of persons falling into the given age cohorts or groups.

MALE/FEMALE: Percentage of population by gender.

URBAN/RURAL: Urban statistics include people living in inner suburbs.

NET MIGRATION RATE: Persons leaving (emigrants) versus persons arriving (immigrants). A negative rate means more people are leaving than arriving.

IDENTITY

Where no percentages are given, the items listed are from largest to smallest. Where it says "official," the language listed is the language of government, and not necessarily spoken by a significant percentage of the population.

ETHNICITY: Refers to cultural and ethnic groups as defined by the national government.

LANGUAGE: Those who speak a given language as their primary tongue.

RELIGION: Includes practitioners and those who are born into a given faith, though they may not practice it. "Indigenous" refers to local faiths.

VITAL STATISTICS

BIRTH RATE: Births per 1,000 persons.

INFANT MORTALITY RATE: Deaths of babies in their first year of life per 1,000 babies born.

ABORTION RATE: Legally induced abortions per 1,000 live births.

LIFE EXPECTANCY AT BIRTH: Life expectancy for all persons.

MARRIAGE RATE: Marriages per 1,000 persons.

DIVORCE RATE: Divorces per 1,000 persons.

AVERAGE AGE AT MARRIAGE: Marrying ages, including persons who have married more than once.

DEATH RATE: Deaths per 1,000 persons.

HOUSEHOLDS

HOUSEHOLDS: Persons living within a single residence, including family members and others.

SINGLE: Households headed by a person who has never married.

MARRIED: Households with parents living at home.

WIDOWED: Households headed by a widow or widower.

DIVORCED: Households headed by a person who has separated or been divorced from his or her spouse.

ECONOMICS AND LABOR

GDP PER CAPITA US$: Gross domestic product (GDP); average income per person in 1995 dollars.

LABOR FORCE: Persons participating in the commercial economy. Excludes those who primarily rely on subsistence farming, fishing, hunting, or gathering.

AGRICULTURE: Persons engaged in agriculture, including farmers, pastoralists, and foresters.

MINING: Persons engaged in underground and surface mining, or quarrying.

MANUFACTURING: Persons working in the production of goods, including handicrafts.

UTILITIES: Persons employed in industries producing or providing energy, fuel, or water.

CONSTRUCTION: Persons involved in the construction of temporary and permanent buildings.

TRADE/FOOD/TOURISM: Includes persons in retail and wholesale trades, retail and wholesale food sales and distribution, restaurants, hotels, hostels, and other tourist services.

TRANSPORT/COMMUNICATIONS: Persons involved in the transport of passengers, the transport and storage of goods, and the provision or production of electronic and print communications and media, including newspapers and magazines; books; recordings; films and videos; telephone, telegraph, television, radio, and Internet service.

FINANCE/INSURANCE/REAL ESTATE: Persons involved in banking; securities; commodity exchanges; insurance of all types; and the buying, selling, and brokering of real property.

SOCIAL AND PERSONAL SERVICES: Persons involved in the provision of welfare, health, education, and personal services.

UNEMPLOYMENT: Percentage as determined by the national government. This does not include individuals who have given up looking for work and those who are not involved in the commercial economy. *Note: Official rates usually underestimate the number of people needing or wanting paid employment.*

UNION DENSITY: Percentage of the commercial workforce who are members of independent or government-run unions.

TRANSPORT

RAILROAD PASSENGER TRIPS: A statistic reached by multiplying the number of passenger trips times the distance times one million.

AIR PASSENGER TRIPS: A statistic reached by multiplying the number of passenger trips times 1,000.

PRIVATE CARS: Vehicles licensed for noncommercial purposes (excludes two- and three-wheeled vehicles).

COMMERCIAL: All vehicles—regardless of the number of wheels or axles—licensed for commercial use.

HEALTH AND HEALTH CARE

HEALTH CARE: Statistics concerning the provision of health care services.

ACCESS TO SANITATION: Percentage of persons living in housing with adequate sanitation, as defined by the United Nations.

MEASLES IMMUNIZATION: Percentage of children under 12 who have received at least one immunization against measles.

RATE OF PHYSICIANS: Number of physicians per 1,000 residents.

RATE OF HOSPITAL BEDS: Number of hospital beds per 1,000 residents.

HEALTH: Statistics concerning the health of a country's population.

LOW-BIRTH-WEIGHT BABIES: Percentage of babies born underweight, as defined by the United Nations.

CHILD MALNUTRITION: Percentage of children under 5 years of age who are not receiving an adequate diet, as defined by the United Nations.

SMOKING PREVALENCE: Percentage of persons who smoke tobacco on a regular basis.

TUBERCULOSIS INCIDENCE RATE: Sufferers from all forms of tuberculosis per 1,000 persons.

AIDS/HIV CASES: Persons afflicted with acquired immune deficiency syndrome (AIDS) or known to be infected by human immunodeficiency virus (HIV). *Note: All figures in the 1980 column are for 1993.*

TOTAL DEATHS: Persons dying from all causes in a given year.

EDUCATION

Note: Figures for this column may exceed 100 percent, because persons outside the school-age group considered may be attending school.

PRIMARY: Percentage of primary school-age children attending primary school.

SECONDARY: Percentage of secondary school-age children attending secondary school.

HIGHER: Percentage of young persons attending institutions of higher learning, including colleges, universities, military academies, and technical institutions.

FEMALES IN SCHOOL: *Note: Due to discrepancies in the sources, data in this section are defined in two ways. See immediately below.*

OF (OR IN) PRIMARY/SECONDARY/ HIGHER: Percentage of school-age girls attending a given school level.

PRIMARY/SECONDARY/HIGHER: Percentage of school-age children and young persons who are female.

COMMUNICATIONS

RATE OF NEWSPAPERS: Newspapers sold on a regular basis (usually daily or weekly) per 1,000 persons.

RATE OF RADIOS: Radios owned per 1,000 persons.

RATE OF TELEVISIONS: Television sets owned per 1,000 persons.

Note: Metric Conversions

The following conversion rates are used in this volume:

1 square mile = 2.59 square kilometers

1 linear mile = 1.6 linear kilometers

Table Bibliography and Sources

The bibliography provides full citations for the information given in the tables that follow. The short citation in parentheses corresponds to the bibliographic sources given at the end of each table.

BIBLIOGRAPHY

Central Intelligence Agency. *The World Factbook, 1997–98.* Washington DC: Brassey's, 1997. (CIA, *The World Factbook,* 1997)

International Labour Office. *World Labour Report: Industrial Relations, Democracy and Social Stability.* Geneva: International Labour Organization, 1997. (ILO. *World Labour Report,* 1997)

Department for Economic and Social Information and Policy Analysis, Statistics Division. *1995 Demographic Yearbook.* New York: United Nations, 1997. (UN, *Demographic Yearbook,* 1997)

———. *1994 Statistical Yearbook.* New York: United Nations, 1996. (UN, *Statistical Yearbook,* 1996)

World Bank. *World Development Indicators, 1998.* Washington DC: World Bank, 1998. (World Bank, *World Development Indicators,* 1998)

TABLE SOURCES

Geography

AREA: CIA, *The World Factbook,* 1997

LAND AREA: CIA, *The World Factbook,* 1997

COASTLINE: CIA, *The World Factbook,* 1997

CITIES: UN, *Demographic Yearbook,* 1997

Population

POPULATION: UN, *Demographic Yearbook,* 1997, 1981, 1966

DENSITY: UN, *Demographic Yearbook,* 1997, 1981, 1966

ANNUAL GROWTH: UN, *Demographic Yearbook,* 1997, 1981, 1966

AGE COHORTS: UN, *Demographic Yearbook,* 1997, 1981, 1966

MALE/FEMALE: UN, *Demographic Yearbook,* 1997, 1981, 1966

URBAN/RURAL: UN, *Demographic Yearbook,* 1997, 1981, 1966

NET MIGRATION: 1995: CIA, *The World Factbook,* 1997; 1980, 1965: UN *Demographic Yearbook,* 1981, 1966

Identity

ETHNICITY: CIA, *The World Factbook,* 1997

LANGUAGE: CIA, *The World Factbook,* 1997

RELIGION: CIA, *The World Factbook,* 1997

Vital Statistics

BIRTH RATE: UN, *Demographic Yearbook,* 1997, 1981, 1966

INFANT MORTALITY RATE: UN, *Demographic Yearbook,* 1997, 1981, 1966

ABORTION: UN, *Demographic Yearbook,* 1997

LIFE EXPECTANCY: UN, *Demographic Yearbook,* 1997, 1981, 1966

MARRIAGE RATE: UN, *Demographic Yearbook,* 1997, 1981, 1966

DIVORCE RATE: UN, *Demographic Yearbook,* 1997, 1981, 1966

AVERAGE AGE AT MARRIAGE: UN, *Demographic Yearbook,* 1997, 1981, 1966

DEATH RATE: UN, *Demographic Yearbook,* 1997, 1981, 1966

Households

HOUSEHOLDS: UN, *Demographic Yearbook,* 1997, 1981, 1966

SINGLE: UN, *Demographic Yearbook,* 1997, 1981, 1966

MARRIED: UN, *Demographic Yearbook,* 1997, 1981, 1966

WIDOWED: UN, *Demographic Yearbook,* 1997, 1981, 1966

DIVORCED: UN, *Demographic Yearbook,* 1997, 1981, 1966

Economics and Labor

GDP PER CAPITA US$: CIA, *The World Factbook,* 1997

LABOR FORCE: UN, *Statistical Yearbook,* 1996

UNEMPLOYMENT: UN, *Statistical Yearbook,* 1996

UNION DENSITY: ILO, *World Labour Report,* 1997

POVERTY: World Bank, *World Development Indicators,* 1998

Transport

RAILROAD PASSENGER TRIPS: UN, *Statistical Yearbook,* 1996

AIR PASSENGER TRIPS: UN, *Statistical Yearbook,* 1996

PRIVATE CARS: UN, *Statistical Yearbook,* 1996, 1981, 1966

COMMERCIAL: UN, *Statistical Yearbook,* 1996, 1981, 1966

Health and Health Care

ACCESS TO SANITATION: World Bank, *World Development Indicators,* 1998

MEASLES IMMUNIZATION: World Bank, *World Development Indicators,* 1998

RATE OF PHYSICIANS: World Bank, *World Development Indicators,* 1998

RATE OF HOSPITAL BEDS: World Bank, *World Development Indicators,* 1998

Health

LOW BIRTHWEIGHT BABIES: World Bank, *World Development Indicators,* 1998

CHILD MALNUTRITION: World Bank, *World Development Indicators,* 1998

SMOKING PREVALENCE: World Bank, *World Development Indicators,* 1998

TUBERCULOSIS INCIDENCE RATE: World Bank, *World Development Indicators,* 1998

AIDS/HIV CASES: UN, *Statistical Yearbook,* 1996

TOTAL DEATHS: World Bank, *World Development Indicators,* 1998

Education

PRIMARY: UN, *Statistical Yearbook,* 1996, 1981, 1966

SECONDARY: UN, *Statistical Yearbook,* 1996, 1981, 1966

HIGHER: UN, *Statistical Yearbook,* 1996, 1981, 1966

Females in School

OF PRIMARY/SECONDARY/HIGHER: UN, *Statistical Yearbook,* 1996, 1981, 1966

PRIMARY/SECONDARY/HIGHER: UN, *Statistical Yearbook,* 1996, 1981, 1966

Communications

RATE OF NEWSPAPERS: UN, *Statistical Yearbook,* 1996, 1981, 1966

RATE OF RADIOS: UN, *Statistical Yearbook,* 1996, 1981, 1966

RATE OF TELEVISIONS: UN, *Statistical Yearbook,* 1996, 1981, 1966

I.

World Data, Graphs, and Tables

The world's population, distributed across six of its seven continents, as well as numerous large and small islands, is roughly six billion. The total area of the planet is 197 million square miles, with land masses accounting for about 30 percent of that. Most of the planet's land area is in the northern hemisphere, largely in the tropical and temperate zones. Following World War II, the global economy underwent a roughly 30-year period of sustained growth. Since the 1970s, the various regions of the world have experienced varying economic growth rates. While much of the developed and developing world went through sustained recession for 20 years, the Middle East and the Far East experienced rapid economic growth. In the 1990s, as the developed world appears to be coming out of recession, East Asia appears to be sinking into it. Still, in the past 50 years, the combination of overall economic growth, decolonization, and improved agricultural and health care practices have allowed the population to skyrocket, as death rates fell dramatically in comparison to slowly declining birth rates.

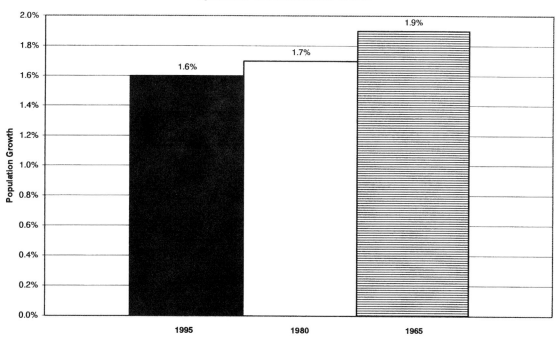

Population Growth Rates: World

Population growth rates have been gradually coming down since 1965, but they remain high. To translate growth rates into doubling time, divide the annual growth rate into 70. Thus, a growth rate of 1.9 percent divided into 70 equals a doubling period of 36.84 years.

Growth in Population: World

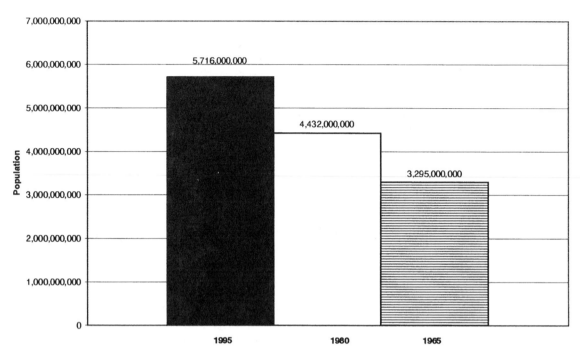

The time it takes the world's population to double has been rapidly getting shorter. While it once took millennia, and later centuries, doubling now occurs in decades. Though global population has not doubled since 1965, it is expected to do so shortly after the turn of the turn of the century.

Gender: World

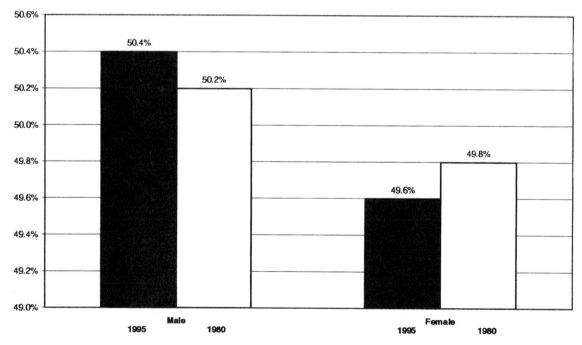

The rising percentage of males in the global population may be the result of birth control. That is, in many world cultures, boy children are valued over girl children. If parents decide to keep their families small, they may stop after one or two boy children, but will continue to reproduce even after they have a girl child or two.

Birth and Death Rates: World

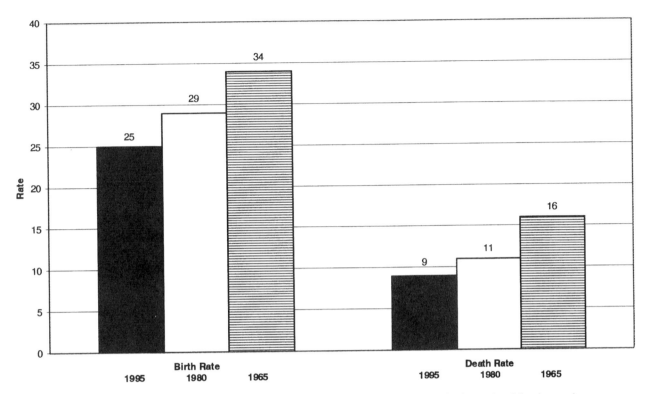

While the birth rate has come down by more than 25 percent since 1965, the death rate has fallen by nearly half. Thus, the gap between the two remains barely unchanged, promising further rapid population growth in coming decades, until the birth rate drops further.

	1995	1980	1965

GEOGRAPHY

AREA (square miles/kilometers)	196,938,990/510,072,000		
LAND AREA (square miles/kilometers)	57,505,791/148,940,000		
COASTLINE	222,500/356,000		

POPULATION

	1995	1980	1965
TOTAL	5,716,000,000	4,432,000,000	3,295,000,000
DENSITY (per square mile/kilometer)	109/42	85/33	65/25
ANNUAL GROWTH	1.6%	1.7%	1.9%
AGE COHORTS			
0–14	32%	35%	n/a
15–64	62%	59%	n/a
65 AND OVER	6%	6%	n/a

	1995	1980	1965
MALE	50.4%	50.2%	n/a
FEMALE	49.6%	49.8%	n/a

VITAL STATISTICS

	1995	1980	1965
BIRTH RATE	25	29	34
DEATH RATE	9	11	16

Source: CIA, The World Factbook, 1997; UN, Demographic Yearbook, 1997; UN, Statistical Yearbook, 1996.

2.
The Regions of the World: Data, Graphs, and Tables

AFRICA

Africa, the world's second largest continent, lies astride the equator surrounded by the Red Sea and the Indian Ocean to the east, the Atlantic Ocean to the west, and the Mediterranean Sea to the north. Largely ruled by Europeans until the 1960s—who did little to develop the continent except in areas that benefited the colonizers directly—independent Africa emerged onto the world scene burdened by a host of problems unfamiliar to other regions. First, its national borders had little correspondence to ethnicity, so that many different peoples were forced to live under one government. Second, much of its infrastructure was designed to serve foreign exploiters.

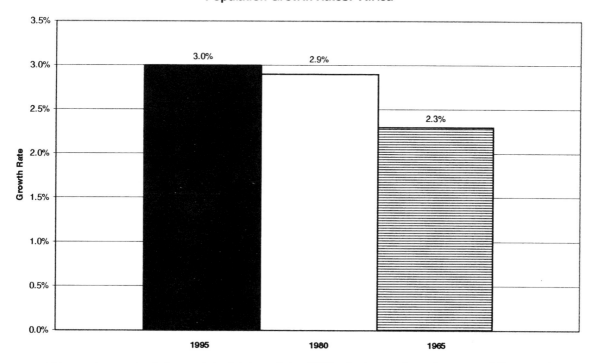

Population Growth Rates: Africa

Africa continues to buck the trends in global population. While all other continents have seen a falling rate of growth in recent decades, Africa's growth rate continues to climb. The key factor here is health care. Colonized by Europeans until the 1960s, Africans were unable to develop health care policies. Since then, independent African governments have made great strides in bringing down the death rates of their nations' populations.

Railroads, for example, usually connected mines or other sources of wealth with ports, rather than providing the continent with an integrated transportation system. Third, the colonizers did little to educate the people of the continent. Not surprisingly, given these handicaps, Africa has been plagued by war and underdevelopment for much of the past 30 years. Most of the world's poorest countries are located in Africa, below the Sahara Desert. (North Africa is often lumped together with the Middle East, or Southwest Asia, for reasons of culture and levels of economic and social development.) Still, recent trends are promising. More of Africa lives under democratic rule, and South Africa, potentially the economic powerhouse of the continent, is under black rule for the first time in its history.

Density: Africa

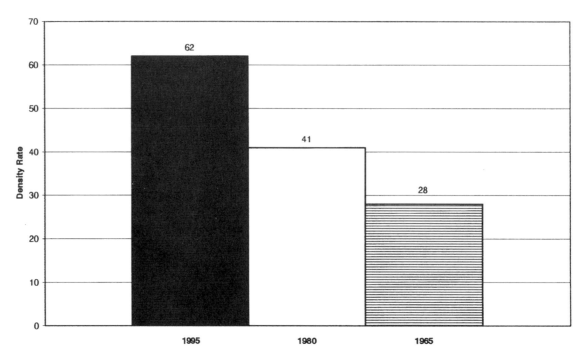

While the world bemoans rapid population growth in Africa, many African demographers and population experts are less concerned. They point to the fact that the continent—by world standards—remains less densely populated than some other areas, a legacy of slavery and colonialism. There is some truth to their claims. Compare Africa's density to that of Europe (minus Russia) and Asia.

AFRICA

	1995	1980	1965

GEOGRAPHY

AREA (square miles/kilometers)   11,701,545/30,306,000

	1995	1980	1965
POPULATION			
TOTAL	728,000,000	470,000,000	311,000,000
DENSITY (per square mile/kilometer)	62/24	41/16	28/11
ANNUAL GROWTH	3%	2.9%	2.3%
AGE COHORTS			
0–14	44%	45%	n/a
15–64	53%	52%	n/a
65 AND OVER	3%	3%	n/a
MALE	49.9%	49.6%	n/a
FEMALE	50.1%	50.4%	n/a

VITAL STATISTICS

	1995	1980	1965
BIRTH RATE	42	46	46
DEATH RATE	14	17	23

WEST AFRICA

GEOGRAPHY

AREA (square miles/kilometers)	2,369,884/6,138,000

POPULATION

	1995	1980	1965
TOTAL	211,000,000	141,000,000	98,000,000
DENSITY (per square mile/kilometer)	88/34	62/24	28/11
ANNUAL GROWTH	3.0%	3.1%	2.3%

	1995	**1980**	**1965**
AGE COHORTS			
0–14	46%	46%	n/a
15–64	51%	51%	n/a
65 AND OVER	3%	3%	n/a
MALE		49.6%	n/a
FEMALE		50.4%	n/a

VITAL STATISTICS

BIRTH RATE	46	49	50
DEATH RATE	16	14	27

EAST AFRICA

GEOGRAPHY

AREA (square miles/kilometers)	2,454,054/6,356,000

POPULATION

	1995	1980	1965
TOTAL	227,000,000	134,000,000	86,000,000
DENSITY (per square mile/kilometer)	93/36	57/22	36/14
ANNUAL GROWTH	3.0%	2.9%	2.4%
AGE COHORTS			
0–14	46%	46%	n/a
15–64	51%	51%	n/a
65 AND OVER	3%	3%	n/a
MALE	49.8%	49.3%	n/a
FEMALE	50.2%	50.7%	n/a

VITAL STATISTICS

BIRTH RATE	46	48	45
DEATH RATE	16	19	21

	1995	1980	1965

NORTH AFRICA

GEOGRAPHY

AREA (square miles/kilometers)   3,291,506/8,525,000

POPULATION

	1995	1980	1965
TOTAL	161,000,000	109,000,000	75,000,000
DENSITY (per square mile/kilometer)	49/19	34/13	23/9
ANNUAL GROWTH	2.3%	2.9%	2.4%
AGE COHORTS			
0–14	39%	43%	n/a
15–64	57%	53%	n/a
65 AND OVER	4%	4%	n/a
MALE	50.6%	50.5%	n/a
FEMALE	49.4%	49.5%	n/a

VITAL STATISTICS

	1995	1980	1965
BIRTH RATE	31	43	43
DEATH RATE	9	14	19

CENTRAL AFRICA

GEOGRAPHY

AREA (square miles/kilometers)   2,553,282/6,613,000

POPULATION

	1995	1980	1965
TOTAL	82,000,000	53,000,000	32,000,000
DENSITY (per square mile/kilometer)	31/12	21/8	13/5
ANNUAL GROWTH	3.1%	2.5%	1.9%

	1995	1980	1965
AGE COHORTS			
0–14	47%	44%	n/a
15–64	50%	53%	n/a
65 AND OVER	3%	3%	n/a
MALE	48.8%	49.1%	n/a
FEMALE	51.2%	50.9%	n/a

VITAL STATISTICS

BIRTH RATE	46	45	42
DEATH RATE	15	20	23

SOUTHERN AFRICA

GEOGRAPHY

AREA (square miles/kilometers)	1,032,819/2,675,000

POPULATION

	1995	1980	1965
TOTAL	47,000,000	33,000,000	20,000,000
DENSITY (per square mile/kilometer)	47/18	34/13	21/8
ANNUAL GROWTH	2.3%	2.8%	2.5%
AGE COHORTS			
0–14	38%	42%	n/a
15–64	58%	54%	n/a
65 AND OVER	4%	4%	n/a
MALE	48.9%	48.5%	n/a
FEMALE	51.1%	51.5%	n/a

VITAL STATISTICS

BIRTH RATE	32	39	42
DEATH RATE	9	11	17

Source: UN, Demographic Yearbook, 1997; UN, Statistical Yearbook, 1996.

ASIA

The largest continent on earth, Asia is surrounded by the Arctic Sea to the north; the Pacific Ocean to the east; Australia and the Indian Ocean to the south; and Europe, Africa, and the Mediterranean Sea to the west. With the largest population of any continent by a factor of nearly five, Asia is really several continents in one: East Asia (dominated by China), South Asia (dominated by India), Southeast Asia, and Southwest Asia (the Middle East and the former Central Asian republics of the Soviet Union). Each region presents a different profile to the world. East Asia and Southeast Asia, though still divided between countries calling themselves communist and capitalist, have—until the last couple of years—been experiencing rapid economic growth. This growth has brought a host of other developments in its wake, including declining birth rates and better educational and health care services. Southwest Asia presents a mixed picture. While the rise in oil prices brought wealth to some countries of the Middle East—and, with that wealth, better education and health care—it left others behind. Plagued by continuing high rates of population growth and declining oil prices, the region is currently experiencing a prolonged slump. South Asia, though showing some signs of economic life, lags behind the other regions. Still, its dominant country—India—has managed to retain its democratic institutions through trying times.

Annual Growth: East Asia and Southwest Asia

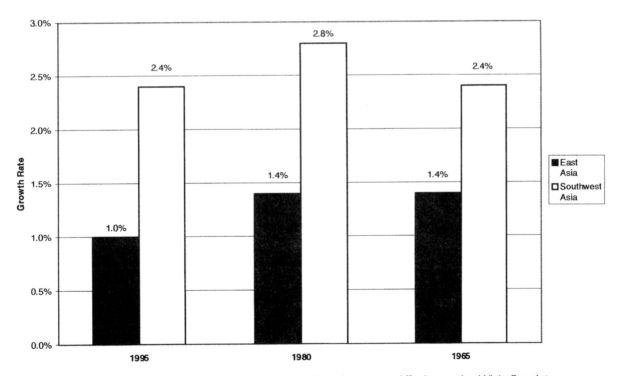

Asia is such an immense and varied continent, generalities about it are difficult to make. While East Asia—dominated numerically by China and its tough birth-control practices—has seen its growth rate drop significantly, Southwest Asia—roughly the Middle East and the former Muslim republics of the Soviet Union—has witnessed continued high growth rates.

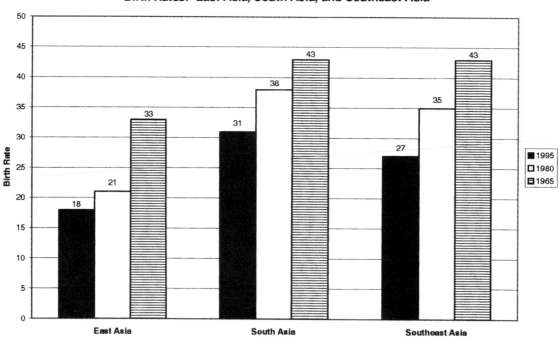

Birth Rates: East Asia, South Asia, and Southeast Asia

With its various regions, Asia presents several models for dealing with population control. In East Asia, China has imposed harsh pro-birth-control laws; in South Asia, democratic India has attempted to bring down the birth rate by education; in Southeast Asia, rapid economic growth is having an impact on birth rates.

ASIA

	1995	1980	1965

GEOGRAPHY

AREA (square miles/kilometers) 12,229,343/31,764,000			

POPULATION

	1995	1980	1965
TOTAL	3,458,000,000	2,579,000,000	1,830,000,000
DENSITY (per square mile/kilometer)	282/109	246/95	176/68
ANNUAL GROWTH	1.6%	n/a	2%
AGE COHORTS			
0–14	32%	37%	n/a
15–64	63%	59%	n/a
65 AND OVER	5%	4%	n/a
MALE	51.1%	51%	n/a
FEMALE	48.9%	49%	n/a

	1995	1980	1965

VITAL STATISTICS

	1995	1980	1965
BIRTH RATE	25	n/a	38
DEATH RATE	8	n/a	18

EAST ASIA[1]

GEOGRAPHY

AREA (square miles/kilometers)   4,541,313/11,762,000

POPULATION

	1995	1980	1965
TOTAL	1,424,000,000	1,190,000,000	864,000,000
DENSITY (per square mile/kilometer)	313/121	262/101	189/73
ANNUAL GROWTH	1%	1.4%	1.4%
AGE COHORTS			
0–14	25%	33%	n/a
15–64	68%	61%	n/a
65 AND OVER	7%	6%	n/a
MALE	51.1%	50.9%	n/a
FEMALE	48.9%	49.1%	n/a

VITAL STATISTICS

	1995	1980	1965
BIRTH RATE	18	21	33
DEATH RATE	7	7	19

SOUTH ASIA[2]

GEOGRAPHY

AREA (square miles/kilometers)   4,160,618/10,776,000

	1995	1980	1965
POPULATION			
TOTAL	1,381,000,000	944,000,000	681,000,000
DENSITY (per square mile/kilometer)	332/128	225/87	262/101
ANNUAL GROWTH	2.1%	2.2%	2.4%
AGE COHORTS			
0–14	37%	41%	n/a
15–64	59%	56%	n/a
65 AND OVER	4%	3%	n/a
MALE	51.5%	51.7%	n/a
FEMALE	49.5%	48.3%	n/a
VITAL STATISTICS			
BIRTH RATE	31	38	43
DEATH RATE	10	16	18

SOUTHEAST ASIA[3]

GEOGRAPHY

AREA (square miles/kilometers)   1,735,521/4,495,000

POPULATION

	1995	1980	1965
TOTAL	484,000,000	369,000,000	255,000,000
DENSITY (per square mile/kilometer)	280/108	212/82	148/57
ANNUAL GROWTH	1.8%	2.1%	2.6%
AGE COHORTS			
0–14	35%	40%	n/a
15–64	61%	57%	n/a
65 AND OVER	4%	3%	n/a
MALE	49.8%	49.9%	n/a
FEMALE	50.2%	50.1%	n/a

	1995	**1980**	**1965**
VITAL STATISTICS			
BIRTH RATE	27	35	43
DEATH RATE	8	14	17

SOUTHWEST ASIA[4]

GEOGRAPHY

AREA (square miles/kilometers)   1,826,641/4,731,000

POPULATION

	1995	**1980**	**1965**
TOTAL	168,000,000	101,000,000	68,000,000
DENSITY (per square mile/kilometer)	93/36	57/22	39/15
ANNUAL GROWTH	2.4%	2.8%	2.4%
AGE COHORTS			
0–14	38%	42%	n/a
15–64	58%	54%	n/a
65 AND OVER	4%	4%	n/a
MALE	51.2%	51%	n/a
FEMALE	48.8%	49%	n/a

VITAL STATISTICS

	1995	**1980**	**1965**
BIRTH RATE	32	40	42
DEATH RATE	7	12	18

FOOTNOTES
1. Includes China, Japan, and the two Koreas.
2. Includes Bangladesh, India, Nepal, Pakistan, and Sri Lanka.
3. Includes all countries to the east of India, south of China, north of Australia, and west of the Pacific.
4. Includes the Middle East, Iran, Afghanistan, and former Central Asian republics of the Soviet Union.

Source: UN, *Demographic Yearbook, 1997;* UN, *Statistical Yearbook, 1996.*

EUROPE

Europe lies at the western extreme of the Eurasian land mass and is surrounded by Asia to the east, the Mediterranean Sea to the south, the Atlantic Ocean to the west, and the Arctic Ocean to the north. (Note that Europe is often considered to include all of Russia, which actually stretches across Asia to the Pacific.) Until the overthrow of East European communism in 1989 and the collapse of the Soviet Union in 1991, Europe was largely divided along a line that divided the capitalist West from the communist East. In the former, market economies boomed through the 1970s, before entering a period of prolonged economic slump. Despite high unemployment and slow rates of economic growth, the people in the region continued to enjoy some of the highest social indices and standards of living in the world. The southern parts of capitalist Europe have never been as prosperous as those to the north. In the East, there was also economic development through the 1970s, but not nearly as rapid. This region also enjoyed good health care and educational services, though its rate of consumption was below that of the West. The two regions do share one phenomenon: They remain the only regions of the world where population growth has approached zero and, especially in the East, actually begun to decline.

Birth and Death Rates: Europe

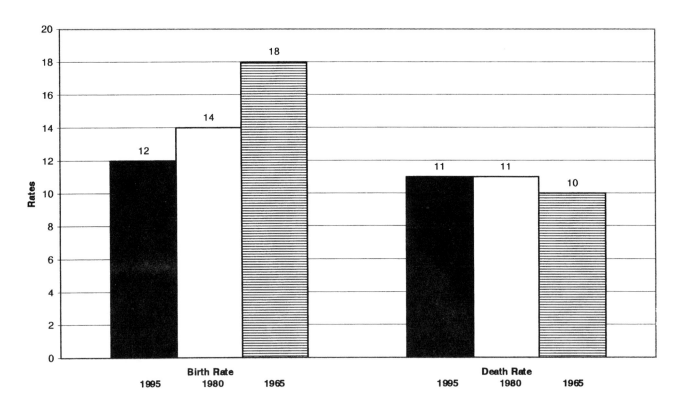

With its highly developed economies and small families, Europe has essentially achieved zero population growth as far as natural increase is concerned. Continued immigration from other regions of the world is now largely responsible for population increases.

Age Distribution: Europe

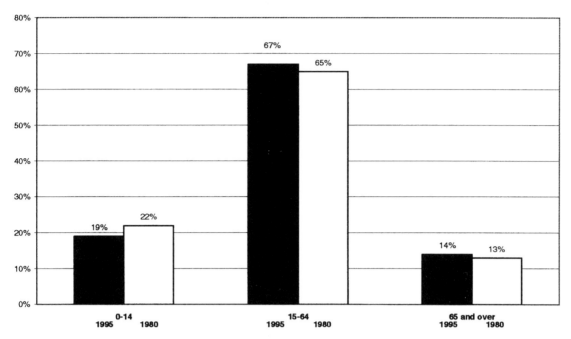

Because of declining birth rates and longer lives, Europe has the oldest population of any world region. In another 20 years, it is expected that the number of persons over the age of 65 will equal the number under 15.

EUROPE[1]

	1995	1980	1965

GEOGRAPHY

AREA (square miles/kilometers)   8,874,903/22,986,000[2]

POPULATION

	1995	1980	1965
TOTAL	727,000,000	484,000,000	445,000,000
DENSITY (per square mile/kilometer)	83/32	254/98	236/91
ANNUAL GROWTH	0.2%	0.4%	0.9%
AGE COHORTS			
0–14	19%	22%	n/a
15–64	67%	65%	n/a
65 AND OVER	14%	13%	n/a
MALE	48.3%	48.8%	n/a
FEMALE	51.7%	51.2%	n/a

	1995	1980	1965

VITAL STATISTICS

	1995	1980	1965
BIRTH RATE	12	14	18
DEATH RATE	11	11	10

EASTERN EUROPE[2]

GEOGRAPHY

AREA (square miles/kilometers)   7,263,707/18,813,000

POPULATION

	1995	1980	1965
TOTAL	309,000,000	110,000,000	100,000,000
DENSITY (per square mile/kilometer)	41/16	290/112	264/102
ANNUAL GROWTH	−0.1%	0.7%	0.6%
AGE COHORTS			
0–14	21%	23%	n/a
15–64	67%	65%	n/a
65 AND OVER	12%	12%	n/a
MALE	47.4%	49.1%	n/a
FEMALE	52.6%	50.9%	n/a

VITAL STATISTICS

	1995	1980	1965
BIRTH RATE	12	18	17
DEATH RATE	12	10	9

NORTHERN EUROPE[3]

GEOGRAPHY

AREA (square miles/kilometers)   675,290/1,749,000

	1995	1980	1965

POPULATION

	1995	1980	1965
TOTAL	94,000,000	82,000,000	79,000,000
DENSITY (per square mile/kilometer)	137/53	130/50	124/48
ANNUAL GROWTH	0.3%	0.1%	0.7%
AGE COHORTS			
0–14	20%	23%	n/a
15–64	65%	65%	n/a
65 AND OVER	15%	12%	n/a
MALE	48.4%	48.8%	n/a
FEMALE	51.6%	51.2%	n/a

VITAL STATISTICS

	1995	1980	1965
BIRTH RATE	14	13	16
DEATH RATE	11	12	11

SOUTHERN EUROPE[4]

GEOGRAPHY

AREA (square miles/kilometers)	508,108/1,316,000

POPULATION

	1995	1980	1965
TOTAL	144,000,000	139,000,000	123,000,000
DENSITY (per square mile/kilometer)	282/109	275/106	243/94
ANNUAL GROWTH	0.1%	0.7%	0.8%
AGE COHORTS			
0–14	17%	21.0%	n/a
15–64	68%	65.0%	n/a
65 AND OVER	15%	14.0%	n/a
MALE	49%	48.9%	n/a
FEMALE	51%	51.1%	n/a

	1995	1980	1965
VITAL STATISTICS			
BIRTH RATE	11	16	21
DEATH RATE	10	9	9

WESTERN EUROPE[5]

GEOGRAPHY

AREA (square miles/kilometers)   427,413/1,107,000

POPULATION

	1995	1980	1965
TOTAL	181,000,000	153,000,000	143,000,000
DENSITY (per square mile/kilometer)	422/163	396/153	381/147
ANNUAL GROWTH	0.6%	0.1%	1.2%
AGE COHORTS			
0–14	18%	21%	n/a
15–64	67%	65%	n/a
65 AND OVER	15%	14%	n/a
MALE	48.9%	48.4%	n/a
FEMALE	51.1%	51.6%	n/a

VITAL STATISTICS

	1995	1980	1965
BIRTH RATE	12	12	18
DEATH RATE	11	12	11

UNION OF SOVIET SOCIALIST REPUBLICS (USSR)

GEOGRAPHY

AREA (square miles/kilometers)   8,649,421/22,402,000

	1995	**1980**	**1965**

POPULATION

	1995	1980	1965
TOTAL	n/a	265,000,000	231,000,000
DENSITY (per square mile/kilometer)	n/a	31/12	26/10
ANNUAL GROWTH	n/a	0.9%	1.4%
AGE COHORTS			
0–14	n/a	24%	n/a
15–64	n/a	66%	n/a
65 AND OVER	n/a	10%	n/a
MALE	n/a	46.8%	n/a
FEMALE	n/a	53.2%	n/a

VITAL STATISTICS

	1995	1980	1965
BIRTH RATE		18	22
DEATH RATE		9	7

FOOTNOTES

1. Statistics for 1965 and 1980 do not include the USSR (statistics for 1995 include both European and Asiatic areas of the Russian Federation; Eastern Europe designates all former communist countries, including republics of the former Yugoslavia and European republics of the former Soviet Union).
2. Includes European and Asiatic areas of the Russian Federation.
3. Includes Scandinavia and the British Isles.
4. Includes Iberia, Italian peninsula, and Greece.
5. Includes German- and French-speaking countries, as well as the Netherlands.

Source: UN, *Demographic Yearbook, 1997;* UN, *Statistical Yearbook, 1996.*

LATIN AMERICA

The southern half of the so-called New World, or the Western Hemisphere, Latin America lies to the south of North America, with the Atlantic and Pacific oceans to its east and west, respectively. It includes Central America (including Mexico), the Caribbean, and South America. It is also divided by economic development. While the nations of the southern cone (Chile, Argentina, and Uruguay) are relatively prosperous, the countries of Central America and the Andean Mountains are not. United by a common culture combining elements of Iberia (Spain and Portugal), Native America, and Africa (the latter especially prevalent in Brazil and the Caribbean), Latin America is the only significant part of the developing world that has been politically independent since the nineteenth century. Still, its history since 1965 has been troubling. Though it experienced substantial economic growth through the 1970s, most of the region was governed by military dictatorships. In many countries, these governments nearly bankrupted the economy, as they put the governments there into deep debt to first-world lending institutions. Since the 1980s, however, virtually all of Latin America has been liberated from dictatorship, though the economic problems created by the dictatorial governments continue to stifle growth. Latin America has also been making great strides toward developing its human potential, especially in the field of education.

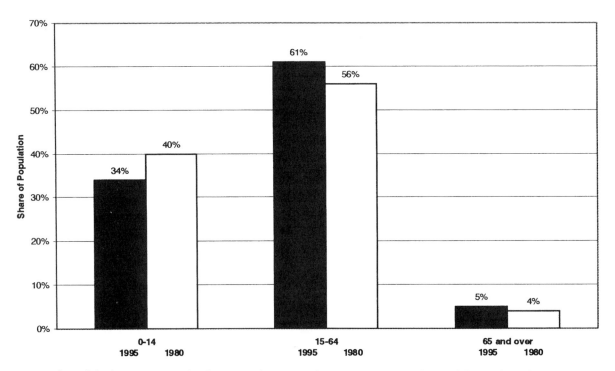

Age Distribution: Latin America

One of the key ways to predict future population growth is to examine age cohorts. If the number of young persons is on the rise, population is likely to grow rapidly. In Latin America, the percentage of persons under the age of 15 is falling, thereby promising slower growth rates in the coming century.

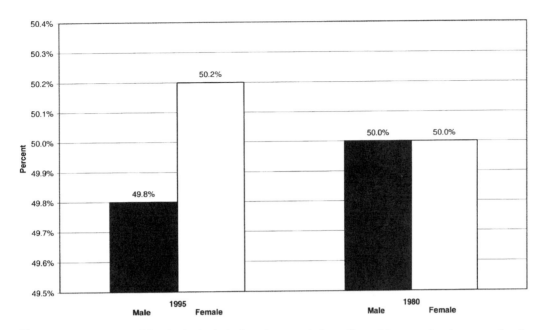

The growing percentage of females in the Latin American population reflects rising out-migration rates, since it is men who are most likely to seek educational and job opportunities by moving to other regions of the world, largely, in this case, the United States

LATIN AMERICA

	1995	1980	1965
GEOGRAPHY			
AREA (square miles/kilometers)	7,927,799/20,533,000		
POPULATION			
TOTAL	482,000,000	364,000,000	246,000,000
DENSITY (per square mile/kilometer)	60/23	47/18	31/12
ANNUAL GROWTH	1.8%	2.5%	2.8%
AGE COHORTS			
0–14	34%	40%	n/a
15–64	61%	56%	n/a
65 AND OVER	5%	4%	n/a
MALE	49.8%	50%	n/a
FEMALE	50.2%	50%	n/a

	1995	1980	1965

VITAL STATISTICS

BIRTH RATE	26	34	41
DEATH RATE	7	9	13

CARIBBEAN

GEOGRAPHY

AREA (square miles/kilometers)	90,734/235,000

POPULATION

	1995	1980	1965
TOTAL	36,000,000	31,000,000	23,000,000
DENSITY (per square mile/kilometer)	394/152	339/131	256/99
ANNUAL GROWTH	1.3%	1.8%	2.3%
AGE COHORTS			
0–14	30%	37%	n/a
15–64	63%	58%	n/a
65 AND OVER	7%	5%	n/a
MALE	48.6%	48.4%	n/a
FEMALE	51.4%	51.6%	n/a

VITAL STATISTICS

BIRTH RATE	24	28	38
DEATH RATE	8	9	14

CENTRAL AMERICA[1]

GEOGRAPHY

AREA (square miles/kilometers)	957,529/2,480,000

	1995	1980	1965

POPULATION

	1995	1980	1965
TOTAL	126,000,000	93,000,000	57,000,000
DENSITY (per square mile/kilometer)	132/51	98/38	62/24
ANNUAL GROWTH	2.2%	3.0%	3.5%
AGE COHORTS			
0–14	38%	45%	n/a
15–64	58%	52%	n/a
65 AND OVER	4%	3%	n/a
MALE	50.8%	50.5%	n/a
FEMALE	49.2%	49.5%	n/a

VITAL STATISTICS

	1995	1980	1965
BIRTH RATE	30	39	45
DEATH RATE	6	8	10

SOUTH AMERICA

GEOGRAPHY

AREA (square miles/kilometers)   6,879,923/17,819,000

POPULATION

	1995	1980	1965
TOTAL	320,000,000	240,000,000	171,000,000
DENSITY (per square mile/kilometer)	47/18	35/14	26/10
ANNUAL GROWTH	1.7%	2.3%	2.7%
AGE COHORTS			
0–14	33%	39%	n/a
15–64	62%	57%	n/a
65 AND OVER	5%	4%	n/a
MALE	49.7%	50%	n/a
FEMALE	50.3%	50%	n/a

	1995	1980	1965
VITAL STATISTICS			
BIRTH RATE	25	32	40
DEATH RATE	7	9	13

FOOTNOTES
1. Includes Mexico.

Source: UN, *Demographic Yearbook, 1997;* UN, *Statistical Yearbook, 1996.*

NORTH AMERICA

North America—the world's third largest continent—is surrounded by the Arctic Ocean to the north, the Atlantic Ocean to the east, the Pacific Ocean to the west, and Mexico and the Gulf of Mexico to the south. Consisting almost entirely of two highly developed countries—the United States and Canada—North America is the richest continent on earth, by per capita income. Long a home to immigrants from around the world, the continent's population represents a melange of distinct ethnic groups from around the world, as well as a tiny minority of native peoples. Until the 1960s, most of this population represented people of European and African (largely in the United States) descent. In the years since, the presence of people from Latin America and Asia have become more common. Indeed, it is expected that Hispanics will soon outnumber blacks to become the largest ethnic minority in the region. The North American economy, having almost entirely escaped the ravages of World War II, dominated the globe until the 1970s, when competitors in Europe and Japan revived. Following two decades of economic crisis, North America appears to be economically dominant again. Its population also continues to grow more rapidly than that of Europe, though most of the population growth comes from immigration.

Age Distribution: North America

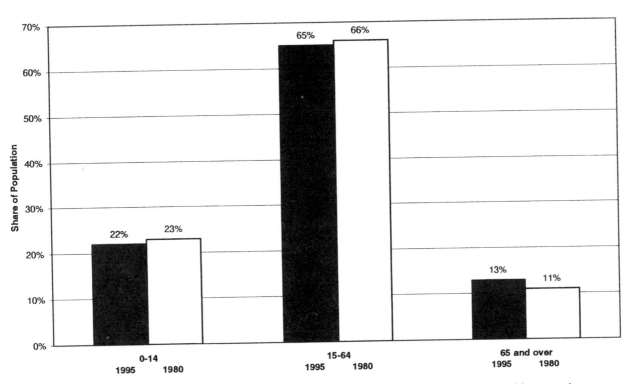

The aging population in North America reflects a phenomenon of developed nations. Better health care and falling birth rates mean more older people, along with strains on the economy caused by taking care of them.

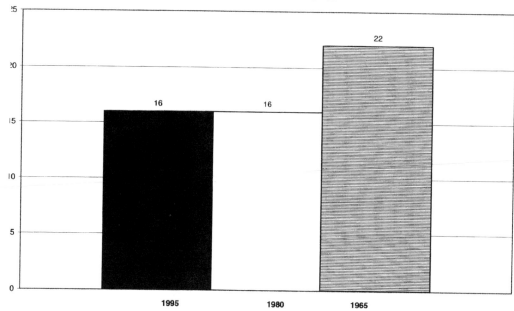

Birth Rate: North America

The birth rate graph reflects one of the most significant demographic developments in recent North American history—the baby boom. In 1965, the post–World War II reversal in declining birth rates was still being felt. By 1980, it had disappeared.

	1995	1980	1965
GEOGRAPHY			
AREA (square miles/kilometers) 8,307,722/21,517,000			
POPULATION			
TOTAL	293,000,000	248,000,000	214,000,000
DENSITY (per square mile/kilometer)	36/14	31/12	26/10
ANNUAL GROWTH	1%	1%	1.5%
AGE COHORTS			
0–14	22%	23%	n/a
15–64	65%	66%	n/a
65 AND OVER	13%	11%	n/a
MALE	49%	48.8%	n/a
FEMALE	51%	51.2%	n/a
VITAL STATISTICS			
BIRTH RATE	16	16	22
DEATH RATE	9	9	9

Source: UN, *Demographic Yearbook, 1997;* UN, *Statistical Yearbook, 1996.*

OCEANIA

The smallest region of the world by territory and especially population, Oceania lies in the southwestern Pacific Ocean, off the southeast coast of Asia. It consists of three distinct areas. The first and largest is Australia and New Zealand, a continent and series of large islands initially inhabited by Aborigines and Polynesians but eventually colonized and settled by European immigrants, who became predominant. In recent years, Australia has become a popular destination for Asian immigrants as well. Both countries developed economic and social profiles much like those in Europe and North America, with good social indices and high standards of living. Melanesia, consisting of large and small islands to the northeast of Australia and New Zealand, is the most impoverished part of Oceania. Most of its people make their living through subsistence farming and fishing, and have social indices comparable to middle tier countries of the developing world. Micronesia and Polynesia are made up of hundreds of tiny islands scattered across immense stretches of the southern and western Pacific Ocean. Largely divided into newly independent republics or possessions of France and the United States, the people of Micronesia and Polynesia generally enjoy moderate standards of income and social indexes. While many of the people in this region also support themselves through subsistence fishing and farming, their national economies are heavily subsidized by tourism or, in the case of French Polynesia, revenues from the home country.

Birth Rates: Australia and New Zealand, and Melanesia

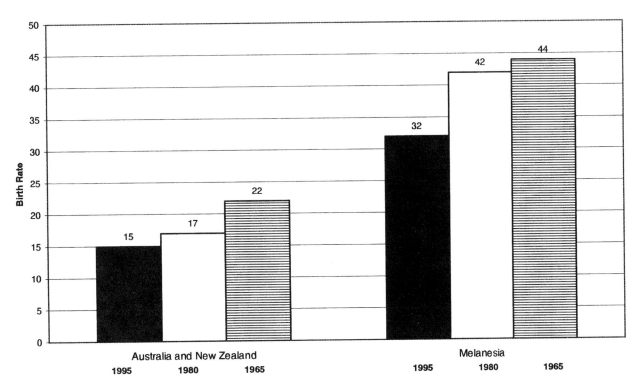

Like Asia, Oceania is highly diverse as a world region. Numerically dominated by Australia—a developed economy—it also includes the impoverished islands of Melanesia. Thus, while Australia and New Zealand have birth rates equivalent to those of North America, Melanesia has rates equivalent to those of South Asia.

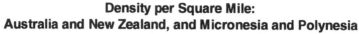

Density per Square Mile:
Australia and New Zealand, and Micronesia and Polynesia

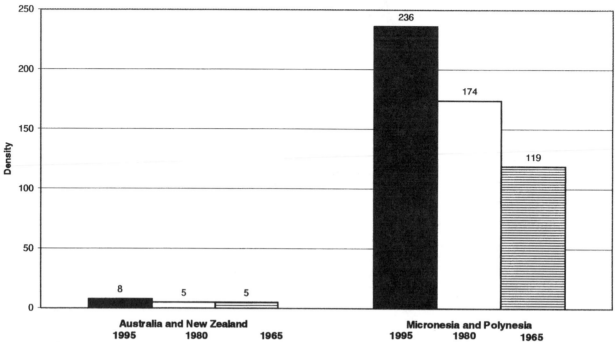

Density rates for Oceania are as varied as birth rates. While Australia remains the least densely populated continent on earth (aside from uninhabited Antarctica), the tiny islands of Micronesia and Polynesia are among the most densely populated nations of the world.

OCEANIA

	1995	1980	1965
GEOGRAPHY			
AREA (square miles/kilometers)	3,296,139/8,537,000		
POPULATION			
TOTAL	28,500,000	22,800,000	17,500,000
DENSITY (per square mile/kilometer)	8.0/3.0	8.0/3.0	5.0/2.0
ANNUAL GROWTH	1.5%	1.5%	2.1%
AGE COHORTS			
0–14	26%	29%	n/a
15–64	64%	63%	n/a
65 AND OVER	10%	8%	n/a

	1995	**1980**	**1965**
MALE	50.2%	50.4%	n/a
FEMALE	49.8%	49.6%	n/a

VITAL STATISTICS

	1995	**1980**	**1965**
BIRTH RATE	19	22	40
DEATH RATE	8	9	10

AUSTRALIA AND NEW ZEALAND

GEOGRAPHY

AREA (square miles/kilometers)   3,082,625/7,984,000

POPULATION

	1995	**1980**	**1965**
TOTAL	21,700,000	17,800,000	14,300,000
DENSITY (per square mile/kilometer)	8/3	5/2	5/2
ANNUAL GROWTH	1.4%	1.2%	2.0%
AGE COHORTS			
0–14	22%	26%	n/a
15–64	66%	65%	n/a
65 AND OVER	12%	9%	n/a
MALE	49.5%	50%	n/a
FEMALE	50.5%	50%	n/a

VITAL STATISTICS

	1995	**1980**	**1965**
BIRTH RATE	15	17	22
DEATH RATE	8	8	9

MELANESIA

GEOGRAPHY

AREA (square miles/kilometers)   208,880/541,000

	1995	1980	1965

POPULATION

	1995	1980	1965
TOTAL	5,800,000	3,600,000	2,500,000
DENSITY (per square mile/kilometer)	28/11	18/7	13/5
ANNUAL GROWTH	2.2%	2.7%	2.4%
AGE COHORTS			
0–14	39%	43%	n/a
15–64	58%	54%	n/a
65 AND OVER	3%	3%	n/a
MALE	50%	52.8%	n/a
FEMALE	50%	47.2%	n/a

VITAL STATISTICS

	1995	1980	1965
BIRTH RATE	32	42	44
DEATH RATE	9	15	20

MICRONESIA AND POLYNESIA

GEOGRAPHY

AREA (square miles/kilometers)   4,633/12,000

POPULATION

	1995	1980	1965
TOTAL	1,100,000	800,000	550,000
DENSITY (per square mile/kilometer)	236/91	174/67	119/46
ANNUAL GROWTH	1.9%	1.7%	3.0%
AGE COHORTS			
0–14	40%	41%	n/a
15–64	57%	56%	n/a
65 AND OVER	3%	3%	n/a
MALE	50%	50%	n/a
FEMALE	50%	50%	n/a

	1995	1980	1965
VITAL STATISTICS			
BIRTH RATE	32	34	40
DEATH RATE	6	7	10

Source: UN, Demographic Yearbook, 1997; UN, Statistical Yearbook, 1996.

3.
The Countries of the World, Statistical Tables

AFGHANISTAN

Afghanistan is a landlocked country located in South-Central Asia, north of Pakistan, east of Iran, and south of the former Soviet Republics of Turkmenistan, Uzbekistan, and Tajikistan. The 250,000-square-mile (647,000-square-kilometer) country borders China on the extreme northeast. Since the country gained independence in 1919, its economic and social development has languished, primarily as a result of Cold War disputes between the West and the Soviet Union. Since the fall of the Soviet Union, the country has been racked by factional conflicts among competing adherents of Sunni Islam. Over the past de-

cade, the military conflicts have produced millions of refugees. In part due to the long period of unbroken conflict, the country lacks basic necessities and health services, and is mired in abject poverty and neglect. In 1996, life expectancy at birth was 45.9 years in Afghanistan, significantly lower than in nearby Iran and Pakistan. The infant mortality rate was estimated at 163.4 deaths per 1,000 live births. The national economy is dominated by agricultural production. Only 20 percent of all Afghanis reside in urban areas.

	1995	1980	1965
GEOGRAPHY			
AREA (square miles/kilometers)	250,000/647,000		
LAND AREA (square miles/kilometers)	250,000/647,000		
COASTLINE	Landlocked		
CITIES			
CAPITAL	Kabul	1,424,400 (88)	
MAJOR CITIES	Kandahar	225,500	
	Herat	177,300	
	Mazar-I-Sharif	130,600	

	1995	1980	1965

POPULATION

	1995	1980	1965
TOTAL	20,141,000	13,051,058 (79)	n/a
DENSITY (per square mile/kilometer)	81/31	52/20	n/a
ANNUAL GROWTH	4.78%	2.6%	1.8%
AGE COHORTS			
0–14	43%		
15–64	54%		
65 AND OVER	3%		
MALE	51%		
FEMALE	49%		
URBAN	20%	15.4%	n/a
RURAL	80%	84.6%	n/a
NET MIGRATION RATE	22.9	n/a	n/a

IDENTITY

	1995	1980	1965
ETHNICITY			
PASHTUN	38%		
TAJIK	25%		
HAZARA	19%		
LANGUAGE			
AFGHAN-PERSIAN (Dari)	50%		
PASHTU	35%		
UZBEK-TURKMEN	11%		
RELIGION			
SUNNI MUSLIM	84%		
SHI'A MUSLIM	15%		

VITAL STATISTICS

	1995	1980	1965
BIRTHS			
BIRTH RATE	43	48.1	n/a
INFANT MORTALITY RATE	163.4	181.6	n/a
LIFE EXPECTANCY AT BIRTH	45.9	37	n/a

	1995	1980	1965
MARRIAGES			
MARRIAGE RATE	4.6	n/a	n/a
DIVORCE RATE	0.9	n/a	n/a
DEATHS			
DEATH RATE	18.2	22.3	n/a

ECONOMICS AND LABOR

GDP PER CAPITA US$	$600		

TRANSPORT

	1995	1980	1965
JOURNEYS (by transport mode)			
AIR PASSENGER TRIPS (thousands)	238		
VEHICLES (thousands)			
CARS	35	n/a	12.8
COMMERCIAL VEHICLES	41	n/a	12.6

EDUCATION

	1995	1980	1965
SCHOOL AGE IN SCHOOL			
PRIMARY	n/a	36%	16%
SECONDARY	n/a	11%	2%
HIGHER	n/a	0.4%	0.2%
FEMALES IN SCHOOL			
IN PRIMARY	n/a	13%	5%
IN SECONDARY	n/a	4%	1%
ADULT ILLITERACY M/F	n/a	69.7/95% (79)	n/a

COMMUNICATIONS

	1995	1980	1965
RATE OF NEWSPAPERS	12	6	6
RATE OF RADIOS	118	75	n/a
RATE OF TELEVISIONS	10	3	n/a

Source: CIA, *The World Factbook, 1997;* ILO, *World Labour Report, 1997;* UN, *Demographic Yearbook, 1997;* UN, *Statistical Yearbook, 1996;* World Bank, *World Development Indicators, 1998.*

ALBANIA

Albania occupies a land area of 11,100 square miles (28,750 square kilometers) in Southeastern Europe, west of the Adriatic Sea and the Ionian sea. The country borders Serbia and Montenegro to the north, the former Yugoslav Republic of Macedonia to the east, and Greece to the southeast. The country's population of 3.25 million is dominated by ethnic Albanians, who compose over 95 percent of all residents. Large Albanian minorities live in nearby regions of Serbia and Montenegro, the former Yugoslav Republic of Macedonia, and Greece. In the Kosovo region of southern Serbia, ethnic Albanians have been wag-

ing a decade-long war for autonomy from the Serbian Republic. Albania was one of Europe's most isolated countries for most of the Cold War period between 1946 and 1991. As Albania's economy has opened to the West and reverted from state control to the free market in the 1990s, the country's population has suffered severe hardships, including astronomical rates of inflation and high unemployment. In 1997, the collapse of Albania's highly speculative capitalist market economy led to an economic depression, civil war, and mass out-migration of political and economic refugees.

	1995	1980	1965
GEOGRAPHY			
AREA (square miles/kilometers)	11,100/28,750		
LAND AREA (square miles/kilometers)	10,579/27,400		
COASTLINE (miles/kilometers)	226/362		
CITIES			
CAPITAL	Tirane	244,153 (90)	
POPULATION			
TOTAL	3,249,126	n/a	1,626,315 (60)
DENSITY (per square mile/kilometer)	329/127	268/103	174/67
ANNUAL GROWTH	1.34 %	2.1%	3 %
AGE COHORTS			
0–14	34%		
15–4	60%		
65 AND OVER	6%		
MALE	51%		
FEMALE	49%		
URBAN	38%	33.6%	32%
RURAL	62%	n/a	68%

	1995	1980	1965
NET MIGRATION RATE	−1.17%	n/a	n/a

IDENTITY

ETHNICITY

ALBANIAN	95%		
GREEKS	3%		

LANGUAGE

ALBANIAN	97%		
GREEK	2%		

RELIGION

SUNNI MUSLIM	70%		
ALBANIAN ORTHODOX	20%		
ROMAN CATHOLIC	10%		

VITAL STATISTICS

BIRTHS

BIRTH RATE	22.2	26.2 (85)	34
URBAN BIRTH RATE	18.9 (91)		
RURAL BIRTH RATE	26.6 (91)		
INFANT MORTALITY RATE	49.2	86.8 (85)	86.8
LIFE EXPECTANCY AT BIRTH	67.9	66	64.9

MARRIAGES

MARRIAGE RATE	7.6	8.5 (85)	6.8
DIVORCE RATE	0.7	0.8 (85)	0.6

DEATHS

DEATH RATE	7.6	5.8 (85)	8.6

ECONOMICS AND LABOR

GDP PER CAPITA US$	$1,210		

LABOR FORCE M/F (thousands)	494.1/356.4 (91)		
UNEMPLOYMENT (official)	9.1%		

	1995	1980	1965

HEALTH AND HEALTH CARE

HEALTH CARE

	1995	1980	1965
RATE OF PHYSICIANS	1.3	0.9	0.3 (60)
RATE OF HOSPITAL BEDS	3	n/a	5.1 (60)
MEASLES IMMUNIZATION	91 %		

HEALTH INDICATORS

LOW-BIRTH-WEIGHT BABIES	7%		
SMOKING PREVALENCE M/F	50/8%		
TUBERCULOSIS RATE	0.4		

EDUCATION

SCHOOL AGE IN SCHOOL

	1995	1980	1965
PRIMARY	87%	113%	84% (60)
SECONDARY	35%	67%	8% (60)
HIGHER	10%	8%	6.80%

FEMALES IN SCHOOL

| PRIMARY | 48%[1] | 47 %[1] | 75% (60) |
| SECONDARY | 54 %[1] | 59 %[1] | 4% (60) |

COMMUNICATIONS

	1995	1980	1965
RATE OF NEWSPAPERS	49	54	47
RATE OF RADIOS	177	150	47
RATE OF TELEVISIONS	89	36	0.6

FOOTNOTE
1. Percentage of students who are female.

Source: CIA, The World Factbook, 1997; ILO, World Labour Report, 1997; UN, Demographic Yearbook, 1997; UN, Statistical Yearbook, 1996; World Bank, World Development Indicators, 1998.

ALGERIA

Algeria is located in north Africa on the coast of the Mediterranean Sea, bordering Tunisia, Libya, Niger, Mali, Mauritania, and Morocco. Algeria has benefited from huge natural gas and oil reserves. However, the national economy has stagnated following the decline in world oil prices in the early 1980s, which has precipitated a national austerity program aimed at reducing government subsidies and economic assistance programs. The national economy is also burdened by onerous debt obligations to the International Monetary Fund and foreign banks. In 1992, the government refused to honor the results of elections that would have brought fundamentalist Muslims to power. This refusal led to a bloody civil war that has taken thousands of civilian lives. Between 1980 and 1995, the national birth rate fell from 42.7 births 28.5 births per 1,000 residents. Over the same period, life expectancy at birth increased from 59.9 years to 68.3 years.

Secondary Education

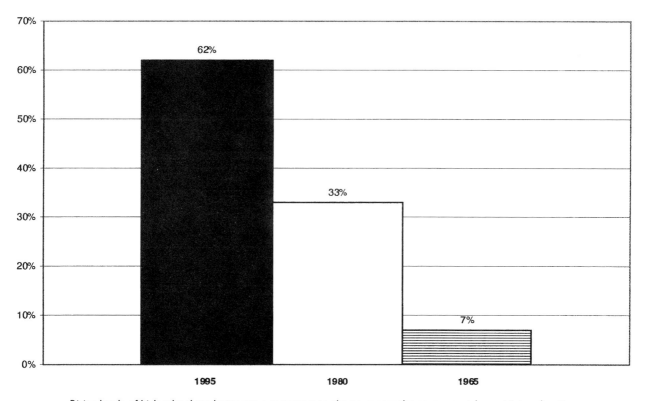

Rising levels of high school graduates are a testament to the resources the government has put into education since independence from France in 1962. However, rising graduation rates have not been matched by rising job opportunities. This is one of the sources of frustration that led to the rise of Muslim militancy in the country in the 1990s.

Private Cars

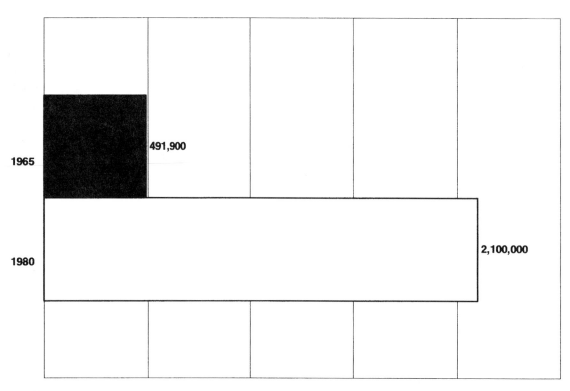

Massive increases in oil revenues in the 1970s raised living standards for a substantial minority of Algeria's population, a trend reflected in the rapidly rising rates of private car ownership during that period.

CHRONOLOGY

1962   Algeria wins independence from France after eight-year war.
1965   Socialist coup; Houari Boumedienne takes power.
1974   Rise in oil and natural gas prices brings new wealth to country.
1978   Boumedienne dies suddenly; replaced by close associate Chadli Benjedid.
1985   Collapsing oil/gas prices hit Algerian economy.
1988   Rioting over economic dislocations; army guns down hundreds.
1989   Government announces political liberalization.
1992   Army cancels elections that Islamic fundamentalists appear about to win; war breaks out between government and fundamentalists.
1996   New elections fail to end fighting.

	1995	**1980**	**1965**

GEOGRAPHY

AREA (square miles/kilometers)	1,093,336/2,831,740		
LAND AREA (square miles/kilometers)	1,093,336/2,381,740		
COASTLINE (miles/kilometers)	624/998		

CITIES
CAPITAL	Algiers		
MAJOR CITIES	Algiers	1,740,461 (77)	
	Oran	543485 (77)	
	Constantine	378,668 (77)	
	Annaba	246,049 (77)	
	Blida	138240 (77)	

POPULATION

	1995	**1980**	**1965**
TOTAL	29,183,032	16,948,000 (77)	12,101,994
DENSITY (per square mile/kilometer)	31/12	23/9	13/5
ANNUAL GROWTH	2.2%	3.10%	2%

AGE COHORTS
0–14	40%		
15–64	56%		
65 AND OVER	4%		

URBAN	56%	40%	n/a
RURAL	44%	60%	n/a

NET MIGRATION RATE	2.2	−3.5	n/a

IDENTITY

ETHNICITY
ARAB	80%		
BERBER	20%		

LANGUAGE
ARABIC	85%		
BERBER	12%		
FRENCH	2%		

RELIGION
SUNNI MUSLIM	99%		

	1995	1980	1965

VITAL STATISTICS

BIRTHS

BIRTH RATE	28.5	42.7	n/a
INFANT MORTALITY RATE	48.7	88	n/a
LIFE EXPECTANCY AT BIRTH	68.3	59.9	n/a

MARRIAGES

MARRIAGE RATE	5.6	6.3	n/a
AVERAGE AGE OF MARRIAGE M/F	n/a	27.7/23.7	n/a
DIVORCE RATE	n/a	8.5	n/a

DEATHS

DEATH RATE	5.9	10.7	n/a

HOUSEHOLDS

NUMBER	n/a	3,283,409 (87)	n/a
AVERAGE SIZE	n/a	7 (87)	n/a

ECONOMICS AND LABOR

GDP PER CAPITA US$	$3,800		

LABOR FORCE M/F

AGRICULTURE	18/57%		
INDUSTRY	38/7%		
SERVICES	44/36%		

UNEMPLOYMENT (official)	23.8%		

POVERTY

UNDER $1/DAY	2%		
UNDER $2/DAY	17.6%		

TRANSPORT

VEHICLES

PRIVATE CARS	n/a	491,900	2,100,000
COMMERCIAL	n/a	91,000	251,500

	1995	**1980**	**1965**

HEALTH AND HEALTH CARE

HEALTH CARE

	1995	**1980**	**1965**
ACCESS TO SAFE WATER	n/a	77%	n/a
MEASLES IMMUNIZATION	69%	n/a	n/a
RATE OF PHYSICIANS	0.8	n/a	0.2 (60)
RATE OF HOSPITAL BEDS	2.1	n/a	3.1 (60)

HEALTH INDICATORS

	1995	**1980**
PREGNANT WOMEN WITH ANEMIA	42%	
LOW-BIRTH-WEIGHT BABIES	9%	
CHILD MALNUTRITION	10%	
SMOKING PREVALENCE M/F	53/10%	
TUBERCULOSIS INCIDENCE RATE	0.53	
AIDS/HIV CASES	217	138 (93)

EDUCATION

SCHOOL AGE IN SCHOOL

	1995	**1980**	**1965**
PRIMARY	107%	94%	68%
SECONDARY	62%	33%	7%
HIGHER	11%	6%	0.7%

FEMALES IN SCHOOL

	1995	**1980**	**1965**
OF PRIMARY STUDENTS	99%	86%	53%
OF SECONDARY STUDENTS	47%	26%	5%

ADULT ILLITERACY M/F	**1995**	**1980**	**1965**
	26/51%	42.7/68.3%	70.1/92%

COMMUNICATIONS

	1995	**1980**	**1965**
RATE OF NEWSPAPERS	38	24	15
RATE OF RADIOS	236	197	12
RATE OF TELEVISIONS	79	52	n/a

Source: CIA, *The World Factbook, 1997;* ILO, *World Labour Report, 1997;* UN, *Demographic Yearbook, 1997;* UN, *Statistical Yearbook, 1996;* World Bank, *World Development Indicators, 1998.*

ANDORRA

The principality of Andorra is located in Southwestern Europe between France and Spain. The country is the size of a large city, occupying a land area of 174 square miles (450 square kilometers). Due to a large inflow of foreigners, Andorra's population grew twelvefold from 5,664 to 72,766 between 1954 and 1995. However, this population growth has moderated in the last decade because of a slow rate of natural growth. The leading ethnic groups in Andorra are Spanish (61 percent), Andorran (30 percent), and French (6 percent). Andorra has a vibrant economy with a relatively high standard of living. In 1996, Andorra's per capita gross domestic product was $16,200. Tourism and banking are the principality's leading economic sectors.

	1995	1980	1965
GEOGRAPHY			
AREA (square miles/kilometers)	174/450		
LAND AREA (square miles/kilometers)	174/450		
COASTLINE (miles/kilometers)	Landlocked		
CITIES			
CAPITAL	Andorra la Vella	n/a	16,151 (86)	n/a
POPULATION			
TOTAL	72,766	n/a	5,664 (54)
DENSITY (per square mile/kilometer)	389/150	199/77	62/24
ANNUAL GROWTH	3.0%	−0.30%	5.80%
AGE COHORTS			
0–14	16%	n/a	29% (66)
15–64	73%	n/a	61.9% (66)
65 AND OVER	11%	n/a	9.1% (66)[1]
NET MIGRATION RATE	22.3	n/a	n/a
IDENTITY			
ETHNICITY			
SPANISH	61%		
ANDORRAN	30%		
FRENCH	6%		

	1995	1980	1965
RELIGION			
ROMAN CATHOLIC	99%		

VITAL STATISTICS

	1995	1980	1965
BIRTHS			
BIRTH RATE	10.2	14.8	n/a
LIFE EXPECTANCY AT BIRTH	90.9	n/a	n/a
MARRIAGES			
MARRIAGE RATE	2	3.8	n/a
DEATHS			
DEATH RATE	2.9	4.1	n/a

ECONOMICS AND LABOR

	1995	1980	1965
GDP PER CAPITA US$	$16,200		

COMMUNICATIONS

	1995	1980	1965
RATE OF NEWSPAPERS	67	n/a	n/a
RATE OF RADIOS	206	194	n/a
RATE OF TELEVISIONS	367	118	90 (70)

FOOTNOTE
1. Age 60 and over.

Source: CIA, *The World Factbook, 1997*; ILO, *World Labour Report, 1997*; UN, *Demographic Yearbook, 1997*; UN, *Statistical Yearbook, 1996*; World Bank, *World Development Indicators, 1998*.

ANGOLA

Angola is located in southwestern Africa, bordering Zaire, Zambia, and Namibia. The 481,351-square-mile (1,246,700-square-kilometer) country lies on the coast of the South Atlantic Ocean. For much of the period since it received independence from Portugal in 1975, a civil war between the Angolan government and Union for the Total Independence of Angola (UNITA), an insurgent group, has destabilized the economy, wreaked havoc on the population, and obstructed national economic development. UNITA has continued to wage a guerrilla war against the national government, despite signing an agreement to end the conflict in 1994. Like many other African countries south of the Sahara, Angola has experienced rapid population growth in the last four decades of the twentieth century. Between 1960 and 1995, Angola's population increased from 4,840,719 to 10,342,899. National population growth increased from 1.7 percent in 1960 to 2.7 percent in 1995. In 1995, life expectancy at birth was only 46.8 years and the country had an infant mortality rate of 124.2 per 1,000 live births. The leading ethnic minorities are the Ovimbundu (37 percent), the Kimbundu (25 percent), and the Bakongo (13 percent).

Ethnic Groups, 1995

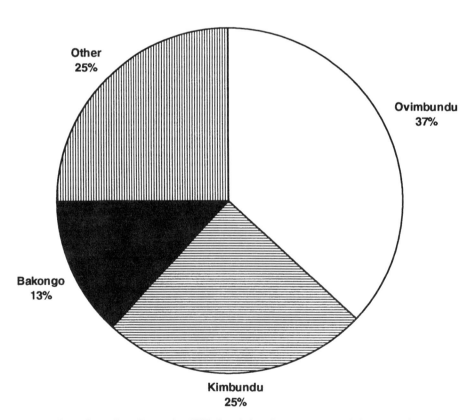

Since winning independence from Portugal in 1975, Angola has almost continuously been torn by civil war. While a host of factors have contributed to the fighting, the battlelines have often fallen along ethnic lines. Like many African countries, Angola is divided into several major ethnic groups.

Rate of Hospital Beds

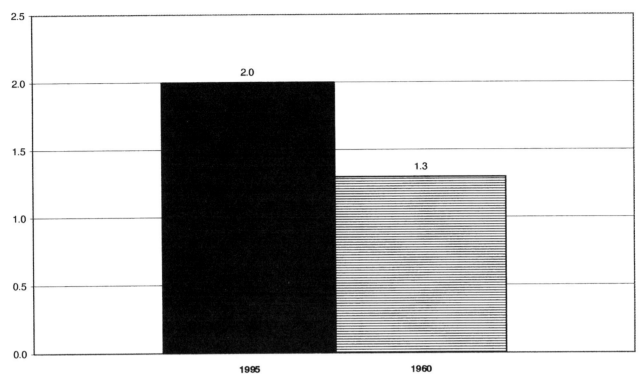

One of the goals of the rebel Union for the Total Liberation Movement of Angola (UNITA) has been the destruction of government-provided social services like health care, as reflected in the decline in hospital beds between 1965 and 1995.

CHRONOLOGY

1961	Uprising against Portuguese rule begins.
1974	Leftist coup ends pro-colonial dictatorship in Portugal.
1975	Angola wins independence from Portugal; war between liberation groups breaks out.
1979	Fighting between rightist rebel movement and leftist government is renewed.
1987–1988	South Africa invades; defeated by combined Cuban/Angolan forces.
1992	Government party defeats rightist rebel-led party in first national elections; rightist rebels return to fighting.
1994	Peace treaty signed, but fails to fully end fighting.

		1995	1980	1965
GEOGRAPHY				
AREA (square miles/kilometers)	481,351/1,246,700			
LAND AREA (square miles/kilometers)	481,351/1,246,700			
COASTLINE (miles/kilometers)	1,000/1,600			
CITIES				
CAPITAL	Luanda	n/a	n/a	475,328 (70)
POPULATION				
TOTAL		10,342,899	8,664,318	4,840,719 (60)
DENSITY (per square mile/kilometer)		23/9	18/7	10.0/4.0 (60)
ANNUAL GROWTH		2.7%	2.5%	1.7%
AGE COHORTS				
0–14		45%	n/a	33%
15–64		53%	n/a	64%
65 AND OVER		2%	n/a	3%
MALE		52%		
FEMALE		48%		
URBAN		32%		
RURAL		68%		
NET MIGRATION RATE		−0.1	n/a	0.2
IDENTITY				
ETHNICITY				
OVIMBUNDU		37%		
KIMBUNDU		25%		
BAKONGO		13%		
RELIGION				
ANIMIST		47%		
ROMAN CATHOLIC		38%		
PROTESTANT		15%		

	1995	1980	1965
VITAL STATISTICS			
BIRTHS			
BIRTH RATE	44.6	47.3	n/a
INFANT MORTALITY RATE	124.2	149	n/a
LIFE EXPECTANCY AT BIRTH	46.8	42	n/a
MARRIAGES			
MARRIAGE RATE	n/a	4.5	n/a
DEATHS			
DEATH RATE	17.7	22.2	n/a
ECONOMICS AND LABOR			
GDP PER CAPITA US$	$700		
LABOR FORCE M/F			
AGRICULTURE	65/86%		
INDUSTRY	14/2%		
SERVICES	21/13%		
TRANSPORT			
JOURNEYS (by transport mode)			
RAILROAD PASSENGER TRIPS			
(millions of miles/kilometers)	76/122 (93)		
AIR PASSENGER TRIPS (thousands)	519 (94)		
VEHICLES			
PRIVATE CARS	n/a	n/a	42,500
COMMERCIAL	n/a	n/a	17,500
HEALTH AND HEALTH CARE			
HEALTH CARE			
ACCESS TO SAFE WATER	32%		
ACCESS TO SANITATION	16%		

	1995	**1980**	**1965**
MEASLES IMMUNIZATION	32%		
RATE OF HOSPITAL BEDS	1.3	n/a	2 (60)
HEALTH INDICATORS			
PREGNANT WOMEN WITH ANEMIA	29%		
LOW-BIRTH-WEIGHT BABIES	19%		
CHILD MALNUTRITION	35%		
TUBERCULOSIS INCIDENCE RATE	2.25		
AIDS/HIV CASES	1,181	703 (93)	

EDUCATION

SCHOOL AGE IN SCHOOL			
PRIMARY	88%	174%	41%
SECONDARY	14%	21%	5%
HIGHER	1%	n/a	0.10%
FEMALES IN SCHOOL			
PRIMARY STUDENTS	n/a	47%	27%
SECONDARY STUDENTS	n/a	33%	4%
ADULT ILLITERACY	n/a	59% (85)	n/a

COMMUNICATIONS

RATE OF NEWSPAPERS	12	20	9
RATE OF RADIOS	29	21	16.5
RATE OF TELEVISIONS	7	4	0

Source: CIA, The World Factbook, 1997; ILO, World Labour Report, 1997; UN, Demographic Yearbook, 1997; UN, Statistical Yearbook, 1996; World Bank, World Development Indicators, 1998.

ANTIGUA AND BARBUDA

Antigua and Barbuda are in the Lesser Antilles, an archipelago bordered by the Atlantic Ocean to the east and the Caribbean Sea to the west. The country (including Antigua, Barbuda, and Redonda, a small island southeast of Antigua) covers a land area of 170 square miles (440 square kilometers). Since Antigua received independence from the United Kingdom in 1981, the country's economy has depended extensively on tourism from North America and Western Europe. Industrial development and new construction are tied heavily to the country's tourist sector. In 1995, per capita income was $6,600. Between 1960 and 1995, Antigua and Barbuda's population grew from 54,304 to 65,647, the vast majority of whom reside on the island of Antigua. Despite limited economic development, the country has a relatively healthy population. In 1995, life expectancy at birth was 73.6 years, comparable with developed industrialized countries.

	1995	1980	1965
GEOGRAPHY			
AREA (square miles/kilometers)	170/440		
LAND (square miles/kilometers)	170/440		
COASTLINE (miles/kilometers)	96/153		
CITIES			
CAPITAL	Saint John's	22,342 (91)	
POPULATION			
TOTAL	65,647	n/a	54,304 (60)
DENSITY (per square mile/kilometer)	386/149	n/a	352/136
ANNUAL GROWTH	0.8%	1.2%	1.6%
AGE COHORTS			
0–14	25%	n/a	43%
15–64	69%	n/a	53%
65 AND OVER	6%	n/a	4%
URBAN	36%		
RURAL	64%		
NET MIGRATION RATE	−0.1	n/a	2.4

	1995	1980	1965

IDENTITY

ETHNICITY
BLACK   n/a
BRITISH   n/a
PORTUGUESE   n/a

LANGUAGE
ENGLISH (official)   n/a

RELIGION
ANGLICAN   n/a
OTHER PROTESTANT   n/a
ROMAN CATHOLIC   n/a

VITAL STATISTICS

	1995	1980	1965
BIRTHS			
BIRTH RATE	16.8	15 (83)	30.4 (60)
INFANT MORTALITY RATE	24.4	7.7 (83)	45.4 (60)
LIFE EXPECTANCY AT BIRTH	73.6	70 (83)	62.5 (60)
MARRIAGES			
MARRIAGE RATE	5.4	2.4 (83)	3.7 (60)
DIVORCE RATE	0.7	0.4 (83)	0.4
DEATHS			
DEATH RATE	5.3	5.2 (83)	8.4

HOUSEHOLDS

	1995	1980	1965
NUMBER	19,501 (91)	n/a	10,579 (46)
AVERAGE SIZE	3.1 (91)	n/a	3.9

ECONOMICS AND LABOR

	1995
GDP PER CAPITA US$	$6,600
UNION DENSITY	53.80%

	1995	**1980**	**1965**

TRANSPORT

JOURNEYS (by transport mode)
AIR PASSENGER TRIPS (thousands)   1,000 (94)

VEHICLES
ALL TYPES   15,100

HEALTH AND HEALTH CARE

HEALTH CARE

	1995	1980	1965
RATE OF PHYSICIANS	n/a	n/a	0.3 (60)
RATE OF HOSPITAL BEDS	n/a	n/a	7.6 (60)

HEALTH INDICATORS

	1995	1980	1965
HIV INFECTION	45	34 (93)	

EDUCATION

SCHOOL AGE IN SCHOOL

	1995	1980	1965
PRIMARY	n/a	n/a	145% (63)
SECONDARY	n/a	n/a	96% (63)
HIGHER	n/a	n/a	0.80%

FEMALES IN SCHOOL

	1995	1980	1965
PRIMARY	n/a	n/a	160% (63)
SECONDARY	n/a	n/a	101% (63)

COMMUNICATIONS

	1995	1980	1965
RATE OF NEWSPAPERS	94 (90)	98	22
RATE OF RADIOS	425	279	70
RATE OF TELEVISIONS	369	262	28

Source: CIA, *The World Factbook, 1997*; ILO, *World Labour Report, 1997*; UN, *Demographic Yearbook, 1997*; UN, *Statistical Yearbook, 1996*; World Bank, *World Development Indicators, 1998*.

ARGENTINA

Argentina lies in southern South America, bordering the South Atlantic Ocean. Uruguay and Brazil are on the east, Bolivia and Paraguay are on the north, and Chile is on the west and south. The country covers a land area of 1,056,637 square miles (2,736,690 square kilometers). Along with Brazil and Mexico, Argentina has one of Latin America's most advanced economies, with a mature industrial sector. During the last decade of the twentieth century, the government of Carlos Saul Menem has introduced free market reforms and privatized state-run enterprises. Under President Menem's economic liberalization program, inflation declined from double-digit levels. However, unemployment increased significantly, and by the mid-1990s, Argentina's unemployment rate exceeded 10 percent. In 1995, Argentina's per capita income was $8,100. Between 1960 and 1995, the country's population increased from just over 20 million to 34.7 million; however, annual population growth rates have declined from 1.6 percent to 1.1 percent. In 1995, Argentina's average life expectancy was 71.7 years at birth. The country has an infant mortality rate of 20.3 per 1,000 live births.

Infant Mortality Rate

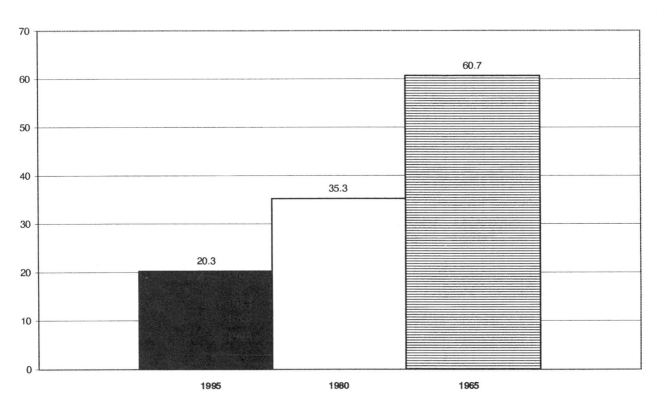

Falling rates of infant mortality reflect the growing health awareness of Argentinian mothers.

Life Expectancy at Birth

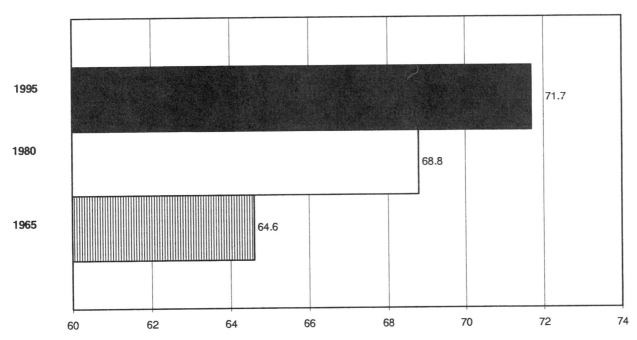

Gradually rising income and educational levels in Argentina over the past 30 years have translated into greater life expectancy.

CHRONOLOGY

1966   Military coup ends decades of civilian rule.
1974   Widow of Juan Peron takes power.
1976   Army ousts Peron widow after she fails to curb inflation.
1982   Argentina invades Falklands/Malvinas Islands; defeated by Great Britain
       in subsequent war.
1983   Military rule ends.
1989   Transfer of power from one civilian government to next.
1993   Major privatization campaign of state-owned companies accelerates.

	1995	1980	1965

GEOGRAPHY

AREA (square miles/kilometers)	1,068,397/2,766,890		
LAND AREA (square miles/kilometers)	1,056,637/2,736,690		
COASTLINE (miles/kilometers)	31,000/84,989		

CITIES

CAPITAL	Buenos Aires	2,690,976 (91)		
MAJOR CITIES	Córdoba	1,148,305		
	La Matanza	1,111,811		
	Rosario	894,645		
	Moron	641,541		

POPULATION

	1995	1980	1965
TOTAL	34,672,997	27,947,446	20,005,691 (60)
DENSITY (per square mile/kilometer)	31/12	28/11	21/8
ANNUAL GROWTH	1.1%	1.6%	1.6%

AGE COHORTS

	1995	1980	1965
0–14	28%	n/a	30%
15–64	63%	n/a	64%
65 AND OVER	9%	n/a	6%

	1995	1980	1965
MALE	49%		
FEMALE	51%		

	1995	1980	1965
URBAN	88%	83%	n/a
RURAL	12%	17%	n/a

	1995	1980	1965
NET MIGRATION RATE	0.2	n/a	3.6

IDENTITY

ETHNICITY

EUROPEAN	85%
MESTIZO/INDIAN	15%

LANGUAGE

SPANISH (official)	n/a
ENGLISH	n/a
GERMAN	n/a

	1995	**1980**	**1965**
RELIGION			
ROMAN CATHOLIC	90%		
PROTESTANT	2%		
JEWISH	2%		

VITAL STATISTICS

	1995	**1980**	**1965**
BIRTHS			
BIRTH RATE	9.4	23.7	23
INFANT MORTALITY RATE	20.3	35.3	60.7
LIFE EXPECTANCY AT BIRTH	71.7	68.8	64.6
MARRIAGES			
MARRIAGE RATE	4.6	6	6.6
AVERAGE AGE OF MARRIAGE M/F	225.8/23.3 (19)		
DEATHS			
DEATH RATE	8.6	8.4	9

HOUSEHOLDS

	1995	**1980**	**1965**
NUMBER	8,927,289 (91)	n/a	5,232,222 (60)
AVERAGE SIZE	3.7	n/a	3.7
FEMALE HEADED	22.3%		

ECONOMICS AND LABOR

	1995	**1980**	**1965**
GDP PER CAPITA US$	$8,100		
LABOR FORCE M/F			
AGRICULTURE	16/3%		
INDUSTRY	39/17%		
SERVICES	46/80%		
UNEMPLOYMENT (official)	10.1% (93)		
UNION DENSITY	25.4		

TRANSPORT

	1995	**1980**	**1965**
JOURNEYS (by transport mode)			
RAILROAD PASSENGER TRIPS			
(millions of miles/kilometers)	3,908/6,253		
AIR PASSENGER TRIPS (thousands)	6,460.00		

	1995	1980	1965
VEHICLES			
PRIVATE CARS	n/a	3,024,000	927,500
COMMERCIAL	n/a	1,334,00	625,800

HEALTH AND HEALTH CARE

	1995	1980	1965
HEALTH CARE			
ACCESS TO SAFE WATER	64%		
ACCESS TO SANITATION	89%		
MEASLES IMMUNIZATION	76%		
RATE OF PHYSICIANS	2.7	n/a	1.3 (60)
RATE OF HOSPITAL BEDS	4.6	n/a	6.3(60)
HEALTH INDICATORS			
PREGNANT WOMEN WITH ANEMIA	26%		
LOW-BIRTH-WEIGHT BABIES	7%		
CHILD MALNUTRITION	2%		
SMOKING PREVALENCE M/F	40/23%		
TUBERCULOSIS INCIDENCE RATE	0.5		
AIDS/HIV CASES	7,966	4,313 (93)	

EDUCATION

	1995	1980	1965
SCHOOL AGE IN SCHOOL			
PRIMARY	108%	106%	100%
SECONDARY	72%	56%	38%
HIGHER	38%	22%	10.9%
FEMALES IN SCHOOL			
PRIMARY	n/a	49%	101%
SECONDARY	n/a	64%	40%
ADULT ILLITERACY M/F	4/4%	5.7/6.4%	n/a

COMMUNICATIONS

	1995	1980	1965
RATE OF NEWSPAPERS	143	142	148
RATE OF RADIOS	672	427	310
RATE OF TELEVISIONS	220	183	80

Source: CIA, The World Factbook, 1997; ILO, World Labour Report, 1997; UN, Demographic Yearbook, 1997; UN, Statistical Yearbook, 1996; World Bank, World Development Indicators, 1998.

ARMENIA

Armenia is located in Southwestern Asia, bordering Azerbaijan, Georgia, Iran, and Turkey. It covers an area of 11,506 square miles (29,800 square kilometers). The country, which first received independence in 1918 from the Ottoman Empire, was subsumed as a socialist republic under the Soviet Union following World War II. In 1991, after the breakup of the Soviet Union, Armenia regained full autonomy. Armenia's economy fell into a recession after independence was achieved, due to the decline of state support for the industrial sector. Armenia also fell into a dispute with Azerbaijan over the future of Nagorno Karabakh, an Armenian enclave in Azerbaijan. The ethnic dispute with Azerbaijan has led to a chronic energy shortage and intensified the decline of Armenia's economy. The country has a life expectancy of 69.1 years and an infant mortality rate of 15.1 infant deaths per 1,000 live births.

1995[1]

GEOGRAPHY

AREA (square miles/kilometers)	11,506/29,800	
LAND AREA (square miles/kilometers)	10,96/528,400	
COASTLINE (miles/kilometers)	Landlocked	
CITIES		
CAPITAL	Yerevan	1,254,400 (90)
MAJOR CITIES	Leninakan	206,600
	Kirovakan	170,200

POPULATION

TOTAL	3,463,574
DENSITY (per square mile/kilometer)	326/126
ANNUAL GROWTH	0.02%
AGE COHORTS	
0–14	28%
15–64	64%
65 AND OVER	8%
MALE	49%
FEMALE	51%
URBAN	68.5% (92)
RURAL	31.5 (92)
NET MIGRATION RATE	−8.3

1995

IDENTITY

ETHNICITY
ARMENIAN	93%
AZERI	3%
RUSSIAN	2%

LANGUAGE
ARMENIAN	96%
RUSSIAN	2%

RELIGION
ARMENIAN ORTHODOX	94%
MUSLIM	3%
RUSSIAN ORTHODOX	2%

VITAL STATISTICS

BIRTHS
BIRTH RATE	16.3
URBAN BIRTH RATE	17.4 (92)
RURAL BIRTH RATE	22.9 (92)
INFANT MORTALITY RATE	15.1
ABORTION RATE	358.4
LIFE EXPECTANCY AT BIRTH	69.1

MARRIAGES
MARRIAGE RATE	4.6
DIVORCE RATE	0.9

DEATHS
DEATH RATE	7.7

TRANSPORT

JOURNEYS (by transport mode)
AIR PASSENGER TRIPS (thousands)	435

HEALTH AND HEALTH CARE

HEALTH CARE
MEASLES IMMUNIZATION	95%

	1995
RATE OF PHYSICIANS	3.1
RATE OF HOSPITAL BEDS	7.8

HEALTH INDICATORS
| TUBERCULOSIS INCIDENCE RATE | 0.4 |
| TOTAL DEATHS | 24,648 (94) |

EDUCATION

SCHOOL AGE IN SCHOOL
PRIMARY	82%
SECONDARY	79%
HIGHER	49%

FEMALES IN SCHOOL
| OF PRIMARY STUDENTS | 50% |

COMMUNICATIONS

RATE OF NEWSPAPERS   24

FOOTNOTE
1. Part of the Soviet Union in 1965 and 1980.

Source: CIA, *The World Factbook, 1997;* ILO, *World Labour Report, 1997;* UN, *Demographic Yearbook, 1997;* UN, *Statistical Yearbook, 1996;* World Bank, *World Development Indicators, 1998.*

AUSTRALIA

The Commonwealth of Australia occupies the entire continent of Australia, in Oceania, between the Indian and the South Pacific oceans. The country has an area of 2,967,896 square miles (7,686,850 square kilometers). It has a low density of 6 persons per square mile (2 persons per square kilometer). Most of the country's population is concentrated in five major metropolitan areas. While about 95 percent of Australia's population is of European descent, the growth in Asian migration is diversifying the nation's ethnic composition. Between 1965 and 1995, Australia's migration rate increased from 2.2 to 2.7 per 1,000 residents. The Australian economy is highly dependent on the export of raw materials and primary products, chiefly fossil fuels, minerals, and agricultural products. The country has strong social service and health care sectors relative to the region, contributing to a fairly high life expectancy at birth of 79.4 years.

Ethnic Groups, 1995

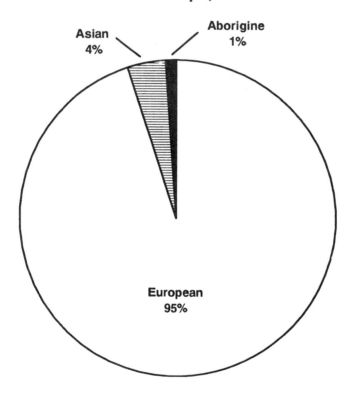

Always a haven for immigrants, Australia has lately seen the source of that immigration change. Whereas most immigrants came from Europe through the 1960s, a rapidly growing number have come from East and South Asia in recent decades, reflecting the country's shift from a European outpost to a Pacific-centered nation.

Net Migration

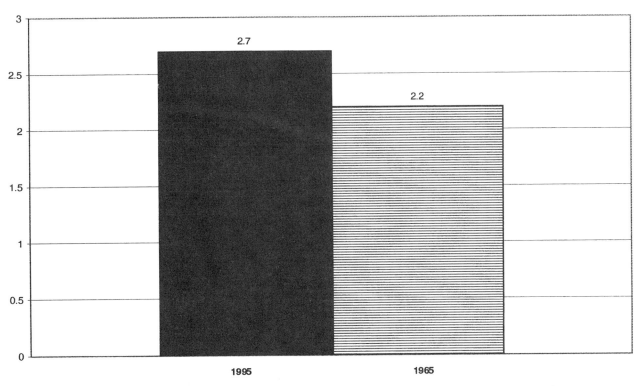

With just 6 persons per square mile, Australia remains one of the most underpopulated nations on the planet, though much of the country's territory is desert. This has led to consistently high rates of in-migration.

CHRONOLOGY

1965   Australia begins sending troops to Southeast Asia to help the United States and South Vietnam.

1972   Labour Party takes power.

1975   Liberal-Country coalition takes power.

1983   Radical Labour Prime Minister Bob Hawke wins national elections.

1988   Native aborigines protest Australian bicentennial.

1991   High inflation leads to ouster of Hawke government.

1998   Right-wing, anti-Asian immigration party wins seats in parliament.

	1995	**1980**	**1965**

GEOGRAPHY

AREA (square miles/kilometers)	2,967,896/7,686,850			
LAND AREA (square miles/kilometers)	2,941,286/7,617,930			
COASTLINE (miles/kilometers)	16,100/25,760			

CITIES				
CAPITAL	Canberra	298,200 (93)		
MAJOR CITIES	Sydney	3,713,500		
	Melbourne	3,189,200		
	Brisbane	1,421,600		
	Perth	1,221,200		

POPULATION

	1995	**1980**	**1965**
TOTAL	18,260,863	14,576,330 (81)	11,540,764 (66)
DENSITY (per square mile/kilometer)	6.0/2.0	5.0/2.0	5.0/2.0
ANNUAL GROWTH	1.00%	1.40%	2%

AGE COHORTS			
0–14	21%	n/a	30%
15–64	66%	n/a	62%
65 AND OVER	13%	n/a	8%

MALE	50%		
FEMALE	50%		

URBAN	85%	85.7	n/a
RURAL	15%	14.30%	n/a

NET MIGRATION RATE	2.7	n/a	2.2

IDENTITY

ETHNICITY	
EUROPEAN	95%
ASIAN	4%
ABORIGINE	1%

LANGUAGE	
ENGLISH	99%

	1995	**1980**	**1965**
RELIGION			
ANGLICAN	26%		
ROMAN CATHOLIC	26%		
OTHER PROTESTANT	24%		

VITAL STATISTICS

BIRTHS			
BIRTH RATE	14	15 (84)	19.3
INFANT MORTALITY RATE	5.9 (94)	9.2 (84)	18.2
LIFE EXPECTANCY AT BIRTH	79.4	75.9 (84)	70.9

MARRIAGES			
MARRIAGE RATE	6.8	7 (84)	8.3
AVERAGE AGE OF MARRIAGE M/F	29.2/27 (94)		
DIVORCE RATE	2.7	2.8 (84)	0.7

DEATHS			
DEATH RATE	6.9	7.1 (84)	9

HOUSEHOLDS

NUMBER	n/a	n/a	2,781,945 (61)
AVERAGE SIZE	n/a	n/a	3.7 (61)

ECONOMICS AND LABOR

GDP PER CAPITA US$	$22,100

LABOR FORCE M/F (thousands)	4,545.4/3,375.2 (94)
AGRICULTURE	281.0/122.6
MINING	76.6/9.7
MANUFACTURING	811.5/294.5
UTILITIES	73.3/13.0
CONSTRUCTION	490.0/79.6
TRADE/FOOD/TOURISM	1,066.1/948.5
TRANSPORT/COMMUNICATIONS	384.2/126.5
FINANCE/INSURANCE/REAL ESTATE	537.5/488.7
SOCIAL AND PERSONAL SERVICES	800.1/1,278.1

UNEMPLOYMENT (official)	9.8 (94)
UNION DENSITY	28.60%

	1995	1980	1965

TRANSPORT

JOURNEYS (by transport mode)

	1995	1980	1965
AIR PASSENGER TRIPS (thousands)	26,816.0 (94)		
VEHICLES (thousands)			
PRIVATE CARS	8,209	5,800.60	2,894.2
COMMERCIAL	2,151	1,425.10	872.4

HEALTH AND HEALTH CARE

HEALTH CARE

	1995	1980	1965
RATE OF PHYSICIANS	2.2	1.8	1.4
RATE OF HOSPITAL BEDS	8.9	n/a	11.9
ACCESS TO SAFE WATER	95%		
ACCESS TO SANITATION	90%		
MEASLES IMMUNIZATION	n/a	68%	n/a
HEALTH INDICATORS			
SMOKING PREVALENCE M/F	29/21%		
TUBERCULOSIS INCIDENCE RATE	0.06		
AIDS/HIV CASES	6,442	5,006 (93)	
TOTAL DEATHS	126,692 (94)		

EDUCATION

SCHOOL AGE IN SCHOOL

	1995	1980	1965
PRIMARY	108%	112%	106%
SECONDARY	72%	56%	72%
HIGHER	n/a	25%	11.6%
FEMALES IN SCHOOL			
OF PRIMARY STUDENTS	49%	49%	50%
OF SECONDARY STUDENTS	49%	49%	49%

COMMUNICATIONS

	1995	1980	1965
RATE OF NEWSPAPERS	265	323	373
RATE OF RADIOS	1,290	1,098	219
RATE OF TELEVISIONS	489	384	169

Source: CIA, *The World Factbook, 1997;* ILO, *World Labour Report, 1997;* UN, *Demographic Yearbook, 1997;* UN, *Statistical Yearbook, 1996;* World Bank, *World Development Indicators, 1998.*

AUSTRIA

Austria is located in central Europe, bordering Italy, Switzerland, Germany, the Czech Republic, Hungary, and Slovenia. The country has an area of 32,375 square miles (83,850 square kilometers). Persons of German and Austrian descent compose the vast majority (99 percent) of the nation's residents. In recent decades, the national birth rate has declined significantly, leading to a slow rate of growth. Migration accounts for a large share of the nation's population growth. In 1995, the country had a net migration rate of 3.3 per 1,000 residents. Austria is one of Europe's wealth-iest nations, with a high standard of living. In 1995, the country had a per capita gross domestic product of $19,000. The country has one of the most comprehensive systems of social protection in the world. A large share of the national economy is under the control of the state, and the national government provides one of the strongest social safety nets in the world. Like its counterparts in Western Europe, the Austrian government has come under pressure to cut budget deficits by reducing social benefits.

	1995	1980	1965
GEOGRAPHY			
AREA (square miles/kilometers)	32,375/83,850		
LAND AREA (square miles/kilometers)	31,942/82,730		
COASTLINE (miles/kilometers)	Landlocked		
CITIES			
CAPITAL	Vienna	1,750,000	
MAJOR CITIES	Graz	237,810	
	Linz	203,044	
	Salzburg	143,973	
	Innsbruck	118,112	
POPULATION			
TOTAL	8,023,244	7,555,338 (81)	7,073,807 (61)
DENSITY (per square mile/kilometer)	249/96	233/90	225/87
ANNUAL GROWTH	0.4 %	0 %	0.5 %
AGE COHORTS			
0–14	18 %	n/a	23 %
15–64	67 %	n/a	64%
65 AND OVER	15 %	n/a	13 %
MALE	48%		
FEMALE	52%		

	1995	1980	1965
URBAN	56%	55.10%	n/a
RURAL	44%	44.90%	n/a
NET MIGRATION	3.3	n/a	−0.2

IDENTITY

ETHNICITY
GERMAN-AUSTRIAN	99%		
CROATIAN AND SLOVENE	1%		

LANGUAGE
GERMAN	n/a		

RELIGION
ROMAN CATHOLIC	85%		
PROTESTANT	6%		

VITAL STATISTICS

BIRTHS
BIRTH RATE	11.2	11.5 (85)	17.6
INFANT MORTALITY RATE	5.5	11 (85)	28.1
LIFE EXPECTANCY AT BIRTH	76.5	73.7 (85)	69.3

MARRIAGES
MARRIAGE RATE	5.4	5.9 (85)	7.6
AVERAGE AGE OF MARRIAGE M/F	28.9/26.1		
DIVORCE RATE	2	2 (85)	1.2

DEATHS
DEATH RATE	10.4	11.8 (85)	12.5

HOUSEHOLDS

NUMBER	n/a	n/a	2,306,000 (61)
AVERAGE SIZE	n/a	n/a	3 (61)

ECONOMICS AND LABOR

GDP PER CAPITA US$	$19,000

	1995	**1980**	**1965**
LABOR FORCE M/F (thousands)	2,078.8/1496.6 (93)		
AGRICULTURE	129.3/117.2		
MINING	9.3/0.9		
MANUFACTURING	658.0/244.8		
UTILITIES	31.8/4.1		
CONSTRUCTION	280.7/25.1		
TRADE/FOOD/TOURISM	273.2/401.1		
TRANSPORT/COMMUNICATIONS	188.1/44.4		
FINANCE/INSURANCE/REAL ESTATE	133.7/131.6		
SOCIAL AND PERSONAL SERVICES	366.4/516.0		
UNEMPLOYMENT (official)	6.5 % (94)		
UNION DENSITY	36.60 %		

TRANSPORT

JOURNEYS (by transport mode)			
RAILROAD PASSENGER TRIPS			
(millions of miles/kilometers)	2,343/3,748.0 (94)		
AIR PASSENGER TRIPS (thousands)	9,384.0 (94)		
VEHICLES (thousands)			
PRIVATE CARS	3,479.60	2,247.00	789.7
COMMERCIAL	698.2	526.1	297.3

HEALTH AND HEALTH CARE

HEALTH CARE			
RATE OF PHYSICIANS	2.6	2.3	1.8 (60)
RATE OF HOSPITAL BEDS	9.4	11.2	10.8 (60)
ACCESS TO SAFEWATER	n/a	100	n/a
ACCESS TO SANITATION	100		
MEASLES IMMUNIZATION	60		
HEALTH INDICATORS			
LOW-BIRTH-WEIGHT BABIES	6%		
SMOKING PREVALENCE M/F	42/27%		
TUBERCULOSIS INCIDENCE RATE	0.2		
AIDS/HIV CASES	1,515	1,176 (93)	
TOTAL DEATHS	80,368		

	1995	1980	1965
EDUCATION			
SCHOOL AGE IN SCHOOL			
PRIMARY	101%	99%	105%
SECONDARY	104%	99%	69%
HIGHER	4.5%	26%	6.8%
FEMALES IN SCHOOL			
OF PRIMARY STUDENTS	49%	49%	49%
OF SECONDARY STUDENTS	49%	49%	48%
COMMUNICATIONS			
RATE OF NEWSPAPERS	398	351	249
RATE OF RADIOS	618	507	305
RATE OF TELEVISIONS	479	391	101

Source: CIA, The World Factbook, 1997; ILO, World Labour Report, 1997; UN, Demographic Yearbook, 1997; UN, Statistical Yearbook, 1996; World Bank, World Development Indicators, 1998.

AZERBAIJAN

Azerbaijan is located in the Transcaucasus of Southwestern Asia, bordered by the Caspian Sea on the east, Russia and Georgia on the North, Armenia on the west, and Iran on the south. The country occupies an area of 33,436 square miles (86,600 square kilometers). In 1995, it had a population of 7.6 million and a growth rate of 0.8 percent. Azerbaijan was a soviet socialist republic of the Soviet Union until 1991, when the Soviet Union collapsed and the country gained independence. People of Azeri descent compose the vast majority of the nation's residents (90 percent). Da-

gestanis (3 percent), Russians (3 percent), and Armenians (2.3 percent) are Azerbaijan's three leading minorities. In 1995, the country had an out-migration rate of 5.8 persons per 1,000 residents. The country has a birth rate of 22.3 and a death rate of 8.7 persons per 1,000 residents. Life expectancy at birth is 64.8 years. Although Azerbaijan is less economically developed than bordering states in the region, the country has extensive petroleum and natural gas reserves now under development and expansion.

1995[1]

GEOGRAPHY

AREA (square miles/kilometers)	33,436/86,600	
LAND AREA (square miles/kilometers)	33,243/86,100	
COASTLINE (miles/kilometers)	500/800	

CITIES
CAPITAL	Baku	1,149,000 (90)
MAJOR CITIES	Giyandja	281,000
	Sumgait	235,000

POPULATION

TOTAL	7,676,953
DENSITY (per square mile/kilometer)	225/87
ANNUAL GROWTH	0.8%

AGE COHORTS
0–14	32%
15–64	61%
65 AND OVER	7%

MALE	49%
FEMALE	51%

URBAN	56%
RURAL	44%

	1995
NET MIGRATION RATE	−5.8%

IDENTITY

ETHNICITY

AZERI	90%
DAGESTANI	3%
RUSSIAN	3%
ARMENIAN	2.3%

LANGUAGE

AZERI	89%
RUSSIAN	3%
ARMENIAN	2%

RELIGION

SUNNI MUSLIM	93%
RUSSIAN ORTHODOX	3%
ARMENIAN ORTHODOX	2%

VITAL STATISTICS

BIRTHS

BIRTH RATE	22.3
INFANT MORTALITY RATE	26.1
LIFE EXPECTANCY AT BIRTH	64.8

MARRIAGES

MARRIAGE RATE	6.4
DIVORCE RATE	1.6

DEATHS

DEATH RATE	8.7

ECONOMICS AND LABOR

GDP PER CAPITA US$	$1,480

LABOR FORCE M/F

AGRICULTURE	27/36%
INDUSTRY	35/21%
SERVICES	38/43%

UNEMPLOYMENT (official)	13.6 (94)
UNION DENSITY	75.40%

1995

TRANSPORT

JOURNEYS (by transport mode)
RAILROAD PASSENGER TRIPS
   (millions of miles/kilometers)   863/1,380 (94)

HEALTH AND HEALTH CARE

HEALTH CARE
MEASLES IMMUNIZATION   91
RATE OF PHYSICIANS   3.8
RATE OF HOSPITAL BEDS   10

HEALTH INDICATORS
CHILD MALNUTRITION   10%
TUBERCULOSIS INCIDENCE RATE   0.47
AIDS/HIV CASES   2
TOTAL DEATHS   54,921 (94)

EDUCATION

SCHOOL AGE IN SCHOOL
PRIMARY   104%
SECONDARY   74%
HIGHER   20%

FEMALES IN SCHOOL
OF PRIMARY STUDENTS   47%
OF SECONDARY STUDENTS   48%

COMMUNICATIONS

RATE OF NEWSPAPERS   59

FOOTNOTE
1. Part of the Soviet Union in 1965 and 1980.

Source: CIA, *The World Factbook, 1997;* ILO, *World Labour Report, 1997;* UN, *Demographic Yearbook, 1997;* UN, *Statistical Yearbook, 1996;* World Bank, *World Development Indicators, 1998.*

THE BAHAMAS

The Bahamas is an island archipelago located in the Caribbean, southeast of Florida and north of Cuba. The country occupies a total area of 5,382 square miles (13,940 square kilometers) in the Atlantic Ocean. The country's population increased from 136,368 in 1965 to 259,367 in 1995. Blacks compose a majority (85 percent) of the national population. In 1995, the country had a relatively high life expectancy of 72.5 years. The Bahamian economy is dependent on tourism from North America and Western Europe, which accounts for about 50 percent of the nation's gross domestic product. Compared to other regional states, the Bahamas had a high gross domestic product of $18,700 in 1995. Only 13 percent of the population resides in rural areas.

	1995	1980	1965
GEOGRAPHY			
AREA (square miles/kilometers)	5,382/13,940		
LAND AREA (square miles/kilometers)	3,888/10,070		
COASTLINE (miles/kilometers)	2,214/3,542		
CITIES			
CAPITAL	New Providence	n/a	
MAJOR CITIES	Nassau	172,196 (90)	
POPULATION			
TOTAL	259,367	223,455	136,368 (63)
DENSITY (per square mile/kilometer)	52/20	44/17	31/12
ANNUAL GROWTH	1.1%	1.90%	4%
AGE COHORTS			
0–14	28%	n/a	44%
15–64	67%	n/a	52%
65 AND OVER	5%	n/a	4%
MALE	49%		
FEMALE	51%		
URBAN	87%	75.3%	n/a
RURAL	13%	24.7%	n/a
NET MIGRATION RATE	−2.5	n/a	35.7

	1995	**1980**	**1965**

IDENTITY

ETHNICITY
BLACK	85%		
WHITE	15%		

LANGUAGE
ENGLISH	n/a		
CREOLE	n/a		

RELIGION
BAPTIST	32%		
ANGLICAN	20%		
ROMAN CATHOLIC	19%		

VITAL STATISTICS

BIRTHS
BIRTH RATE	18.7	22.2 (84)	32.6 (66)
INFANT MORTALITY RATE	27.3	22.9 (84)	36.5 (66)
LIFE EXPECTANCY AT BIRTH	72.5	66.6 (84)	n/a

MARRIAGES
MARRIAGE RATE	9.1	7.4 (84)	7.5 (66)
AVERAGE AGE OF MARRIAGE M/F	29.1/27.2		
DIVORCE RATE	1.2	0.8 (84)	0.1 (66)

DEATHS
DEATH RATE	5.7	5 (84)	7.1 (66)

HOUSEHOLDS

NUMBER	61,910 (90)	n/a	32,035 (63)
AVERAGE SIZE	4.1 (90)	n/a	4.1 (63)

TYPE OF HOUSEHOLD
SINGLE	25%		
MARRIED	43%		
WIDOWED	9%		
DIVORCED/SEPARATED	13%		

FEMALE HEADED	36%		

	1995	1980	1965

ECONOMICS AND LABOR

GDP PER CAPITA US$	$18,700		
UNEMPLOYMENT (official)	13.3% (94)		

TRANSPORT

JOURNEYS (by transport mode)			
AIR PASSENGER TRIPS (thousands)	862 (94)		
VEHICLES			
PRIVATE CARS	46,100	47,100	19,800
COMMERCIAL	11,900	8,000	3,500

HEALTH AND HEALTH CARE

HEALTH CARE			
RATE OF PHYSICIANS	n/a	n/a	0.5 (60)
RATE OF HOSPITAL BEDS	n/a	n/a	5.5 (60)
HEALTH INDICATORS			
AIDS/HIV CASES	2,101	1,389 (93)	
TOTAL DEATHS	1,538 (94)		

EDUCATION

SCHOOL AGE IN SCHOOL			
PRIMARY	n/a	n/a	106%
SECONDARY	n/a	n/a	42%
HIGHER	n/a	n/a	0.20%
FEMALES IN SCHOOL			
PRIMARY	n/a	n/a	105%
SECONDARY	n/a	n/a	46%

	1995	**1980**	**1965**
COMMUNICATIONS			
RATE OF NEWSPAPERS	133	157	113
RATE OF RADIOS	545	486	220
RATE OF TELEVISIONS	226	148	23

Source: CIA, *The World Factbook, 1997;* ILO, *World Labour Report, 1997;* UN, *Demographic Yearbook, 1997;* UN, *Statistical Yearbook, 1996;* World Bank, *World Development Indicators, 1998.*

BAHRAIN

Bahrain is an archipelago located in the Persian Gulf, east of Saudi Arabia and north of Qatar. The country covers an area of 293 square miles (620 square kilometers). Much of the country's terrain is desert. In the three decades between 1965 and 1995, the national population increased from 182,203 to 590,042. Ninety percent of the population resides in urban areas. Manama, located on Bahrain's north shore, is the country's capital and the largest population center. From 1980 to 1995, Bahrain's annual population growth declined from 3.8 percent to 2.3 percent. Bahrain's national economy is dominated by petroleum production and processing for export. The oil economy contributes to Bahrain's high per capita gross domestic product of $12,000. However, the country is dependent on stable oil prices. Frequent shifts in world oil prices in the last two decades of the twentieth century have subjected the economy to frequent and unpredictable changes. In 1995, the country had a net migration rate of 2.4 per 1,000 residents. Males compose a significant 58 percent majority of the country's population. Islam is the major religion. About 75 percent of Bahrain's population is Shi'a Muslim and 25 percent is Sunni Muslim.

	1995	1980	1965
GEOGRAPHY			
AREA (square miles/kilomters)	293/620		
LAND AREA (square miles/kilometers)	293/620		
COASTLINE (miles/kilometers)	100/161		
CITIES			
CAPITAL	Manamah 140,402 (92)		
POPULATION			
TOTAL	590,042	350,798 (81)	182,203
DENSITY (per square mile/kilometer)	2,186/844	1,738/671	837/323
ANNUAL GROWTH	2.3%	3.8%	1.4%
AGE COHORTS			
0–14	31%		
15–64	67%		
65 AND OVER	2%		
MALE	58%		
FEMALE	42%		
URBAN	90%	80.7%	n/a
RURAL	10%	19.3%	n/a

	1995	**1980**	**1965**
NET MIGRATION RATE	2.4	n/a	0.2

IDENTITY

ETHNICITY

BAHRAINI	63%		
ASIAN	13%		
OTHER ARAB	10%		

LANGUAGE

ARABIC	n/a		
ENGLISH	n/a		
FARSI	n/a		

RELIGION

SHI'A MUSLIM	75%		
SUNNI MUSLIM	25%		

VITAL STATISTICS

BIRTHS

BIRTH RATE	23.6	32.2	n/a
INFANT MORTALITY RATE	18	32	
LIFE EXPECTANCY AT BIRTH	74.3	67.4	n/a

MARRIAGES

MARRIAGE RATE	5.9		
AVERAGE AGE AT MARRIAGE M/F	28.4/25.6		
DIVORCE RATE	1.1		

DEATHS

DEATH RATE	3.3	4.5	n/a

HOUSEHOLDS

NUMBER	78,776 (91)	
AVERAGE SIZE	5.6 (91)	

ECONOMICS AND LABOR

GDP PER CAPITA US$	$12,000	

	1995	1980	1965
LABOR FORCE M/F (thousands)	104.0/11.8 (94)		
AGRICULTURE	0.9/0.3		
MINING	0.5/0.0		
MANUFACTURING	22.4/3.7		
UTILITIES	3.3/0.7		
CONSTRUCTION	33.0/0.3		
TRADE/FOOD/TOURISM	19.3/1.6		
TRANSPORT/COMMUNICATIONS	8.3/2.3		
FINANCE/INSURANCE/REAL ESTATE	5.0/1.6		
SOCIAL AND PERSONAL SERVICES	10.0/2.1		

TRANSPORT

	1995	1980	1965
JOURNEYS (by transport mode)			
AIR PASSENGER TRIPS (thousands)	1,151 (94)		
VEHICLES			
PRIVATE CARS	125,500 (94)	47,000	n/a
COMMERCIAL	29,400	18,400	n/a

HEALTH AND HEALTH CARE

	1995	1980	1965
HEALTH CARE			
RATE OF PHYSICIANS	n/a	n/a	0.5 (60)
RATE OF HOSPITAL BEDS	n/a	n/a	4.7 (60)
HEALTH INDICATORS			
AIDS/HIV CASES	28	15 (93)	
TOTAL DEATHS	1,695 (94)		

EDUCATION

	1995	1980	1965
SCHOOL AGE IN SCHOOL			
PRIMARY	n/a	104%	103%
SECONDARY	n/a	64%	33%
HIGHER	n/a	4.7%	1.7 (70)
FEMALES IN SCHOOL			
PRIMARY	n/a	97%	82%
SECONDARY	n/a	58%	21%
HIGHER	n/a	4.9%	2.2% (70)
ADULT ILLITERACY M/F	n/a	23.5/41.4% (81)	63.9/81.8%

	1995	**1980**	**1965**
COMMUNICATIONS			
RATE OF NEWSPAPERS	83	40	n/a
RATE OF RADIOS	553	360	494
RATE OF TELEVISIONS	430	259	71

Source: CIA, *The World Factbook, 1997;* ILO, *World Labour Report, 1997;* UN, *Demographic Yearbook, 1997;* UN, *Statistical Yearbook, 1996;* World Bank, *World Development Indicators, 1998.*

BANGLADESH

Bangladesh is located in southern Asia on the Bay of Bengal. The 55,598-square-mile (144,000-square-kilometer) country is bordered by India on the east, west, and north, and by Myanmar on the southeast. Bangladesh is one of the most densely populated countries in the world, with a rate of 2,165 persons per square mile (836 per square kilometer). The country received independence in 1971 following a civil war with Pakistan. However, the Bangladeshi government has experienced frequent internal political unrest and domestic turmoil for much of the period since independence. The high density often forces Bangladeshis to reside in regions susceptible to regular seasonal flooding. Frequently, water is polluted, intensifying sanitation problems and promoting communicable diseases. Residents who live near the Bay of Bengal suffer from cyclones and flooding during the summer monsoon season. Although Bangladesh's economic growth rate dropped from 2.2 percent in 1981 to 1.9 percent in 1995, the population increased from 87,119,965 to 123,062,800 over the same period. Nearly all the country's residents are of Bengali origin; however, 83 percent of the population is Sunni Muslim and 16 percent is Hindu. Due to the lack of economic development, the country's population is mired in a state of poverty. Most of the country's population is made up of agricultural workers who produce mainly rice and other grain products for personal use. In 1995, per capita gross domestic product was only $1,130.

Density

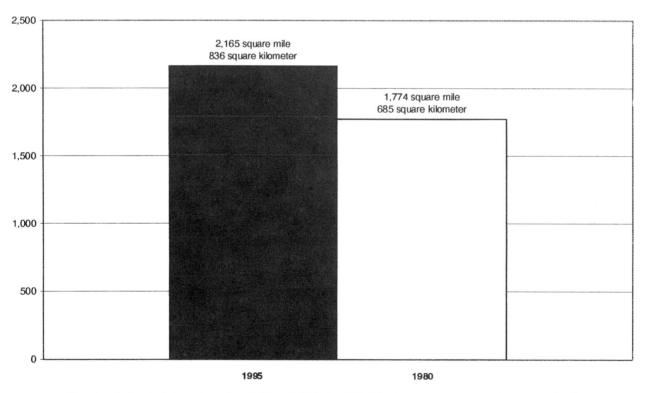

Since long before its independence from Pakistan in 1971, Bangladesh has been among the most densely populated countries on the planet.

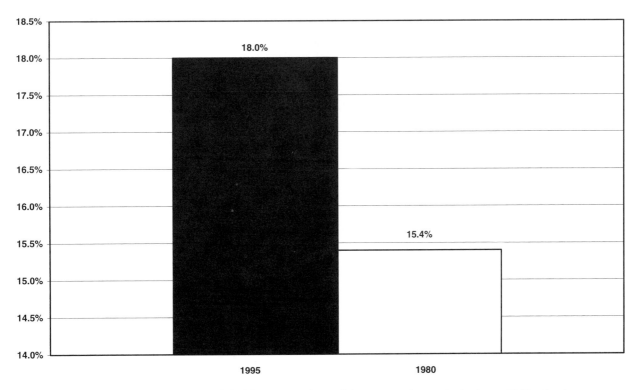

Percent Urban

Like its giant neighbor India, Bangladesh has remained one of the most rural countries in the world. Despite the fertile delta land on which it lives, Bangladesh's rising population is causing reduced average farm size and setting off the beginnings of urban migration.

CHRONOLOGY

1971   With help from India, Bangladesh fights war with and wins independence from Pakistan.
1975   Military coup ends in assassination of country's first prime minister.
1979   Martial law lifted and democratic government reinstated.
1981   Prime Minister Ziaur Rahman assassinated.
1982   Military coup leads to renewed martial law.
1987   State of Emergency declared after antigovernment protests break out around country.
1991   Rahman's widow elected prime minister.

	1995	1980[1]

GEOGRAPHY

AREA (square miles/kilometers)   55,598/144,000
LAND AREA (square miles/kilometers)   51,703/133,910
COASTLINE (miles/kilometers)   363/580

CITIES
CAPITAL   Dhaka   3,397,187 (91)
MAJOR CITIES   Chittagong   1,363,998
                         Khulna   545,849
                         Rajshahi   299,671
                         Narayanganj   268,952

POPULATION

	1995	1980[1]
TOTAL	123,062,800	87,119,965 (81)
DENSITY (per square mile/kilometer)	2,165/836	1,774/685
ANNUAL GROWTH	1.9%	2.20%

AGE COHORTS
0–14   39%
15–64   58%
65 AND OVER   3%

MALE   51%
FEMALE   49%

	1995	1980[1]
URBAN	18%	15.4%
RURAL	82%	84.6%

NET MIGRATION RATE   −0.8%

IDENTITY

ETHNICITY
BENGALI   98%
TRIBALS   1%

LANGUAGE
BANGLA   n/a
ENGLISH   n/a

	1995	1980[1]
RELIGION		
SUNNI MUSLIM	83%	
HINDU	16%	

VITAL STATISTICS

	1995	1980[1]
BIRTHS		
BIRTH RATE	30.5	44.8
INFANT MORTALITY RATE	107.5	128
LIFE EXPECTANCY AT BIRTH	55.9	54.9
MARRIAGES		
MARRIAGE RATE	10.9	9
DEATHS		
DEATH RATE	11.2	17.5

ECONOMICS AND LABOR

	1995	1980[1]
GDP PER CAPITA US$	$1,130	
LABOR FORCE M/F		
AGRICULTURE	59/74%	
INDUSTRY	14/19%	
SERVICES	26/7%	
UNION DENSITY	4.3%	

TRANSPORT

	1995	1980[1]
JOURNEYS (by transport mode)		
RAILROAD PASSENGER TRIPS	3,343/5,348	
(millions of miles/kilometers)		
AIR PASSENGER TRIPS (thousands)	1,216 (94)	
VEHICLES		
PRIVATE CARS	46,600 (93)	45,100
COMMERCIAL	59,500 (93)	36,500

HEALTH AND HEALTH CARE

	1995	1980[1]
HEALTH CARE		
RATE OF PHYSICIANS	0.2	0.1
RATE OF HOSPITAL BEDS	0.3	0.2

	1995	**1980**[1]
ACCESS TO SAFE WATER	79%	
ACCESS TO SANITATION	35%	
MEASLES IMMUNIZATION	96%	

HEALTH INDICATORS

	1995	**1980**[1]
PREGNANT WOMEN WITH ANEMIA	53%	
LOW-BIRTH-WEIGHT BABIES	34%	
CHILD MALNUTRITION	68%	
SMOKING PREVALENCE M/F	60/15%	
TUBERCULOSIS INCIDENCE RATE	2.2	
AIDS/HIV CASES	7	1 (93)

EDUCATION

SCHOOL AGE IN SCHOOL

	1995	**1980**[1]
PRIMARY	n/a	61%
SECONDARY	n/a	18%
HIGHER	n/a	3%

FEMALES IN SCHOOL

	1995	**1980**[1]
PRIMARY		37%

	1995	**1980**[1]
ADULT ILLITERACY M/F	51/74%	60.3/82% (81)

COMMUNICATIONS

	1995	**1980**[1]
RATE OF NEWSPAPERS	6	3
RATE OF RADIOS	47	17
RATE OF TELEVISIONS	6	1

FOOTNOTE
1. Part of Pakistan in 1965.

Source: CIA, The World Factbook, 1997; ILO, World Labour Report, 1997; UN, Demographic Yearbook, 1997; UN, Statistical Yearbook, 1996; World Bank, World Development Indicators, 1998.

BARBADOS

Barbados is a tropical island located in the eastern Caribbean east of the Windward Islands. The island's northeast shores border the Atlantic Ocean. The 166-square-mile (430-square-kilometer) country is located approximately 200 miles northeast of Trinidad. The country received independence from the United Kingdom in November 1966. Barbados's leading economic activities are sugar production and tourism, making the country highly dependent on world market prices for sugar and tourism from North America and Western Europe. In 1995, the national per capita gross domestic product was $9,800. Although Barbados's population has grown slowly at a pace of 0.3 percent in recent years, the country has a relatively high density of 1,590 persons per square mile (614 per square kilometer). Persons of African descent compose nearly 84 percent of the country's population.

	1995	1980	1965
GEOGRAPHY			
AREA (square miles/kilometers)	166/430		
LAND AREA (square miles/kilometers)	166/430		
COASTLINE (miles/kilometers)	60/97		
CITIES			
CAPITAL	Bridgetown	n/a	7,466	n/a
POPULATION			
TOTAL	257,030	248,983	243,810
DENSITY (per square mile/kilometer)	1,590/614	1,520/587	n/a
ANNUAL GROWTH	0.3%	0.3%	n/a
AGE COHORTS			
0–14	24%	n/a	39%
15–64	66%	n/a	54%
65 AND OVER	10%	n/a	7%
URBAN	47%	32.2%	n/a
RURAL	53%	68.8%	n/a
NET MIGRATION RATE	−4.5	n/a	28.6

	1995	1980	1965

IDENTITY

ETHNICITY
AFRICAN	84%		
EUROPEAN	4%		

LANGUAGE
ENGLISH	100%		

RELIGION
ANGLICAN	40%		
PENTECOSTAL	8%		
METHODIST	7%		

VITAL STATISTICS

BIRTHS
BIRTH RATE	15.3	16.7 (84)	29–32
INFANT MORTALITY RATE	13.2	10.9 (84)	49.3
LIFE EXPECTANCY AT BIRTH	74.4	69.8 (84)	65.1

MARRIAGES
MARRIAGE RATE	11.2	5 (84)	3.9
DIVORCE RATE	1.4	1.3 (84)	0.3

DEATHS
DEATH RATE	8.2	7.8 (84)	9

HOUSEHOLDS

NUMBER	n/a	n/a	57,622 (60)
AVERAGE SIZE	n/a	n/a	4 (60)

ECONOMICS AND LABOR

GDP PER CAPITA US$	$9,800		

LABOR FORCE M/F (thousands)
LABOR FORCE M/F	54.1/46.6 (94)		
AGRICULTURE	3.5/2.4		
MINING	0.0/0.0		
MANUFACTURING	5.2/4.8		
UTILITIES	0.9/0.1		

	1995	1980	1965
CONSTRUCTION	7.4/0.3		
TRADE/FOOD/TOURISM	6.9/8.4		
TRANSPORT/COMMUNICATIONS	3.1/1.1		
FINANCE/INSURANCE/REAL ESTATE	2.2/4.1		
SOCIAL AND PERSONAL SERVICES	10.8/19.8		
UNEMPLOYMENT (official)	21.9% (94)		

TRANSPORT

	1995	1980	1965
JOURNEYS (by transport mode)			
AIR PASSENGER TRIPS (thousands)	46 (80)		
VEHICLES (thousands)			
PRIVATE CARS	42,600	29,400 (79)	10,500
COMMERCIAL	6,800	2,300	3,200

HEALTH AND HEALTH CARE

	1995	1980	1965
HEALTH CARE			
RATE OF PHYSICIANS	n/a	n/a	0.3 (60)
RATE OF HOSPITAL BEDS	n/a	n/a	5.9 (60)
HEALTH INDICATORS			
AIDS/HIV CASES	632	418 (93)	
TOTAL DEATHS	2,481		

EDUCATION

	1995	1980	1965
SCHOOL AGE IN SCHOOL			
PRIMARY	n/a	100%	89%
SECONDARY	n/a	84%	34%
HIGHER	n/a	14.5%	1.5%
FEMALES IN SCHOOL			
PRIMARY	n/a	100%	93%
SECONDARY	n/a	84%	31%
HIGHER	n/a	15.3	n/a
ADULT ILLITERACY M/F	n/a	n/a	0.3/0.3% (70)

	1995	1980	1965
COMMUNICATIONS			
RATE OF NEWSPAPERS	160	156	112
RATE OF RADIOS	877	542	176
RATE OF TELEVISIONS	279	209	25

Source: CIA, The World Factbook, 1997; ILO, World Labour Report, 1997; UN, Demographic Yearbook, 1997; UN, Statistical Yearbook, 1996; World Bank, World Development Indicators, 1998.

BELARUS

Belarus is a landlocked country, located in Eastern Europe, west of the Russian Federation. Latvia and Lithuania border the 80,154-square-mile (207,600-square-kilometer) country on the north. Poland borders it on the west and the Ukraine on the south. Although Belarus had nominal independence as a soviet socialistic republic of the Soviet Union, the country gained formal independence in August 1991 amid the breakup of the Soviet Union. Belarus is one of the most economically developed countries of the former Soviet Union. In 1995, Belarus had a per capita gross domestic product of $4,700. In 1993, the official unemployment rate was under 1 percent and only 6.4 percent of the country's population lived on less than $2 a day. Under the leadership of President Aleksandr Lukashenko, the government has resisted market reforms that have been implemented elsewhere in the region. Byelorussians (78 percent) are the country's leading ethnic group, followed by Russians (13 percent) and Poles (4 percent). In 1993, life expectancy at birth was 68.6 percent, and the infant mortality rate was 13.3 per 1,000 live births.

		1995	1980[1]	1965[1]
GEOGRAPHY				
AREA (square miles/kilometers)		80,154/207,600		
LAND AREA (square miles/kilometers)		80,154/207,600		
COASTLINE (miles/kilometers)		Landlocked		
CITIES				
CAPITAL	Minsk	1,659,700 (93)		
MAJOR CITIES	Gomel	503,900 (93)		
	Mogilev	364,600 (93)		
	Vitebsk	362,700 (93)		
	Grodno	298,400 (93)		
POPULATION				
TOTAL		10,415,973	0,543 (79)	8,054,648 (59)
DENSITY (per square mile/kilometer)		125/49	n/a	109/42
ANNUAL GROWTH		0.2%	n/a	1%
AGE COHORTS				
0–14		21%		
15–64		66%		
65 AND OVER		13%		
MALE		47%		
FEMALE		53%		

	1995	1980[1]	1965[1]
URBAN	71%	56.8%	n/a
RURAL	29%	43.2%	n/a
NET MIGRATION RATE	3.5		

IDENTITY

ETHNICITY
BYELORUSSIAN	78%
RUSSIAN	13%
POLISH	4%

LANGUAGE
BYELORUSSIAN	n/a
RUSSIAN	n/a

RELIGION
EASTERN ORTHODOX	60%
ROMAN CATHOLIC	40%

VITAL STATISTICS

BIRTHS
	1995	1980[1]	1965[1]
BIRTH RATE	12.2	n/a	17.7
URBAN BIRTH RATE	11.6 (93)		
RURAL BIRTH RATE	10.9 (93)		
INFANT MORTALITY RATE	13.3 (93)	n/a	22
ABORTION RATE	732.4		
LIFE EXPECTANCY AT BIRTH	68.6		

MARRIAGES
	1995	1980[1]	1965[1]
MARRIAGE RATE	7.3	n/a	8.3
AVERAGE AGE AT MARRIAGE M/F	24.5/21.9		
DIVORCE RATE	3.9	n/a	1

DEATHS
	1995	1980[1]	1965[1]
DEATH RATE	13.6	n/a	6.7

HOUSEHOLDS

NUMBER	2,796,121 (89)
AVERAGE SIZE	3.6 (89)

	1995	**1980**[1]	**1965**[1]

ECONOMICS AND LABOR

GDP PER CAPITA US$	$4,700		
LABOR FORCE (thousands)	4,696,000 (94)		
AGRICULTURE	995.7		
MINING	27.2		
MANUFACTURING	1,245.60		
UTILITIES	38.7		
CONSTRUCTION	328.9		
TRADE/FOOD/TOURISM	422.3		
TRANSPORT/COMMUNICATIONS	318		
FINANCE/INSURANCE/REAL ESTATE	40.9		
SOCIAL AND PERSONAL SERVICES	1,099.70		
UNEMPLOYMENT (official)	0.7% (93)		
UNION DENSITY	96.1%		
POVERTY			
UNDER $2/DAY	6.4% (93)		

TRANSPORT

JOURNEYS (by transport mode)			
RAILROAD PASSENGER TRIPS			
(millions of miles/kilometers)	10,039/16,063 (94)		
AIR PASSENGER TRIPS (thousands)	805.0 (94)		

HEALTH AND HEALTH CARE

HEALTH CARE			
RATE OF PHYSICIANS	4.1	3.4	n/a
RATE OF HOSPITAL BEDS	12.4	12.5	n/a
ACCESS TO SANITATION	100%		
MEASLES IMMUNIZATION	96%		
HEALTH INDICATORS			
LOW-BIRTH-WEIGHT BABIES	5%		
TUBERCULOSIS INCIDENCE RATE	0.5		
AIDS/HIV CASES	15	10 (93)	
TOTAL DEATHS	130,003 (94)		

	1995	1980[1]	1965[1]
EDUCATION			
SCHOOL AGE IN SCHOOL			
PRIMARY	97%	104%	n/a
SECONDARY	n/a	98%	n/a
HIGHER	n/a	39%	12.1%
FEMALES IN SCHOOL			
OF PRIMARY STUDENTS	48%		
OF SECONDARY STUDENTS	50%		
COMMUNICATIONS			
RATE OF NEWSPAPERS	186	243	n/a
RATE OF RADIOS	313	223	n/a
RATE OF TELEVISIONS	272	218	n/a

FOOTNOTE
1. Part of Union of Soviet Socialist Republics.

Source: CIA, The World Factbook, 1997; ILO, World Labour Report, 1997; UN, Demographic Yearbook, 1997; UN, Statistical Yearbook, 1996; World Bank, World Development Indicators, 1998.

BELGIUM

Belgium is located in Western Europe on the North Sea. The 11,780-square-mile (30,510-square-kilometer) country is bordered by the Netherlands on the north; Germany, and Luxembourg on the east; and France on the south and southwest. Belgium received its independence in October 1830 from the Netherlands. It has few natural resources, and its highly industrialized economy is linked to Western European and global markets. The country has a density of 857 persons per square mile (331 per square kilometer). The leading social division is between the Dutch-speaking Flemish (56 percent) in the

industrial north and the French-speaking Walloons (32 percent) in the less economically developed southern region. Although the Flemish are an ethnic majority, about 75 percent of the country's population are Roman Catholic and 25 percent are Protestant. The country is almost entirely urban, with 97 percent of the population living in cities and only 3 percent in rural zones. In 1995, Belgium had a relatively slow annual population growth rate of 0.33 percent. Belgium has a high average life expectancy at birth of 77.1 years and a low infant mortality rate of 7.6 per 1,000 live births.

	1995	1980	1965
GEOGRAPHY			
AREA (square miles/kilometers)	11,780/30,510		
LAND AREA (square miles/kilometers)	11,672/30,230		
COASTLINE (miles/kilometers)	40/64		
CITIES			
CAPITAL	Brussels (91) 136,488		
MAJOR CITIES	Antwerp (90) 470,349		
	Ouvers (91) 467,875		
	Gent 230,466		
	Charleroi 206,928		
POPULATION			
TOTAL	10,170,241	9,848,647 (81)	9,189,741 (61)
DENSITY (per square mile/kilometer)	857/331	842/325	808/312
ANNUAL GROWTH	0.3%		
AGE COHORTS			
0–14	18%	n/a	23.8% (64)
15–64	66%	n/a	64% (64)
65 AND OVER	16%	12.4% (64)	n/a
URBAN	97%	94.6 (76)	n/a
RURAL	3%	5.4 (76)	n/a

	1995	1980	1965
NET MIGRATION RATE	1.6	n/a	0.6 (64)

IDENTITY

ETHNICITY

FLEMING	55%		
WALLOON	33%		

LANGUAGE

DUTCH	56%		
FRENCH	32%		
GERMAN	1%		

RELIGION

ROMAN CATHOLIC	75%		
PROTESTANT	25%		

VITAL STATISTICS

BIRTHS

BIRTH RATE	12	11.5 (85)	15.8
INFANT MORTALITY RATE	7.6	9.4 (85)	24.1
LIFE EXPECTANCY AT BIRTH	77.1	73.4 (85)	70.5

MARRIAGES

MARRIAGE RATE	5.1	5.8 (85)	7.2
AVERAGE AGE AT MARRIAGE M/F	27.5/25.1 (91)		
DIVORCE RATE	2.1	1.9 (85)	0.6

DEATHS

DEATH RATE	10.3	11.2 (85)	12

ECONOMICS AND LABOR

GDP PER CAPITA US$	$19,500

LABOR FORCE M/F (thousands)	2,236.0/1,517.1 (92)
AGRICULTURE	68.5/26.4
MINING	6.3/0.3
MANUFACTURING	576.1/175.6
UTILITIES	25.7/3.4
CONSTRUCTION	229.6/15.7
TRADE/FOOD/TOURISM	318.0/316.2
TRANSPORT/COMMUNICATIONS	211.3/45.8

	1995	**1980**	**1965**
FINANCE/INSURANCE/REAL ESTATE	196.8/144.8		
SOCIAL AND PERSONAL SERVICES	603.7/788.8		
UNEMPLOYMENT (official)	13.9% (94)		
UNION DENSITY	38.1%		

TRANSPORT

	1995	**1980**	**1965**
JOURNEYS (by transport mode)			
RAILROAD PASSENGER TRIPS			
(millions of miles/kilometers)	4,149/6,638 (94)		
AIR PASSENGER TRIPS (thousands)	4,193 (94)		
VEHICLES (thousands)			
PRIVATE CARS	4,281.1	3,315.00	1,340
COMMERCIAL	444.4	318.6	233.5

HEALTH AND HEALTH CARE

	1995	**1980**	**1965**
HEALTH CARE			
RATE OF PHYSICIANS	3.7	2.5	1.3 (60)
RATE OF HOSPITAL BEDS	7.6	9.4	8 (60)
ACCESS TO SANITATION	100%		
MEASLES IMMUNIZATION	70%		
HEALTH INDICATORS			
LOW-BIRTH-WEIGHT BABIES	6%		
SMOKING PREVALENCE M/F	31/19%		
TUBERCULOSIS INCIDENCE RATE	0.16		
AIDS/HIV CASES	2,072	1,631 (93)	
TOTAL DEATHS	105,933		

EDUCATION

	1995	**1980**	**1965**
SCHOOL AGE IN SCHOOL			
PRIMARY	103%	104%	109%
SECONDARY	144%	91%	75%
HIGHER	4.9%	26%	8.9%
FEMALES IN SCHOOL			
OF PRIMARY STUDENTS	49%	49%	49%
OF SECONDARY STUDENTS	n/a	49%	49%

	1995	1980	1965
COMMUNICATIONS			
RATE OF NEWSPAPERS	310	232	285
RATE OF RADIOS	771	731	329
RATE OF TELEVISIONS	453	387	168

Source: CIA, *The World Factbook, 1997*; ILO, *World Labour Report, 1997*; UN, *Demographic Yearbook, 1997*; UN, *Statistical Yearbook, 1996*; World Bank, *World Development Indicators, 1998*.

BELIZE

Belize is located on the Central American isthmus on the Caribbean Sea. Mexico borders the 8,865-square-mile (22,960-square-kilometer) country on the north, and Guatemala borders it on the south. In 1995, the country's population of 219,296 was growing at a relatively rapid 2.4 percent per year. Belize has a low density of 26 persons per square mile (10 persons per square kilometer). Once known as British Honduras, Belize gained independence from the United Kingdom in September 1981. The country's southwestern border with Guatemala is in dispute. Belize is an ethnically and linguistically divided country. The three leading ethnic minorities in the country are Mestizo (44 percent), Creole (30 percent), and Maya (11 percent). The leading languages spoken are English, Spanish, and indigenous Mayan. Average life expectancy at birth has increased dramatically over the last four decades of the twentieth century, from 47 years in 1960 to 68.5 years in 1995. The national economy is highly dependent on the production of sugar for sale in North American and other export markets. The per capita gross domestic product in 1995 was $2,750.

	1995	**1980**	**1965**
GEOGRAPHY			
AREA (square miles/kilometers)	8,865/22,960		
LAND AREA (square miles/kilometers)	8,803/22,800		
COASTLINE (miles/kilometers)	241/386		
CITIES			
CAPITAL	Belmopan	44,087 (91)	
POPULATION			
TOTAL	219,296	142,847	90,505 (60)
DENSITY (per square mile/kilometer)	26/10	18/7	n/a
ANNUAL GROWTH	2.4%	2.7%	n/a
AGE COHORTS			
0–14	43%	n/a	45%
15–64	53%	n/a	51%
65 AND OVER	4%	n/a	4%
MALE	51%		
FEMALE	49%		
URBAN	47%		
RURAL	53%		
NET MIGRATION RATE	−2.9	n/a	3.7

	1995	1980	1965
IDENTITY			
ETHNICITY			
MESTIZO	44%		
CREOLE	30%		
MAYA	11%		
LANGUAGE			
ENGLISH	n/a		
SPANISH	n/a		
MAYA	n/a		
RELIGION			
ROMAN CATHOLIC	62%		
ANGLICAN	12%		
METHODIST	6%		
VITAL STATISTICS			
BIRTHS			
BIRTH RATE	32.8	40.1 (85)	n/a
INFANT MORTALITY RATE	32.5	18.9 (85)	n/a
LIFE EXPECTANCY AT BIRTH	68.5	n/a	47 (60)
MARRIAGES			
MARRIAGE RATE	6.5	5.2 (85)	n/a
DIVORCE RATE	0.6	0.4 (85)	n/a
DEATHS			
DEATH RATE	n/a	5.7 (85	4 (60)
HOUSEHOLDS			
NUMBER	39,929 (91)	n/a	19,187 (60)
AVERAGE SIZE	4.8(91)	n/a	4.7 (61)
TYPE OF HOUSEHOLD			
SINGLE	35.6%		
MARRIED	54.3%		
WIDOWED	6.4%		
DIVORCED/SEPARATED	3.7%		

	1995	1980	1965

ECONOMICS AND LABOR

GDP PER CAPITA US$	$2,750		
LABOR FORCE M/F (thousands)	43.0/19.0 (94)		
AGRICULTURE	13.3/0.8		
MINING	0.3/0.0		
MANUFACTURING	5.0/1.7		
UTILITIES	1.0/0.2		
CONSTRUCTION	3.5/0.1		
TRADE/FOOD/TOURISM	1.3/1.9		
TRANSPORT/COMMUNICATIONS	3.2/0.5		
FINANCE/INSURANCE/REAL ESTATE	0.5/0.7		
SOCIAL AND PERSONAL SERVICES	1.4/1.4		
UNEMPLOYMENT (official)	11.1% (94)		

TRANSPORT

	1995	1980	1965
VEHICLES			
PRIVATE CARS	n/a	1,400	1,300
COMMERCIAL	n/a	1,200	700

HEALTH AND HEALTH CARE

	1995	1980	1965
HEALTH CARE			
RATE OF PHYSICIANS	n/a	n/a	0.3 (60)
RATE OF HOSPITAL BEDS	n/a	n/a	4.7 (60)
HEALTH INDICATORS			
AIDS/HIV CASE	138	92 (93)	
TOTAL DEATHS	863 (94)		

EDUCATION

	1995	1980	1965
SCHOOL AGE IN SCHOOL			
PRIMARY	n/a	n/a	114%
SECONDARY	n/a	n/a	26%
HIGHER	n/a	n/a	0.6%
FEMALES IN SCHOOL			
PRIMARY	n/a	n/a	111%
SECONDARY	n/a	n/a	27%

	1995	1980	1965
ADULT ILLITERACY M/F	n/a	n/a	8.8/8.8 (70)

COMMUNICATIONS

	1995	1980	1965
RATE OF NEWSPAPERS	578	21	58
RATE OF RADIOS	167	486	72

Source: CIA, The World Factbook, 1997; ILO, World Labour Report, 1997; UN, Demographic Yearbook, 1997; UN, Statistical Yearbook, 1996; World Bank, World Development Indicators, 1998.

BENIN

Benin, formerly known as Dahomey, is located in western Africa on the Bight of Benin, an inlet of the North Atlantic Ocean. Nigeria borders the narrow 48,483-square-mile (112,620-square-kilometer) country on the east. Niger and Burkina Faso lie to the north, and Togo to the west. Benin received independence from France in December 1960. Most residents depend on subsistence agriculture for survival. Cotton, the leading crop, is sold to regional West African markets. The national economy is in heavy debt to external lenders, including the International Monetary Fund and Western banks. In 1995, the nation's per cap-

ita gross domestic product was $1,380. Benin's population growth has continued to accelerate in the 1990s from an annual rate of 2.8 percent in 1979 to 3.3 percent in 1995. In 1995, the national population exceeded 5.7 million. French is Benin's official language. The Fon, Adja, and Yoruba are Benin's leading ethnic minorities. Most of the national population practices indigenous African religions (70 percent), followed by Christianity (15 percent) and Muslim (15 percent). Average life expectancy at birth increased from 44 years in 1965 to 52.7 years in 1995.

	1995	**1980**	**1965**
## GEOGRAPHY			
AREA (square miles/kilometers)	43,483/112,620		
LAND AREA (square miles/kilometers)	42,710/110,620		
COASTLINE (miles/kilometers)	76/121		
CITIES			
CAPITAL	Porto-Novo	179,138	
MAJOR CITIES	Cotonou	536,827 (90)	
	Djougou	134,099 (90)	
	Parakou	103,577 (90)	
## POPULATION			
TOTAL	5,709,529	3,331,210 (79)	2,082,511 (61)
DENSITY (per square mile/kilometer)	49	35	n/a
ANNUAL GROWTH	3.3%	2.8%	n/a
AGE COHORTS			
0–14	48%	n/a	46%
15–64	50%	n/a	50%
65 AND OVER	2%	n/a	4%
MALE	49%		
FEMALE	51%		

	1995	1980	1965
URBAN	31%	39.4	n/a
RURAL	69%	60.60%	n/a
NET MIGRATION RATE	0		

IDENTITY

ETHNICITY
FON	n/a
ADJA	n/a
YORUBA	n/a

LANGUAGE
FRENCH (official)	n/a
FON	n/a
YORUBA	n/a

RELIGION
ANIMIST	70%
CHRISTIAN	15%
MUSLIM	15%

VITAL STATISTICS

BIRTHS
	1995	1980	1965
BIRTH RATE	46.8	50.7	n/a
INFANT MORTALITY RATE	85.8	109.6	n/a
LIFE EXPECTANCY AT BIRTH	52.7	44	n/a

DEATHS
	1995	1980	1965
DEATH RATE	13.5	21.2	n/a

HOUSEHOLDS

NUMBER	832,526 (92)
AVERAGE SIZE	5.9 (92)

TYPE OF HOUSEHOLD
SINGLE	9.7%
MARRIED	75.4%
WIDOWED	9.2%
DIVORCED/SEPARATED	4.3%
FEMALE HEADED	21.4%

	1995	**1980**	**1965**

ECONOMICS AND LABOR

GDP PER CAPITA US$

	1995	1980	1965
GDP PER CAPITA US$	$1,380		

LABOR FORCE M/F

	1995	1980	1965
AGRICULTURE	62/65%		
INDUSTRY	12.0/4.0%		
SERVICES	27/30%		

TRANSPORT

JOURNEYS (by transport mode)

	1995	1980	1965
RAILROAD PASSENGER TRIPS (millions of miles/kilometers)	n/a	75/120 (87)	n/a
AIR PASSENGER TRIPS (thousands)	69 (94)		

VEHICLES

	1995	1980	1965
PRIVATE CARS	22,000	n/a	5,700
COMMERCIAL	12,300	n/a	3,900

HEALTH AND HEALTH CARE

HEALTH CARE

	1995	1980	1965
RATE OF PHYSICIANS	0.1	0.1	n/a
RATE OF HOSPITAL BEDS	0.2	1.5	1.3 (60)
ACCESS TO SAFE WATER	50%		
ACCESS TO SANITATION	20%		
MEASLES IMMUNIZATION	81%		

HEALTH INDICATORS

	1995	1980	1965
PREGNANT WOMEN WITH ANEMIA	41%		
LOW-BIRTH-WEIGHT BABIES	10%		
CHILD MALNUTRITION	24%		
TUBERCULOSIS INCIDENCE RATE	1.35%		
AIDS/HIV CASES	1,280	742 (93)	

EDUCATION

SCHOOL AGE IN SCHOOL

	1995	1980	1965
PRIMARY	72%	67%	35%
SECONDARY	16%	16%	3%
HIGHER	3%	1%	0.1%

	1995	1980	1965
FEMALES IN SCHOOL			
PRIMARY	n/a	32%	21%
SECONDARY	n/a	26%	2%
ADULT ILLITERACY M/F	51/74%	74.8/90.5%	

COMMUNICATIONS

	1995	1980	1965
RATE OF NEWSPAPERS	2	0.3	1
RATE OF RADIOS	91	66	17
RATE OF TELEVISIONS	6	1	1 (70)

Source: CIA, The World Factbook, 1997; ILO, World Labour Report, 1997; UN, Demographic Yearbook, 1997; UN, Statistical Yearbook, 1996; World Bank, World Development Indicators, 1998.

BHUTAN

Bhutan is a landlocked country located in the Great Himalaya mountain range of southern Asia. China borders the 18,147-square-mile (47,000-square-kilometer) country on the north, and India borders it on the south, east, and west. The nation's annual rate of population growth increased from 1.8 percent in 1969 to 2.3 percent in 1995, with a population increase from about 1.3 million to over 1.8 million. The country received independence from India in August 1949 and became the Kingdom of Bhutan. Since 1907 the country has been ruled by a monarchy. Bhutan is one of the poorest countries in the world, with an economy that is highly dependent on India for technological assistance and skilled labor. In 1995,

the country's per capita gross domestic product was only $730 per year. Subsistence farming and agriculture are the primary economic activity of the country's population. The country's leading ethnic groups are Bhote (50 percent) and Nepalese (35 percent), and the leading religions are Buddhism (75 percent) and Hinduism (25 percent). In 1965, only 7 percent of the school-aged population was enrolled in primary schools, and a mere 0.3 percent was enrolled in institutions of higher education. Between 1980 and 1995, Bhutan's infant mortality rate fell from 139 to 124 per 1,000 live births, as life expectancy at birth increased from 45.8 years to 51.5 years.

	1995	1980	1965
GEOGRAPHY			
AREA (square miles/kilometers)	18,147/47,000		
LAND AREA (square miles/kilometers)	18,147/47,000		
COASTLINE	Landlocked		
CITIES			
CAPITAL	Thimphu	n/a	8,922 (77)	n/a
POPULATION			
TOTAL	1,822,625	n/a	1,304,774 (69)
DENSITY (per square mile/kilometer)	91/35	78/30	41/16
ANNUAL GROWTH	2.3%	2%	1.8%
AGE COHORTS			
0–14	40%		
15–64	56%		
65 AND OVER	4%		
URBAN	6%		
RURAL	94%		
NET MIGRATION RATE	0		

	1995	1980	1965

IDENTITY

ETHNICITY
BHOTE	50%
NEPALESE	35%
TRIBAL	15%

LANGUAGE
DZONGKHA (official)	n/a
TIBETAN	n/a
NEPALESE	n/a

RELIGION
| BUDDHIST | 75% |
| HINDU | 25% |

VITAL STATISTICS

BIRTHS
BIRTH RATE	38.5	38.4	n/a
INFANT MORTALITY RATE	124	139	n/a
LIFE EXPECTANCY AT BIRTH	51.5	45.8	n/a

DEATH
| DEATH RATE | 15.3 | 18.1 | n/a |

ECONOMICS AND LABOR

| GDP PER CAPITA US$ | $730 |

TRANSPORT

JOURNEYS (by transport mode)
RAILROAD PASSENGER TRIPS   5.6/9 (94)
  (millions of miles/kilometers)

	1995	1980	1965
EDUCATION			
SCHOOL AGE IN SCHOOL			
PRIMARY	n/a	15%	7%
SECONDARY	n/a	n/a	4%
HIGHER	n/a	0.3%	n/a
FEMALES IN SCHOOL			
PRIMARY	n/a	n/a	3%
SECONDARY	n/a	n/a	2%
HIGHER	n/a	0.1%	n/a
COMMUNICATIONS			
RATE OF NEWSPAPERS	17	n/a	n/a
RATE OF RADIOS	n/a	5	n/a

Source: CIA, *The World Factbook, 1997;* ILO, *World Labour Report, 1997;* UN, *Demographic Yearbook, 1997;* UN, *Statistical Yearbook, 1996;* World Bank, *World Development Indicators, 1998.*

BOLIVIA

Bolivia is a landlocked country located in central South America. Brazil borders the 424,162-square-mile (1,098,580-square-kilometer) country on the north and east. Peru borders it on the north and west, Chile on the southwest, Argentina on the south, and Paraguay on the southeast. Although the country's population increased from 4,613,486 million in 1950 to 7,165,257 in 1995, the annual rate of population growth declined from 2.8 percent to 1.8 percent. Since receiving independence from Spain in August 1825, Bolivia has endured frequent internal political turmoil and unrest. In addition, Bolivia has sought to regain a land corridor to the Pacific Ocean, lost to Chile in 1884.

In recent years the country has made the transition from military rule to nominal democracy. The country's leading ethnic minorities are Quechua (30 percent), Aymara (25 percent), and Mestizo (25 percent). About 95 percent of Bolivia's population are Roman Catholic. In 1995, just over 60 percent of the country's population lived in urban areas. Although infant mortality has declined substantially, from 124 per 1,000 live births in 1975 to 75.1 per 1,000 live births in 1995, infant mortality continues to be higher than in other countries in the region. Over the same period, life expectancy increased from 50.8 years to 59.8 years.

	1995	1980	1965
GEOGRAPHY			
AREA (square miles/kilometers)	424,162/1,098,580		
LAND AREA (square miles/kilometers)	418,683/1,084,390		
COASTLINE (miles/kilometers)	Landlocked		
CITIES			
CAPITAL	La Paz 784,976 (93)		
MAJOR CITIES	Santa Cruz 767,260		
	Cochabamba 448,756		
	El Alto 446,189		
	Oruro 201,831		
POPULATION			
TOTAL	7,165,257	4,613,486 (76)	2,704,165 (50)
DENSITY (per square mile/kilometer)	18/7	16/6	8.0/3.0
ANNUAL GROWTH	1.8%	2.8%	1.4%
AGE COHORTS			
0–14	39%		
15–64	56%		
65 AND OVER	5%		

	1995	**1980**	**1965**
MALE	49%		
FEMALE	51%		
URBAN	61%	44.4	n/a
RURAL	39%	55.60%	n/a
MIGRATION	−3.4		

IDENTITY

ETHNICITY	
QUECHUA	30%
AYMARA	25%
MESTIZO	25%

LANGUAGE	
SPANISH	n/a
QUECHUA	n/a
AYMARA	n/a

RELIGION	
ROMAN CATHOLIC	95%
PROTESTANT	5%

VITAL STATISTICS

	1995	**1980**	**1965**
BIRTHS			
BIRTH RATE	32.4	46.6 (75)	45
INFANT MORTALITY RATE	75.1	124 (75)	86
LIFE EXPECTANCY AT BIRTH	59.8	50.8 (75)	49.7
MARRIAGES			
MARRIAGE RATE	5	4.8 (75)	5.5
AVERAGE AGE AT MARRIAGE M/F	25.1/22.7 (92)		
DEATHS			
DEATH RATE	10.8	18 (75)	22

HOUSEHOLDS

NUMBER	1,444,817 (92)
AVERAGE SIZE	4.3 (92)

	1995	1980	1965
TYPE OF HOUSEHOLD			
SINGLE	10.3%		
MARRIED	74.6%		
WIDOWED	10.8%		
DIVORCED/SEPARATE	4%		
FEMALE HEADED	24.5%		

ECONOMICS AND LABOR

	1995	1980	1965
GDP PER CAPITA US$	$2,530		
LABOR FORCE M/F (thousands)	616.3/432 (92)		
AGRICULTURE	16.7/5.4		
MINING	18.8/0.9		
MANUFACTURING	136.5/67.0		
UTILITIES	8.2/1.1		
CONSTRUCTION	95.9/1.3		
TRADE/FOOD/TOURISM	121.8/183.4		
TRANSPORT/COMMUNICATIONS	70.7/4.8		
FINANCE/INSURANCE/REAL ESTATE	26.5/13.9		
SOCIAL AND PERSONAL SERVICES	120.4/154.3		
UNEMPLOYMENT (official)	5.4% (92)		
UNION DENSITY	16.40%		

TRANSPORT

	1995	1980	1965
JOURNEYS (by transport mode)			
RAILROAD PASSENGER TRIPS			
(millions of miles/kilometers)	276.0 (94)		
AIR PASSENGER TRIPS (thousands)	1,175.0 (94)		
VEHICLES			
PRIVATE CARS	261,000	50,200	14,500
COMMERCIAL	66,300	32,500	26,600

HEALTH AND HEALTH CARE

	1995	1980	1965
HEALTH CARE			
RATE OF PHYSICIANS	0.4	0.5	0.2 (60)
RATE OF HOSPITAL BEDS	1.4	n/a	1.6 (60)
ACCESS TO SAFE WATER	60%		
ACCESS TO SANITATION	44%		
MEASLES IMMUNIZATION	83%		

	1995	**1980**	**1965**
HEALTH INDICATORS			
PREGNANT WOMEN WITH ANEMIA	51%		
LOW-BIRTH-WEIGHT BABIES	10%		
CHILD MALNUTRITION	16%		
SMOKING PREVALENCE M/F	50/21%		
TUBERCULOSIS INCIDENCE RATE	3.35		
AIDS/HIV CASES	109	88 (93)	

EDUCATION

	1995	**1980**	**1965**
SCHOOL AGE IN SCHOOL			
PRIMARY	n/a	87%	76%
SECONDARY	n/a	37%	19%
HIGHER		16%	3.70%
	n/a		
FEMALES IN SCHOOL			
PRIMARY	n/a	47%	63%
SECONDARY	n/a	n/a	14%
ADULT ILLITERACY M/F	10.0/24%		

COMMUNICATIONS

	1995	**1980**	**1965**
RATE OF NEWSPAPERS	57	42	26
RATE OF RADIOS	669	523	194
RATE OF TELEVISIONS	113	56	0

Source: CIA, *The World Factbook, 1997;* ILO, *World Labour Report, 1997;* UN, *Demographic Yearbook, 1997;* UN, *Statistical Yearbook, 1996;* World Bank, *World Development Indicators, 1998.*

BOSNIA AND HERZEGOVINA

Bosnia and Herzegovina is located in southeastern Europe in a region that formed part of Yugoslavia before the early 1990s. Although the country declared independence in April 1992, both Yugoslavia (Serbia) and Croatia disputed the country's autonomy. Armed factions loyal to Yugoslavia, Croatia, and the Muslim-led government of Bosnia fought an ongoing regional war from 1992 to March 1994, when a regional settlement was achieved among the warring parties. The March 1994 accords, enforced by North Atlantic Treaty Organization (NATO) forces, created the government of Bosnia and Herzegovina made up of the Muslim/Croat Federation and the Republika Srpska, an autonomous region controlled by Bosnian Serbs. Croatia borders the 19,781-square-mile (51,233-square-kilometer) country on the north and west, and Serbia and Montenegro lie to the east and south. In 1995, the country's population was 2,656,240. In the same year, Bosnia and Herzegovina's population declined by 2.84 percent, primarily as a consequence of out-migration. Serbs (40 percent) are the ethnic majority, followed by Muslims (38 percent) and Croats (22 percent). Despite the ethnic differences, nearly all the population speaks Serbo-Croatian.

1995[1]

GEOGRAPHY

AREA (square miles/kilometers)	19,781/51,233
LAND AREA (square miles/kilometers)	19,781/51,233
COASTLINE (miles/kilometers)	13/20

CITIES

CAPITAL	Sarajevo	529,021 (91)
MAJOR CITIES	Banja Luka	195,994 (91)
	Zenica	145,837 (91)
	Tuzla	131,866 (91)
	Mostar	127,034 (91)

POPULATION

TOTAL	2,656,240
DENSITY (per square mile/kilometer)	228/88
ANNUAL GROWTH	−2.8%

AGE COHORTS

0–14	20%
15–64	68%
65 AND OVER	12%

	1995[1]
URBAN	49%
RURAL	51%
NET MIGRATION RATE	−18.9

IDENTITY

ETHNICITY
SERB	40%
MUSLIM	38%
CROATIAN	22%

LANGUAGE
SERBO-CROATIAN	99%

RELIGION
MUSLIM	40%
EASTERN ORTHODOX	31%
ROMAN CATHOLIC	15%

VITAL STATISTICS

BIRTHS
BIRTH RATE	6.3
INFANT MORTALITY RATE	15.3
LIFE EXPECTANCY AT BIRTH	56.1

DEATHS
DEATH RATE	15.9

ECONOMICS AND LABOR

GDP PER CAPITA US$ $300

LABOR FORCE M/F
AGRICULTURE	9/16%
INDUSTRY	54/37%
SERVICES	37/48%

1995[1]

HEALTH AND HEALTH CARE

HEALTH CARE

RATE OF PHYSICIANS	0.6
RATE OF HOSPITAL BEDS	2
MEASLES IMMUNIZATION	57%

HEALTH INDICATORS

TUBERCULOSIS INCIDENCE RATE	0.8
AIDS/HIV CASES	6

COMMUNICATIONS

RATE OF NEWSPAPERS   131

FOOTNOTE
1. Part of Yugoslavia in 1965 and 1980.

Source: CIA, *The World Factbook, 1997;* ILO, *World Labour Report, 1997;* UN, *Demographic Yearbook, 1997;* UN, *Statistical Yearbook, 1996;* World Bank, *World Development Indicators, 1998.*

BOTSWANA

Botswana is a landlocked country located in southern Africa. South Africa borders the 231,803-square-mile (600,370-square-kilometer) country on the south and east. Zimbabwe borders it on the northeast, and Namibia lies to the north and west. The country received independence in September 1966 from the United Kingdom. Subsistence agriculture and animal husbandry are the primary economic activities of the majority of Botswana's population. The country has a small but growing diamond-mining industry. The leading exports are diamonds, copper, nickel, and livestock. Botswana is relatively more affluent than other African countries south of the Sahara, with a 1995 per capita gross domestic product of $3,200. However, a substantial share of the national population remains mired in poverty. In 1986, 61 percent of the population lived on the equivalent of less than $2 a day, and 33 percent subsisted on $1 a day. Botswana has a relatively small population. Still, the population grew rapidly from 543,105 in 1965 to 1,477,630 in 1981. Over the same period, Botswana's annual population growth rate declined from 3.1 percent to 1.6 percent. Life expectancy at birth is 56 years. Botswana's infant mortality rate has declined steadily to 43 infant deaths per 1,000 live births in 1991 from 76 in 1980. Although the urban population is growing at a rapid pace, Botswana is still primarily a rural country, with 28 percent of the population residing in urban areas.

	1995	1980	1965
GEOGRAPHY			
AREA (square miles/kilometers)	231,803/600,370		
LAND AREA (square miles/kilometers)	226,012/585,370		
COASTLINE (miles/kilometers)	Landlocked		
CITIES			
CAPITAL	Gaborone	133,468 (91)	
POPULATION			
TOTAL	1,477,630 (81)	941,027	543,105
DENSITY (per square mile/kilometer)	8.0/3.0	5.0/2.0	3.0/1.0
ANNUAL GROWTH	1.6%	n/a	3.1%
AGE COHORTS			
0–14	42%	n/a	44%
15–64	54%	n/a	52%
65 AND OVER	4%	n/a	4%
MALE	48%		
FEMALE	52%		

	1995	1980	1965
URBAN	28%	15.9%	n/a
RURAL	72%	84.1%	n/a
NET MIGRATION RATE	0		

IDENTITY

ETHNICITY
BOTSWANA	95%
OTHER AFRICAN	4%
WHITE	1%

LANGUAGE
ENGLISH (official)	n/a
SETSWANA	n/a

RELIGION
ANIMIST	50%
CHRISTIAN	50%

VITAL STATISTICS

BIRTHS
	1995	1980	1965
BIRTH RATE	6,600.00%	49.9	
INFANT MORTALITY RATE	43	76	
LIFE EXPECTANCY AT BIRTH	56	55	

MARRIAGES
MARRIAGE RATE	n/a	1.6 (87)	n/a
AVERAGE AGE AT MARRIAGE M/F	30.9/26.9		

DEATH
DEATH RATE	6.6	12.6	n/a

HOUSEHOLDS

NUMBER	276,209 (91)
AVERAGE SIZE	4.8 (91)
FEMALE HEADED	47.1%

	1995	**1980**	**1965**

ECONOMICS AND LABOR

GDP PER CAPITA US$	$3,200		
LABOR FORCE M/F (thousands)	145.6/81.9 (92)		
AGRICULTURE	4.2/1.8		
MINING	7.3/0.4		
MANUFACTURING	16.1/9.5		
UTILITIES	2.3/0.3		
CONSTRUCTION	28.9/4.8		
TRADE/FOOD/TOURISM	18.4/22.5		
TRANSPORT/COMMUNICATIONS	7.5/2.7		
FINANCE/INSURANCE/REAL ESTATE	11.4/6.2		
SOCIAL AND PERSONAL SERVICES	49.4/33.8		
UNION DENSITY	11.50%		
POVERTY			
UNDER $1/DAY	n/a	33% (86)	n/a
UNDER $2/DAY	n/a	61% (86)	n/a

TRANSPORT

JOURNEYS (by transport mode)			
AIR PASSENGER TRIPS (thousands)	101 (94)		
VEHICLES			
PRIVATE CARS	81,900 (94)	16,400	n/a
COMMERCIAL	27,600 (94)	7,800	n/a

HEALTH AND HEALTH CARE

HEALTH CARE			
ACCESS TO SAFE WATER	70%		
ACCESS TO SANITATION	55%		
MEASLES IMMUNIZATION	68%		
RATE OF PHYSICIANS	0.2	0.1	n/a
RATE OF HOSPITAL BEDS	1.6	2.4	2 (60)
HEALTH INDICATORS			
LOW-BIRTH-WEIGHT BABIES	8%		
CHILD MALNUTRITION	27%		
SMOKING PREVALENCE M/F	21/0%		

	1995	1980	1965
TUBERCULOSIS INCIDENCE RATE	0.04		
AIDS/HIV CASES	3,451	1,948 (93)	

EDUCATION

SCHOOL AGE IN SCHOOL

	1995	1980	1965
PRIMARY	115%	91%	69%
SECONDARY	56%	19%	3%
HIGHER	4%	1%	0%

FEMALES IN SCHOOL

	1995	1980	1965
PRIMARY	50%	91%	76%
SECONDARY	53%	19%	n/a
HIGHER	2%	n/a	n/a

ADULT ILLITERACY M/F	n/a	n/a	63.1/56% (71)

COMMUNICATIONS

	1995	1980	1965
RATE OF NEWSPAPERS	29	21	23
RATE OF RADIOS	119	83	9
RATE OF TELEVISIONS	17	0	0

Source: CIA, *The World Factbook, 1997;* ILO, *World Labour Report, 1997;* UN, *Demographic Yearbook, 1997;* UN, *Statistical Yearbook, 1996;* World Bank, *World Development Indicators, 1998.*

BRAZIL

Brazil is the largest and most populous country in South America. The 3,286,473-square-mile (8,511,965-square-kilometer) country is located in eastern South America. Brazil's boundaries extend north, south, and west, bordering all but two of South America's political units, including French Guyana, Suriname, Guyana, Venezuela, Columbia, Peru, Bolivia, Paraguay, Argentina, and Uruguay. Chile and Ecuador are the only two South American countries that do not have a land boundary with Brazil. The country, which received its independence in 1822, is a study in contrasts. Brazil is one of the most economically advanced nations of South America, with a large service and manufacturing sector. However, due to an inequitable distribution of income, Brazil has one of the most impoverished populations on the continent. In the late 1990s, the government of President Cardoso has reduced Brazil's hyper-inflation and increased economic growth, increasing the spending power of the country's working and peasant classes. The government has imposed a strict monetary policy and has sold large segments of the country's public-sector enterprises to private firms. Still, much of the country's population continues to live in poverty. In 1995, 43.5 percent of Brazil's population subsisted on the equivalent of less than $2 a day. Population growth slowed in the 35 years between 1960 and 1995 from 3 percent to 1.16 percent, but the national population more than doubled, from nearly 71 million to 162.7 million. Brazil's poulation is white (55 percent), mulatto (38 percent), and black (6 percent).

Poverty Rate

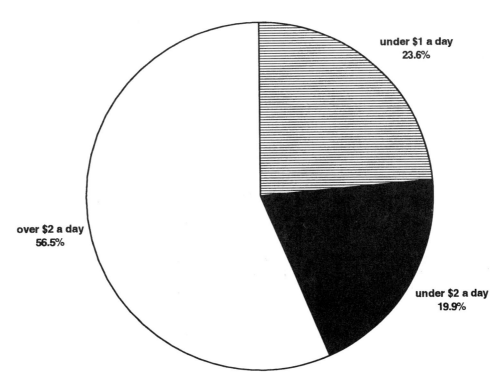

under $1 a day
23.6%

over $2 a day
56.5%

under $2 a day
19.9%

Despite its relatively high gross domestic product of $6,100, Brazil has one of the most unequal distributions of wealth in the world, a fact reflected in its high poverty rates.

Birth Rate per 1,000

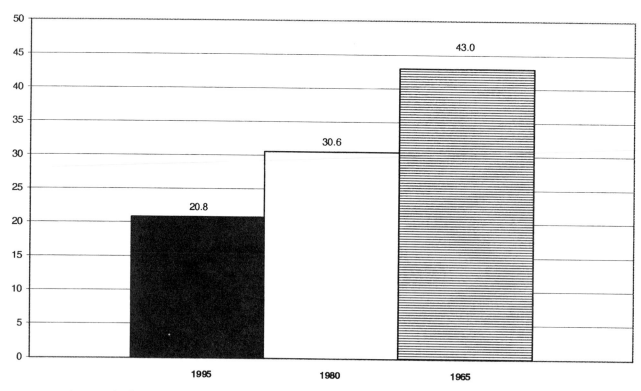

As in much of Latin America, rising educational levels have helped bring down birth rates dramatically over the past 30 years.

CHRONOLOGY

1964	Right-wing military coup ends civilian rule, leads to repressive regime.
1969	Army-approved constitution takes force.
1978	Military begins to prepare country for transfer to civilian rule.
1985	Return to civilian rule.
1990	Conservative Fernando Collor de Mello defeats leftist in national elections.
1992	Collor de Mello is impeached on charges of corruption.

	1995	1980	1965

GEOGRAPHY

AREA (square miles/kilometers)   3,286,473/8,511,965
LAND AREA (square miles/kilometers)   3,265,062/8,456,510
COASTLINE (miles/kilometers)   4,682/7,491

CITIES
CAPITAL   Brasília   1,601,964 (91)
MAJOR CITIES   São Paulo   9,842,059
                           Rio de Janeiro   5,547,033
                           Salvador   2,174,072
                           Belo Horizonte   2,060,804

POPULATION

	1995	1980	1965
TOTAL	162,661,214	118,674,604	70,967,185 (60)
DENSITY (per square mile/kilometer)	47/18	41/16	26/10
ANNUAL GROWTH	1.16%	2.30%	3%
AGE COHORTS			
0–14	31%	n/a	43%
15–64	65%	n/a	54%
65 AND OVER	4%	n/a	3%
MALE	49%		
FEMALE	51%		
URBAN	78%	67.60%	n/a
RURAL	22%	32.40%	n/a
NET MIGRATION RATE	0		

IDENTITY

	1995
ETHNICITY	
WHITE	55%
MULATTO	38%
BLACK	6%
LANGUAGE	
PORTUGUESE (official)	n/a
SPANISH	n/a

	1995	1980	1965
RELIGION			
ROMAN CATHOLIC	70%		
SYNCRETIC AFRICAN FAITHS	5%		

VITAL STATISTICS

	1995	1980	1965
BIRTHS			
BIRTH RATE	20.8	30.6	43
INFANT MORTALITY RATE	57.7	71	170
LIFE EXPECTANCY AT BIRTH	61.6	59.4	42.4
MARRIAGES			
MARRIAGE RATE	5	n/a	7.1
DIVORCE RATE	0.6		
DEATHS			
DEATH RATE	9.2	8.4	12

HOUSEHOLDS

	1995	1980	1965
NUMBER	34,734,715 (91)	n/a	13,475,472 (60)
AVERAGE SIZE	4.2 (91)	n/a	5.1 (60)
FEMALE HEADED	18.1%		

ECONOMICS AND LABOR

	1995
GDP PER CAPITA US$	$6,100
LABOR FORCE M/F (thousands)	40,018.0/22,083.0 90
AGRICULTURE	11,235.0/2,945.0
MINING	764.0/96.0
MANUFACTURING	6,774/2,637.0
UTILITIES	
CONSTRUCTION	3,726.0/97.0
TRADE/FOOD/TOURISM	5,060.0/2,916.0
TRANSPORT/COMMUNICATIONS	2,246.0/194.0
FINANCE/INSURANCE/REAL ESTATE	1,151.0/565.0
SOCIAL AND PERSONAL SERVICES	9,062.0/12,633.0
UNEMPLOYMENT (official)	3.7% (90)
UNION DENSITY	32.1%

	1995	1980	1965
POVERTY			
UNDER $1/DAY	23.6%		
UNDER $2/DAY	43.5%		

TRANSPORT

	1995	1980	1965
JOURNEYS (by transport mode)			
RAILROAD PASSENGER TRIPS			
(millions of miles/kilometers)	8,774/14,038 (94)		
AIR PASSENGER TRIPS (thousands)	17,885 (94)		
VEHICLES (thousands)			
PRIVATE CARS	8,098.4	8,004.6	1,140.8
COMMERCIAL	1,839	1,569.8	989.7

HEALTH AND HEALTH CARE

	1995	1980	1965
HEALTH CARE			
RATE OF PHYSICIANS	1.4	0.8	0.4 (60)
RATE OF HOSPITAL BEDS	3	n/a	3.2 (60)
ACCESS TO SAFE WATER	72%		
ACCESS TO SANITATION	41%		
MEASLES IMMUNIZATION	78%		
HEALTH INDICATORS			
PREGNANT WOMEN WITH ANEMIA	33%		
LOW-BIRTH-WEIGHT BABIES	11%		
CHILD MALNUTRITION	7%		
SMOKING PREVALENCE M/F	40/25%		
TUBERCULOSIS INCIDENCE RATE	0.8		
AIDS/HIV CASES	79,908	58,321 (93)	
TOTAL DEATHS	912,110 (94)		

EDUCATION

	1995	1980	1965
SCHOOL AGE IN SCHOOL			
PRIMARY	112%	98%	120%
SECONDARY	45%	33%	19%
HIGHER	11%	11%	1.9%
FEMALES IN SCHOOL			
OF PRIMARY STUDENTS	n/a	49%	49%
OF SECONDARY STUDENTS	n/a	51%	50%
ADULT ILLITERACY M/F	17/17%	23.7/27.2%	n/a

	1995	1980	1965
COMMUNICATIONS			
RATE OF NEWSPAPERS	55	45	32
RATE OF RADIOS	390	313	106
RATE OF TELEVISIONS	209	124	32

Source: CIA, *The World Factbook, 1997;* ILO, *World Labour Report, 1997;* UN, *Demographic Yearbook, 1997;* UN, *Statistical Yearbook, 1996;* World Bank, *World Development Indicators, 1998.*

BRUNEI DARUSSALAM

The sultanate of Brunei Darussalam is located on two noncontiguous territories in Southeastern Asia on the northeast coast of the island of Borneo. Brunei shares the island with Indonesia and Malaysia. The two 2,228-square-mile (5,770-square-kilometer) territories that compose Brunei border the South China Sea and Malaysia. Brunei's economy is almost totally dominated by the export of unrefined petroleum products. Due to the presence of abundant oil reserves and the relatively small population, Brunei has one of the wealthiest populations in the world, with a per capita gross domestic product of $15,800 in 1995.

As a result of the abundant oil reserves, the government provides the population with an advanced social safety net, including medical care, subsidized housing, and other social services. Brunei's population, which expanded at a rapid annual rate of about 4 percent from the early 1960s to the 1980s, more than tripled from 83,877 in 1960 to nearly 300,000 in 1995. From 1980 to 1995, net migration has declined from 7.8 per 1,000 to 5.2 per 1,000 residents. Malay is the official language, although English and Chinese are also spoken.

		1995	1980	1965
GEOGRAPHY				
AREA (square miles/kilometers)	2,228/5,770			
LAND AREA (square miles/kilometers)	2,035/5,270			
COASTLINE (miles/kilometers)	100/161			
CITIES				
CAPITAL	Bandar Seri Begawan	n/a	49,902 (81)	n/a
POPULATION				
TOTAL		299,939	192,832 (81)	83,877 (60)
DENSITY (per square mile/kilometer)		127/49	101/39	47/18
ANNUAL GROWTH		2.6%	3.9%	4%
AGE COHORTS				
0–14		33%	47%	n/a
15–64		62%	50%	n/a
65 AND OVER		5%	n/a	3%
MALE		53%		
FEMALE		47%		
URBAN		58%	59.4%	n/a
RURAL		42%	40.1%	n/a

	1995	1980	1965
NET MIGRATION RATE	5.2	n/a	7.8

IDENTITY

ETHNICITY

MALAY	64%		
CHINESE	20%		

LANGUAGE

MALAY (official)	n/a		
ENGLISH	n/a		
CHINESE	n/a		

RELIGION

MUSLIM	64%		
BUDDHIST	14%		
CHRISTIAN	8%		

VITAL STATISTICS

BIRTHS

BIRTH RATE	25.5	29.8 (85)	39.3
URBAN BIRTH RATE	39 (91)		
RURAL BIRTH RATE	4 (91)		
INFANT MORTALITY RATE	11.2	12 (85)	75.8
LIFE EXPECTANCY AT BIRTH	71.4	71.4	n/a

MARRIAGES

MARRIAGE RATE	7.1	4.6	8.5 (85)
AVERAGE AGE OF MARRIAGE M/F	27.3/25.1		
DIVORCE RATE	1.1	0.7 (85)	0.5

DEATHS

DEATH RATE	5.1	3.5 (85)	6.3

HOUSEHOLDS

NUMBER	n/a	n/a	8,091 (60)
AVERAGE SIZE	n/a	n/a	4.5 (60)

ECONOMICS AND LABOR

GDP PER CAPITA US$	$15,800

	1995	1980	1965

TRANSPORT

JOURNEYS (by transport mode)
AIR PASSENGER TRIPS (thousands)	769.0 94		

VEHICLES (thousands)
PRIVATE CARS	134,000	43,600	5,400
COMMERCIAL	14,500	7,000	1,600

HEALTH AND HEALTH CARE

HEALTH CARE
RATE OF PHYSICIANS	n/a	n/a	0.1 (60)
RATE OF HOSPITAL BEDS	n/a	n/a	4.8 (60)

HEALTH INDICATORS
AIDS/HIV CASES	6	2 (93)	
TOTAL DEATHS	1,018 (93)		

EDUCATION

SCHOOL AGE IN SCHOOL
PRIMARY	n/a	n/a	134%
SECONDARY	n/a	n/a	44%

FEMALES IN SCHOOL
PRIMARY	n/a	n/a	125%
SECONDARY	n/a	n/a	33%

ADULT ILLITERACY M/F
	n/a	14.8/31.0%	n/a

COMMUNICATIONS

RATE OF NEWSPAPERS	74	n/a	n/a
RATE OF RADIOS	270	212	107
RATE OF TELEVISIONS	241	135	n/a

Source: CIA, *The World Factbook, 1997;* ILO, *World Labour Report, 1997;* UN, *Demographic Yearbook, 1997;* UN, *Statistical Yearbook, 1996;* World Bank, *World Development Indicators, 1998.*

BULGARIA

Bulgaria is located in Southeastern Europe on the western shores of the Black Sea. The 42,822-square-mile (110,910-square-kilometer) country is bordered by Romania on the north, Serbia and Macedonia on the west, and Greece and Turkey on the south. Bulgaria received its independence from the Ottoman Empire in September 1908. For much of the post–World War II era, Bulgaria was in the orbit of the Soviet Union. Following the breakup of the Soviet Union in 1991, Bulgaria adopted a new constitutional system that allowed for greater party competition. During the 1990s, Bulgaria has moved more slowly than its Eastern European counterparts in implementing structural adjustment policies and other economic market reforms. Overall, the country's population remained relatively static between 1965 and 1995. It grew from 8.2 million to 8.7 million between 1965 and 1975, but declined to 8.6 million over the next 20 years. The decline was caused in part by an excess of deaths over births due to a high abortion rate. The country has a life expectancy at birth of 71 years. The vast majority (85 percent) of the country's residents are Bulgarians, but Turks (9 percent) and Gypsies (3 percent) represent large ethnic minorities.

		1995	1980	1965
GEOGRAPHY				
AREA (square miles/kilometers)		42,822/110,910		
LAND AREA (square miles/kilometers)		42,683/110,550		
COASTLINE (miles/kilometers)		221/354		
CITIES				
CAPITAL	Sofia	1,113,674 (93)		
MAJOR CITIES	Plovdiv	345,205		
	Varna	307,200		
	Bourgas	198.439		
	Ruse	170,209		
POPULATION				
TOTAL		8,612,757	8,729,666 (75)	8,226,564
DENSITY (per square mile/kilometer)		197/76	210/81	192/74
ANNUAL GROWTH		0.5%	0.2%	0.8%
AGE COHORTS				
0–14		17%	n/a	24%
15–64		68%	n/a	67%
65 AND OVER		15%	n/a	9%
URBAN		71%	62.1	n/a
RURAL		29%	27.9%	n/a

	1995	1980	1965
NET MIGRATION RATE	9.8	n/a	0

IDENTITY

ETHNICITY

BULGARIAN	85%		
TURKISH	9%		
ROMANISM (Gypsy)	3%		

LANGUAGE

BULGARIAN	n/a		
TURKISH	n/a		

RELIGION

BULGARIAN ORTHODOX	85%		
MUSLIM	13%		
JEWISH	1%		

VITAL STATISTICS

BIRTHS

BIRTH RATE	8.3	13.2 (85)	14.9
URBAN BIRTH RATE	10.2 (93)		
RURAL BIRTH RATE	9.5 (93)		
INFANT MORTALITY RATE	15.8	15.8 (85)	32.2
ABORTION RATE	1,278.80		
LIFE EXPECTANCY AT BIRTH	71	70.9 (85)	69.1

MARRIAGES

MARRIAGE RATE	5	7.2 (85)	8.2
AVERAGE AGE AT MARRIAGE M/F	n/a	24.9/21.1	n/a
DIVORCE RATE	1.1	1.7 (85)	1

DEATHS

DEATH RATE	13.6	12	8.3

HOUSEHOLDS

NUMBER

NUMBER	n/a	3,020,335 (85)	1,964,551 (56)
AVERAGE SIZE	n/a	2.9 (85)	3.7 (56)

TYPE OF HOUSEHOLD

SINGLE	n/a	6.7%	n/a
MARRIED	n/a	74.1%	n/a
WIDOWED	n/a	13.4%	n/a

	1995	1980	1965
DIVORCED/SEPARATED	n/a	5.8%	n/a
FEMALE HEADED	n/a	17.6%	n/a

ECONOMICS AND LABOR

GDP PER CAPITA US$ $4,920

LABOR FORCE (thousands)	3,157.9 (94)
AGRICULTURE	698.1
MANUFACTURING	934.9
CONSTRUCTION	177.8
TRADE/FOOD/TOURISM	389.2
TRANSPORT/COMMUNICATIONS	230.8
FINANCE/INSURANCE/REAL ESTATE	68
SOCIAL AND PERSONAL SERVICES	659.1

UNEMPLOYMENT (official)	12.4% (94)
UNION DENSITY	51.4%

POVERTY	
UNDER $1/DAY	2.6% (92)
UNDER $2/DAY	23.5% (92)

TRANSPORT

JOURNEYS (by transport mode)
RAILROAD PASSENGER TRIPS

(millions of miles/kilometers)	3,162/5,059 (94)
AIR PASSENGER TRIPS (thousands)	789 (94)

VEHICLES (thousands)	
PRIVATE CARS	1,587.9 94
COMMERCIAL	255.4

HEALTH AND HEALTH CARE

HEALTH CARE

	1995	1980	1965
RATE OF PHYSICIANS	3.3	2.5	1.4 (60)
RATE OF HOSPITAL BEDS	10.2	11.1	6.2 (60)
ACCESS TO SAFE WATER	n/a	96	n/a
ACCESS TO SANITATION	99%		
MEASLES IMMUNIZATION	93%		

	1995	**1980**	**1965**
HEALTH INDICATORS			
LOW-BIRTH-WEIGHT BABIES	6%		
SMOKING PREVALENCE M/F	49/17%		
TUBERCULOSIS INCIDENCE RATE	0.4		
AIDS/HIV CASES	35	24 (93)	
TOTAL DEATHS	112,632		

EDUCATION

	1995	**1980**	**1965**
SCHOOL AGE IN SCHOOL			
PRIMARY	94%	98%	105%
SECONDARY	78%	84%	90%
HIGHER	39.0%	16%	12.2%
FEMALES IN SCHOOL			
OF PRIMARY STUDENTS	48%	49%	49%
OF SECONDARY STUDENTS	45%	44%	48%
HIGHER	n/a	18%	14.8 (70)
ADULT ILLITERACY M/F	n/a	n/a	4.8/14.7%

COMMUNICATIONS

	1995	**1980**	**1965**
RATE OF NEWSPAPERS	164	253	172
RATE OF RADIOS	450	395	250
RATE OF TELEVISIONS	260	243	23

Source: CIA, *The World Factbook, 1997;* ILO, *World Labour Report, 1997;* UN, *Demographic Yearbook, 1997;* UN, *Statistical Yearbook, 1996;* World Bank, *World Development Indicators, 1998.*

BURKINA FASO

Burkina Faso is a vast, 105,869-square-mile (274,200-square-kilometer) landlocked country in West Africa. It is north of Côte d'Ivoire, Ghana, Togo, and Benin; west of Niger; and south and east of Mali. Formerly known as Upper Volta, Burkina Faso gained independence from France in August 1960. The country's 1995 population of 10.6 million is continuing to grow at a high annual rate of 2.5 percent. Burkina Faso is one of the poorest countries in the world, with an estimated 1995 per capita gross domestic product of only $700. Nearly three-quarters of Burkina Faso's population resides in rural areas. Most of the population is engaged in subsistence farming and agriculture. The country has a very limited

and unproductive industrial base with few exports. In 1996, the country's leading exports were cotton, gold, and animal products. The population remains mired in poverty. Life expectancy at birth increased from 31.6 years in 1980 to 43.2 years in 1995, but remains one of the lowest in the world. In 1995, the country had a rate of 129.9 infant deaths per 1,000 live births. The leading causes of illness and premature death in Burkina Faso are communicable diseases, due in part to the lack of access to clean water and sanitation facilities. The three major religions in Burkina Faso are Muslim (50 percent), Animism (40 percent), and Roman Catholicism (10 percent).

	1995	1980	1965
GEOGRAPHY			
AREA (square miles/kilometers)	105,869/274,200		
LAND AREA (square miles/kilometers)	105,714/273,800		
COASTLINE	Landlocked		
CITIES			
CAPITAL	Ouagadougou	634,479 (91)	
MAJOR CITY	Bobo Dioulasso	268,926	
POPULATION			
TOTAL	10,623,323	7,919,895 (85)	4,300,000
DENSITY (per square mile/kilometer)	96/37	62/24	n/a
ANNUAL GROWTH	2.5%		
AGE COHORTS			
0–14	48%	n/a	42%
15–64	49%	n/a	55%
65 AND OVER	3%	n/a	3%
MALE	48%		
FEMALE	52%		

	1995	**1980**	**1965**
URBAN	27%		
RURAL	73%		
NET MIGRATION RATE	−1.7		

IDENTITY

ETHNICITY	
MOSSI	n/a
GURUNSI	n/a
SENUFO	n/a

LANGUAGE	
FRENCH (official)	n/a
SUDANIC LANGUAGES	n/a

RELIGION	
MUSLIM	50%
ANIMIST	40%
ROMAN CATHOLIC	10%

VITAL STATISTICS

BIRTHS	**1995**	**1980**	**1965**
BIRTH RATE	47	47.8	n/a
INFANT MORTALITY RATE	129.9	182	n/a
LIFE EXPECTANCY AT BIRTH	43.2	31.6	n/a

MARRIAGES	
MARRIAGE RATE	
AVERAGE AGE AT MARRIAGE M/F	27.6/19

DEATHS			
DEATH RATE	20	20.1	n/a

ECONOMICS AND LABOR

GDP PER CAPITA US$	$700

TRANSPORT

JOURNEYS (by transport mode)	
AIR PASSENGER TRIPS (thousands)	130 (94)

	1995	**1980**	**1965**
VEHICLES			
PRIVATE CARS	32,000	14,700	4,200
COMMERCIAL	24,000	15,200	4,800

HEALTH AND HEALTH CARE

HEALTH CARE			
ACCESS TO SAFE WATER	78%		
ACCESS TO SANITATION	18%		
MEASLES IMMUNIZATION	55%		
RATE OF HOSPITAL BEDS	0.3	n/a	0.5 (60)
HEALTH INDICATORS			
PREGNANT WOMEN WITH ANEMIA	24%		
LOW-BIRTH-WEIGHT BABIES	21%		
CHILD MALNUTRITION	33%		
TUBERCULOSIS INCIDENCE RATE	2.89		
AIDS/HIV CASES	3,966	3,722 (93)	

EDUCATION

SCHOOL AGE IN SCHOOL			
PRIMARY	38%	17%	12%
SECONDARY	8%	3%	1%
HIGHER	1%	negligible	negligible
FEMALES IN SCHOOL			
PRIMARY	39%	37%	8%
SECONDARY	3.4%	3.3%	1.0%
ADULT ILLITERACY M/F	71/91%	79.3/93.9%	n/a

COMMUNICATIONS

	1995	1980	1965
RATE OF NEWSPAPERS	0.3	0.2	0.1
RATE OF RADIOS	27	18	12
RATE OF TELEVISIONS	6	3	0.1

Source: CIA, *The World Factbook, 1997;* ILO, *World Labour Report, 1997;* UN, *Demographic Yearbook, 1997;* UN, *Statistical Yearbook, 1996;* World Bank, *World Development Indicators, 1998.*

BURUNDI

Burundi is a landlocked country located on the eastern shores of Lake Tanganyika in east Central Africa. The 10,733-square-mile (27,830-square-kilometer) country is bordered by the Democratic Republic of the Congo (formerly Zaire) on the northwest, Rwanda on the north, and Tanzania on the east and south. Burundi received independence from a U.N. trusteeship under Belgian administration in July 1962. Since independence, Burundi has been rife with ethnic strife between the Hutu (85 percent of the population) and the Tutsi (14 percent of the population), the country's two leading ethnic groups. The escalation of ethnic unrest in 1993 created mass waves of refugees who fled to Rwanda, Tanzania, and the Democratic Republic of the Congo. The country's economy is dominated by agricultural production, chiefly for subsistence use. The leading export product is coffee, which generates minimal income. At $600 a year, Burundi's per capita gross domestic product is one of the lowest in the world. The country is densely populated, and the population was growing at a pace of 1.5 percent a year in 1995. In the same year, Burundi's life expectancy at birth was 49.3 years, and the country's infant mortality rate was 102 infant deaths per 1,000 live births.

	1995	1980	1965
GEOGRAPHY			
AREA (square miles/kilometers)	10,733/27,830		
LAND AREA (square miles/ kilometers)	9,869/25,650		
COASTLINE (miles/kilometers)	Landlocked		
CITIES			
CAPITAL	Bujumbura	235,440 (90)	
POPULATION			
TOTAL	5,943,057	4,114,135 (79)	3,210,090
DENSITY (per square mile/kilometer)	557/215	438/169	306,118
ANNUAL GROWTH	1.5%	2.7%	2.0%
AGE COHORTS			
0–14	47%	n/a	47%
15–64	50%	n/a	49%
65 AND OVER	3%	n/a	4%
MALE	48%		
FEMALE	52%		

	1995	**1980**	**1965**
URBAN	8%	3.90%	n/a
RURAL	92%	96.10%	n/a
NET MIGRATION RATE	−12.5		

IDENTITY

ETHNICITY
HUTU	85%		
TUTSI	14%		
TWA (PYGMY)	1%		

LANGUAGE
KIRUNDI	n/a		
FRENCH	n/a		

RELIGION
ROMAN CATHOLIC	62%		
ANIMIST	32%		
PROTESTANT	5%		

VITAL STATISTICS

BIRTHS
BIRTH RATE	43	20.4	46.1 (71)
INFANT MORTALITY RATE	102	150	150 (71)
LIFE EXPECTANCY AT BIRTH	49.3	41.5	36.8 (71)

MARRIAGES
MARRIAGE RATE			
AVERAGE AGE AT MARRIAGE M/F	25.7/22.5		

DEATH
DEATH RATE	15.2	20.4	25.6 (71)

HOUSEHOLDS

NUMBER	1,145,479 (90)		
AVERAGE SIZE	4.5 (90)		

ECONOMICS AND LABOR

GDP PER CAPITA US$	$600	

	1995	1980	1965
LABOR FORCE (thousands)	44.7 (91)		
AGRICULTURE	6.6		
MINING	0.3		
MANUFACTURING	6.2		
UTILITIES	0.9		
CONSTRUCTION	2.4		
TRADE/FOOD/TOURISM	3.8		
TRANSPORT/COMMUNICATIONS	2.9		
FINANCE/INSURANCE/REAL ESTATE	1.9		
SOCIAL AND PERSONAL SERVICES	17.7		
UNEMPLOYMENT (official)	7.30%		

TRANSPORT

	1995	1980	1965
JOURNEYS (by transport mode)			
AIR PASSENGER TRIPS (thousands)	9 (94)		
VEHICLES			
PRIVATE CARS	17,000	5,600	n/a
COMMERCIAL	17,500	2,700	n/a

HEALTH AND HEALTH CARE

	1995	1980	1965
HEALTH CARE			
MEASLES IMMUNIZATION	44%		
RATE OF PHYSICIANS	0.1	n/a	negligible (60)
RATE OF HOSPITAL BEDS	0.7	n/a	1.1 (60)
HEALTH INDICATORS			
PREGNANT WOMEN WITH ANEMIA	68%		
CHILD MALNUTRITION	38%		
TUBERCULOSIS INCIDENCE RATE	3.67		
AIDS/HIV CASES	7,024	6,880 (93)	

EDUCATION

	1995	1980	1965
SCHOOL AGE IN SCHOOL			
PRIMARY	70%	26%	26%
SECONDARY	7%	3%	%
HIGHER	1%	1%	negligible
FEMALES IN SCHOOL			
PRIMARY	45%	39%	15%
SECONDARY	38%	25%	0.70%

	1995	1980	1965
ADULT ILLITERACY M/F	51/78%	57.2/74.3% (82)	n/a

COMMUNICATIONS

	1995	1980	1965
RATE OF NEWSPAPERS	3	0.2	0.1 (70)
RATE OF RADIOS	62	39	18 (70)
RATE OF TELEVISIONS	2	0	0

Source: CIA, The World Factbook, 1997; ILO, World Labour Report, 1997; UN, Demographic Yearbook, 1997; UN, Statistical Yearbook, 1996; World Bank, World Development Indicators, 1998.

CAMBODIA

Cambodia is located in Southeastern Asia on the Gulf of Thailand. The 69,900-square-mile (181,040-square-kilometer) country is bordered by Vietnam on the east, Laos on the north, and Thailand on the north and west. Cambodia's fate was inextricably tied to the war between Vietnam and the United States. The secret bombing of alleged Vietcong bases in Cambodia by U.S. war planes gave rise to animosity toward the United States, and caused an escalation of internal hostilities and rivalries for leadership over the nation. The resulting civil war contributed to mass killings of civilians, foreign invasions, and intrigue that continued into the late 1990s. The conflicts have severely eroded Cambodia's economy, leaving the population in abject poverty. In 1995, the country had an estimated per capita gross domestic product of only $660. Most of the population is engaged in subsistence farming. In 1995, Cambodia's population of 10,861,218 was growing at a rate of 2.8 percent. The vast majority of Cambodians are Khmer (90 percent). Vietnamese (5 percent) and Chinese (1 percent) are Cambodia's leading minorities.

	1995	1980	1965
GEOGRAPHY			
AREA (square miles/kilometers)	69,900/181,040		
LAND AREA (square miles/kilometers)	68,154/176,520		
COASTLINE (miles/kilometers)	277/443		
CITIES			
CAPITAL	Phnom Penh	n/a	n/a	393,995 (62)
POPULATION			
TOTAL	10,861,218	n/a	5,740,115 (62)
DENSITY (per square mile/kilometer)	140/54	n/a	91/35 (59)
ANNUAL GROWTH	2.8%	n/a	2.6% (59)
AGE COHORTS			
0–14	45%	n/a	43.8% (59)
15–64	51%	n/a	53% (59)
65 AND OVER	4%	n/a	3% (59)
MALE	50%		
FEMALE	50%		
URBAN	21%		
RURAL	79%		
NET MIGRATION MIGRATION	0		

	1995	1980	1965

IDENTITY

ETHNICITY
KHMER	90%		
VIETNAMESE	5%		
CHINESE	1%		

LANGUAGE
KHMER (official)	n/a		
FRENCH	n/a		

RELIGION
BUDDHIST	95%		

VITAL STATISTICS

BIRTHS
BIRTH RATE	43.5	n/a	41.4 (59)
INFANT MORTALITY RATE	115.7	n/a	127 (59)
LIFE EXPECTANCY AT BIRTH	49.9	n/a	43.8 (59)

DEATHS
DEATH RATE	15.8	n/a	19.7 (59)

ECONOMICS AND LABOR

GDP PER CAPITA US$
	$660		

LABOR FORCE M/F
AGRICULTURE	69/78%		
INDUSTRY	7/8%		
SERVICES	24/14%		

TRANSPORT

VEHICLES
PRIVATE CARS	n/a	n/a	16,400 (59)
COMMERCIAL	n/a	n/a	9,300 (59)

	1995	1980	1965

HEALTH AND HEALTH CARE

HEALTH CARE

	1995	1980	1965
ACCESS TO SAFE WATER	13%		
MEASLES IMMUNIZATION	75		
RATE OF PHYSICIANS	0.1	0.1	n/a
RATE OF HOSPITAL BEDS	2.1		

HEALTH INDICATORS

	1995	1980	1965
CHILD MALNUTRITION	38		
TUBERCULOSIS INCIDENCE RATE	2.35		
AIDS/HIV CASES	86	1 (93)	

EDUCATION

SCHOOL AGE IN SCHOOL

	1995	1980	1965
PRIMARY	122%	n/a	74% (59)
SECONDARY	27%	32%	9% (59)
HIGHER	2%	1%	1.20%

FEMALES IN SCHOOL

	1995	1980	1965
OF PRIMARY STUDENTS	110%	n/a	54% (59)
SECONDARY	38%	n/a	6% (59)

ADULT ILLITERACY M/F	20/47%	n/a	30.1/87.3% (62)

COMMUNICATIONS

	1995	1980	1965
RATE OF NEWSPAPERS	n/a	n/a	7 (59)
RATE OF RADIOS	108	92	168 (59)
RATE OF TELEVISIONS	8	5	1 (59)

Source: CIA, *The World Factbook, 1997;* ILO, *World Labour Report, 1997;* UN, *Demographic Yearbook, 1997;* UN, *Statistical Yearbook, 1996;* World Bank, *World Development Indicators, 1998.*

CAMEROON

Cameroon is located in West Africa on the Gulf of Guinea, an inlet of the Atlantic Ocean. The 183,568-square-mile (475,440-square-kilometer) country is bordered by the Central African Republic on the east; Chad on the north; Nigeria on the west; and Equitorial Guinea, Gabon, and Congo (Brazzaville) on the south. Prior to gaining independence in January 1960, Cameroon was a U.N. trusteeship under French administration. Paul Biya has been president since November 1982. The economy is dominated by the export of oil, petroleum, and agricultural products, including lumber, aluminum, cocoa, beans, coffee, and cotton. Due to the revenue generated from offshore oil drilling, the country's per capita gross domestic product of $1,200 is higher than the GDPs of most other African countries south of the Sahara. The country's population grew rapidly from 4.8 million in 1965 to over 14.2 million in 1995. Cameroon's annual population growth, which approached 3 percent in the mid-1990s, continues to be among the highest in the world in the late 1990s. Cameroon tends to have a healthier population than neighboring African countries. In 1995, the country's average life expectancy at birth was 52.6 years, and its infant mortality rate of 63 per 1,000 live births, high by Western standards, was lower than that of other impoverished countries in Africa.

		1995	1980	1965
GEOGRAPHY				
AREA (square miles/kilometers)		183,568/475,440		
LAND AREA (square miles/kilometers)		181,236/469,400		
COASTLINE (miles/kilometers)		251/402		
CITIES				
CAPITAL	Yaounde	653,670 (86)		
MAJOR CITIES	Douala	1,029,731 (86)		
	Nkongsamba	123,149		
	Maroua	103,653		
POPULATION				
TOTAL		14,261,557	7,090,115 (76)	4,807,000
DENSITY (per square mile/kilometer)		73/28	54/21	28/11
ANNUAL GROWTH		2.9%	3.5%	2.2%
AGE COHORTS				
0–14		46%		
15–64		51%		
65 AND OVER		3%		

	1995	**1980**	**1965**
URBAN	45%	28% (76)	n/a
RURAL	55%	72% (76)	n/a
NET MIGRATION RATE	0	n/a	n/a

IDENTITY

ETHNICITY
CAMEROON HIGHLANDERS	31%
EQUATORIAL BANTU	19%
KIRDI	11%

LANGUAGE
ENGLISH (official)	n/a
FRENCH (official)	n/a

RELIGION
ANIMIST	51%
CHRISTIAN	33%
MUSLIM	16%

VITAL STATISTICS

BIRTHS
	1995	1980	1965
BIRTH RATE	42.5	42.9	49.9
INFANT MORTALITY RATE	63	103	137.2
LIFE EXPECTANCY AT BIRTH	52.6	50.9	35.8

DEATHS
DEATH RATE	13.6	n/a	25.7

ECONOMICS AND LABOR

GDP PER CAPITA US$ $1,200

LABOR FORCE M/F
AGRICULTURE	62/83%
INDUSTRY	12/3%
SERVICES	26/14%

UNION DENSITY 14.7%

	1995	1980	1965

TRANSPORT

JOURNEYS (by transport mode)
RAILROAD PASSENGER TRIPS

(millions of miles/kilometers)	3,162/5,059 (94)		
AIR PASSENGER TRIPS (thousands)	789 (94)		

VEHICLES

PRIVATE CARS	90,000	n/a	17,300
COMMERCIAL	79,000	n/a	21,900

HEALTH AND HEALTH CARE

HEALTH INDICATORS

PREGNANT WOMEN WITH ANEMIA	44%		
LOW-BIRTH-WEIGHT BABIES	13%		
CHILD MALNUTRITION	15%		
TUBERCULOSIS INCIDENCE RATE	1.94		
AIDS/HIV CASES	5,375	3,958 (93)	

HEALTH CARE

ACCESS TO SAFE WATER	41%		
ACCESS TO SANITATION	40%		
MEASLES IMMUNIZATION	51%		
RATE OF PHYSICIANS	0.1	n/a	negligible (60)

RATE OF HOSPITAL BEDS

	2.6	n/a	2.2 (60)

EDUCATION

SCHOOL AGE IN SCHOOL

PRIMARY	88%	98%	78%
SECONDARY	27%	18%	5%
HIGHER	n/a	2	0.3

FEMALES IN SCHOOL

PRIMARY	47	45%	44%
SECONDARY	40%	34%	40%

ADULT ILLITERACY M/F

	25/48%	45.4/70.9%	n/a

	1995	1980	1965
COMMUNICATIONS			
RATE OF NEWSPAPERS	4	8	4
RATE OF RADIOS	146	88	n/a
RATE OF TELEVISIONS	25	n/a	n/a

Source: CIA, *The World Factbook, 1997;* ILO, *World Labour Report, 1997;* UN, *Demographic Yearbook, 1997;* UN, *Statistical Yearbook, 1996;* World Bank, *World Development Indicators, 1998.*

CANADA

Canada is located in North America, north of the United States. The 3,851,792-square-mile (9,976,140-square-kilometer) country has coastlines on the Pacific, Atlantic, and Arctic oceans. Although Canada is the world's second largest country in total area, it is one of the most sparsely populated countries in the world. The country received independence from the United Kingdom in July 1867. It is divided primarily along linguistic lines, and much of Quebec's French-speaking population continues to seek autonomy from the rest of the confederation, where English tends to be the dominant language. Although

Canada continues to depend on exports of natural resources, it has a diversified and industrialized national economy. However, the national economy has been mired in a recession through much of the 1990s. In 1995, Canada had a density of only 3 persons per square mile. Canada's 28.8 million people tend to live in the southern tier of the country along the border with the United States. Canada has a higher average life expectancy at birth (79.1 years) and a lower infant mortality rate (6.2 persons per 1,000 live births) than the United States.

Life Expectancy at Birth

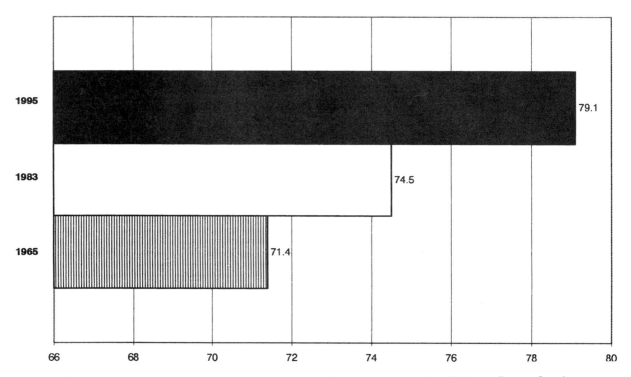

With one of the most admired and successful national health care programs outside of Western Europe, Canada has seen its life expectancy rates climb dramatically in the past three decades.

Divorce Rate

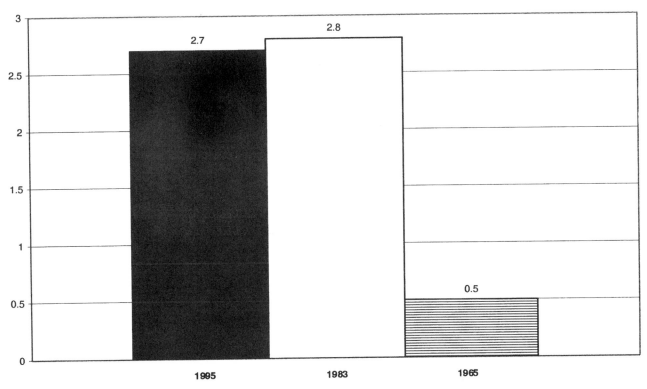

Like its vast neighbor to the south, Canada has seen a significant liberalization of social attitudes in recent decades, including those concerning marriage. Divorce rates have climbed substantially in the past 30 years.

CHRONOLOGY

1966 Canada unveils new maple leaf flag as symbol of break with British heritage.

1967 Nations hosts World's Fair in Montreal, celebrating 100 years of nationhood.

1968 Charismatic Liberal Party candidate Pierre Trudeau wins election and becomes prime minister.

1969 French and English declared official languages of Canada.

1976 Separatist party wins provincial elections in French-speaking Quebec.

1979 Trudeau loses power for last time.

1990 Meech Lake Accords, designed to give Quebec special status, fails to be ratified by provinces.

1997 Separatist referendum in Quebec defeated by narrow majority.

	1995	1980	1965

GEOGRAPHY

AREA (square miles/kilometers)   3,851,792/9,976,140
LAND AREA (square miles/kilometers)   3,569,220/9,220,970
COASTLINE (miles/kilometers)   152,369/243,791

CITIES

		1995
CAPITAL	Ottawa	1,010,288 (94)
MAJOR CITIES	Toronto	4,281,906
	Montreal	3,127,424
	Vancouver	1,774,672
	Edmonton	888,465

POPULATION

	1995	1980	1965
TOTAL	28,820,671	24,343,180 (81)	19,919,000 (66)
DENSITY (per square mile/kilometer)	3	3	n/a
ANNUAL GROWTH	1.1%	1.1%	n/a
AGE COHORTS			
0–14	21%	n/a	33%
15–64	67%	n/a	59%
65 AND OVER	12%	n/a	8%
URBAN	77%	75.7	n/a
RURAL	23%	24.3%	n/a
NET MIGRATION RATE	4.5	n/a	n/a

IDENTITY

ETHNICITY
	1995
BRITISH	40%
FRENCH	27%
OTHER EUROPEAN	20%

LANGUAGE
ENGLISH (official)	n/a
FRENCH (official)	n/a

RELIGION
ROMAN CATHOLIC	45%
UNITED CHURCH	12%
ANGLICAN	8%

	1995	1980	1965

VITAL STATISTICS

BIRTHS

	1995	1980	1965
BIRTH RATE	13.3	15 (83)	19.6
INFANT MORTALITY RATE	6.2	8.5 (83)	23.6
LIFE EXPECTANCY AT BIRTH	79.1	74.5 (83)	71.4

MARRIAGES

	1995	1980	1965
MARRIAGE RATE	5.4	7.4 (83)	7.8
AVERAGE AGE AT MARRIAGE M/F	28.9/26.2		
DIVORCE RATE	2.7	2.8 (83)	0.5

DEATHS

	1995	1980	1965
DEATH RATE	7.2	n/a	7.5

HOUSEHOLDS

	1995	1980	1965
NUMBER	10,018,265 (91)	n/a	4,554,493 (61)
AVERAGE SIZE	2.7 (91)	n/a	3.9 (61)

TYPE OF HOUSEHOLD

	1995
SINGLE	14.9%
MARRIED	56.7%
WIDOWED	10.1%
DIVORCED/SEPARATED	11.3%

ECONOMICS AND LABOR

	1995
GDP PER CAPITA US$	$24,400
LABOR FORCE M/F (thousands)	6,753/5,630 (93)
AGRICULTURE	395.0/155.0
MINING	129.0/20.0
MANUFACTURING	1,297.0/503.0
UTILITIES	108.0/34.0
CONSTRUCTION	585.0/75.0
TRADE/FOOD/TOURISM	1,514.0/1,398.0
TRANSPORT/COMMUNICATIONS	559.0/208.0
FINANCE/INSURANCE/REAL ESTATE	699.0/767.0
SOCIAL AND PERSONAL SERVICES	1,468.0/2,469.0
UNEMPLOYMENT (official)	10.4% (94)
UNION DENSITY	31%

	1995	1980	1965

TRANSPORT

JOURNEYS (by transport mode)
RAILROAD PASSENGER TRIPS
  (millions of miles/kilometers)
AIR PASSENGER TRIPS (thousands)

	1995	1980	1965
RAILROAD PASSENGER TRIPS (millions of miles/kilometers)	900/1,440 (94)		
AIR PASSENGER TRIPS (thousands)	18,105 (94)		

VEHICLES (thousands)

	1995	1980	1965
PRIVATE CARS	13,639.4	10,255.50	5,279.40
COMMERCIAL	3,764.9	2,955.30	1,348.70

HEALTH AND HEALTH CARE

HEALTH CARE

	1995	1980	1965
RATE OF PHYSICIANS	2.2	1.8	1.1 (60)
RATE OF HOSPITAL BEDS	5.4	n/a	11.1 (60)
ACCESS TO SAFE WATER	100%		
ACCESS TO SANITATION	85%		
MEASLES IMMUNIZATION	98%		

HEALTH INDICATORS

	1995	1980	1965
LOW-BIRTH-WEIGHT BABIES	6%		
SMOKING PREVALANCE M/F	31/29%		
TUBERCULOSIS INCIDENCE RATE	0.08		
AIDS/HIV CASES	13,235	10,781 (93)	
TOTAL DEATHS	211,535 (94)		

EDUCATION

SCHOOL AGE IN SCHOOL

	1995	1980	1965
PRIMARY	102%	99%	117%
SECONDARY	106%	88%	52%
HIGHER	n/a	n/a	18.60%

FEMALES IN SCHOOL

	1995	1980	1965
PRIMARY	49%	49%	49%
SECONDARY	49%	49%	51%

	1995	1980	1965
COMMUNICATIONS			
RATE OF NEWSPAPERS	204	221	227
RATE OF RADIOS	992	721	502
RATE OF TELEVISIONS	618	432	267

Source: CIA, *The World Factbook, 1997;* ILO, *World Labour Report, 1997;* UN, *Demographic Yearbook, 1997;* UN, *Statistical Yearbook, 1996;* World Bank, *World Development Indicators, 1998.*

CAPE VERDE

Cape Verde is an island group situated in the Atlantic Ocean about 300 miles (500 kilometers) west of the African country of Senegal. The 1,556-square-mile (4,030-square-kilometer) country received independence from Portugal in July 1975. Cape Verde is lacking in natural resources and produces few agricultural commodities for foreign export. Moreover, the country experiences frequent droughts and water shortages. Much of the country's revenue base is generated through remittances from workers living abroad. In 1995, Cape Verde's out-migration rate was 6.7 percent, owing to the country's limited economic development and lack of job opportunities. The country has a high birth rate of 44.3 live births per 1,000 residents. Creoles (71 percent) and Africans of various nationalities (28 percent) are Cape Verde's two leading ethnic groups. About 54 percent of Cape Verde's national population of nearly 450,000 reside in urban areas.

	1995	1980	1965
GEOGRAPHY			
AREA (square miles/kilometers)	1,556/4,030		
LAND AREA (square miles/kilometers)	1,556/4,030		
COASTLINE (miles/kilometers)	603/965		
CITIES			
CAPITAL	Praia	61,644	
POPULATION			
TOTAL	449,066	295,703	199,661
DENSITY (per square mile/kilometer)	97	81	
ANNUAL GROWTH	2.9%	1.9%	2.0%
AGE COHORTS			
0–14	50%		
15–64	46%		
65 AND OVER	4%		
MALE	47%		
FEMALE	53%		
URBAN	54%		
RURAL	46%		
NET MIGRATION RATE	−6.7	n/a	−0.9

	1995	1980	1965

IDENTITY

ETHNICITY
CREOLE ... 71%
AFRICAN ... 28%
EUROPEAN ... 1%

LANGUAGE
PORTUGUESEA ... n/a
CRIOULO ... n/a

RELIGION
ROMAN CATHOLIC ... n/a

VITAL STATISTICS

BIRTHS

	1995	1980	1965
BIRTH RATE	44.3	31	42.9
INFANT MORTALITY RATE	65.1 (92)	71.4	109.7
LIFE EXPECTANCY AT BIRTH	69.4	60	n/a

MARRIAGES

	1995	1980	1965
MARRIAGE RATE	3.8 (92)	5.4	3.8
AVERAGE AGE AT MARRIAGE M/F	28.1/25.7		

DEATHS

	1995	1980	1965
DEATH RATE	8.3	7.6	10.6

HOUSEHOLDS

NUMBER ... 67,619 (90)
URBAN HOUSEHOLDS ... 30,659
RURAL HOUSEHOLDS ... 36,900

AVERAGE SIZE ... 5 (90)
URBAN ... 4.9
RURAL ... 5.1

FEMALE HEADED ... 38.4%

	1995	1980	1965
ECONOMICS AND LABOR			
GDP PER CAPITA US$	$1,040		
UNION DENSITY	16.90%		
TRANSPORT			
JOURNEYS (by transport mode)			
AIR PASSENGER TRIPS (thousands)	118 (94)		
VEHICLES			
PRIVATE CARS	10,000 (92)	4,000 (81)	
COMMERCIAL	10,000 (92)	1,300 (81)	
HEALTH AND HEALTH CARE			
HEALTH CARE			
RATE OF PHYSICIANS	n/a	n/a	0.1 (60)
RATE OF HOSPITAL BEDS	n/a	n/a	2.5 (60)
HEALTH INDICATORS			
AIDS/HIV CASES	117	82 (93)	
TOTAL DEATHS	2,843 (92)		
EDUCATION			
SCHOOL AGE IN SCHOOL			
PRIMARY	n/a	66%	71%
SECONDARY	n/a	10%	7%
FEMALES IN SCHOOL			
PRIMARY	n/a	n/a	56%
SECONDARY	n/a	n/a	7%
ADULT ILLITERACY M/F	n/a	38.6/61.4%	60.7/82.6% (60)

	1995	1980	1965
COMMUNICATIONS			
RATE OF RADIOS	176	142	18
RATE OF TELEVISIONS	3	0	0

Source: CIA, *The World Factbook, 1997;* ILO, *World Labour Report, 1997;* UN, *Demographic Yearbook, 1997;* UN, *Statistical Yearbook, 1996;* World Bank, *World Development Indicators, 1998.*

CENTRAL AFRICAN REPUBLIC

The Central African Republic (CAR) is a land-locked country located in central Africa. The two Congos (Republic of Congo and Democratic Republic of Congo) border the 240,533-square-mile (622,980-square-kilometer) country on the south, Sudan on the east, Chad on the north, and Cameroon on the west. CAR gained nominal independence from France in December 1958, but the economy remains dependent on French foreign assistance. Between 1975 and 1995, CAR's population expanded from just over 2 million to nearly 3.3 million. But CAR's annual growth rate de-

clined from 2.5 percent in 1975 to 2.1 percent in 1995. In the late 1990s, the majority of the country's population remain subsistence farmers. CAR's principal exports are diamonds, timber products, and agricultural commodities. Throughout the 1970s and 1980s, a military dictatorship plundered the wealth of much of CAR's natural resources for personal use. The country has a low average life expectancy of only 45.9 years and a high infant mortality rate of 101.7 infant deaths per 1,000 live births.

	1995	1980	1965
GEOGRAPHY			
AREA (square miles/kilometers)	240,533/622,980		
LAND AREA (square miles/kilometers)	240,533/622,980		
COASTLINE (miles/kilometers)	landlocked		
CITIES			
CAPITAL	Bangui	n/a	473,817 (84)	n/a
POPULATION			
TOTAL	3,274,426	2,054,610 (75)	1,202,910
DENSITY (per square mile/kilometer)	13/5	10.0/4.0	5.0/2.0
ANNUAL GROWTH	2.10%	2.50%	2.20%
AGE COHORTS			
0–14	44%	n/a	26%
15–64	52%	n/a	73%
65 AND OVER	4%	n/a	1%
MALE	49%		
FEMALE	51%		
URBAN	39%	35.3%	n/a

	1995	**1980**	**1965**
RURAL	61%	64.70%	n/a
NET MIGRATION RATE	−1.5		

IDENTITY

ETHNICITY

BAYA	34%
BANDA	27%
MANDIJA	21%
OTHER	18%

LANGUAGE

FRENCH (official)	n/a
SANGHO	n/a
ARABIC	n/a

RELIGION

PROTESTANT	25%
ROMAN CATHOLIC	25%
ANIMIST	24%
OTHER	26%

VITAL STATISTICS

BIRTHS

BIRTH RATE	40	44.6	48
INFANT MORTALITY RATE	101.7	190	190
LIFE EXPECTANCY AT BIRTH	45.9	34.5	34.5

MARRIAGES

AVERAGE AGE AT MARRIAGE M/F	24.1/19.1 (88)

DEATHS

DEATH RATE	17.6	21.8	30 (60)

HOUSEHOLDS

NUMBER

	519,314 (88)
URBAN	170,149 (88)
RURAL	349,165 (88)

AVERAGE SIZE

	4.7 (88)
URBAN	5.3 (88)
RURAL	4.4 (88)

	1995	1980	1965
TYPE OF HOUSEHOLD			
SINGLE	13.1%		
MARRIED	71.4%		
WIDOWED	8.6%		
DIVORCED/SEPARATED	6.5%		
FEMALE HEADED	18.7%		

ECONOMICS AND LABOR

	1995	1980	1965
GDP PER CAPITA US$	$800		
LABOR FORCE (thousands)	13 (90)		
AGRICULTURE	2.3		
MINING	n/a		
MANUFACTURING	n/a		
UTILITIES	0.8		
CONSTRUCTION	1.3		
TRADE/FOOD/TOURISM	4.3		
TRANSPORT/COMMUNICATIONS	1.5		
FINANCE/INSURANCE/REAL ESTATE	0.3		

TRANSPORT

	1995	1980	1965
JOURNEYS (by transport mode)			
AIR PASSENGER TRIPS (thousands)	123 (94)		
VEHICLES			
PRIVATE CARS	11,900	14,500	3,600
COMMERCIAL	2,800	n/a	5,900

HEALTH AND HEALTH CARE

	1995	1980	1965
HEALTH INDICATORS			
PREGNANT WOMEN WITH ANEMIA	67%		
LOW-BIRTH-WEIGHT BABIES	15%		
CHILD MALNUTRITION	23%		
TUBERCULOSIS INCIDENCE RATE	1.39		
AIDS/HIV CASES	4,939	4,240 (93)	
HEALTH CARE			
ACCESS TO SAFE WATER	18%	n/a	n/a
MEASLES IMMUNIZATION	70%		

	1995	**1980**	**1965**
RATE OF PHYSICIANS	negligible	negligible	negligible (60)
RATE OF HOSPITAL BEDS	0.9	1.6	1.5 (60)

EDUCATION

SCHOOL AGE IN SCHOOL			
PRIMARY	58%	71%	59%
SECONDARY	10%	14%	2%
HIGHER	1%	1%	n/a

FEMALES IN SCHOOL			
PRIMARY	n/a	37%	26%
SECONDARY	n/a	25%	1%

ADULT ILLITERACY M/F	32/48%	67/85%	n/a

COMMUNICATIONS

	1995	**1980**	**1965**
RATE OF NEWSPAPERS	1	n/a	0.3 (62)
RATE OF RADIOS	72	52	25
RATE OF TELEVISIONS	5	0	0

Source: CIA, *The World Factbook, 1997;* ILO, *World Labour Report, 1997;* UN, *Demographic Yearbook, 1997;* UN, *Statistical Yearbook, 1996;* World Bank, *World Development Indicators, 1998.*

CHAD

Chad, a landlocked country in north central Africa, is bounded by six countries: Libya on the north, Sudan on the east, Central African Republic on the south, Cameroon and Nigeria on the southwest, and Niger on the west. Chad has a land area of 495,753 square miles (1,284,000 square kilometers). Chad gained independence from France in August 1960 and has since been ruled by a series of military governments supported by competing internal and external groups. In the late 1990s, Chad was undergoing an uneasy transition to democracy. Nearly 80 percent of Chad's population resides in rural areas and engages in subsistence farming as a primary economic activity. In 1995, Chad's per capita gross domestic product (GDP) was only $600 per year, among the lowest in the world. Between 1964 and 1995, Chad's population nearly doubled from 3,254,000 to 6,976,845. By 1995, the country's population was continuing to grow at a rapid rate of 2.7 percent per year. French and Arab are Chad's two official languages. Half of the country's people are Muslim, 25 percent are Christian, and 25 percent are adherents of various Animist faiths.

	1995	1980	1965
GEOGRAPHY			
AREA (square miles/kilometers)	495,753/1,284,000		
LAND AREA (square miles/kilometers)	486,178/1,259,200		
COASTLINE (miles/kilometers)	landlocked		
CITIES			
CAPITAL	N'Djamena 613,000	n/a	179,000 (72)
POPULATION			
TOTAL	6,976,845	n/a	3,254,000 (64)
DENSITY	13/5	10.0/4	n/a
CHANGE	2.7%	2.3%	1.5%
AGE COHORTS			
0–14	44%		46%
15–64	53%		50%[1]
65 AND OVER	3%		3.6%[2]
MALE	48%		
FEMALE	52%		
URBAN	21%	18.4% (78)	n/a
RURAL	79%	81.6% (78)	n/a

	1995	1980	1965
NET MIGRATION RATE	0		

IDENTITY

ETHNICITY
ARAB	n/a		
SARA	n/a		

LANGUAGE
FRENCH (official)	n/a		
ARABIC (official)	n/a		
SARA	n/a		

RELIGION
MUSLIM	50%		
CHRISTIAN	25%		
ANIMIST	25%		

VITAL STATISTICS

BIRTHS
BIRTH RATE	44.3	44.2	45
INFANT MORTALITY RATE	122	160	160
LIFE EXPECTANCY AT BIRTH	47.6	32	31

DEATHS
DEATH RATE	17.4	21.4	31 (64)

ECONOMICS AND LABOR

GDP PER CAPITA US$	$600		

LABOR FORCE M/F (thousands)	11.8/0.7 (91)		
AGRICULTURE	1.3/0.1		
MINING	0.2/0.0		
MANUFACTURING	5.2/0.1		
UTILITIES	0.0/0.0		
CONSTRUCTION	1.0/0.0		
TRADE/FOOD/TOURISM	0.6/0.1		
TRANSPORT/COMMUNICATIONS	0.9/0.1		
FINANCE/INSURANCE/REAL ESTATE	0.3/0.0		
SOCIAL AND PERSONAL SERVICES	2.1/0.3		

	1995	1980	1965

TRANSPORT

JOURNEYS (by transport mode)
RAILROAD PASSENGER TRIPS   86 (94)
  (millions of miles/kilometers)

VEHICLES

PRIVATE CARS	9,000	n/a	3,300
COMMERCIAL	7,000	n/a	4,800

HEALTH AND HEALTH CARE

HEALTH CARE

ACCESS TO SAFE WATER	24%		
ACCESS TO SANITATION	21%		
MEASLES IMMUNIZATION	24%		
RATE OF PHYSICIANS	0.7		
RATE OF HOSPITAL BEDS	n/a	n/a	0.7 (60)

HEALTH INDICATORS

PREGNANT WOMEN WITH ANEMIA	37%		
LOW-BIRTH-WEIGHT BABIES	11%		
TUBERCULOSIS INCIDENCE RATE	1.67		
AIDS/HIV CASES	3,457	1,597 (93)	

EDUCATION

SCHOOL AGE IN SCHOOL

PRIMARY	55%	38% (84)	30%
SECONDARY	9%	6% (84)	1%
HIGHER	1%	0.3% (84)	negligible

FEMALES IN SCHOOL

PRIMARY	32%	18% (84)	11%
SECONDARY	1.7%	2% (84)	0.2%

ADULT ILLITERACY M/F   38/65%   59.5/89.1%   n/a

	1995	1980	1965
COMMUNICATIONS			
RATE OF NEWSPAPERS	0.4	0.2	0.4
RATE OF RADIOS	245	168	7
RATE OF TELEVISIONS	1	0	0

FOOTNOTES
1. Ages 15–59.
2. Age 60 and over.

Source: CIA, *The World Factbook, 1997;* ILO, *World Labour Report, 1997;* UN, *Demographic Yearbook, 1997;* UN, *Statistical Yearbook, 1996;* World Bank, *World Development Indicators, 1998.*

CHILE

Chile consists of a long coastal strip of land that extends about 3,750 miles (6,000 kilometers) from the Pacific Coast border with Peru southeast to the Strait of Magellan on the South Atlantic Ocean border with Argentina. Peru and Bolivia border the 292,259-square-mile (756,950-square-kilometer) country on the north and northeast, and Argentina borders it on the east. In 1973, the Chilean military, in a bloody coup backed by the United States, overthrew the democratically elected government of Salvador Allende. In 1989, the military junta was forced to turn power over to a democratically elected government. Though democratic rule was suspended for nearly two decades, the government was credited with accelerating economic growth through market reforms and privatization. Although Chile has a fairly high annual per capita gross domestic product (GDP) of $8,000, income inequality remains extremely high for a modern economy. In 1992, nearly 40 percent of the country's population subsisted on less than the equivalent of $2 a day. The country has almost doubled in population from 1965 to 1995, but annual growth rates have significantly declined from 2.3 percent to 1.2 percent. Chile has a comparatively high average life expectancy and a low infant mortality rate.

	1995	1980	1965
GEOGRAPHY			
AREA (square miles/kilometers)	292,259/756,950		
LAND AREA (square miles/kilometers)	289,252/748,900		
COASTLINE (miles/kilometers)	4,022/6,435		
CITIES			
CAPITAL	Santiago 4,229,970		
MAJOR CITIES	Concepción 350,268		
	Viña del Mar 322,220		
	Puente Alto 318,898		
	Valparaíso 282,168		
POPULATION			
TOTAL	14,333,528	11,275,440 (82)	7,374,115 (60)
DENSITY (per square mile/kilometer)	49/19	41/16	31/12
ANNUAL CHANGE	1.2%	1.7%	2.3%
AGE COHORTS			
0–14	29%	n/a	28%
15–64	65%	n/a	68%
65 AND OVER	6%	n/a	4%

	1995	1980	1965
MALE	49%		
FEMALE	51%		
URBAN	84%	81%	n/a
RURAL	16%	19%	n/a
NET MIGRATION RATE	0	n/a	0.2 (64)

IDENTITY

ETHNICITY	
EUROPEAN/EUROPEAN-INDIAN	95%
INDIAN	3%

LANGUAGE	
SPANISH	100%

RELIGION	
ROMAN CATHOLIC	89%
PROTESTANT	11%

VITAL STATISTICS

	1995	1980	1965
BIRTHS			
BIRTH RATE	18.1	22.3 (84)	36
URBAN BIRTH RATE	21.2 (94)		
RURAL BIRTH RATE	17.6 (94)		
INFANT MORTALITY RATE	12	19.6	107.1
ABORTION RATE	0.22		
LIFE EXPECTANCY AT BIRTH	74.5	64.4	52.3
MARRIAGES			
MARRIAGE RATE	6.7	7.3 (84)	7.6
AVERAGE AGE AT MARRIAGE M/F	25.8/23.4		
DEATHS			
DEATH RATE	5.7	6.3 (84)	12

HOUSEHOLDS

	1995	1980	1965
NUMBER	3,293,779 (92)	n/a	1,322,896 (60)
AVERAGE SIZE	4 (92)	n/a	5.4 (62)
FEMALE HEADED	25.3%		

	1995	1980	1965

ECONOMICS AND LABOR

	1995	1980	1965
GDP PER CAPITA US$	$8,000		
LABOR FORCE M/F (thousands)	3,375.0/1,614.8 (94)		
AGRICULTURE	720.1/88.8		
MINING	82.9/3.5		
MANUFACTURING	594.9/223.9		
UTILITIES	30.6/3.0		
CONSTRUCTION	350.7/10.2		
TRADE/FOOD/TOURISM	530.0/410.7		
TRANSPORT/COMMUNICATIONS	328.2/43.1		
FINANCE/INSURANCE/REAL ESTATE	192.5/106.0		
SOCIAL AND PERSONAL SERVICES	542.8/725.6		
UNEMPLOYMENT (official)	5.9% (94)		
UNION DENSITY	15.9%		
POVERTY			
UNDER $1/DAY	15% (92)		
UNDER $2/DAY	38.5 (92)		

TRANSPORT

	1995	1980	1965
JOURNEYS (by transport mode)			
RAILROAD PASSENGER TRIPS	510/816.0 (94)		
(millions of miles/kilometers)			
AIR PASSENGER TRIPS (thousands)	2,962.0 (94)		
VEHICLES			
PRIVATE CARS	914,000	448,500	97,700
COMMERCIAL	208,300	219,600	105,400

HEALTH AND HEALTH CARE

	1995	1980	1965
HEALTH CARE			
ACCESS TO SANITATION	83%		
MEASLES IMMUNIZATION	93%		
RATE OF PHYSICIANS	1.1	n/a	0.6 (60)
RATE OF HOSPITAL BEDS	3.2	3.4	3.6 (60)

	1995	**1980**	**1965**
HEALTH INDICATORS			
PREGNANT WOMEN WITH ANEMIA	13%		
LOW-BIRTH-WEIGHT BABIES	7%		
CHILD MALNUTRITION	1%		
SMOKING PREVALENCE M/F	38/25%		
TUBERCULOSIS INCIDENCE RATE	0.67		
AIDS/HIV CASES	1,429	970 (93)	
TOTAL DEATHS	75,445 (94)		

EDUCATION

SCHOOL AGE IN SCHOOL			
PRIMARY	99%	109%	116%
SECONDARY	69%	53%	33%
HIGHER	27%	12%	5.1%
FEMALES IN SCHOOL			
PRIMARY STUDENTS	49%	49%	49%
SECONDARY STUDENTS	54%	55%	51%
ADULT ILLITERACY	5%	5.6%	n/a

COMMUNICATIONS

RATE OF NEWSPAPERS	147	115 (82)	118
RATE OF RADIOS	345	292	203
RATE OF TELEVISIONS	211	110	7

Source: CIA, *The World Factbook, 1997;* ILO, *World Labour Report, 1997;* UN, *Demographic Yearbook, 1997;* UN, *Statistical Yearbook, 1996;* World Bank, *World Development Indicators, 1998.*

CHINA

China, the world's most populous country, is located in east central Asia. China is the world's third largest country, following Russia and Canada, with a land area of 3,705,390 square miles (9,596,960 square kilometers). China continues to be governed by the Communist Party that gained power in the 1949 revolution that defeated the Chinese Nationalists. Since the late 1970s, however, the Communist Party has opened the economy to foreign trade and investment, implemented market reforms that have eroded many social protections and, as a result of a lack of reg- ulations, degraded the physical environment. Though the economy has industrialized rapidly, poverty, particularly in rural areas, has increased dramatically. By the mid-1990s, up to 100 million migrant workers roamed the countryside and cities in search of work. China is the world's most populous country with over 1.2 million people in 1995. The country's population growth has declined from 1.5 percent in 1953 to 1.0 percent in 1995, equivalent to growth rates in most industrialized countries. About 70 percent of the national population continues to live in rural areas.

Population Growth

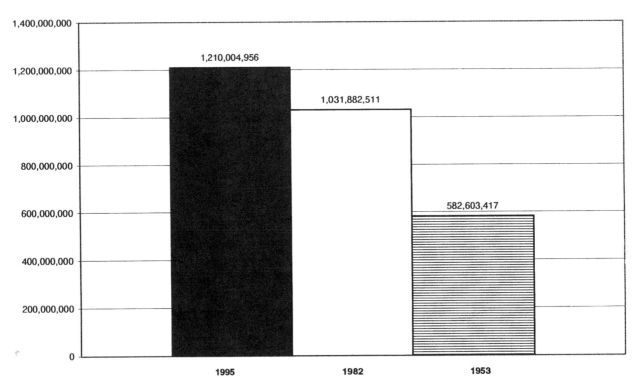

Though it has instituted one of the most draconian birth-control policies in the world, China is still experiencing population growth on an epic scale. This is due to demographic lag, whereby a generally young population means a high fertility rate.

Higher Education

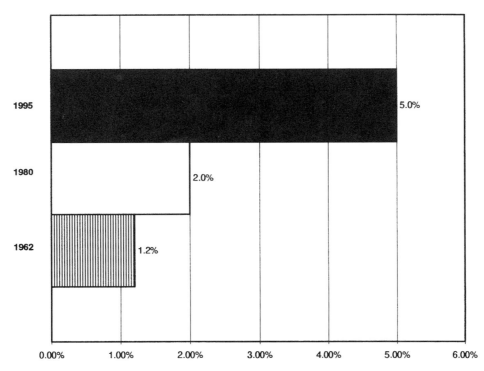

Since the rise of reformist, pro-market governments, China has put a great deal of resources into higher education, partly to help the country progress economically and partly to overcome the anti-intellectualism of the Cultural Revolution of the 1960s.

CHRONOLOGY

1966 Communist Party Chairman Mao Zedong launches radical Cultural Revolution.

1970 Cultural Revolution ends.

1971 Mainland China takes over Taiwan's seat at United Nations.

1972 President Richard Nixon visits China.

1976 Mao and Zhou Enlai, architects of China's communist revolution, die.

1979 Conservative Deng Xiaoping defeats radical Gang of Four to take power in China; he launches economic reforms.

1989 Chinese pro-democracy movement crushed when troops open fire on protesters in Tiananmen Square in Beijing, killing thousands.

1997 Chinese economic progress undermined by economic crisis in Asia.

	1995	**1980**	**1965**

GEOGRAPHY

AREA (square miles/kilometers)   3,705,390/9,596,960
LAND AREA (square miles/kilometers)   3,600,931/9,326,410
COASTLINE (miles/kilometers)   9,063/14,500

CITIES
CAPITAL	Beijing	7,362,426 (90)
MAJOR CITIES	Shanghai	8,205,598
	Tianjin	5,804,023
	Qingdao	5,124,668
	Shenyang	4,655,280

POPULATION

	1995	**1980**	**1965**
TOTAL	1,210,004,956	1,031,882,511 (82)	582,603,417 (53)
DENSITY (per square mile/kilometer)	329/127	285/110	192/74
ANNUAL GROWTH	1.00%	1.2%	1.5%

AGE COHORTS
0–14	26%
15–64	67%
65 AND OVER	7%

	1995	**1980**	**1965**
URBAN	30%	20.6% (82)	n/a
RURAL	70%	79.4% (82)	n/a

NET MIGRATION RATE	−0.3

IDENTITY

ETHNICITY
HAN CHINESE	91.9%
ZHUANG	n/a
UYGUR	n/a

LANGUAGE
MANDARIN	n/a
CANTONESE	n/a
WU	n/a

	1995	**1980**	**1965**
RELIGION			
TAOIST	n/a		
BUDDHIST	n/a		
MUSLIM	n/a		

VITAL STATISTICS

BIRTHS			
BIRTH RATE	17	19	34 (57)
INFANT MORTALITY RATE	44.5	39	n/a
LIFE EXPECTANCY AT BIRTH	69.6	67.8	n/a

MARRIAGES			
AVERAGE AGE AT MARRIAGE M/F	23.8/22.1		

DEATHS			
DEATH RATE	6.9	6.7	11 (57)

HOUSEHOLDS

NUMBER	276,911,767 (90)
AVERAGE SIZE	4 (90)

ECONOMICS AND LABOR

GDP PER CAPITA US$	$2,900

LABOR FORCE M/F (thousands)	66,867.0/34,220 (89)
AGRICULTURE	5,076/2867
MINING	6,218/1,589
MANUFACTURING	20,292/13,144
UTILITIES	1,089/395
CONSTRUCTION	4,550/1,233
TRADE/FOOD/TOURISM	5,639/4,167
TRANSPORT/COMMUNICATIONS	4,947/1,453
FINANCE/INSURANCE/REAL ESTATE	864/492
SOCIAL AND PERSONAL SERVICES	17,396/8,637

UNEMPLOYMENT M/F (official)	0.8/1.1 (94)
UNION DENSITY	54.70%

	1995	1980	1965
POVERTY			
UNDER $1/DAY	22.2%		
UNDER $2/DAY	57.8%		

TRANSPORT

	1995	1980	1965
JOURNEYS (by transport mode)			
RAILROAD PASSENGER TRIPS	227,253/363,605 (94)		
(millions of miles/kilometers)			
AIR PASSENGER TRIPS (thousands)	37,498 (94)		

HEALTH AND HEALTH CARE

	1995	1980	1965
HEALTH CARE			
ACCESS TO SAFE WATER	90%		
ACCESS TO SANITATION	21%		
MEASLES IMMUNIZATION	89%		
RATE OF PHYSICIANS	1.6	0.9	n/a
RATE OF HOSPITAL BEDS	2.4	2	n/a
HEALTH INDICATORS			
PREGNANT WOMEN WITH ANEMIA	52%		
LOW-BIRTH-WEIGHT BABIES	6%		
CHILD MALNUTRITION	16%		
SMOKING PREVALENCE M/F	61/7%		
TUBERCULOSIS INCIDENCE RATE	0.85		
AIDS/HIV CASES	117	36 (93)	
TOTAL DEATHS	7,800,000 (93)		

EDUCATION

	1995	1980	1965
SCHOOL AGE IN SCHOOL			
PRIMARY	118%	113%	89% (70)
SECONDARY	67%	46%	24%
HIGHER	5%	2	1.2% (62)
FEMALES IN SCHOOL			
PRIMARY STUDENTS	47%	45%	n/a
SECONDARY STUDENTS	44%	40%	n/a
ADULT ILLITERACY M/F	27.0/10.0%	20.8/48.9% (82)	n/a

	1995	1980	1965
COMMUNICATIONS			
RATE OF NEWSPAPERS	43	34	19 (55)
RATE OF RADIOS	184	55	14
RATE OF TELEVISIONS	38	4	0.2

Source: CIA, The World Factbook, 1997; ILO, World Labour Report, 1997; UN, Demographic Yearbook, 1997; UN, Statistical Yearbook, 1996; World Bank, World Development Indicators, 1998.

COLOMBIA

Colombia, located in northwestern South America, borders the Caribbean Sea on the north and the Pacific Ocean on the west. Venezuela borders the 439,737-square-mile (1,138,920-square-kilometer) country on the northeast, Panama on the northwest, Ecuador on the southwest, Peru on the South, and Brazil on the southeast. Colombia's government has been embroiled in a civil war against rebels who control large regions of the country. In 1995, the country's annual per capita gross national product (GNP) was $5,300. Still, over 21 percent of the population survives on incomes of under $2 a day. Colombia has a comparatively high life expectancy at birth of 72.8 years and an infant mortality rate of 37 infant deaths per 1,000 live births. The three primary ethnic divisions in Colombia are mestizo (58 percent), white (20 percent), and mulatto (14 percent). About 95 percent of the country's population is Roman Catholic.

		1995	1980	1965
GEOGRAPHY				
AREA (square miles/kilometers)		439,737/1,138,920		
LAND AREA (square miles/kilometers)		401,042/1,038,700		
COASTLINE (miles/kilometers)		2,005/3,208		
CITIES				
CAPITAL	Bogotá	n/a	3,974,813 (85)	n/a
MAJOR CITIES	Medellín	n/a	1,452,392 (85)	n/a
	Cali	n/a	1,369,331 (85)	n/a
	Barranquilla	n/a	917,486 (85)	n/a
	Cartagena	n/a	513,986 (85)	n/a
POPULATION				
TOTAL		36,813,161	22,551,811 (73)	17,484,508 (64)
DENSITY (per square mile/kilometer)		80/31	65/25	41/16
ANNUAL GROWTH		1.7%		
AGE COHORTS				
0–14		32%	n/a	47%
15–64		64%	n/a	48%
65 AND OVER		4%	n/a	5%
MALE		49%		
FEMALE		51%		
URBAN		73%	65.4% (83)	n/a
RURAL		27%	34.6% (83)	n/a

	1995	**1980**	**1965**
NET MIGRATION RATE	−0.1	n/a	0

IDENTITY

ETHNICITY
MESTIZO	58%		
WHITE	20%		
MULATTO	14%		

LANGUAGE
SPANISH	n/a		

RELIGION
ROMAN CATHOLIC	95%		

VITAL STATISTICS

BIRTHS
BIRTH RATE	21.3	31	44
INFANT MORTALITY RATE	37	50	82.4
LIFE EXPECTANCY AT BIRTH	72.8	63.7	45

MARRIAGES
MARRIAGE RATE	2.3	3.6	4.8

DEATHS
DEATH RATE	4.7	7.7	14

HOUSEHOLDS

NUMBER	n/a	5,251,273 (85)	n/a
AVERAGE SIZE	n/a	5.2	n/a

ECONOMICS AND LABOR

GDP PER CAPITA US$	$5,300		

LABOR FORCE M/F (thousands)   2,819.5/2,021.7 (92)
AGRICULTURE	53.0/15.4		
MINING	15.0/4.3		
MANUFACTURING	660.8/477.9		
UTILITIES	27.1/5.4		
CONSTRUCTION	288.3/16.3		

	1995	1980	1965
TRADE/FOOD/TOURISM	680.0/552.7		
TRANSPORT/COMMUNICATIONS	266.2/32.1		
FINANCE/INSURANCE/REAL ESTATE	216.0/130.0		
SOCIAL AND PERSONAL SERVICES	604.4/781.3		
UNION DENSITY	7%		
POVERTY			
UNDER $1/DAY	7.4% (91)		
UNDER $2/DAY	21.7% (91)		

TRANSPORT

	1995	1980	1965
JOURNEYS (by transport mode)			
RAILROAD PASSENGER TRIPS	10/16 (92)		
(millions of miles/kilometers)			
AIR PASSENGER TRIPS (thousands)	7,686 (94)		
VEHICLES (thousands)			
PRIVATE CARS	761.7	522.7	112.9
COMMERCIAL	672.6	294.9	104.4

HEALTH AND HEALTH CARE

	1995	1980	1965
HEALTH CARE			
ACCESS TO SAFE WATER	76%		
ACCESS TO SANITATION	63%		
MEASLES IMMUNIZATION	77%		
RATE OF PHYSICIANS	0.9	n/a	0.4 (60)
RATE OF HOSPITAL BEDS	1.4	1.6	2.8 (60)
HEALTH INDICATORS			
PREGNANT WOMEN WITH ANEMIA	24		
LOW-BIRTH-WEIGHT BABIES	9		
CHILD MALNUTRITION	8		
SMOKING PREVALENCE M/F	35/19		
TUBERCULOSIS INCIDENCE RATE	167		
AIDS/HIV CASES	6,541	4,453 (93)	
TOTAL DEATHS	163,692 (91)		

	1995	1980	1965
EDUCATION			
SCHOOL AGE IN SCHOOL			
PRIMARY	114%	124%	88%
SECONDARY	67%	41%	17%
HIGHER	17%	9%	2.40%
FEMALES IN SCHOOL			
PRIMARY	114%	124%	90%
SECONDARY	n/a	41%	16%
ADULT ILLITERACY M/F	9/9%	13.6/16.1% (81)	25.2/28.9%
COMMUNICATIONS			
RATE OF NEWSPAPERS	63	53	52
RATE OF RADIOS	177	124	172
RATE OF TELEVISIONS	118	85	20

Source: CIA, *The World Factbook, 1997*; ILO, *World Labour Report, 1997*; UN, *Demographic Yearbook, 1997*; UN, *Statistical Yearbook, 1996*; World Bank, *World Development Indicators, 1998*.

COMOROS

The Comoros are a group of islands located in the Indian Ocean northeast of southern Africa. The Comoros, with a total area of 839 square miles (2,170 square kilometers) are located on the northern extension of the Mozambique Channel, east of the African coast and northwest of Madagascar. Comoros, which gained independence from France in July 1975, claims sovereignty over Mayotte, an island to the southeast that continues to be administered by France. The Comoros have few natural resources, and most of the population is engaged in subsistence agriculture. In 1995, the annual per capita gross domestic product (GDP) was $700, among the lowest in the world. Between 1966 and 1995, the population of the Comoros increased from 183,133 to 569,237. The country is continuing to grow at a rapid annual rate of 3.6 percent. In 1995, the country's life expectancy at birth was 58.7 years. Although the Comoros education system is limited by global standards, access to education has significantly improved. By 1980, nearly 75 percent of all children were attending primary schools.

	1995	1980	1965
GEOGRAPHY			
AREA (square miles/kilometers)	839/2,170		
LAND AREA (square miles/kilometers)	839/2,170		
COASTLINE (miles/kilometers)	213/340		
CITIES			
CAPITAL	Moroni	n/a	17,267	n/a
POPULATION			
TOTAL	569,237	385,890	183,133 (66)
DENSITY (per square mile/kilometer)	756/292	531/205	n/a
ANNUAL GROWTH	3.6%	3.1%	2.7%
AGE COHORTS			
0–14	48%	n/a	44%
15–64	49%	n/a	49%
65 AND OVER	3%	n/a	5%
MALE	49%		
FEMALE	51%		
URBAN	31%	23.3	n/a
RURAL	69%	77.70%	n/a
NET MIGRATION RATE	0	n/a	0 (63)

	1995	1980	1965

IDENTITY

ETHNICITY
ANTALOTE	n/a		
CAFRE	n/a		
MAKOA	n/a		

LANGUAGE
ARABIC (official)	n/a		
FRENCH (official)	n/a		
COMORAN	n/a		

RELIGION
SUNNI MUSLIM	86%		
ROMAN CATHOLIC	14%		

VITAL STATISTICS

BIRTHS
BIRTH RATE	45.8	46.4	n/a
INFANT MORTALITY RATE	88.9	88	n/a
LIFE EXPECTANCY AT BIRTH	58.7	50	n/a

MARRIAGES
MARRIAGE RATE	n/a	8.3	n/a
AVERAGE AGE AT MARRIAGE M/F	28.6/22.4		
DIVORCE RATE	n/a	1.3	n/a

DEATHS
DEATH RATE	10.3	15.9	n/a

HOUSEHOLDS

NUMBER	71,995 (91)		
AVERAGE SIZE	6.2 (91)		

TYPE OF HOUSEHOLD
SINGLE	2.7%		
MARRIED	82.6%		
WIDOWED	3.3%		
DIVORCED/SEPARATED	11.4%		

FEMALE HEADED	24.5%		

	1995	1980	1965
ECONOMICS AND LABOR			
GDP PER CAPITA US$	$700		
TRANSPORT			
JOURNEYS (by transport mode) AIR PASSENGER TRIPS (thousands)	26.0 (94)		
VEHICLES			
PRIVATE CARS	n/a	1,000 (87)	n/a
COMMERCIAL	n/a	4,000 (87)	n/a
HEALTH AND HEALTH CARE			
HEALTH CARE			
RATE OF PHYSICIANS	n/a	n/a	0.1 (60)
RATE OF HOSPITAL BEDS	n/a	n/a	2.1 (60)
HEALTH INDICATORS			
AIDS/HIV CASES	15	10 (93)	
EDUCATION			
SCHOOL AGE IN SCHOOL			
PRIMARY	n/a	91%	27%
SECONDARY	n/a	23%	3%
FEMALES IN SCHOOL			
PRIMARY	n/a	76%	14%
SECONDARY	n/a	36%	1%
ADULT ILLITERACY M/F	n/a	44/60%	33.9/48.3%
COMMUNICATIONS			
RATE OF NEWSPAPERS	n/a	n/a	n/a
RATE OF RADIOS	129	120	n/a
RATE OF TELEVISIONS	0	0	0

Source: CIA, *The World Factbook, 1997;* ILO, *World Labour Report, 1997;* UN, *Demographic Yearbook, 1997;* UN, *Statistical Yearbook, 1996;* World Bank, *World Development Indicators, 1998.*

CONGO, DEMOCRATIC REPUBLIC OF (ZAIRE)

The second largest country in Africa (after Sudan), the Democratic Republic of Congo (formerly Zaire), is located in the heart of the continent, bordered by no less than nine countries. A collection of various kingdoms and ethnic groups in the precolonial era, the Congo was conquered by the Belgians in the late nineteenth century. In 1960, it received its independence from its colonial master and plunged immediately into a civil war between factions and regions. With the rise to power of Joseph Mobutu (later Mobutu Sese Seko), the country, covering some 905,564 square miles, achieved a certain amount of political stability, but at a high price. One of the most repressive and corrupt of African dictators, Mobutu systematically robbed the country of much of its mineral wealth. In the early 1990s, protests among the nation's 46.5 million persons—

up from 12.73 million in 1965—spread from the capital to the eastern reaches of the vast Central African realm. In 1997, rebel leader Laurent Kabila, backed by the armed forces of Rwanda, swept across the country, eventually forcing Mobutu into exile. Kabila revived the original independence name of the country—Mobutu had changed the name of the country to Zaire in 1971—and attempted to establish a less corrupt regime. The international community claimed that Kabila's Rwandan forces had massacred tens of thousands of political and ethnic opponents. But an international commission trying to unearth the truth was forced to leave the country in 1998. During the summer of that year, a new rebellion broke out, this time against Kabila by his former Rwandan backers.

	1995	1980	1965
GEOGRAPHY			
AREA (square miles/kilometers)	905,564/2,345,410		
LAND AREA (square miles/kilometers)	875,521/2,267,600		
COASTLINE (miles/kilometers)	23/37		
CITIES			
CAPITAL	Kinshasa	n/a	2,664,309 (84)	
MAJOR CITIES	Lubumbashi	n/a	564,830	
	Luluabourg	n/a	n/a	506,033 (72)
	Mbuji-Mayi	n/a	486,235	
	Kisangani	n/a	317,581	
POPULATION			
TOTAL	46,498,539	29,671,407 (84)	12,733,590 (57)
DENSITY (per square mile/kilometer)	53/21	33/13	15/6
ANNUAL GROWTH	1.67%	2.9	

	1995	1980	1965
AGE COHORTS			
0–14	48%	n/a	39.4%
15–64	49%	n/a	n/a
65 AND OVER	3%	5.6%[1]	n/a
MALE	49%		
FEMALE	51%		
URBAN	n/a	34.2%	n/a
RURAL	n/a	65.8%	n/a
NET MIGRATION RATE	−14.56		

IDENTITY

ETHNICITY

BANTU (Mongo, Luba, Kongo)	55%
HAMITIC (Mangbetu-Azande)	45%

LANGUAGE

FRENCH	n/a
LINGALA	n/a
KINGWANA	n/a
KIKONGO	n/a
TSHILUBA	n/a

RELIGION

ROMAN CATHOLIC	50%
PROTESTANT	20%
KIMBANGUIST	10%
MUSLIM	10%
OTHER INDIGENOUS	10%

VITAL STATISTICS

BIRTH

	1995	1980	1965
BIRTH RATE	48.1	45.1	n/a
INFANT MORTALITY RATE	108	104	n/a
LIFE EXPECTANCY AT BIRTH	46.7	50	n/a

DEATHS

	1995	1980	1965
DEATH RATE	16.9	15.8	n/a

	1995	1980	1965

ECONOMICS AND LABOR

GDP PER CAPITA US$	$400		

TRANSPORT

JOURNEYS (by transport mode)	469. (90)		
RAILROAD PASSENGER TRIPS	178. (94)		
(millions of miles/kilometers)			
VEHICLES (thousands)			
CARS	145.1	75.4	42.5
COMMERCIAL VEHICLES	92.8	n/a	32.9

HEALTH AND HEALTH CARE

RATE OF PHYSICIANS	0.1	n/a	0 (60)
RATE OF HOSPITAL BEDS	1.4	n/a	6.1 (60)
AIDS/HIV CASES	29,434	26,161 (93)	

EDUCATION

SCHOOL AGE IN SCHOOL			
PRIMARY	72%	80%	86%
SECONDARY	26%	24%	6%
HIGHER	2%	1%	24%
FEMALES IN SCHOOL			
PRIMARY	43%	72% (75)	58%
SECONDARY	30%	8% (75)	2%
ADULT ILLITERACY M/F	13/32%	21.4/55.3% (85)	n/a

	1995	1980	1965
COMMUNICATIONS			
RATE OF NEWSPAPERS	3	2	n/a
RATE OF RADIOS	97	56	3
RATE OF TELEVISIONS	2	0	n/a

FOOTNOTE
1. 1957, 55 and over.

Source: CIA, *The World Factbook, 1997*; ILO, *World Labour Report, 1997*; UN, *Demographic Yearbook, 1997*; UN, *Statistical Yearbook, 1996*; World Bank, *World Development Indicators, 1998*.

CONGO, REPUBLIC OF

The Republic of Congo is located in West Africa, northwest of the Democratic Republic of Congo (formerly Zaire). The 132,046-square-mile (342,000-square-kilometer) country borders the Atlantic Ocean on the southwest, Gabon on the west, Cameroon on the northwest, and the Central African Republic on the northeast. In 1992, Congo made the transition from military rule to democracy with national elections. In 1997, however, hostilities broke out between two competing parties backed by militias. Elections were suspended after the conflict escalated into armed bat-tles in Brazzaville, Congo's capital, and in major cities. The vast majority of Congo's productive population is engaged in subsistence agricultural activities. The country has a growing oil industry, which generates a significant share of foreign reserves. Congo's per capita gross domestic product (GDP) is $3,100 per year, higher than other countries in Africa, owing to the substantial revenues earned from oil exploration and extraction and the relatively small population. The country has a population of 2.5 million that was growing at an annual rate of 2.2 percent in 1995.

	1995	1980	1965
GEOGRAPHY			
AREA (square miles/kilometers)	132,046/342,000		
LAND AREA (square miles/kilometers)	131,853/341,500		
COASTLINE (miles/kilometers)	106/169		
CITIES			
CAPITAL	Brazzaville n/a	596,200 (84)	n/a
MAJOR CITIES	Pointe-Noire n/a	298,014	n/a
POPULATION			
TOTAL	2,527,841	1,300,120 (74)	581,600 (61)
DENSITY (per square mile/kilometer)	19/7	10/4	4/2
ANNUAL GROWTH	2.2%	2.6%	1.6%
AGE COHORTS			
0–14	43%	n/a	41%
15–64	53%	n/a	57%
65 AND OVER	4%	n/a	2%
URBAN	59%		
RURAL	41%		
NET MIGRATION RATE	0		

	1995	1980	1965
IDENTITY			
ETHNICITY			
KONGO	48%		
SANGHA	20%		
TEKE	17%		
LANGUAGE			
FRENCH (official)	n/a		
LINGALA	n/a		
KIKONGO	n/a		
RELIGION			
CHRISTIAN	50%		
ANIMIST	48%		
MUSLIM	2%		
VITAL STATISTICS			
BIRTHS			
BIRTH RATE	39.2	44.5	43 (58)
INFANT MORTALITY RATE	91.7	180	104 (58)
LIFE EXPECTANCY AT BIRTH	45.8	46.5	38.9 (58)
DEATHS			
DEATH RATE	17.4	18.6	20 (58)
HOUSEHOLDS			
NUMBER	n/a	n/a	13,428 (58)
AVERAGE SIZE	n/a	n/a	4 (58)
ECONOMICS AND LABOR			
GDP PER CAPITA US$	$3,100		
LABOR FORCE M/F			
AGRICULTURE	58/81%		
INDUSTRY	20/5%		
SERVICES	23/14%		

	1995	1980	1965

TRANSPORT

JOURNEYS (by transport mode)
RAILROAD PASSENGER TRIPS   272/435 (91)
  (millions of miles/kilometers)

AIR PASSENGER TRIPS (thousands)   232 (94)

VEHICLES
PRIVATE CARS   26,000
COMMERCIAL   20,100

HEALTH AND HEALTH CARE

HEALTH CARE

	1995	1980	1965
MEASLES IMMUNIZATION	41		
RATE OF PHYSICIANS	0.3	n/a	0.1 (60)
RATE OF HOSPITAL BEDS	3.3	n/a	4.9 (60)

HEALTH INDICATORS

PREGNANT WOMEN WITH ANEMIA	76		
LOW-BIRTH-WEIGHT BABIES	15		
CHILD MALNUTRITION	34		
TUBERCULOSIS INCIDENCE RATE	3.33		
AIDS/HIV CASES	7,773		

EDUCATION

SCHOOL AGE IN SCHOOL

	1995	1980	1965
PRIMARY	114%	n/a	123%
SECONDARY	53%	n/a	10%
HIGHER	n/a	n/a	1.20%

FEMALES IN SCHOOL

	1995	1980	1965
PRIMARY	110%	n/a	100%
SECONDARY	41%	n/a	5%

ADULT ILLITERACY M/F   17/33%

	1995	1980	1965
COMMUNICATIONS			
RATE OF NEWSPAPERS	8	n/a	0.5 (63)
RATE OF RADIOS	115	6,473	n/a
RATE OF TELEVISIONS	7	n/a	0.9

Source: CIA, *The World Factbook, 1997;* ILO, *World Labour Report, 1997;* UN, *Demographic Yearbook, 1997;* UN, *Statistical Yearbook, 1996;* World Bank, *World Development Indicators, 1998.*

COSTA RICA

Costa Rica is located in Central America, bordering the Caribbean Sea on the east and the Pacific Ocean on the southwest. Nicaragua borders the 19,730-square-mile (51,100-square-kilometer) country on the north, and Panama borders on the southeast. Under the constitution of 1949, Costa Rica has a democratic government. The country has a national guard and police force but no standard army. Costa Rica has a vibrant economy that produces a significantly higher standard of living than any country in Central America and a social welfare system that has produced higher levels of economic equality than other countries in the region. Still, 43.8 percent of the population remains in poverty. Between 1963 and 1995, Costa Rica's population increased nearly threefold from just over 1.3 million to nearly 3.5 million. Though the population continues to expand at a rapid annual rate of 2.1 percent, growth is almost half the rate of the early 1960s. Due in part to the universal availability of quality health care, Costa Rica has a comparatively high life expectancy at birth of 75.7 years and a low infant mortality rate of 13 deaths per 1,000 live births.

	1995		**1980**	**1965**
GEOGRAPHY				
AREA (square miles/kilometers)	19,730/51,100			
LAND AREA (square miles/kilometers)	19,560/50,660			
COASTLINE (miles/kilometers)	806/1,290			
CITIES				
CAPITAL	San Jose	n/a	315,909 (94)	n/a
MAJOR CITIES	Alajuela	n/a	170,080	n/a
	Cartago	n/a	117,004	n/a
POPULATION				
TOTAL	3,463,083 (93)		2,416,809 (84)	1,336,274
DENSITY (per square mile/kilometer)	175/68		122/47	68/26
ANNUAL GROWTH	2.1%		n/a	4.1%
AGE COHORTS				
0–14	35%		n/a	48%
15–64	61%		n/a	49%
65 AND OVER	4%		n/a	3%
MALE	50%			
FEMALE	50%			

	1995	1980	1965
URBAN	50%	43.8%	n/a
RURAL	50%	56.2%	n/a
NET MIGRATION RATE	0.9	n/a	0

IDENTITY

ETHNICITY
WHITE AND MESTIZO	96%
BLACK	2%
INDIAN	1%

LANGUAGE
SPANISH	n/a
ENGLISH	n/a

RELIGION
ROMAN CATHOLIC	95%
PROTESTANT	5%

VITAL STATISTICS

BIRTHS
BIRTH RATE	23.8	32.7 (84)	n/a
URBAN BIRTH RATE	25.2	32.7 (84)	n/a
RURAL BIRTH RATE	30.7	32.7 (84)	n/a
INFANT MORTALITY RATE	13		
LIFE EXPECTANCY AT BIRTH	75.7	68.4 (84)	63.4 (63)

MARRIAGES
MARRIAGE RATE	6.5	8.5 (84)	6 (63)
DIVORCE RATE	1.1	1 (84)	0.1 (63)

DEATHS
DEATH RATE	4.1	4.5 (84)	9

ECONOMICS AND LABOR

GDP PER CAPITA US$	$5,400

LABOR FORCE M/F (thousands)	801.2/336.4 (94)
AGRICULTURE	226.4/17.2
MINING	2.1/0.0
MANUFACTURING	131.6/71.9
UTILITIES	14.7/2.2

	1995	1980	1965
CONSTRUCTION	73.1/1.4		
TRADE/FOOD/TOURISM	126.1/83.6		
TRANSPORT/COMMUNICATIONS	51.3/7.1		
FINANCE/INSURANCE/REAL ESTATE	37.7/12.9		
SOCIAL AND PERSONAL SERVICES	130.8/137.2		
UNEMPLOYMENT (official)	4.2% (94)		
UNION DENSITY	13.1%		
POVERTY			
UNDER $1/DAY	18.9% (89)		
UNDER $2/DAY	43.8% (89)		

TRANSPORT

	1995	1980	1965
JOURNEYS (by transport mode)			
RAILROAD PASSENGER TRIPS	483/773 (94)		
(millions of miles/kilometers)			
VEHICLES			
PRIVATE CARS	238,500	88,100	22,700
COMMERCIAL	127,100	65,900	12,100

HEALTH AND HEALTH CARE

	1995	1980	1965
HEALTH CARE			
ACCESS TO SANITATION	94%		
RATE OF PHYSICIANS	0.9	n/a	0.4 (60)
RATE OF HOSPITAL BEDS	2.5	3.3	4.5
HEALTH INDICATORS			
PREGNANT WOMEN WITH ANEMIA	28		
LOW-BIRTH-WEIGHT BABIES	7		
CHILD MALNUTRITION	2		
SMOKING PREVALENCE M/F	35/20		
TUBERCULOSIS INCIDENCE RATE	15		
AIDS/HIV CASES	922	586 (93)	
TOTAL DEATHS	12,253		

EDUCATION

	1995	1980	1965
SCHOOL AGE IN SCHOOL			
PRIMARY	107%	105%	110%
SECONDARY	59%	48%	31%
HIGHER	32%	21%	4.90%

	1995	**1980**	**1965**
FEMALES IN SCHOOL			
PRIMARY	105%	103%	106%
SECONDARY	52%	54%	31%
ADULT ILLITERACY M/F	5/5%	6.0/6.8% (85)	11.4/11.8% (73)

COMMUNICATIONS

	1995	1980	1965
RATE OF NEWSPAPERS	101	110	77
RATE OF RADIOS	258	83	97
RATE OF TELEVISIONS	142	68	37

Source: CIA, The World Factbook, 1997; ILO, World Labour Report, 1997; UN, Demographic Yearbook, 1997; UN, Statistical Yearbook, 1996; World Bank, World Development Indicators, 1998.

CÔTE D'IVOIRE

Côte d'Ivoire is located in West Africa on the Gulf of Guinea, a part of the Atlantic Ocean. Ghana borders the 124,502-square-mile (322,460-square-kilometer) country on the east, Burkino Faso on the northeast and Mali on the northwest, and Guinea and Liberia on the west. The country gained independence from France in August 1960. Felix Houphouet-Boigny served as the country's president from November 1960 to his death in December 1993, a period under which Côte d'Ivoire's economy prospered relative to its neighbors in West Africa. Much of the economic growth is attributed to the export of coffee, cocoa, and other agricultural commodities, primarily to France and other Western European markets.

During the 1990s, however, the country's economy has been subject to downward fluctuations in international market prices for its agricultural exports. Côte d'Ivoire's relative prosperity has not significantly alleviated the poverty among most of the country's population. In 1995, nearly 55 percent of the country's population was subsisting on the equivalent of less than $2 a day. Due to the growth in fertility and the growing access to medicine and clean water between 1965 and 1995, the country's population more than quadrupled to 14,762,445. But by 1995, the country's average life expectancy of 46.7 years continued to remain low.

	1995	1980	1965
GEOGRAPHY			
AREA (square miles/kilometers)	124,502/322,460		
LAND AREA (square miles/kilometers)	122,780/318,000		
COASTLINE (miles/kilometers)	199/515		
CITIES			
CAPITAL	Yamoussoukro	106,786 (88)	
MAJOR CITIES	Abidjan	1,929,079	
	Bouaké	329,850	
	Daloa	121,842	
	Korhogo	109,445	
POPULATION			
TOTAL	14,762,445	6,709,600 (75)	3,300,000
DENSITY (per square mile/kilometer)	114/44	78/30	27/10
ANNUAL GROWTH	2.9%	3.7%	3.0%
AGE COHORTS			
0–14	48%	n/a	43%
15–64[1]	50%	n/a	53%
65 AND OVER[2]	2%	n/a	3.6%

	1995	1980	1965
MALE	51%		
FEMALE	49%		
URBAN	44%	42.5% (83)	n/a
RURAL	56%	57.5% (83)	n/a
NET MIGRATION RATE	2.4		

IDENTITY

ETHNICITY

BAOULE	23%
BETE	18%
SENOUFOU	15%

LANGUAGE

FRENCH (official)	n/a
DIOULA	n/a

RELIGION

MUSLIM	60%
ANIMIST	25%
CHRISTIAN	12%

VITAL STATISTICS

BIRTHS

	1995	1980	1965
BIRTH RATE	42.5	45.6	56.1
INFANT MORTALITY RATE	91.7	138	
LIFE EXPECTANCY AT BIRTH	46.7	50.5	

MARRIAGES

AVERAGE AGE AT MARRIAGE M/F	27.6/19.8

DEATHS

	1995	1980	1965
DEATH RATE	15.7	15.6	33.3

HOUSEHOLDS

NUMBER	1,798,799 (88)
AVERAGE SIZE	66 (88)

	1995	1980	1965

ECONOMICS AND LABOR

GDP PER CAPITA US$	$1,500		
LABOR FORCE (thousands)	385.0 (90)		
AGRICULTURE	53.3		
MANUFACTURING	60		
CONSTRUCTION	17.4		
TRADE/FOOD/TOURISM	25.9		
TRANSPORT/COMMUNICATIONS	53.5		
SOCIAL AND PERSONAL SERVICES	174.9		
UNEMPLOYED	140,300		
UNION DENSITY	13%		
POVERTY			
UNDER $1/DAY	17.7% (88)		
UNDER $2/DAY	54.8% (88)		

TRANSPORT

JOURNEYS (by transport mode)			
RAILROAD PASSENGER TRIPS	n/a	361/578 (87)	n/a
(millions of miles/kilometers)			
AIR PASSENGER TRIPS (thousands)	157 (94)		
VEHICLES			
PRIVATE CARS	155,300	146,100	32,000
COMMERCIAL	90,300	70,600	23,200

HEALTH AND HEALTH CARE

HEALTH CARE			
ACCESS TO SAFE WATER	72%		
ACCESS TO SANITATION	54%		
MEASLES IMMUNIZATION	57%		
RATE OF PHYSICIANS	0.1	n/a	0 (60)
RATE OF HOSPITAL BEDS	0.8	n/a	1.7 (60)
HEALTH INDICATORS			
LOW-BIRTH-WEIGHT BABIES	14%		
CHILD MALNUTRITION	24		
TUBERCULOSIS INCIDENCE RATE	1.96		
AIDS/HIV CASES	25,236	18,670 (93)	

	1995	1980	1965
EDUCATION			
SCHOOL AGE IN SCHOOL			
PRIMARY	69%	75%	60%
SECONDARY	23%	19%	6%
HIGHER	4%	3%	0.40%
FEMALES IN SCHOOL			
PRIMARY	67%	60%	60%
SECONDARY	15%	13%	2%
ADULT ILLITERACY M/F	50/70%	46.9/68.9%	n/a
COMMUNICATIONS			
RATE OF NEWSPAPERS	7	10	3
RATE OF RADIOS	143	122	18
RATE OF TELEVISIONS	60	38	0.5

FOOTNOTES
1. Ages 15–59.
2. Ages 60 and over.

Source: CIA, The World Factbook, 1997; ILO, World Labour Report, 1997; UN, Demographic Yearbook, 1997; UN, Statistical Yearbook, 1996; World Bank, World Development Indicators, 1998.

CROATIA

Croatia is located in southeastern Europe on the Adriatic Sea. The 21,829-square-mile (56,538-square-kilometer) country is located in the southwestern region of the former Yugoslavia on the western border of Bosnia and Herzegovina. Croatia borders Serbia on the northeast and Hungary and Slovenia on the north. The country achieved formal independence in June 1991 amid the breakup of Yugoslavia. Croatia has a developed industrial economy; however, the continued instability in the region has hindered economic stability and renewed growth. In 1995, Croatia's population of 5 million was growing at the slow annual rate of 0.6 percent, due in part to a low birth rate. In the same year, the country had a relatively high life expectancy at birth of 72.8 years and a low infant mortality rate of 10.2 infant deaths per 1,000 residents. Croatians are the country's dominant ethnic majority (78 percent), although there is a sizable Serbian minority (12 percent).

1995[1]

GEOGRAPHY

AREA (square miles/kilometers)	21,829/56,538	
LAND AREA (square miles/kilometers)	21,780/56,410	
COASTLINE (miles/kilometers)	3,619/5,790	
CITIES		
CAPITAL	Zagreb	867,717 (91)
MAJOR CITIES	Split	200,459
	Rijeka	167,964
	Osijek	129,792

POPULATION

TOTAL	5,004,112
DENSITY (per square mile/kilometer)	132/51
ANNUAL GROWTH	0.6%
AGE COHORTS	
0–14	18%
15–64	69%
65 AND OVER	13%
MALE	48%
FEMALE	52%

	1995[1]
URBAN	64%
RURAL	36%
NET MIGRATION RATE	7.3

IDENTITY

ETHNICITY
CROAT	78%
SERB	12%
MUSLIM	1%

LANGUAGE
SERBO-CROATIAN	96%

RELIGION
ROMAN CATHOLIC	77%
EASTERN ORTHODOX	11%
MUSLIM	1%
OTHER	11%

VITAL STATISTICS

BIRTHS
BIRTH RATE	9.8
URBAN BIRTH RATE	12.2 (91)
RURAL BIRTH RATE	9.2 (91)
INFANT MORTALITY RATE	10.2
LIFE EXPECTANCY AT BIRTH	72.8

MARRIAGES
MARRIAGE RATE	4.8
AVERAGE AGE AT MARRIAGE M/F	28/23.8
DIVORCE RATE	1

DEATHS
DEATH RATE	11.3

ECONOMICS AND LABOR

GDP PER CAPITA US$	$4,300
LABOR FORCE M/F (thousands)	601.6/506.8 (93)
AGRICULTURE	42.9/14.6
MINING	5.8/1.1

	1995[1]
MANUFACTURING	214.2/156.4
UTILITIES	21.9/4.9
CONSTRUCTION	58.3/8.7
TRADE/FOOD/TOURISM	73.6/101.2
TRANSPORT/COMMUNICATIONS	74.8/23.7
FINANCE/INSURANCE/REAL ESTATE	16.2/24.7
SOCIAL AND PERSONAL SERVICES	93.9/171.5
UNEMPLOYMENT (official)	17% (93)

TRANSPORT

JOURNEYS (by transport mode)

RAILROAD PASSENGER TRIPS	601/962 (94)
(millions of miles/kilometers)	
AIR PASSENGER TRIPS (thousands)	624 (94)

VEHICLES

| PRIVATE CARS | 698,400 (94) |
| COMMERCIAL | 68,500 (94) |

HEALTH AND HEALTH CARE

HEALTH CARE

ACCESS TO SAFE WATER	96%
ACCESS TO SANITATION	68%
MEASLES IMMUNIZATION	90%
RATE OF PHYSICIANS	2
RATE OF HOSPITAL BEDS	5.9

HEALTH INDICATORS

LOW-BIRTH-WEIGHT BABIES	8%
SMOKING PREVALENCE M/F	37/38%
TUBERCULOSIS INCIDENCE RATE	0.65
AIDS/HIV CASES	92
TOTAL DEATHS	49,482 (94)

EDUCATION

SCHOOL AGE IN SCHOOL

PRIMARY	86%
SECONDARY	82%
HIGHER	28%

	1995[1]
FEMALES IN SCHOOL	
PRIMARY	85%
SECONDARY	65%

COMMUNICATIONS

RATE OF NEWSPAPERS	532
RATE OF RADIOS	301
RATE OF TELEVISIONS	338

FOOTNOTE

1. Part of Yugoslavia; no data available for 1980 and 1965.

Source: CIA, *The World Factbook, 1997;* ILO, *World Labour Report, 1997;* UN, *Demographic Yearbook, 1997;* UN, *Statistical Yearbook, 1996;* World Bank, *World Development Indicators, 1998.*

CUBA

Cuba is located on a large island 90 miles south of the U.S. State of Florida. Cuba borders the Caribbean Sea on the south, the Gulf of Mexico on the northwest, and the Atlantic Ocean on the east. The 42,803-square-mile (110,860-square-kilometer) island country is the largest in the Caribbean. Since the July 1959 Cuban Revolution, the country has nationalized the economy and has instituted programs to foster economic equality, including universal access to health care, education, and housing. The economic programs have contributed to the improvement of the quality of life of the majority of the population. In the early 1990s, however, due to the continuation of a 40-year U.S. embargo and the sudden suspension of Soviet economic assistance, Cuba has endured a period of severe economic retrenchment. The government responded by instituting "special programs" that included some market reforms that did not interfere with the strong system of social protection. By the late 1990s, the country was beginning to emerge from the economic hardships earlier in the decade. The country has a high average life expectancy at birth of 75.1 years and a low infant mortality of 9.4 infant deaths per 1,000 live births. The strong education system trains many Cubans for professional careers. The country's literacy rate is about the same as that of the United States.

Ethnicity

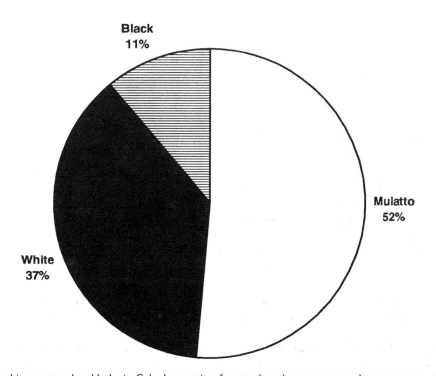

Though whites outnumber blacks in Cuba by a ratio of more than three to one, mulattos, persons of mixed European and African heritage, make up more than 50 percent of the country's population. In the years following the 1959 Cuban Revolution, social reforms significantly improved the socioeconomic status of both blacks and mulattos.

Infant Mortality Rate

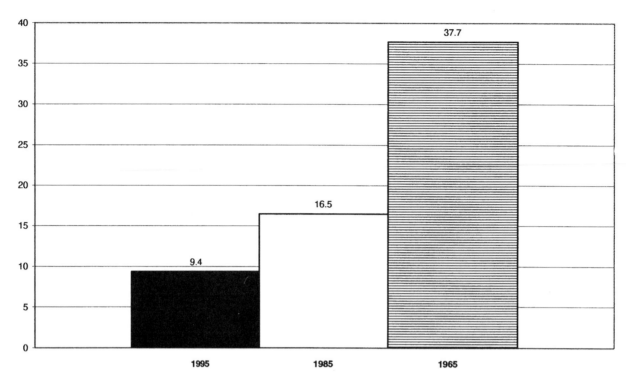

Health care has been another major priority of the Cuban government in recent decades. Its emphasis on rural health care has done much to create dramatically lower rates of infant mortality.

CHRONOLOGY

1959   Revolution. Fidel Castro takes power in Cuba.
1961   The United States severs ties with Cuba; U.S.-sponsored invasion of right-wing exiles at the Bay of Pigs ends in defeat.
1962   The United States announces economic boycott of Cuba; Soviet efforts to place nuclear missiles on island blocked by United States.
1965   Refugees to United States pass 300,000 in number.
1967   Ernesto "Che" Guevara, popular revolutionary leader of Cuba, is killed in Bolivia.
1975   Castro sends troops to defend Angolan government.
1976   Right-wing Cuban exiles blow up Cuban jetliner in Barbados.
1988   Cuba withdraws troops from Africa after signing agreement with United States and South Africa.
1991   Collapse of Soviet Union leads to cutoff in aid and collapse in economy.
1997   Helms-Burton law reenforces economic boycott and angers U.S.'s European trading partners.
1998   Pope John Paul II visits islands and advocates closer ties between United States and Cuba.

	1995	1980	1965

GEOGRAPHY

AREA (square miles/kilometers)	42,803/110,860		
LAND AREA (square miles/kilometers)	42,803/110,860		
COASTLINE (miles/kilometers)	2,334/3,735		

CITIES				
CAPITAL	Havana	2,175,888 (93)		
MAJOR CITIES	Santiago de Cuba	430,494		
	Camagüey	294,332		
	Holguín	242,085		
	Guantánamo	207,796		

POPULATION

	1995	1980	1965
TOTAL	10,951,334	9,723,605 (81)	7,630,700
DENSITY (per square mile/kilometer)	259/100	236/91	178/69
ANNUAL GROWTH	n/a	0.7%	n/a

AGE COHORTS			
0–14	22%	n/a	37%
15–64	68%	n/a	59%
65 AND OVER	10%	n/a	4%

	1995	1980	1965
MALE	51%		
FEMALE	49%		

	1995	1980	1965
URBAN	76%	68.40%	n/a
RURAL	24%	31.60%	n/a

	1995	1980	1965
NET MIGRATION RATE	−1.5	n/a	2.3

IDENTITY

ETHNICITY			
MULATTO	51%		
WHITE	37%		
BLACK	11%		

LANGUAGE			
SPANISH	n/a		

	1995	1980	1965
RELIGION			
ROMAN CATHOLIC	85%		
SANTERIA	n/a		
PROTESTANT	n/a		

VITAL STATISTICS

	1995	1980	1965
BIRTHS			
BIRTH RATE	13.4	18 (85)	34–36
URBAN BIRTH RATE	15.5 (91)		
RURAL BIRTH RATE	18.1 (91)		
INFANT MORTALITY RATE	9.4	16.5 (85)	37.7
ABORTION RATE	843.9 (94)		
LIFE EXPECTANCY AT BIRTH	75.1	74 (85)	n/a
MARRIAGES			
MARRIAGE RATE	17.7	7.9 (85)	8.8
DIVORCE RATE	6	2.9 (85)	1.2
DEATHS			
DEATH RATE	7.4	6.4 (85)	9

ECONOMICS AND LABOR

	1995
GDP PER CAPITA US$	$1,300
LABOR FORCE M/F (thousands)	2,135.6/1,309.8 (88)
AGRICULTURE	519.4/142.7
MINING	29.9/5.3
MANUFACTURING	452.2/230.9
UTILITIES	29.2/9.7
CONSTRUCTION	280.1/42.5
TRADE/FOOD/TOURISM	223.3/213.2
TRANSPORT/COMMUNICATIONS	187.4/54.8
FINANCE/INSURANCE/REAL ESTATE	33.5/29.6
SOCIAL AND PERSONAL SERVICES	380.6/581.1
UNION DENSITY	70.2%

TRANSPORT

	1995
JOURNEYS (by transport mode)	
RAILROAD PASSENGER TRIPS	1,807/2,891 (89)
(millions of miles/kilometers)	
AIR PASSENGER TRIPS (thousands)	731.0 (94)

	1995	1980	1965
VEHICLES			
PRIVATE CARS	241,300	159,400 (88)	162,000
COMMERCIAL	208,400	132,600	103,700

HEALTH AND HEALTH CARE

	1995	1980	1965
HEALTH CARE			
ACCESS TO SAFE WATER	93%		
ACCESS TO SANITATION	66%		
MEASLES IMMUNIZATION	100%		
RATE OF PHYSICIANS	3.6	1.4	1 (60)
RATE OF HOSPITAL BEDS	5.4	n/a	4.5 (60)
HEALTH INDICATORS			
PREGNANT WOMEN WITH ANEMIA	47%		
LOW-BIRTH-WEIGHT BABIES	8%		
CHILD MALNUTRITION	8%		
SMOKING PREVALENCE M/F	39/25		
TUBERCULOSIS INCIDENCE RATE	0.2		
AIDS/HIV CASES	440	261 (93)	
TOTAL DEATHS	78,504 (93)		

EDUCATION

	1995	1980	1965
SCHOOL AGE IN SCHOOL			
PRIMARY	105%	106%	117%
SECONDARY	80%	81%	23%
HIGHER	14%	17%	3.3%
FEMALES IN SCHOOL			
PRIMARY	103%	102%	116%
SECONDARY	88%	83%	21%
ADULT ILLITERACY M/F	5/4%		

COMMUNICATIONS

	1995	1980	1965
RATE OF NEWSPAPERS	122	108	88 (61)
RATE OF RADIOS	346	300	176
RATE OF TELEVISIONS	170	131	72

Source: CIA, The World Factbook, 1997; ILO, World Labour Report, 1997; UN, Demographic Yearbook, 1997; UN, Statistical Yearbook, 1996; World Bank, World Development Indicators, 1998.

CYPRUS

Cyprus is an island country located in the Mediterranean Sea, south of Turkey. The 3,571-square-mile (9,250-square-kilometer) country gained independence from the United Kingdom in August 1960. Since 1974, however, the country has been divided between the Greek majority (78 percent) and Turkish minority (18 percent). The Greeks control about 59 percent of the island, and the Turks control about 37 percent. Although the country is formally constituted as a republic, in 1975 the Turkish Cypriots, with the support of Turkish troops, established an autonomous political entity in the north nominally known as the "Turkish Republic." The country's diversified economy produces agricultural goods and clothing goods primarily for export to Western European and Middle Eastern markets. In 1995, Cyprus's population of 744,609 was growing at an annual rate of 1.1 percent. The country has a high average life expectancy at birth and a low infant mortality rate.

	1995[1]	1980[1]	1965
GEOGRAPHY			
AREA (square miles/kilometers)	3,571/9,250		
LAND AREA (square miles/kilometers)	3,568/9,240		
COASTLINE	405/648		
CITIES			
CAPITAL	Nicosia	47,036 (92)	
MAJOR CITIES	Limassol	87,136 (92)	
POPULATION			
TOTAL	744,609	612,851 (76)	577,615 (60)
DENSITY (per square mile/kilometer)	207/80	186/72	168/65
ANNUAL GROWTH	1.1%	1.2%	1.0%
AGE COHORTS			
0–14	25%	n/a	37%
15–64	64%	n/a	57%
65 AND OVER	11%	n/a	6%
MALE	50%		
FEMALE	50%		
URBAN	54%		
RURAL	46%		
NET MIGRATION RATE	3.4	n/a	−0.2

	1995[1]	1980[1]	1965

IDENTITY

ETHNICITY
GREEK	78%		
TURKISH	18%		

LANGUAGE
GREEK	n/a		
TURKISH	n/a		
ENGLISH	n/a		

RELIGION
GREEK ORTHODOX	78%		
MUSLIM	18%		
OTHER CHRISTIAN	4%		

VITAL STATISTICS

BIRTHS
BIRTH RATE	15.4	20.7	n/a
INFANT MORTALITY RATE	8.6	17	n/a
LIFE EXPECTANCY AT BIRTH	76.3	74.6	n/a

MARRIAGES
MARRIAGE RATE	8.4	6.3	n/a
AVERAGE AGE AT MARRIAGE M/F	27/23.1	n/a	n/a
DIVORCE RATE	0.7	0.4	n/a

DEATHS
DEATH RATE	7.7	8.5	n/a

HOUSEHOLDS

NUMBER
	185,459 (92)	n/a	145,709 (60)
URBAN	125,484		
RURAL	59,933		

AVERAGE SIZE
	3.2 (95)	n/a	4 (60)
URBAN	3.2		
RURAL	3.2		

TYPE OF HOUSEHOLD
SINGLE	4.9%		
MARRIED	81.2%		

	1995[1]	1980[1]	1965
WIDOWED	10.8%		
DIVORCED/SEPARATED	3%		
FEMALE HEADED	14%		

ECONOMICS AND LABOR

	1995[1]	1980[1]	1965
GDP PER CAPITA US$	$11,000		
LABOR FORCE M/F (thousands)	163.8/106.6 (93)		
AGRICULTURE	19.3/15.7		
MINING	0.7/0.0		
MANUFACTURING	25.0/20.5		
UTILITIES	1.4/0.1		
CONSTRUCTION	21.9/1.4		
TRADE/FOOD/TOURISM	37.3/30.5		
TRANSPORT/COMMUNICATIONS	12.1/4.1		
FINANCE/INSURANCE/REAL ESTATE	10.3/9.1		
SOCIAL AND PERSONAL SERVICES	33.1/24.5		
UNEMPLOYMENT (official)	2.7% (94)		
UNION DENSITY	53.7%		

TRANSPORT

	1995[1]	1980[1]	1965
JOURNEYS (by transport mode)			
AIR PASSENGER TRIPS (thousands)	1,234 (94)		
VEHICLES			
PRIVATE CARS	210,000	92,200	30,500
COMMERCIAL	97,100	25,200	11,200

HEALTH AND HEALTH CARE

	1995[1]	1980[1]	1965
HEALTH CARE			
RATE OF PHYSICIANS	n/a	n/a	0.7 (60)
RATE OF HOSPITAL BEDS	n/a	n/a	4.5 (60)
HEALTH INDICATORS			
AIDS/HIV CASES	50	38 (93)	
TOTAL DEATHS	4,924 (94)		

	1995[1]	**1980**[1]	**1965**
EDUCATION			
SCHOOL AGE IN SCHOOL			
PRIMARY	n/a	n/a	86%
SECONDARY	n/a	n/a	42%
HIGHER	n/a	n/a	0.50%
FEMALES IN SCHOOL			
PRIMARY	n/a	n/a	84%
SECONDARY	n/a	n/a	37%
ADULT ILLITERACY M/F	n/a	4.0/17.0 (76)	n/a
COMMUNICATIONS			
RATE OF NEWSPAPERS	107	127	217
RATE OF RADIOS	296	258	225
RATE OF TELEVISIONS	152	135	24

FOOTNOTE

1. Since 1974, Cyprus has been divided into Greek and Turkish ethnic sectors; statistics for 1980 and 1995 are for both sectors.

Source: CIA, *The World Factbook, 1997*; ILO, *World Labour Report, 1997*; UN, *Demographic Yearbook, 1997*; UN, *Statistical Yearbook, 1996*; World Bank, *World Development Indicators, 1998*.

CZECH REPUBLIC

The Czech Republic is a landlocked country located in east central Europe in the western half of the former Czechoslovakia. In 1993, the country formally seceded from Czechoslovakia to form the Czech Republic. In the same year, Slovakia, occupying the eastern region of the country, also declared independence. Germany borders the 30,426-square-mile (78,703-square-kilometer) country on the northwest, Poland on the northeast, Slovakia on the southeast, and Austria on the south. In the early 1990s, Czechoslovakia emerged from the Soviet orbit and embraced a pluralist democratic system and instituted market reforms by privatizing large segments of the economy. Even before independence, Czechoslovakia had developed one of the most advanced industrial economies in the Soviet bloc. In 1995, the Czech Republic's population of more than 10.3 million was contracting by an annual rate of 0.3 percent, due in part to a declining birth rate. The country had a high average life expectancy and a low infant mortality rate.

		1995	1980[1]	1965[1]

GEOGRAPHY

AREA (square miles/kilometers)	30,426/78,703		
LAND AREA (square miles/kilometers)	30,365/78,645		
COASTLINE (miles/kilometers)	landlocked		
CITIES			
CAPITAL	Prague	1,216,568 (94)	
MAJOR CITIES	Brno	390,073	
	Ostrava	326,049	
	Pilsen	172,055	
	Olomouc	105,998	

POPULATION

TOTAL	10,321,120		
DENSITY (per square mile/kilometer)	339/131		
ANNUAL GROWTH	−0.3		
AGE COHORTS			
0–14	18%		
15–64	68%		
65 AND OVER	14%		
MALE	49%		
FEMALE	51%		

	1995	1980[1]	1965[1]
URBAN	65%		
RURAL	35%		
NET MIGRATION RATE	0.2		

IDENTITY

ETHNICITY			
CZECH	94%		
SLOVAK	3%		
POLISH	1%		
LANGUAGE			
CZECH	n/a		
SLOVAK	n/a		
RELIGION			
ATHEIST	40%		
ROMAN CATHOLIC	39%		
PROTESTANT	5%		

VITAL STATISTICS

BIRTHS			
BIRTH RATE	10.4		
URBAN BIRTH RATE	11.6 (93)		
RURAL BIRTH RATE	12.2 (93)		
INFANT MORTALITY RATE	7.4		
ABORTION RATE	512.5 (94)		
LIFE EXPECTANCY AT BIRTH	73.8		
MARRIAGES			
MARRIAGE RATE	5.6		
AVERAGE AGE AT MARRIAGE M/F	26/23		
DIVORCE RATE	2.9		
DEATHS			
DEATH RATE	10.9 per 1,000		

HOUSEHOLDS

NUMBER	4,051,583 (91)		
AVERAGE SIZE	2.5 (91)		
FEMALE HEADED	25.60%		

	1995	1980[1]	1965[1]

ECONOMICS AND LABOR

GDP PER CAPITA US$ $10,200

LABOR FORCE M/F
AGRICULTURE   13/9%
INDUSTRY   54/36%
SERVICES   33/55%

UNEMPLOYMENT (official)   3.2% (94)
UNION DENSITY   36.30%

TRANSPORT

JOURNEYS (by transport mode)
RAILROAD PASSENGER TRIPS 5,301/8,481 (94)
 (millions of miles/kilometers)
AIR PASSENGER TRIPS (thousands) 1,067 (94)

VEHICLES (thousands)
PRIVATE CARS   2,917.3 (94) 2,273.0 (90)
COMMERCIAL   336.2   340.1

HEALTH AND HEALTH CARE

HEALTH CARE
MEASLES IMMUNIZATION   96%
RATE OF PHYSICIANS   2.9
RATE OF HOSPITAL BEDS   7.4

HEALTH INDICATORS
PREGNANT WOMEN WITH ANEMIA 23%
LOW-BIRTH-WEIGHT BABIES   6%
CHILD MALNUTRITION   1%
SMOKING PREVALENCE M/F   43/31%
TUBERCULOSIS INCIDENCE RATE 0.25
AIDS/HIV CASES   72   47 (93)
TOTAL DEATHS   117,913

	1995	1980[1]	1965[1]

EDUCATION

SCHOOL AGE IN SCHOOL

	1995	1980[1]	1965[1]
PRIMARY	96%	92%	98% (70)
SECONDARY	96%	45%	31%
HIGHER	21%	18%	10.4%

FEMALES IN SCHOOL

PRIMARY	95%	91%	98% (70)
SECONDARY	100%	51%	39%
HIGHER	n/a	14.60%	8%

COMMUNICATIONS

	1995	1980[1]	1965[1]
RATE OF NEWSPAPERS	583	313	254 (70)
RATE OF RADIOS	631	509	n/a
RATE OF TELEVISIONS	476	385	216 (70)

FOOTNOTE
1. Statistics for 1980 and 1985 are for Czechoslovakia.

Source: CIA, *The World Factbook, 1997;* ILO, *World Labour Report, 1997;* UN, *Demographic Yearbook, 1997;* UN, *Statistical Yearbook, 1996;* World Bank, *World Development Indicators, 1998.*

DENMARK

Denmark is located on the Baltic Sea and North Sea in northern Europe. Germany borders the 16,629-square-mile (43,070-square-kilometer) country on the south. Denmark is a member state of the European Union and has a modern industrial economy with one of the highest per capita gross domestic products (GDP) in the world. The country is a major producer of agricultural and industrial products. Nearly 70 percent of all employed workers are members of trade unions.

Denmark also has a comprehensive system of social protection that includes universal access to health care and education. Denmark's population of 5,249,632 in 1995 was growing at a slow annual rate of 0.4 percent owing to a slow birth rate. In 1995, deaths outnumbered births by a ratio approaching 2 to 1. Due in part to the broad social safety net, Denmark has one of the highest average life expectancies in Europe and among the lowest infant mortality rates in the world.

		1995	1980	1965
GEOGRAPHY				
AREA (square miles/kilometers)		16,629/43,070		
LAND AREA (square miles/kilometers)		16,243/42,070		
COASTLINE (miles/kilometers)		2,109/3,379		
CITIES				
CAPITAL	Copenhagen	1,353,333		
MAJOR CITIES	Odense	182,617		
	Ålborg	159,056		
	Århus	27,477		
POPULATION				
TOTAL		5,249,632	5,123,989 (81)	4,767,597
DENSITY (per square mile/kilometer)		313/121	308/119	287/111
ANNUAL GROWTH		0.4%	0%	0.8%
AGE COHORTS				
0–14		17%	n/a	23.8% (64)
15–64		67%	n/a	65% (64)
65 AND OVER		16%	n/a	11% (64)
MALE		49%		
FEMALE		51%		

	1995	1980	1965
URBAN	85%	83.90%	n/a
RURAL	15%	16.10%	n/a
NET MIGRATION RATE	2	n/a	0 (64)

IDENTITY

ETHNICITY
DANISH	n/a
INUIT	n/a
FAEROESE	n/a

LANGUAGE
DANISH	n/a
INUIT	n/a

RELIGION
LUTHERAN	91%

VITAL STATISTICS

BIRTHS
	1995	1980	1965
BIRTH RATE	12.2	10.6 (85)	18.4
INFANT MORTALITY RATE	5.3	7.7 (85)	18.7
LIFE EXPECTANCY AT BIRTH	77.3	74.5 (85)	72.5

MARRIAGES
	1995	1980	1965
MARRIAGE RATE	6.8	5.8 (85)	8.8
AVERAGE AGE AT MARRIAGE M/F	27.7/25		
DIVORCE RATE	2.5	2.8 (85)	1.4

DEATHS
	1995	1980	1965
DEATH RATE	10.4	11.4 (85)	10.3

HOUSEHOLDS

NUMBER	2,274,265 (91)		1,544,370 (60)
AVERAGE SIZE	2.3 (91)		3 (60)
FEMALE HEADED	41.6%		
SINGLE	14.6%		
MARRIED	55.5%		
WIDOWED	13.2%		
DIVORCED/SEPARATED	7.3%		

	1995	1980	1965

ECONOMICS AND LABOR

GDP PER CAPITA US$ $21,700

LABOR FORCE M/F (thousands)   1,383.1/1,200.9 (93)
AGRICULTURE   100.5/31.3
MINING   1.8/0.7
MANUFACTURING   346.6/155.1
UTILITIES   13.9/2.3
CONSTRUCTION   131.9/15.9
TRADE/FOOD/TOURISM   216.5/185.6
TRANSPORT/COMMUNICATIONS   132.5/51.5
FINANCE/INSURANCE/REAL ESTATE   134.6/122.9
SOCIAL AND PERSONAL SERVICES   300.2/632.0

UNEMPLOYMENT (official)   12.2% (94)
UNION DENSITY   68.2%

TRANSPORT

JOURNEYS (by transport mode)
RAILROAD PASSENGER TRIPS   2,873/4,596 (93)
   (millions of miles/kilometers)
AIR PASSENGER TRIPS (thousands)   5,456 (94)

VEHICLES (thousands)

	1995	1980	1965
PRIVATE CARS	1,622.3	1,397.9	743.8
COMMERCIAL	339.7	267.5	236

HEALTH AND HEALTH CARE

HEALTH CARE

	1995	1980	1965
ACCESS TO SAFE WATER	100%		
ACCESS TO SANITATION	100%		
MEASLES IMMUNIZATION	88%		
RATE OF PHYSICIANS	2.9	2.4	1.2 (60)
RATE OF HOSPITAL BEDS	5	n/a	9.3 (60)

HEALTH INDICATORS
LOW-BIRTH-WEIGHT BABIES   5%
SMOKING PREVALENCE M/F   37/37%
TUBERCULOSIS INCIDENCE RATE   0.12

	1995	**1980**	**1965**
AIDS/HIV CASES	1,843	1,399 (93)	
TOTAL DEATHS	63,216		

EDUCATION

SCHOOL AGE IN SCHOOL

	1995	**1980**	**1965**
PRIMARY	99%	96%	100%
SECONDARY	118%	105%	66%
HIGHER	45%	28%	10.1%

FEMALES IN SCHOOL

	1995	**1980**	**1965**
PRIMARY	100%	100%	100%
SECONDARY	102%	101%	67%
HIGHER	n/a	28.5%	7%

COMMUNICATIONS

	1995	**1980**	**1965**
RATE OF NEWSPAPERS	332	366	347
RATE OF RADIOS	1,035	927	333
RATE OF TELEVISIONS	538	498	227

Source: CIA, *The World Factbook, 1997;* ILO, *World Labour Report, 1997;* UN, *Demographic Yearbook, 1997;* UN, *Statistical Yearbook, 1996;* World Bank, *World Development Indicators, 1998.*

DJIBOUTI

Djibouti, formerly known as French Somaliland, is located in East Africa in a region known as the Horn of Africa on the Gulf of Aden and the Red Sea. Ethiopia borders the 8,424-square-mile (22,000-square-kilometer) country on the south and west. The country also maintains a border with Somalia on the south and Eritrea on the north. Yemen is located to the northeast across the Bab el Mandeb Strait. The country formally gained independence from France in June 1977. Located strategically in East Africa and the Middle East, Djibouti is a major trans-shipment and trading point. Djibouti is lacking in arable land and natural resources. The per capita gross domestic product (GDP), dependent on foreign assistance, is about $1,200 a year. Because of substantial out-migration, the population of 427,642 in 1995 was growing at a relatively slow rate by African standards. The Somali (60 percent) and the Afar (35 percent) are Djibouti's two leading ethnic groups. The country has a low average life expectancy and a high infant mortality rate.

	1995	1980[1]	1965[1]
GEOGRAPHY			
AREA (square miles/kilometers)	8,424/22,000		
LAND AREA (square miles/kilometers)	8,486/21,980		
COASTLINE (miles/kilometers)	196/314		
CITIES			
CAPITAL	Djibouti	n/a	n/a	62,000 (70)
POPULATION			
TOTAL	427,642		
DENSITY (per square mile/kilometer)	65/25		
ANNUAL GROWTH	1.5%	6.7%	n/a
AGE COHORTS			
0–14	43%	n/a	37%
15–64	55%	n/a	62%
65 AND OVER	2%	n/a	1%
URBAN	83%		
RURAL	17%		
NET MIGRATION RATE	−12.3		

	1995	1980[1]	1965[1]

IDENTITY

ETHNICITY
SOMALI	60%		
AFAR	35%		

LANGUAGE
FRENCH (official)	n/a		
ARABIC (official)	n/a		
SOMALI	n/a		

RELIGION
MUSLIM	94%		
CHRISTIAN	6%		

VITAL STATISTICS

BIRTHS
BIRTH RATE	42.5	n/a	42 (70)
INFANT MORTALITY RATE	114.9		
LIFE EXPECTANCY AT BIRTH	50.2		

DEATHS
DEATH RATE	15.3	n/a	7.6 (70)

ECONOMICS AND LABOR

GDP PER CAPITA US$	$1,200		

TRANSPORT

VEHICLES
PRIVATE CARS	13,000	14,500	3,700
COMMERCIAL	3,000	4,700	1,100

HEALTH AND HEALTH CARE

HEALTH CARE
RATE OF PHYSICIANS	n/a	n/a	0.2 (60)
RATE OF HOSPITAL BEDS	n/a	n/a	8.1 (60)

	1995	1980[1]	1965[1]
HEALTH INDICATORS			
AIDS/HIV CASES	880	453 (93)	

COMMUNICATIONS

	1995	1980[1]	1965[1]
RATE OF RADIOS	81	75	3
RATE OF TELEVISIONS	45	18	11 (70)

FOOTNOTE
1. Under French rule.

Source: CIA, The World Factbook, 1997; ILO, World Labour Report, 1997; UN, Demographic Yearbook, 1997; UN, Statistical Yearbook, 1996; World Bank, World Development Indicators, 1998.

DOMINICA

Dominica is a small island country located in the Windward Island archipelago of the eastern Caribbean Sea. The island borders the Atlantic Ocean on the east. The 290-square-mile (750-square-kilometer) island is located north of the island of Martinique and south of the island of Guadeloupe. Dominica gained independence from the United Kingdom in November 1978. The two leading sectors of Dominica's economy are agriculture and tourism. In 1995, the country's per capita gross domestic product (GDP) of $2,450 was among the lowest in the West Indies. Dominica's population of 82,926 is growing at a slow rate, due in part to the shortage of economic opportunity on the island that leads to out-migration. The country has a large annual net out-migration rate of 9.3 per 1,000 residents. Dominica has a relatively low infant mortality rate and a high average life expectancy. Roman Catholicism and various Protestant denominations are Dominica's leading religions.

	1995	**1980**	**1965**
GEOGRAPHY			
AREA (square miles/kilometers)	290/750		
LAND AREA (square miles/kilometers)	290/750		
COASTLINE (miles/kilometers)	93/148		
CITIES			
CAPITAL Roseau	16,243 (91)		
POPULATION			
TOTAL	82,926	73,795 (81)	59,916 (60)
DENSITY (per square mile/kilometer)	246/95	262/101	236/91
ANNUAL GROWTH	0.4%	0.8%	2.0%
AGE COHORTS			
0–14	28%	n/a	45%
15–64	64%	n/a	49%
65 AND OVER	8%	n/a	6%
MALE	50%		
FEMALE	50%		
NET MIGRATION RATE	−9.3	n/a	0.2

	1995	1980	1965

IDENTITY

ETHNICITY
BLACK	n/a		
CARIB INDIANS	n/a		

LANGUAGE
ENGLISH	n/a		
FRENCH	n/a		
PATOIS	n/a		

RELIGION
ROMAN CATHOLIC	77%		
METHODIST	5%		
PENTECOSTAL	3%		

VITAL STATISTICS

BIRTHS
BIRTH RATE	18.4	21.4 (78)	42.7 (60)
INFANT MORTALITY RATE	18.4	19.6 (78)	53.6 (60)
LIFE EXPECTANCY AT BIRTH	77.4	58 (78)	58 (60)

MARRIAGES
MARRIAGE RATE	3.1	3.2 (78)	3.7 (60)
DIVORCE RATE	0.4		

DEATHS
DEATH RATE	5.3	5.3 (78)	8.9

HOUSEHOLDS

NUMBER	n/a	n/a	14,218 (60)
AVERAGE SIZE	n/a	n/a	4.2

ECONOMICS AND LABOR

GDP PER CAPITA US$	$2,450		

	1995	1980	1965
TRANSPORT			
VEHICLES			
PRIVATE CARS	2,800 (94)		
COMMERCIAL	2,800 (94)		
HEALTH AND HEALTH CARE			
HEALTH CARE			
RATE OF PHYSICIANS	n/a	n/a	0.1 (60)
RATE OF HOSPITAL BEDS	n/a	n/a	4.6 (60)
HEALTH INDICATORS			
AIDS/HIV CASES	31	26 (93)	
EDUCATION			
SCHOOL AGE IN SCHOOL			
PRIMARY	n/a	n/a	162%
SECONDARY	n/a	n/a	18%
ADULT ILLITERACY M/F	n/a	n/a	6.0/5.8% (70)
COMMUNICATIONS			
RATE OF RADIOS	599	419	n/a
RATE OF TELEVISIONS	75	n/a	n/a

Source: CIA, The World Factbook, 1997; ILO, World Labour Report, 1997; UN, Demographic Yearbook, 1997; UN, Statistical Yearbook, 1996; World Bank, World Development Indicators, 1998.

DOMINICAN REPUBLIC

The Dominican Republic is located in the Caribbean Sea on the eastern two-thirds of the island of Hispaniola. Haiti occupies the western one-third of the island. The Dominican Republic, which covers an area of 18,815 square miles (48,730 square kilometers), borders the Atlantic Ocean on the north and the Caribbean Sea on the south. National elections held in 1996 produced the first significant shift in government leadership in more than two decades. The Dominican Republic's national economy is dominated by the production of sugar, coffee, and other commodities and a small but growing manufacturing sector. In 1995, the Dominican Republic's population of 8,088,881 was growing at an annual rate of 1.7 percent. Almost three-quarters of the country's population are mulatto (mixed European and African racial heritage). Whites compose about 16 percent of the population, and Africans account for 11 percent of the national population. The country's social service and public health system, though better than Haiti's, is not as advanced as other countries' in the region. Thus, although life expectancy is increasing, it is still lower than Cuba, Jamaica, and the smaller island countries to the southeast.

	1995	1980	1965
GEOGRAPHY			
AREA (square miles/kilometers)	18,815/48,730		
LAND AREA (square miles/ kilometers)	18,680/48,380		
COASTLINE (miles/kilometers)	805/1,288		
CITIES			
CAPITAL	Santo Domingo (93) 2,134,977 (93)		
MAJOR CITIES	Santiago de los		
	Cabelleros 650,548		
	San Cristóbal 409,381		
	La Vega 335,140		
	Duarte 277,270		
POPULATION			
TOTAL	8,088,881	5,647,977 (81)	3,047,070 (60)
DENSITY (per square mile/kilometer)	420/162	332/128 (81)	162/63 (60)
ANNUAL GROWTH	1.7%	2.9%	3.6%
AGE COHORTS			
0–14	34%	n/a	47%
15–64	62%	n/a	50%
65 AND OVER	4%	n/a	3%

	1995	1980	1965
MALE	50%		
FEMALE	50%		
URBAN	65%	51.2%	n/a
RURAL	35%	48.8%	n/a
NET MIGRATION RATE	0.5	n/a	0 (63)

IDENTITY

ETHNICITY

MULATTO	73%		
WHITE	16%		
BLACK	11%		

LANGUAGE

SPANISH	n/a		
CREOLE	n/a		

RELIGION

ROMAN CATHOLIC	95%		
PROTESTANT	5%		

VITAL STATISTICS

BIRTHS

	1995	1980	1965
BIRTH RATE	23.5	33.1	45 (60)
INFANT MORTALITY RATE	42	75	72.7 (60)
LIFE EXPECTANCY AT BIRTH	69.1	57.9	57.8 (60)

MARRIAGES

MARRIAGE RATE	3.3	5	3.5 (60)
DIVORCE RATE	1.2	1.7	0.3 (60)

DEATHS

DEATH RATE	5.7	8	14 (60)

HOUSEHOLDS

NUMBER	n/a	n/a	513,779 (55)
AVERAGE SIZE	n/a	n/a	4.9 (55)

	1995	1980	1965

ECONOMICS AND LABOR

GDP PER CAPITA US$ $3,400

LABOR FORCE
AGRICULTURE M/F 31/9%
INDUSTRY M/F 32/23%
SERVICES M/F 38/68%

UNION DENSITY 17.30%

POVERTY
UNDER $1/DAY 19.9 (89)
UNDER $2/DAY 47.7 (89)

TRANSPORT

JOURNEYS (by transport mode)
AIR PASSENGER TRIPS (thousands) 300 (94)

VEHICLES			
PRIVATE CARS	174,400	94,400	29,200
COMMERCIAL	111,400	46,900	12,300

HEALTH AND HEALTH CARE

HEALTH CARE			
ACCESS TO SAFE WATER	71%		
ACCESS TO SANITATION	78%		
MEASLES IMMUNIZATION	100%		
RATE OF PHYSICIANS	1.1	n/a	0.2 (60)
RATE OF HOSPITAL BEDS	2	n/a	2.5 (60)

HEALTH INDICATORS			
LOW-BIRTH-WEIGHT BABIES	16%		
CHILD MALNUTRITION	6%		
SMOKING PREVALENCE M/F	66/14%		
TUBERCULOSIS INCIDENCE RATE	1.1		
AIDS/HIV CASES	3,160	2,446 (93)	
TOTAL DEATHS	23,717 (92)		

EDUCATION

SCHOOL AGE IN SCHOOL			
PRIMARY	103%	118%	91%
SECONDARY	41%	42%	15%
HIGHER	n/a	n/a	1.8%
FEMALES IN SCHOOL			
PRIMARY	103%	90%	92%
SECONDARY	57%	n/a	15%
ADULT ILLITERACY M/F	18/18%	22.3/23.2% (85)	33.3/37.6% (60)

COMMUNICATIONS

RATE OF NEWSPAPERS	36	39	27
RATE OF RADIOS	172	158	46
RATE OF TELEVISIONS	90	70	16

Source: CIA, *The World Factbook, 1997;* ILO, *World Labour Report, 1997;* UN, *Demographic Yearbook, 1997;* UN, *Statistical Yearbook, 1996;* World Bank, *World Development Indicators, 1998.*

ECUADOR

Ecuador is located in northwestern South America on the Pacific Ocean. Colombia borders the 109,483-square-mile (283,560-square-kilometer) country on the north and Peru on the east and south. Throughout much of the 1990s, Ecuador has endured a period of political instability. Recent presidents have been deposed amid charges of corruption, incompetence, and even mental illness. Much of the country's recent political difficulties stem in part from declining prices for the country's major commodities, including petroleum, bananas, coffee, cocoa, and fishing products. These problems have intensified declining wages and eroding living conditions, particularly for the country's urban and rural poor. In 1994, nearly two-thirds of Ecuador's national population was subsisting on the equivalent of less than $2 a day. The country's population of nearly 11.5 million was growing at an average annual rate of 2 percent, down from the 1962 average of 3.3 percent. The country's three leading racial groups are mestizo (55 percent), indigenous Indian (25 percent), and black (10 percent). In 1995, average life expectancy at birth was over 71 years.

		1995	1980	1965
GEOGRAPHY				
AREA (square miles/kilometers)		109,483/283,560		
LAND AREA (square miles/kilometers)		106,888/276,840		
COASTLINE (miles/kilometers)		1,398/2,237		
CITIES				
CAPITAL	Quito	1,100,847 (90)	866,472 (82)	n/a
MAJOR CITIES	Guayaquil	1,508,444	1,199,344	n/a
	Cuenca	194,981	n/a	n/a
	Ambato	124,166	100,454	n/a
	Machala	144,197	105,521	n/a
POPULATION				
TOTAL		11,466,291	8,050,630 (82)	4,476,007 (62)
DENSITY (per square mile/kilometer)		104/40	85/33	49/19
ANNUAL GROWTH		2.0%	2.9%	3.3%
AGE COHORTS				
0–14		35%	n/a	45%
15–64		60%	n/a	52%
65 AND OVER		5%	n/a	3%
MALE		50%		
FEMALE		50%		

	1995	**1980**	**1965**
URBAN	58%	47.1	n/a
RURAL	42%	52.9%	n/a
NET MIGRATION RATE	0		

IDENTITY

ETHNICITY

MESTIZO	55%		
INDIAN	25%		
BLACK	10%		

LANGUAGE

SPANISH (official)	n/a		
QUECHUA	n/a		

RELIGION

ROMAN CATHOLIC	95%		
PROTESTANT	5%		

VITAL STATISTICS

BIRTHS

BIRTH RATE	25.1	36.8	50 (62)
URBAN BIRTH RATE	19.8 (93)		
RURAL BIRTH RATE	15.1 (93)		
INFANT MORTALITY RATE	49.7	70	93 (62)
LIFE EXPECTANCY AT BIRTH	71.1	60.6	n/a

MARRIAGES

MARRIAGE RATE	6.2	5.9	5.9 (62)
AVERAGE AGE AT MARRIAGE	25.2/22		
DIVORCE RATE	0.7	0.4	0.3 (62)

DEATHS

DEATH RATE	5.5	8.1	15 (62)

HOUSEHOLDS

NUMBER	n/a	n/a	877,300 (62)
AVERAGE SIZE	n/a	n/a	5.1 (62)

	1995	1980	1965

ECONOMICS AND LABOR

GDP PER CAPITA US$	$4,100		
LABOR FORCE M/F (thousands)	1,665.2/1,032.3 (94)		
AGRICULTURE	164.0/24.7		
MINING	15.0/1.2		
MANUFACTURING	268.6/146.2		
UTILITIES	10.9/1.4		
CONSTRUCTION	165.6/6.1		
TRADE/FOOD/TOURISM	411.9/402.7		
TRANSPORT/COMMUNICATIONS	146.9/9.6		
FINANCE/INSURANCE/REAL ESTATE	75.6/36.4		
SOCIAL AND PERSONAL SERVICES	406.8/404.0		
UNEMPLOYMENT (official)	7.1% (94)		
UNION DENSITY	9.8% (94)		
POVERTY			
UNDER $1/DAY	30.4% (94)		
UNDER $2/DAY	65.8% (94)		

TRANSPORT

JOURNEYS (by transport mode)			
RAILROAD PASSENGER TRIPS	17/27 (94)		
(millions of miles/kilometers)			
AIR PASSENGER TRIPS (thousands)	1,126 (94)		
VEHICLES			
PRIVATE CARS	219,800	65,100	14,400
COMMERCIAL	243,400	112,200	17,600

HEALTH AND HEALTH CARE

HEALTH CARE			
ACCESS TO SAFE WATER	70		
ACCESS TO SANITATION	64		
MEASLES IMMUNIZATION	100		
RATE OF PHYSICIANS	1.5	n/a	0.4 (60)
RATE OF HOSPITAL BEDS	1.6	1.9	2 (60)

	1995	**1980**	**1965**
HEALTH INDICATORS			
PREGNANT WOMEN WITH ANEMIA	17%		
LOW-BIRTH-WEIGHT BABIES	13%		
CHILD MALNUTRITION	17%		
TUBERCULOSIS INCIDENCE RATE	1.66		
AIDS/HIV CASES	543	357 (93)	
TOTAL DEATHS	52,453 (93)		

EDUCATION

	1995	**1980**	**1965**
SCHOOL AGE IN SCHOOL			
PRIMARY	109%	117%	91%
SECONDARY	50%	53%	17%
HIGHER	n/a	n/a	3%
FEMALES IN SCHOOL			
PRIMARY	107%	115%	88%
SECONDARY	47%	48%	15%
ADULT ILLITERACY	12/8%	15.8/23.8% (82)	27.9/36.9% (62)

COMMUNICATIONS

	1995	**1980**	**1965**
RATE OF NEWSPAPERS	64	70	47
RATE OF RADIOS	326	305	114
RATE OF TELEVISIONS	88	63	9

Source: CIA, *The World Factbook, 1997;* ILO, *World Labour Report, 1997;* UN, *Demographic Yearbook, 1997;* UN, *Statistical Yearbook, 1996;* World Bank, *World Development Indicators, 1998.*

EGYPT

Egypt is located in northeast Africa on the Mediterranean Sea. The 386,660-square-mile (1,001,450-square-kilometer) country is bordered by Libya on the west; Sudan on the south; and the Gaza Strip, Israel, Jordan, and Saudi Arabia on the east. The Red Sea also borders Egypt on the east. Since the assassination of President Sadat in 1991, Egypt has been governed by President Mubarak. The government is heavily indebted to the IMF and Western banks, which have imposed austerity programs on the national economy. Over 50 percent of the population survives on the equivalent of less than $2 a day. Al-though Egypt's major cities are growing rapidly, most of the country's people continue to reside in rural areas. The country's population more than doubled from nearly 26 million in 1960 to nearly 63.6 million in 1995. Despite the continued projected growth in Egypt's population, annual growth rates have declined significantly from the 1970s. Muslims compose the majority (94 percent) of Egypt's population, and Cotpic Christians encompass a substantial minority (6 percent). In 1995, the average life expectancy at birth in Egypt was 61.4 years and the infant mortality rate was 36.3 infant deaths per 1,000 live births.

Major Cities

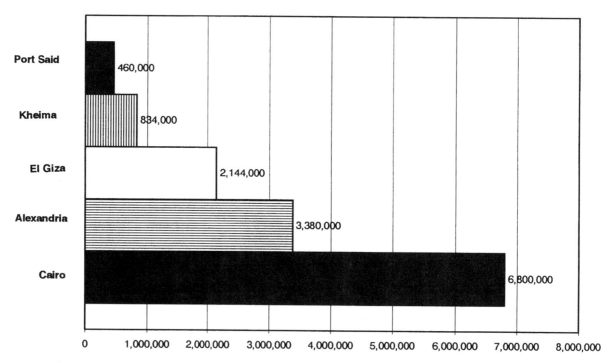

Over 90 percent of Egypt's population lives in the tiny fertile strip of the Nile Valley. Unfortunately, all of Egypt's major cities lie there as well. Thus, as urbanization proceeds, more and more precious farmland is swallowed up. To alleviate the problem, the government has embarked on a major project to irrigate desert lands.

Annual Growth

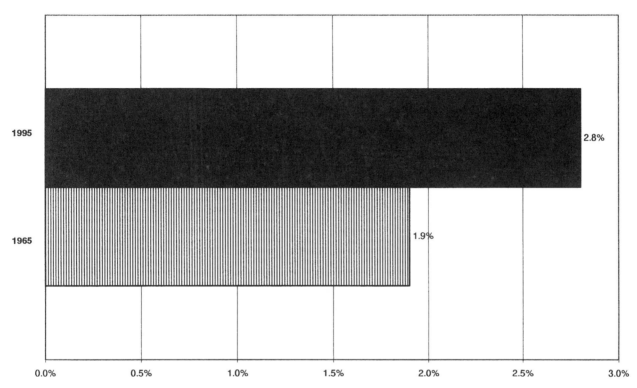

Like many of its fellow Arab countries, Egypt suffers from one of the fastest and, perhaps, most unsustainable rates of population growth in the world. Rising education levels, particularly among women, and birth-control programs have begun to slow this growth in recent years.

CHRONOLOGY

1964   Nationalist Egyptian President Gamel Abdel Nasser sends troops to Yemen.
1967   Egypt defeated in war with Israel; loses Sinai and Gaza.
1970   Nasser dies and is succeeded by lieutenant, Anwar Sadat; Aswan High dam finished with help of Soviets.
1972   Sadat ousts thousands of Soviet advisers from Egypt.
1978   Sadat signs peace treaty with Israel, which leads to Egypt's ostracism from Arab world.
1981   Sadat assassinated by Islamic fundamentalists and succeeded by Vice President Hosni Mubarak.
1982   Sinai returned to Egyptian control.
1990   Egypt allowed to rejoin Arab League.
1997   Islamic fundamentalists launch several terrorist attacks against tourists.

	1995	**1980**	**1965**

GEOGRAPHY

AREA (square miles/kilometers)   386,660/1,001,450
LAND AREA (square miles/kilometers)   384,344/995,450
COASTLINE (miles/kilometers)   1,531/2,450

CITIES
CAPITAL   Cairo   6,800,000 (92)
MAJOR CITIES   Alexandria   3,380,000
                 El Gîza   2,144,000
                 Shubra-El-Kheima   834,000
                 Port Said   460,000

POPULATION

	1995	**1980**	**1965**
TOTAL	63,575,107	36,626,204 (76)	25,984,101 (60)
DENSITY (per square mile/kilometer)	153/59	124/48	n/a
ANNUAL GROWTH	1.9%	2.8%	n/a
AGE COHORTS			
0–14	37%	n/a	43%
15–64	60%	n/a	53%
65 AND OVER	3%	n/a	4%
MALE	51%		
FEMALE	19%		
URBAN	45%	43.80%	n/a
RURAL	55%	56.20%	n/a
NET MIGRATION RATE	−0.35		

IDENTITY

ETHNICITY
EASTERN HAMITIC   99%

LANGUAGE
ARABIC   n/a

RELIGION
MUSLIM   94%
COPTIC CHRISTIAN   6%

	1995	1980	1965

VITAL STATISTICS

BIRTHS

	1995	1980	1965
BIRTH RATE	28.2	36.9	n/a
URBAN BIRTH RATE	24.1 (92)		
RURAL BIRTH RATE	28.9 (92)		
INFANT MORTALITY RATE	36.3	70.3	n/a
LIFE EXPECTANCY AT BIRTH	61.4	52.7	n/a

MARRIAGES

	1995	1980	1965
MARRIAGE RATE	9.2	9.1	n/a
AVERAGE AGE AT MARRIAGE	26.4/21.6		
DIVORCE RATE	1.6	1.6	n/a

DEATHS

	1995	1980	1965
DEATH RATE	8.7	10.3	n/a

HOUSEHOLDS

	1995	1980	1965
NUMBER	n/a	9,732,735 (86)	1,992,491 (60)
AVERAGE SIZE	n/a	4.9 (86)	4.8 (60)

ECONOMICS AND LABOR

GDP PER CAPITA US$	$2,760

LABOR FORCE M/F (thousands)	11,232.1/3,166.8 (92)
AGRICULTURE	3,876.2/1,658.8
MINING	42.6/2.3
MANUFACTURING	1,718.4/296.2
UTILITIES	136.5/10.8
CONSTRUCTION	863.4/20.8
TRADE/FOOD/TOURISM	1,148.5/183.6
TRANSPORT/COMMUNICATIONS	734.8/42.9
FINANCE/INSURANCE/REAL ESTATE	191.3/45.8
SOCIAL AND PERSONAL SERVICES	2,515.1/905.1

UNEMPLOYMENT (official)	9% (92)
UNION DENSITY	29.6%

POVERTY

UNDER $1/DAY	7.6 (91)
UNDER $2/DAY	51.9 (91)

	1995	1980	1965

TRANSPORT

JOURNEYS (by transport mode)

	1995	1980	1965
RAILROAD PASSENGER TRIPS	22,903/36,644 (92)		
(millions of miles/kilometers)			
AIR PASSENGER TRIPS (thousands)	3,538 (94)		
VEHICLES (thousands)			
PRIVATE CARS	1,225.0 (94)	432.4	n/a
COMMERCIAL	445	130	n/a

HEALTH AND HEALTH CARE

HEALTH CARE

	1995	1980	1965
ACCESS TO SAFE WATER	64%		
ACCESS TO SANITATION	11%		
MEASLES IMMUNIZATION	82%		
RATE OF PHYSICIANS	1.8	1.1	0.4 (60)
RATE OF HOSPITAL BEDS	2.1	2	2.1 (60)

HEALTH INDICATORS

	1995	1980	1965
PREGNANT WOMEN WITH ANEMIA	n/a	24%	n/a
LOW-BIRTH-WEIGHT BABIES	n/a	12%	n/a
CHILD MALNUTRITION	n/a	9%	n/a
SMOKING PREVALENCE M/F	n/a	40/1%	n/a
TUBERCULOSIS INCIDENCE RATE	n/a	0.78	n/a
AIDS/HIV CASES	129	91 (93)	
TOTAL DEATHS	414,643 (94)		

EDUCATION

SCHOOL AGE IN SCHOOL

	1995	1980	1965
PRIMARY	100%	73%	72% (70)
SECONDARY	74%	50%	35%
HIGHER	18%	16%	15.10%

FEMALES IN SCHOOL

	1995	1980	1965
PRIMARY	90%	63%	57% (70)
SECONDARY	44%	36%	23%

	1995	1980	1965
ADULT ILLITERACY M/F	36/61%	46.4/77.6% (76)	n/a

	1995	1980	1965
COMMUNICATIONS			
RATE OF NEWSPAPERS	41	39	n/a
RATE OF RADIOS	307	137	n/a
RATE OF TELEVISIONS	113	32	n/a

Source: CIA, *The World Factbook, 1997*; ILO, *World Labour Report, 1997*; UN, *Demographic Yearbook, 1997*; UN, *Statistical Yearbook, 1996*; World Bank, *World Development Indicators, 1998.*

EL SALVADOR

El Salvador is located in Central America, facing the Pacific Ocean, southeast of Guatemala and southwest of Honduras. The 8,124-square-mile (21,040-square-kilometer) country is small but is one of the most densely populated in the world. In 1995, El Salvador's population density was 710 persons per square mile (274 per square kilometer). El Salvador has emerged from a civil war between a military-backed government and an insurgent liberation army seeking land reform and greater socioeconomic equality. The civil war has caused widespread death and suffering and has devastated the national economy. In the 1990s, agricultural commodities (coffee and sugar) remain the leading sectors of El Salvador's economy; however, a large and growing share of the country's workers are employed in manufacturing. The country's textile workers earn extremely low wages by the standards of the developed world. In 1995, the country's population of 5.8 million was growing at an annual rate of 1.8 percent, down from 3.4 percent in the early 1960s. Mestizos (persons of mixed indigenous Indian and European ancestry) constitute 94 percent of El Salvador's population.

	1995	**1980**	**1965**
GEOGRAPHY			
AREA (square miles/kilometers)	8,124/21,040		
LAND AREA (square miles/kilometers)	8,000/20,720		
COASTLINE (miles/kilometers)	192/307		
CITIES			
CAPITAL	San Salvador 415,346 (92)		
MAJOR CITIES	Soyapango 261,122		
	Santa Ana 139,389		
	Mejicanos 131,972		
	San Miguel 127,696		
POPULATION			
TOTAL	5,828,987	3,554,648 (71)	2,510,984 (61)
DENSITY (per square mile/kilometer)	710/274	593/229	308/119 (61)
ANNUAL GROWTH	1.8%	1.3%	3.4%
AGE COHORTS			
0–14	38%	n/a	45%
15–64	57%	n/a	52%
65 AND OVER	5%	n/a	3%
MALE	48%		
FEMALE	52%		

	1995	**1980**	**1965**
URBAN	45%	41	n/a
RURAL	55%	59%	n/a
NET MIGRATION RATE	4.4	n/a	0

IDENTITY

ETHNICITY
MESTIZO	94%		
INDIAN	5%		
WHITE	1%		

LANGUAGE
SPANISH	n/a		
NAHUA	n/a		

RELIGION
ROMAN CATHOLIC	75%		
PROTESTANT	25%		

VITAL STATISTICS

BIRTHS
BIRTH RATE	28.3	29.7 (84)	n/a
URBAN BIRTH RATE	29.1 (92)		
RURAL BIRTH RATE	31 (92)		
INFANT MORTALITY RATE	45.6	35.1 (84)	61.7 (61)
LIFE EXPECTANCY AT BIRTH	68.9	58.5 (84)	58.4 (61)

MARRIAGES
MARRIAGE RATE	4.2	3.5 (84)	3.2 (61)
AVERAGE AGE AT MARRIAGE M/F	25.3/22.3 (92)		
DIVORCE RATE	0.5	0.3 (84)	0.2 (61)

DEATHS
DEATH RATE	5.8	6 (84)	n/a

HOUSEHOLDS

NUMBER	1,236,866 (92)		
AVERAGE SIZE	4.1 (92)		

	1995	1980	1965

ECONOMICS AND LABOR

GDP PER CAPITA US$ $1,950

LABOR FORCE M/F (thousands)	1,134.4/647.2 (92)
AGRICULTURE	542.2/96.1
MINING	2.3/0.3
MANUFACTURING	167.4/141.3
UTILITIES	9.7/1.9
CONSTRUCTION	79.2/1.8
TRADE/FOOD/TOURISM	123.6/184.0
TRANSPORT/COMMUNICATIONS	56.5/4.5
FINANCE/INSURANCE/REAL ESTATE	12.2/7.8
SOCIAL AND PERSONAL SERVICES	139.3/209.4

UNEMPLOYMENT (official)	7.9% (92)
UNION DENSITY	7.20%

TRANSPORT

JOURNEYS (by transport mode)

RAILROAD PASSENGER TRIPS	3.8/6 (94)
(millions of miles/kilometers)	
AIR PASSENGER TRIPS (thousands)	459/734 (94)

VEHICLES	1995	1980	1965
PRIVATE CARS	21,600	n/a	26,200
COMMERCIAL	33,100	n/a	12,000

HEALTH AND HEALTH CARE

HEALTH CARE

	1995	1980	1965
ACCESS TO SAFE WATER	55%		
ACCESS TO SANITATION	68%		
MEASLES IMMUNIZATION	94%		
RATE OF PHYSICIANS	0.7	0.3	0.2 (60)
RATE OF HOSPITAL BEDS	1.5	n/a	2.3 (60)

HEALTH INDICATORS

	1995
PREGNANT WOMEN WITH ANEMIA	14%
LOW-BIRTH-WEIGHT BABIES	11%
CHILD MALNUTRITION	11%
SMOKING PREVALENCE M/F	38/12%

	1995	1980	1965
TUBERCULOSIS INCIDENCE RATE	1.1		
AIDS/HIV CASES	1,372	605 (93)	
TOTAL DEATHS	28,694 (94)		

EDUCATION

SCHOOL AGE IN SCHOOL

	1995	1980	1965
PRIMARY	88%	74%	84%
SECONDARY	32%	25%	11%
HIGHER	4%	1.2%	1.0%

FEMALES IN SCHOOL

	1995	1980	1965
OF PRIMARY STUDENTS	49%	49%	48%
OF SECONDARY STUDENTS	48%	21%	51%

	1995	1980	1965
ADULT ILLITERACY M/F	27/30%	25.0/30.7% (85)	46.1/55.5% (61)

COMMUNICATIONS

	1995	1980	1965
RATE OF NEWSPAPERS	90	64	47 (63)
RATE OF RADIOS	413	343	158
RATE OF TELEVISIONS	94	66	14

Source: CIA, *The World Factbook, 1997;* ILO, *World Labour Report, 1997;* UN, *Demographic Yearbook, 1997;* UN, *Statistical Yearbook, 1996;* World Bank, *World Development Indicators, 1998.*

EQUATORIAL GUINEA

Equatorial Guinea is a country encompassing a mainland enclave in West Africa and an island in the Gulf of Guinea, an inlet of the Atlantic Ocean. Cameroon borders the mainland region of the 10,830-square-mile (28,050-square-kilometer) country to the north, and Gabon to the west and south. The mainland region is known as Rio Muni, and the island to the northwest is known as Bioko, the site of the capital city of Malabo. In the 1990s, the country, which gained independence in October 1968 from Spain, is making the transition to democratic rule. Though Equatorial Guinea is believed to have abundant minerals and natural resources, the economy is undeveloped by most standards. Much of the population

is engaged in various forms of subsistence agricultural and fishing activities. The development of recently discovered oil reserves is expected to increase the country's economic wealth. In 1995, the country's per capita gross domestic product was only $800. In the same year, Equatorial Guinea's population of 431,282 was growing at a relatively high annual rate of 2.6 percent. To help eradicate the high rate of communicable diseases, the country is in need of improved health and sanitation services. Equatorial Guinea has a low life expectancy at birth of 53 years and a high infant mortality rate of 116.6 infant deaths per 1,000 live births.

	1995	1980	1965
GEOGRAPHY			
AREA (square miles/kilometers)	10,830/28,050		
LAND AREA (square miles/kilometers)	10,830/28,050		
COASTLINE (miles/kilometers)	185/296		
CITIES			
CAPITAL	Malabo n/a	30,418 (83)	n/a
POPULATION			
TOTAL	431,282	n/a	245,989 (60)
DENSITY (per square mile/kilometer)	36/14	n/a	23/9
ANNUAL GROWTH	2.6%	n/a	1.9%
AGE COHORTS			
0–14	43%		
15–64	53%		
65 AND OVER	4%		
MALE	48%		
FEMALE	52%		

	1995	1980	1965
URBAN	42%		
RURAL	52%		
NET MIGRATION RATE	0		

IDENTITY

	1995	1980	1965
ETHNICITY			
BIOKO	n/a		
FANG	n/a		
LANGUAGE			
SPANISH (official)	n/a		
PIDGIN ENGLISH	n/a		
FANG	n/a		
RELIGION			
ROMAN CATHOLIC	n/a		
ANIMIST	n/a		

VITAL STATISTICS

	1995	1980	1965
BIRTHS			
BIRTH RATE	39.8	42.5	n/a
INFANT MORTALITY RATE	116.6	137	n/a
LIFE EXPECTANCY AT BIRTH	53	44	n/a
MARRIAGES			
MARRIAGE RATE	n/a	0.8	n/a
DEATHS			
DEATH RATE	14	21	n/a

ECONOMICS AND LABOR

	1995	1980	1965
GDP PER CAPITA US$	$800		

TRANSPORT

	1995	1980	1965
JOURNEYS (by transport mode)			
AIR PASSENGER TRIPS (thousands)	14.0 (94)		

	1995	1980	1965

HEALTH AND HEALTH CARE

HEALTH CARE

	1995	1980	1965
RATE OF PHYSICIANS	n/a	n/a	0.2 (60)
RATE OF HOSPITAL BEDS	n/a	n/a	5.2 (60)

HEALTH INDICATORS

	1995	1980	1965
AIDS/HIV CASES	157	43 (93)	

EDUCATION

SCHOOL AGE IN SCHOOL

	1995	1980	1965
PRIMARY	n/a	n/a	85%
SECONDARY	n/a	11% (75)	8%
HIGHER			

FEMALES IN SCHOOL

	1995	1980	1965
PRIMARY	n/a	n/a	69%
SECONDARY	n/a	4% (75)	3%

ADULT ILLITERACY

	1995	1980	1965
ADULT ILLITERACY	n/a	63%	n/a

COMMUNICATIONS

	1995	1980	1965
RATE OF NEWSPAPERS	3	7	4
RATE OF RADIOS	422	401	n/a
RATE OF TELEVISIONS	10	5	0

Source: CIA, *The World Factbook, 1997*; ILO, *World Labour Report, 1997*; UN, *Demographic Yearbook, 1997*; UN, *Statistical Yearbook, 1996*; World Bank, *World Development Indicators, 1998*.

ERITREA

Eritrea is located in East Africa along the coast of the Red Sea. Ethiopia borders the 46,842-square-mile (121,320-square-kilometer) country on the southwest, Sudan on the northwest, and Djibouti on the southeast. Eritrea received its independence from Ethiopia in May 1993, following a two-decade-long armed struggle against the Ethiopian government. Eritrea was granted formal independence following the collapse of a military government in Ethiopia. The two countries maintained friendly relations for five years before a border war broke out in a remote region in June 1998. Eritrea is one of the poorest countries in the Horn of Africa, a region that is also among the poorest in the world. In 1995, the per capita gross domestic product (GDP) was only $570. The vast majority of the country's population resides in rural areas and is engaged in subsistence agriculture. The country has few agricultural exports. The 1995 population of 3.4 million was growing at a high average annual rate of 2.8 percent. Due in part to the scarcity of modern medicine, poor sanitation, and the high rate of communicable diseases, Eritrea has a low life expectancy and a high infant mortality rate. The country has a limited system of education. While a majority of Eritrean school-aged children attend primary school, fewer than 20 percent attend secondary schools.

1995[1]

GEOGRAPHY

AREA (square miles/kilometers)	46,842/121,320
LAND AREA (square miles/kilometers)	46,842/121,320
COASTLINE (miles/kilometers)	719/1,151

CITIES		
CAPITAL	Asmara	385,100 (90)

POPULATION

TOTAL	3,427,883
DENSITY (per square mile/kilometer)	7,830
ANNUAL GROWTH	2.8%

AGE COHORTS	
0–14	44%
15–64	53%
65 AND OVER	3%

MALE	50%
FEMALE	50%

	1995[1]
URBAN	17%
RURAL	83%
NET MIGRATION RATE	0

IDENTITY

ETHNICITY

TIGRINYA	50%
TIGRE AND KUNAMA	40%
AFAR	4%

LANGUAGE

TIGRINYA	n/a
AMHARIC	n/a
ARABIC	n/a

RELIGION

MUSLIM	n/a
COPTIC CHRISTIAN	n/a
ROMAN CATHOLIC	n/a

VITAL STATISTICS

BIRTHS

BIRTH RATE	43.3
INFANT MORTALITY RATE	105.2
LIFE EXPECTANCY AT BIRTH	50.3

DEATHS

DEATH RATE	15.4

ECONOMICS AND LABOR

GDP PER CAPITA US$	$570

LABOR FORCE M/F

AGRICULTURE	77/85%
INDUSTRY	8/2%
SERVICES	16/13%

UNION DENSITY	7.20%

1995[1]

HEALTH AND HEALTH CARE

HEALTH CARE
MEASLES IMMUNIZATION   29

HEALTH INDICATORS
CHILD MALNUTRITION   41%
TUBERCULOSIS INCIDENCE RATE   1.55
AIDS/HIV CASES   2,021

EDUCATION

SCHOOL AGE IN SCHOOL
PRIMARY   57%
SECONDARY   19%
HIGHER   1%

FEMALES IN SCHOOL
PRIMARY   51%
SECONDARY   15%

FOOTNOTE
1. Part of Ethiopia in 1980 and 1965.

Source: CIA, The World Factbook, 1997; ILO, World Labour Report, 1997; UN, Demographic Yearbook, 1997; UN, Statistical Yearbook, 1996; World Bank, World Development Indicators, 1998.

ESTONIA

Estonia is located in Eastern Europe on the border of the Baltic Sea and the Gulf of Finland. The Russian Federation borders the 17,413-square-mile country on the east, and Latvia borders on the south. Estonia gained formal independence in September 1991 amid the collapse and breakup of the Soviet Union. Estonia's industrialized modern economy produces fabricated goods for regional and Western European markets. Following independence, the institution of market reforms in the early 1990s reduced inflation rates. But the transition to a market economy produced high levels of unemployment. In 1995, the country's population of 1,459,428 was declining at an annual rate of 1.1 percent, due substantially to a net out-migration of 8 percent. Though Estonians constitute a majority of the country's population (62 percent), Russians, who migrated to the region in the post–World War II era, constitute a large (30 percent) minority. The country has a life expectancy at birth of 68.1 years and an infant mortality rate of 14.5 per 1,000 live births.

1995[1]

GEOGRAPHY

AREA (square miles/kilomters)	17,413/45,100	
LAND AREA (square miles/kilometers)	16,680/43,200	
COASTLINE (miles/kilometers)	871/1,393	
CITIES		
CAPITAL	Tallinn	447,672 (93)
MAJOR CITY	Tartu	107,303

POPULATION

TOTAL	1,459,428
DENSITY	34
ANNUAL GROWTH	−1.1%
AGE COHORTS	
0–14	20%
15–64	66%
65 AND OVER	14%
MALE	47%
FEMALE	53%
URBAN	73%
RURAL	27%
NET MIGRATION RATE	−8

1995[1]

IDENTITY

ETHNICITY
ESTONIAN   62%
RUSSIAN   30%
UKRAINIAN   3%

LANGUAGE
ESTONIAN (official)   n/a
RUSSIAN   n/a

RELIGION
LUTHERAN   n/a
EASTERN ORTHODOX   n/a

VITAL STATISTICS

BIRTHS
BIRTH RATE   10.7
URBAN BIRTH RATE   8.9 (93)
RURAL BIRTH RATE   12.4 (93)
INFANT MORTALITY RATE   14.5
ABORTION RATE   1577.9 (92)
LIFE EXPECTANCY AT BIRTH   68.1

MARRIAGES
MARRIAGE RATE   4.5
DIVORCE RATE   3.7

DEATHS
DEATH RATE   14.1

ECONOMICS AND LABOR

GDP PER CAPITA US$ $7,600

LABOR FORCE (thousands)   461.7 (94)
AGRICULTURE   40.2
MINING   11.6
MANUFACTURING   109.4
UTILITIES   14.3
CONSTRUCTION   29.4
TRADE/FOOD/TOURISM   56.7
TRANSPORT/COMMUNICATIONS   43.2

	1995[1]
FINANCE/INSURANCE/REAL ESTATE	27.1
SOCIAL AND PERSONAL SERVICES	129.7
UNEMPLOYMENT (official)	1.9% (93)
UNION DENSITY	26.4%
POVERTY	
UNDER $1/DAY	6% (93)
UNDER $2/DAY	32.5% (93)

TRANSPORT

JOURNEYS (by transport mode)	
RAILROAD PASSENGER TRIPS	336/537 (94)
(millions of miles/kilometers)	
AIR PASSENGER TRIPS (thousands)	157 (94)
PRIVATE CARS	337,800 (94)

HEALTH AND HEALTH CARE

HEALTH CARE	
MEASLES IMMUNIZATION	81%
RATE OF PHYSICIANS	3.1
RATE OF HOSPITAL BEDS	8.4
HEALTH INDICATORS	
SMOKING PREVALENCE M/F	52/24%
TUBERCULOSIS INCIDENCE RATE	0.6
AIDS/HIV CASES	7
TOTAL DEATHS	21,071

EDUCATION

SCHOOL AGE IN SCHOOL	
PRIMARY	91%
SECONDARY	86%
HIGHER	38%
FEMALES IN SCHOOL	
PRIMARY	88%
SECONDARY	86%

1995[1]

COMMUNICATIONS

RATE OF TELEVISIONS   361

FOOTNOTE
1. Part of Soviet Union in 1980 and 1965.

Source: CIA, *The World Factbook, 1997;* ILO, *World Labour Report, 1997;* UN, *Demographic Yearbook, 1997;* UN, *Statistical Yearbook, 1996;* World Bank, *World Development Indicators, 1998.*

ETHIOPIA

Ethiopia is a landlocked country located in the Horn of Africa in East Africa. Sudan borders the 435,184-square-mile (1,127,127-square-kilometer) country on the west, Eritrea on the north, Somalia on the southeast, and Kenya on the south. In 1991, the military government of Mengistu Haile-Mariam was overthrown by the Ethiopian People's Revolutionary Democratic Front and began a process of the transition to democratic rule. National elections were held following the promulgation of a new constitution in 1994. In April 1993, the new government ended a long war in Eritrea by granting that country formal independence. As a result, Ethiopia lost its access to the Red Sea and became landlocked. A border skirmish with Eritrean government troops in June 1998 exposed Ethiopia's dependence on regional states for access to the coast. The national economy remains relatively undeveloped with limited industrial development. Most of Ethiopia's population is engaged in agriculture, primarily for subsistence. In 1995, the population of nearly 57.2 million was growing at a rapid 2.7 annual pace. Due in part to the limited resources available for social and human development, life expectancy is low and infant mortality is high.

Poverty

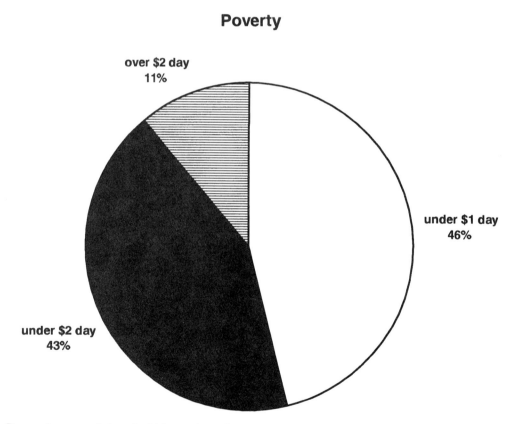

Due to the country's long feudal legacy that only came to an end in 1974, Ethiopia remains one of the most economically destitute countries in the world. Since the mid-1970s, economic modernization and development has been stifled by continuous military conflicts in the region. Nearly 90 percent of the country's population subsists on less than $2 a day.

Religion

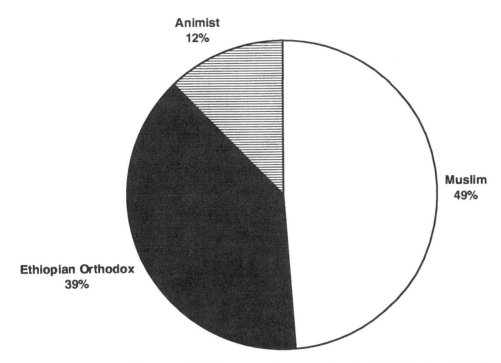

- Animist 12%
- Muslim 49%
- Ethiopian Orthodox 39%

Religious disputes between Christians and Muslims are a major source of conflict in Ethiopia. From the 1970s to the 1990s, Muslim minorities have sought independence from the Ethiopian Orthodox Christian–dominated government. Although Eritrea successfully gained independence, other movements in the north and southwest were quelled militarily. In the early 1990s, most of the Falasha, a small Jewish minority, emigrated to Israel.

CHRONOLOGY

1962	Eritreans launch separatist war against Ethiopian government.
1974	Aging Emperor Haile Selassie overthrown in Marxist military coup.
1977	War breaks out with Somalia over disputed Ogaden region.
1980	War with Tigrean and Eritrean separatists intensifies.
1984	Famine breaks out in much of the country.
1991	Facing defeat in war, Marxist government overthrown.
1993	Eritrea wins independence.

	1995	1980[1]	1965[1]

GEOGRAPHY

AREA (square miles/kilometers)   435,184/1,127,127
LAND AREA (square miles/kilometers)   432,310/1,119,683
COASTLINE (miles/kilometers)   landlocked

CITIES
CAPITAL   Addis Ababa   2,316,400 (94)
MAJOR CITIES   Dire Dawa   194,587
                   Gondar   166,593
                   Nazeret   147,088
                   Harar   122,932

POPULATION

	1995	1980[1]	1965[1]
TOTAL	57,171,662	42,169,203 (84)	n/a
DENSITY (per square mile/kilometer)	132/51	91/35	n/a
CHANGE	2.7%	2.4%	1.7%

AGE COHORTS
	1995
0–14	46%
15–64	51%
65 AND OVER	3%

	1995
MALE	46%
FEMALE	54%

	1995	1980[1]	1965[1]
URBAN	13%	13.6	n/a
RURAL	87%	86.4	n/a

NET MIGRATION RATE   −1.4

IDENTITY

ETHNICITY
	1995
OROMO	40%
MHARA AND TIGREAN	32%
SIDAMO	9%

LANGUAGE
	1995
AMHARIC (official)	n/a
TIGRINYA	n/a
OROMINGA	n/a

	1995	**1980**[1]	**1965**[1]
RELIGION			
MUSLIM	49%		
ETHIOPIAN ORTHODOX	39%		
ANIMIST	12%		

VITAL STATISTICS

	1995	**1980**[1]	**1965**[1]
BIRTHS			
BIRTH RATE	46.1	49.7	n/a
INFANT MORTALITY RATE	119.2	84.2	n/a
LIFE EXPECTANCY AT BIRTH	46.9	40.9	n/a
DEATHS			
DEATH RATE	17.5	23.2	n/a

HOUSEHOLDS

	1995	**1980**[1]	**1965**[1]
NUMBER	n/a	n/a	123,755
AVERAGE SIZE	n/a	n/a	3.5

ECONOMICS AND LABOR

	1995	**1980**[1]	**1965**[1]
GDP PER CAPITA US$	$400		
LABOR FORCE M/F (thousands)	504.6/178.3 (93)		
AGRICULTURE	82.7/17.2		
MINING	0.4/0.1		
MANUFACTURING	96.3/39.0		
UTILITIES	18.2/3.6		
CONSTRUCTION	23.3/4.3		
TRADE/FOOD/TOURISM	18.9/11.4		
TRANSPORT/COMMUNICATIONS	21.2/6.9		
FINANCE/INSURANCE/REAL ESTATE	15.2/6.4		
SOCIAL AND PERSONAL SERVICES	228.6/89.5		
UNEMPLOYMENT (official)	62.9% (93)		
UNION DENSITY	4.10%		
POVERTY			
UNDER $1/DAY	n/a	46% (82)	n/a
UNDER $2/DAY	n/a	89% (82)	n/a

	1995	1980[1]	1965[1]

TRANSPORT

JOURNEYS (by transport mode)
RAILROAD PASSENGER TRIPS   144/230 (93)
  (millions of miles/kilometers)
AIR PASSENGER TRIPS (thousands)   716 (94)

VEHICLES

	1995	1980[1]	1965[1]
PRIVATE CARS	41,000	41,600	23,900
COMMERCIAL	20,300	13,500	8,900

HEALTH AND HEALTH CARE

HEALTH CARE

	1995	1980[1]	1965[1]
ACCESS TO SAFE WATER	10%		
	38%		
RATE OF PHYSICIANS	negligible	negligible	negligible (60)
RATE OF HOSPITAL BEDS	0.2	0.3	0.3 (60)

HEALTH INDICATORS

	1995	1980[1]
PREGNANT WOMEN WITH ANEMIA	42%	
LOW-BIRTH-WEIGHT BABIES	16%	
CHILD MALNUTRITION	48%	
TUBERCULOSIS INCIDENCE RATE	1.55	
AIDS/HIV CASES	19,433	10,008 (93)

EDUCATION

SCHOOL AGE IN SCHOOL

	1995	1980[1]	1965[1]
PRIMARY	31%	36%	12%
SECONDARY	11%	9%	2%
HIGHER	1%	negligible	0.1%

FEMALES IN SCHOOL

	1995	1980[1]	1965[1]
PRIMARY	38%	35%	6%
SECONDARY	9%	6%	1%

ADULT ILLITERACY

	1995	1980[1]	1965[1]
	65%	44.8%	n/a

	1995	1980[1]	1965[1]
COMMUNICATIONS			
RATE OF NEWSPAPERS	1	1	2
RATE OF RADIOS	197	82	6 (70)
RATE OF TELEVISIONS	3	1	1 (70)

FOOTNOTE
1. Includes Eritrea.

Source: CIA, *The World Factbook, 1997;* ILO, *World Labour Report, 1997;* UN, *Demographic Yearbook, 1997;* UN, *Statistical Yearbook, 1996;* World Bank, *World Development Indicators, 1998.*

FIJI

Fiji is an island group located in Oceania, about 1,500 miles (2,400 kilometers) east of Australia. The 7,054-square-mile (18,270-square-kilometer) country is located in the South Pacific Ocean, west of Tonga, south of Tuvalu, east of Vanuatu, and north of New Zealand. The country received independence from the United Kingdom in October 1970. Fiji is rich in agriculture (sugar, coconuts) and minerals (gold), much of which is produced for foreign export primarily to regional countries in Oceania, Japan, Europe, and North America. Tourism remains a large and growing sector of the economy. The country has a relatively high annual per capita gross domestic product (GDP) of $6,100. In 1995, Fiji's population of 782,381 was growing at an annual rate of 1.3 percent, significantly lower than the 3.3 percent annual rate of growth four decades earlier. Fiji has a net out-migration rate of 4.2 per 1,000 residents. In 1995, the country had an average life expectancy at birth of 65.7 years and an infant mortality rate of 13.8 per 1,000 live births.

	1995	1980	1965
GEOGRAPHY			
AREA (square miles/kilometers)	7,054/18,270		
LAND AREA (square miles/kilometers)	7,054/18,270		
COASTLINE (miles/kilometers)	706/1,129		
CITIES			
CAPITAL	Suva	n/a	69,665 (86)	n/a
POPULATION			
TOTAL	782,381	588,068 (76)	345,737 (56)
DENSITY (per square mile/kilometer)	114/44	98/38	67/26
ANNUAL GROWTH	1.3%	1.9%	3.3%
AGE COHORTS			
0–14	35%	n/a	44% (66)
15–64	62%	n/a	53% (66)
65 AND OVER	3%	n/a	3% (66)
MALE	51%		
FEMALE	49%		
URBAN	41%	37.2% (76)	n/a
RURAL	59%	62.8% (76)	n/a
NET MIGRATION RATE	−4.2	n/a	0

	1995	1980	1965

IDENTITY

ETHNICITY

FIJIAN	49%		
INDIAN	46%		

LANGUAGE

ENGLISH (official)	n/a		
FIJIAN	n/a		
HINDI	n/a		

RELIGION

HINDU	38%		
METHODIST	37%		
ROMAN CATHOLIC	9%		

VITAL STATISTICS

BIRTHS

BIRTH RATE	23.4	28.4 (84)	n/a
INFANT MORTALITY RATE	13.8	16.4 (84)	n/a
LIFE EXPECTANCY AT BIRTH	65.7	69 (84)	n/a

MARRIAGES

MARRIAGE RATE	8.7	9.6 (84)	n/a
AVERAGE AGE AT MARRIAGE M/F	n/a	25.3/22.5	n/a
DIVORCE RATE	0.7	0.7 (84)	n/a

DEATHS

DEATH RATE	6.4	4.6 (84)	n/a

ECONOMICS AND LABOR

GDP PER CAPITA US$	$6,100		

LABOR FORCE M/F (thousands)	65.0/27.1 (90)		
AGRICULTURE	2.0/0.3		
MINING	1.6/0.1		
MANUFACTURING	12.4/8.6		
UTILITIES	2.0/0.1		
CONSTRUCTION	5.6/0.1		

	1995	1980	1965
TRADE/FOOD/TOURISM	10.1/4.8		
TRANSPORT/COMMUNICATIONS	8.2/1.3		
FINANCE/INSURANCE/REAL ESTATE	3.6/2.1		
SOCIAL AND PERSONAL SERVICES	19.6/9.7		
UNEMPLOYMENT (official)	6% (94)		

TRANSPORT

	1995	1980	1965
JOURNEYS (by transport mode)			
AIR PASSENGER TRIPS (thousands)	465.0 (94)		
VEHICLES			
PRIVATE CARS	47,700	23,400	7,300
COMMERCIAL	36,800	15,500	3,900

HEALTH AND HEALTH CARE

	1995	1980	1965
HEALTH CARE			
RATE OF PHYSICIANS	n/a	n/a	0.5 (60)
RATE OF HOSPITAL BEDS	n/a	n/a	4 (60)
HEALTH INDICATORS			
AIDS/HIV CASES	7	5 (93)	
TOTAL DEATHS	4,959		

EDUCATION

	1995	1980	1965
SCHOOL AGE IN SCHOOL			
PRIMARY	n/a	110%	92% (63)
SECONDARY	n/a	74%	19% (63)
HIGHER	n/a	2.7%	0.9%
FEMALES IN SCHOOL			
PRIMARY	n/a	109%	78% (63)
SECONDARY	n/a	76%	13% (63)
HIGHER	n/a	2% (81)	1.1%
ADULT ILLITERACY M/F	n/a	16.0/26.0% (76)	n/a

	1995	1980	1965
COMMUNICATIONS			
RATE OF NEWSPAPERS	36	102	17
RATE OF RADIOS	607	473	101
RATE OF TELEVISIONS	17	5.2	0

Source: CIA, *The World Factbook, 1997;* ILO, *World Labour Report, 1997;* UN, *Demographic Yearbook, 1997;* UN, *Statistical Yearbook, 1996;* World Bank, *World Development Indicators, 1998.*

FINLAND

Finland is located on the Gulf of Bothnia and the Gulf of Finland, inlets of the Baltic Sea, in the Scandinavian region of northern Europe. The Russian Federation bounds the 130,127-square-mile (337,030-square-kilometer) country on the east, Norway on the north, and Sweden on the west. The country achieved independence from the Soviet Union in December 1917. The country has a democratic government and a mixed modern and industrialized economy. Finland's key exports are fabricated wood products such as furniture, food products, machinery, and large ships.

The country has one of the highest standards of living in the world. In October 1994, Finns voted in a referendum to join the European Union. In 1995, Finland's population of 5.1 million was growing at a slow rate of 0.1 percent, due in part to a slow birth rate. Finns constitute the ethnic majority. The two leading ethnic minorities in Finland are Swedes and Lapps. In 1995, the country had a high life expectancy at birth of 75.5, and 4.7 infant deaths per 1,000 live births, one of the lowest infant mortality rates in the world.

		1995	1980	1965
GEOGRAPHY				
AREA (square miles/kilometers)		130,127/337,030		
LAND AREA (square miles/kilometers)		117,942/305,470		
COASTLINE (miles/kilometers)		704/1,126		
CITIES				
CAPITAL	Helsinki	512,176 (94)		
MAJOR CITIES	Tampere	175,504		
	Vantaa	162,739		
	Turku	161,380		
	Oulu	105,382		
POPULATION				
TOTAL		5,105,230	4,784,710	4,446,222 (60)
DENSITY (per square mile/kilometer)		39/15	39/15	36/14
CHANGE		0.1%	0.5%	0.8%
AGE COHORTS				
0–14		19%	n/a	27%
15–64		67%	n/a	65%
65 AND OVER		14%	n/a	8%
MALE		49%		
FEMALE		51%		

	1995	1980	1965
URBAN	63%	59.8	n/a
RURAL	37%	40.20%	n/a
NET MIGRATION RATE	0.6	n/a	0 (61)

IDENTITY

ETHNICITY
FINN	n/a		
SWEDE	n/a		
LAPP	n/a		

LANGUAGE
FINNISH	94%		
SWEDISH	6%		

RELIGION
LUTHERAN	89%		

VITAL STATISTICS

BIRTHS
	1995	1980	1965
BIRTH RATE	11.3	13.3 (84)	16.7
URBAN BIRTH RATE	13.2 (94)		
RURAL BIRTH RATE	12.1 (94)		
INFANT MORTALITY RATE	4.7	6.5 (84)	17.6
ABORTION RATE	154 (94)		
LIFE EXPECTANCY AT BIRTH	75.5	74.5 (84)	67.7

MARRIAGES
MARRIAGE RATE	4.7	5.8 (84)	8.2
AVERAGE AGE AT MARRIAGE	31.5/29		
DIVORCE RATE	2.4	2 (84)	1

DEATHS
DEATH RATE	10.9	9.2 (84)	9.4

HOUSEHOLDS

	1995	1980	1965
NUMBER	2,036,732 (90)	n/a	1,315,434 (60)
AVERAGE SIZE	2.5 (90)	n/a	3.3
FEMALE HEADED	37.3%		
SINGLE	20.2%		
MARRIED	4.7%		

	1995	1980	1965
WIDOWED	9.6%		
DIVORCED/SEPARATED	14.2%		

ECONOMICS AND LABOR

GDP PER CAPITA US$	$18,200		

LABOR FORCE M/F (thousands)	1,065.0981 (94)		
AGRICULTURE	110/57		
MINING	5/0		
MANUFACTURING	271/127		
UTILITIES	19/4		
CONSTRUCTION	103/10		
TRADE/FOOD/TOURISM	133/161		
TRANSPORT/COMMUNICATIONS	120/41		
FINANCE/INSURANCE/REAL ESTATE	84/91		
SOCIAL AND PERSONAL SERVICES	216/487		

UNEMPLOYMENT (official)	18.2% (94)		
UNION DENSITY	59.70%		

TRANSPORT

JOURNEYS (by transport mode)			
RAILROAD PASSENGER TRIPS	1,898/3,037 (94)		
(millions of miles/kilometers)			
AIR PASSENGER TRIPS (thousands)	4,492 (94)		

VEHICLES (thousands)			
PRIVATE CARS	1,872.6	1,225.9	n/a
COMMERCIAL	257.5	158.1	n/a

HEALTH AND HEALTH CARE

HEALTH CARE			
ACCESS TO SAFE WATER	100%		
ACCESS TO SANITATION	100%		
MEASLES IMMUNIZATION	98%		
RATE OF PHYSICIANS	2.7	1.9	0.6 (60)
RATE OF HOSPITAL BEDS	10.1	15.5	10 (60)

HEALTH INDICATORS			
LOW-BIRTH-WEIGHT BABIES	5%		
SMOKING PREVALENCE M/F	27/19%		

	1995	**1980**	**1965**
TUBERCULOSIS INCIDENCE RATE	0.15		
AIDS/HIV CASES	230	147	
TOTAL DEATHS	49,352		

EDUCATION

SCHOOL AGE IN SCHOOL
PRIMARY	100%	96%	109%
SECONDARY	116%	100%	57%
HIGHER	67%	32%	8.4%

FEMALES IN SCHOOL
PRIMARY	98%	104%	106%
SECONDARY	122%	106%	79%
HIGHER	n/a	31.5%	13.3% (70)

COMMUNICATIONS

RATE OF NEWSPAPERS	512	505	n/a
RATE OF RADIOS	996	837	347
RATE OF TELEVISIONS	504	414	165

Source: CIA, *The World Factbook, 1997*; ILO, *World Labour Report, 1997*; UN, *Demographic Yearbook, 1997*; UN, *Statistical Yearbook, 1996*; World Bank, *World Development Indicators, 1998*.

FRANCE

France is located in the heart of Western Europe, between the Mediterranean Sea and the Bay of Biscay, an inlet of the Atlantic Ocean. Spain borders the 211,208-square-mile (547,030-square-kilometer) country on the south; Italy and Switzerland on the southeast; and Belgium, Germany, and Luxembourg on the northeast. The United Kingdom lies to France's north, across the English Channel. A new constitution was established in September 1958. The country has a diversified and highly industrialized economy that produces a high standard of living. In 1995, France's annual per capita gross domestic product (GDP) was $20,200. The country is one of the original members of the European Union.

France's 1995 population of more than 58.3 million was growing at an annual rate of less than 0.3 percent, due in part to a steady decline in the birth rate. The French constitute an ethnic majority, although since the 1950s a large and growing number of Africans from the former colonies have migrated to the country. The country has a strong system of social protection that includes universal access to health care and education, although, during the 1990s, the government has sought to curb some of the social benefits as a means to conform to the standards for entry into the European Monetary System. France has a relatively high life expectancy and a low infant mortality rate.

AIDS/HIV

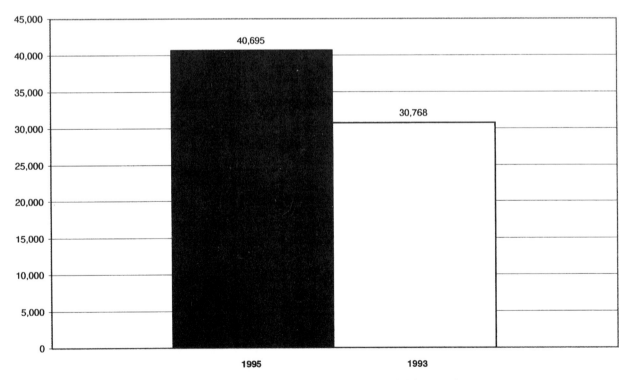

With the highest AIDS/HIV rates in Europe, France has been a leader in AIDS research.

Net Migration Rate

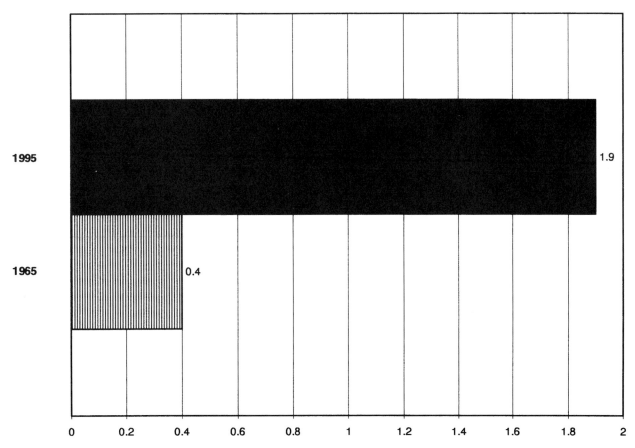

Rising levels of immigration to France from former colonies in the Arab world and sub-Saharan Africa have produced a major anti-immigrant backlash in French politics.

CHRONOLOGY

1962   France defeated in colonial war in Algeria; 1 million Europeans flee Algeria for France.
1966   French President Charles de Gaulle pulls France out of NATO military command.
1968   Radical leftist protests engulf students and workers across France.
1969   De Gaulle forced to resign.
1981   Socialist François Mitterand wins elections as president.
1982   Dozens of French troops killed in terrorist attack in Lebanon.
1989   France celebrates bicentennial of its revolution.
1995   Conservative Jacques Chirac wins presidency.

	1995	1980	1965

GEOGRAPHY

AREA (square miles/kilometers)	211,208/547,030	
LAND AREA (square miles/kilometers)	210,668/545,630	
COASTLINE (miles/kilometers)	2,142/3,427	

CITIES

CAPITAL	Paris	2,152,329 (90)
MAJOR CITIES	Marseille	800,309
	Lyon	415,479
	Toulouse	358,598
	Nice	342,903

POPULATION

	1995	1980	1965
TOTAL	58,317,450	54,334,871 (82)	46,520,271 (62)
DENSITY (per square mile/kilometer)	272/105	259/100	233/90
ANNUAL GROWTH	0.3%	0.3%	1.2%
AGE COHORTS			
0–14	19%	n/a	25%
15–64	66%	n/a	62%
65 AND OVER	15%	n/a	13%
MALE	49%		
FEMALE	51%		
URBAN	73%	73.3% (82)	n/a
RURAL	27%	26.7%	n/a
NET MIGRATION RATE	1.9	n/a	0.4

IDENTITY

	1995
ETHNICITY	
EUROPEAN	n/a
ARAB	n/a
AFRICAN	n/a
LANGUAGE	
FRENCH	n/a
ARABIC	n/a
RELIGION	
ROMAN CATHOLIC	90%

	1995	1980	1965
MUSLIM	n/a		
PROTESTANT	n/a		

VITAL STATISTICS

BIRTHS

	1995	1980	1965
BIRTH RATE	10.8	17.5	14.1 (85)
URBAN BIRTH RATE	13.8 (92)		
RURAL BIRTH RATE	10.5 (92)		
INFANT MORTALITY RATE	4.9	21.7	8 (85)
ABORTION RATE	215.2 (91)		
LIFE EXPECTANCY AT BIRTH	77.9	71.5	74.5

MARRIAGES

	1995	1980	1965
MARRIAGE RATE	4.7	6.9	4.9 (85)
AVERAGE AGE AT MARRIAGE	29.2/27.2		
DIVORCE RATE	1.9	0.7	1.9 (85)

DEATHS

	1995	1980	1965
DEATH RATE	9.3	10.7	10.1 (85)

HOUSEHOLDS

	1995	1980	1965
NUMBER	21,520,700 (92)	n/a	14,561,620 (62)
AVERAGE SIZE	2.6 (90)	n/a	3.1

FEMALE HEADED

	1995
SINGLE	19.2%
MARRIED	59.3%
WIDOWED	14.1%
DIVORCED/SEPARATED	7.4%

ECONOMICS AND LABOR

	1995
GDP PER CAPITA US$	$20,200
LABOR FORCE M/F (thousands)	12,446.3/9,629.9 (93)
AGRICULTURE	748.7/352.1
MANUFACTURING	4,551.8/1,479.8
TRADE/FOOD/TOURISM	7,145.8/7,798.0
UNEMPLOYMENT (official)	12.5% (94)
UNION DENSITY	6.1%

	1995	1980	1965

TRANSPORT

JOURNEYS (by transport mode)

	1995	1980	1965
RAILROAD PASSENGER TRIPS (millions of miles/kilometers)	36,831/58,930 (94)		
AIR PASSENGER TRIPS (thousands)	38,060 (94)		

VEHICLES (thousands)

	1995	1980	1965
PRIVATE CARS	24,900	18,400.00	9,600
COMMERCIAL	4,027	2,710.00	2,181.5

HEALTH AND HEALTH CARE

HEALTH CARE

	1995	1980	1965
ACCESS TO SAFE WATER	100%		
ACCESS TO SANITATION	96%		
MEASLES IMMUNIZATION	78%		
RATE OF PHYSICIANS	2.8	2.2	1.1 (60)
RATE OF HOSPITAL BEDS	9	n/a	8.4 (60)

HEALTH INDICATORS

	1995	1980	1965
LOW-BIRTH-WEIGHT BABIES	5%		
SMOKING PREVALENCE M/F	40/27%		
TUBERCULOSIS INCIDENCE RATE	0.2		
AIDS/HIV CASES	40,695	30,768 (93)	
TOTAL DEATHS	529,000		

EDUCATION

SCHOOL AGE IN SCHOOL

	1995	1980	1965
PRIMARY	106%	111%	135%
SECONDARY	111%	85%	56%
HIGHER	50%	25%	10.5%

FEMALES IN SCHOOL

	1995	1980	1965
PRIMARY	102%	109%	134%
SECONDARY	113%	83%	59%

	1995	1980	1965
COMMUNICATIONS			
RATE OF NEWSPAPERS	205	192	245
RATE OF RADIOS	890	741	330
RATE OF TELEVISIONS	412	353	138

Source: CIA, *The World Factbook, 1997;* ILO, *World Labour Report, 1997;* UN, *Demographic Yearbook, 1997;* UN, *Statistical Yearbook, 1996;* World Bank, *World Development Indicators, 1998.*

GABON

Gabon is located in west central Africa on the Gulf of Guinea, an inlet of the Atlantic Ocean. The Republic of Congo borders the 103,347-square-mile (267,670-square-kilometer) country on the east, and Cameroon and Equatorial Guinea border on the north. In August 1960, the country gained independence from France. Since December 1967, the country has been led by the government of President Omar Bongo. Owing to the presence of rich oil fields in the Gulf of Guinea, Gabon is one of the most economically prosperous countries in Africa. In 1995, the country had an annual per capita gross domestic product (GDP) of $5,200. The petroleum fields are complemented by significant other natural resources, including timber, manganese, uranium, and gold. Despite the country's abundant wealth, a large share of the population continues to live in rural areas under subsistence conditions. In 1995, the country had a relatively small population of 1,172,798 growing at an annual rate of 1.5 percent, of which about 50 percent resided in urban areas. The average life expectancy at birth is 55.6 years, and the infant mortality rate is 50 per 1,000 live births.

	1995	1980	1965
GEOGRAPHY			
AREA (square miles/kilometers)	103,347/267,670		
LAND AREA (square miles/kilometers)	99,486/257,670		
COASTLINE (miles/kilometers)	553/885		
CITIES			
CAPITAL	Libreville	n/a	n/a	57,000 (67)
POPULATION			
TOTAL	1,172,798	n/a	448,564 (61)
DENSITY (per square mile/kilometer)	13/5	10.0/4.0	n/a
ANNUAL GROWTH	1.5%	1.6%	1.5%
AGE COHORTS			
0–14	34%	n/a	36%
15–64	61%	n/a	57%
65 AND OVER	5%	n/a	7%
MALE	49%		
FEMALE	51%		

	1995	1980	1965
URBAN	50%		
RURAL	50%		
NET MIGRATION RATE	0		

IDENTITY

ETHNICITY
FANG	n/a		
ESHIRU	n/a		
BAPOUNOU	n/a		

LANGUAGE
FRENCH (official)	n/a		
FANG	n/a		
MYENE	n/a		

RELIGION
CHRISTIAN	65%		
ANIMIST	34%		
MUSLIM	1%		

VITAL STATISTICS

BIRTHS
	1995	1980	1965
BIRTH RATE	28.2	33.8	35
INFANT MORTALITY RATE	94	229	229
LIFE EXPECTANCY AT BIRTH	55.6	35	35

DEATHS
DEATH RATE	13.6	18.1	30

ECONOMICS AND LABOR

GDP PER CAPITA US$	$5,200		

LABOR FORCE M/F
AGRICULTURE	46/59%		
INDUSTRY	21/10%		
SERVICES	33/32%		

UNION DENSITY	2%		

	1995	1980	1965
TRANSPORT			
JOURNEYS (by transport mode)			
AIR PASSENGER TRIPS (thousands)	481.0 (94)		
VEHICLES			
PRIVATE CARS	23,000	n/a	3,200
COMMERCIAL	17,000	n/a	5,800
HEALTH AND HEALTH CARE			
HEALTH CARE			
ACCESS TO SAFE WATER	67%		
ACCESS TO SANITATION	76%		
MEASLES IMMUNIZATION	50%		
RATE OF PHYSICIANS	0.5	0.5	0.1 (60)
RATE OF HOSPITAL BEDS	3.2	n/a	6.2 (60)
HEALTH INDICATORS			
LOW-BIRTH-WEIGHT BABIES	10%		
CHILD MALNUTRITION	15%		
TUBERCULOSIS INCIDENCE RATE	1		
AIDS/HIV CASES	890	521 (93)	
EDUCATION			
SCHOOL AGE IN SCHOOL			
PRIMARY	142%	115%	136%
SECONDARY	n/a	21%	11%
FEMALES IN SCHOOL			
PRIMARY	142%	113%	120%
SECONDARY	n/a	17%	4%
ADULT ILLITERACY M/F	26/47	29.8/46.6 (85)	n/a
COMMUNICATIONS			
RATE OF NEWSPAPERS	16	19	n/a
RATE OF RADIOS	147	130	80
RATE OF TELEVISIONS	38	12	3

Source: CIA, The World Factbook, 1997; ILO, World Labour Report, 1997; UN, Demographic Yearbook, 1997; UN, Statistical Yearbook, 1996; World Bank, World Development Indicators, 1998.

THE GAMBIA

The Gambia is a narrow strip of land lying inside Senegal on both sides of the Gambia River in western Africa. Senegal envelops the 4,363-square-mile (11,300-square-kilometer) country on the north, east, and south, and on the narrow west coast is the Atlantic Ocean. In 1965, The Gambia received independence from the United Kingdom. A 1981 agreement calling for confederation with Senegal was abandoned in 1989. The majority of the country's population is engaged in subsistence agriculture, though some commodities (e.g., peanuts, cotton) are sold to export markets. In 1995, the densely populated country of 1.2 million was growing at a very high rate of 3.6 percent, owing to a birth rate of 44.4 and a death rate of 13.7 per 1,000 residents. In the same year, The Gambia's life expectancy at birth was 53 years and the infant mortality rate was 132 per 1,000 live births.

	1995	1980	1965
GEOGRAPHY			
AREA (square miles/kilometers)	4,363/11,300		
LAND AREA (square miles/kilometers)	3,861/10,000		
COASTLINE (miles/kilometers)	50/80		
CITIES			
CAPITAL	Banjul	n/a	49,181	n/a
POPULATION			
TOTAL	1,204,984	695,886 (83)	315,486 (63)
DENSITY (per square mile/kilometer)	256/99	145/56	n/a
ANNUAL GROWTH	3.6%	1.4%	1.9%
AGE COHORTS			
0–14	46%		
15–64	51%		
65 AND OVER	3%		
MALE	50%		
FEMALE	50%		
URBAN	26%	18.20%	n/a
RURAL	74%	81.80%	n/a
NET MIGRATION RATE	4.7		

	1995	1980	1965

IDENTITY

ETHNICITY
MADINKA   42%
FULA   18%
WOLOF   16%

LANGUAGE
ENGLISH (official)   n/a
MANDINKA   n/a
WOLOF   n/a

RELIGION
MUSLIM   90%
CHRISTIAN   9%
ANIMIST   1%

VITAL STATISTICS

BIRTHS

	1995	1980	1965
BIRTH RATE	44.4	48.4	38.7
INFANT MORTALITY RATE	132	174	n/a
LIFE EXPECTANCY AT BIRTH	53	35	43

DEATHS

	1995	1980	1965
DEATH RATE	13.7	29	21

ECONOMICS AND LABOR

GDP PER CAPITA US$ $1,100

LABOR FORCE M/F (thousands)   21.1/5.0 (87)
AGRICULTURE   1.4/0.6
MINING   0.0/0.0
MANUFACTURING   1.9/0.5
UTILITIES   0.8/0.1
CONSTRUCTION   2.9/0.0
TRADE/FOOD/TOURISM   3.7/0.8
TRANSPORT/COMMUNICATIONS   2.7/0.4
FINANCE/INSURANCE/REAL ESTATE   0.8/0.3
SOCIAL AND PERSONAL SERVICES   7.0/2.3

	1995	1980	1965

TRANSPORT

JOURNEYS (by transport mode)

AIR PASSENGER TRIPS (thousands)	19.0 (94)		

VEHICLES

PRIVATE CARS	7,000	6,000	2,000
COMMERCIAL	3,000	1,600	1,800

HEALTH AND HEALTH CARE

HEALTH CARE

ACCESS TO SAFE WATER	76%		
ACCESS TO SANITATION	37%		
MEASLES IMMUNIZATION	68%		
RATE OF PHYSICIANS	n/a	n/a	0.1
RATE OF HOSPITAL BEDS	0.6	n/a	1.4

HEALTH INDICATORS

PREGNANT WOMEN WITH ANEMIA	80%		
LOW-BIRTH-WEIGHT BABIES	10%		
CHILD MALNUTRITION	17%		
TUBERCULOSIS INCIDENCE RATE	1.66		
AIDS/HIV CASES	410	295 (93)	

EDUCATION

SCHOOL AGE IN SCHOOL

PRIMARY	73%	53%	26%
SECONDARY	22%	11%	6%
HIGHER	2%	n/a	n/a

FEMALES IN SCHOOL

PRIMARY	41%	35%	15%
SECONDARY	n/a	7%	4%

ADULT ILLITERACY M/F	47/75%	64.4/84.9% (85)	n/a

	1995	1980	1965
COMMUNICATIONS			
RATE OF NEWSPAPERS	2	n/a	5 (59)
RATE OF RADIOS	162	114	95

Source: CIA, The World Factbook, 1997; ILO, World Labour Report, 1997; UN, Demographic Yearbook, 1997; UN, Statistical Yearbook, 1996; World Bank, World Development Indicators, 1998.

GEORGIA

Georgia is located south of the Russian Federation on the Black Sea. Turkey, Armenia, and Azerbaijan border the 26,911-square-mile (69,700-square-kilometer) country on the south. In 1991, Georgia gained independence amid the breakup and collapse of the Soviet Union. Subsequently, civil conflicts between rival ethnic groups and Georgia have destabilized the political and economic transition to independence. Between 1991 and 1994, the Abkhazian and South Osssetian autonomy movements were the two most significant challenges to the new Georgian state. In the mid-1990s, the conflicts subsided. Under Soviet rule, Georgia's economy industrialized and modernized rapidly. The leading exports are citrus and food products and manufactured goods. The country's population of 5,219,810 in 1995 was declining at an annual rate of 1 percent, due in part to a high out-migration rate. Although Georgians are the country's ethnic majority with about 70 percent of the population, Russians (6 percent) and Armenians (8 percent) remain significant ethnic minorities. The country has a fairly high life expectancy of 68.1 and an infant mortality rate of 19.6 deaths per 1,000 live births.

1995[1]

GEOGRAPHY

AREA (square miles/kilometers)	26,911/69,700	
LAND AREA (square miles/kilometers)	26,911/69,700	
COASTLINE (miles/kilometers)	194/310	
CITIES		
CAPITAL	Tbilisi	1,268,000 (90)
MAJOR CITIES	Kutaisi	236,000
	Rustavi	160,000
	Batumi	137,000
	Sukhumi	122,000

POPULATION

TOTAL	5,219,810
DENSITY (per square mile/kilometer)	202/78
ANNUAL GROWTH	−1%
AGE COHORTS	
0–14	22%
15–64	66%
65 AND OVER	12%
MALE	47%
FEMALE	53%

	1995[1]
URBAN	58%
RURAL	42%
NET MIGRATION RATE	−10.8

IDENTITY

ETHNICITY

GEORGIAN	70%
ARMENIAN	8%
RUSSIAN	6%

LANGUAGE

GEORGIAN	71%
RUSSIAN	9%
ARMENIAN	7%

RELIGION

EASTERN ORTHODOX	75%
MUSLIM	11%
ARMENIAN ORTHODOX	8%

VITAL STATISTICS

BIRTHS

BIRTH RATE	12.8
INFANT MORTALITY RATE	19.6
LIFE EXPECTANCY AT BIRTH	68.1

MARRIAGES

MARRIAGE RATE	7
DIVORCE RATE	1.4

DEATHS

DEATH RATE	12.2

ECONOMICS AND LABOR

GDP PER CAPITA US$	$1,080

LABOR FORCE M/F

AGRICULTURE	27/24%
INDUSTRY	38/23%
SERVICES	34/52%

1995[1]

TRANSPORT

JOURNEYS (by transport mode)
RAILROAD PASSENGER TRIPS   627/1,003 (93)
  (millions of miles/kilometers)
AIR PASSENGER TRIPS (thousands)   224.0 (94)

VEHICLES
PRIVATE CARS   468,800 (93)
COMMERCIAL   56,000

HEALTH AND HEALTH CARE

HEALTH CARE
MEASLES IMMUNIZATION   63%
RATE OF PHYSICIANS   4.2
RATE OF HOSPITAL BEDS   8.2

HEALTH INDICATORS
TUBERCULOSIS INCIDENCE RATE   0.7
AIDS/HIV CASES   2

EDUCATION

SCHOOL AGE IN SCHOOL
PRIMARY   82%
SECONDARY   73%
HIGHER   38%

FOOTNOTE
1. Part of Soviet Union in 1950 and 1965.

Source: CIA, The World Factbook, 1997; ILO, World Labour Report, 1997; UN, Demographic Yearbook, 1997; UN, Statistical Yearbook, 1996; World Bank, World Development Indicators, 1998.

GERMANY

Gemany, the most populous country in Western Europe, is located on the North Sea and the Baltic Sea. Poland and the Czech Republic border the 137,803-square-mile   (356,910-square-kilometer) country on the east; Switzerland and Austria on the south; France, Luxembourg, Belgium, and Netherlands on the west; and Denmark on the north. Germany remained divided between east and west from the end of World War II until October 1990. East Germany, known as the German Democratic Republic, was in the Soviet military and economic alliance and developed a state-controlled economy with a strong system of social protection. West Germany, the German Federal Republic, became part of the Western alliance and developed a mixed economy with private enter-

prise and a strong social welfare system. Following unification of the two Germanys in 1990, much of the East German economy was privatized. The Federal Republic financed much of the cost of modernizing East German infrastructure and industry. East Germans have had to bear the cost of foreign speculation and steeply higher unemployment. In 1995, Germany's population of over 83.5 million was growing at a rate of 0.7 percent. Much of this new population growth is due to rising migration. The country has a relatively high life expectancy and a low infant mortality rate. Germans account for 95 percent of the population. A Turkish minority that immigrated in the post–World War II years constitutes 2 percent of the national population.

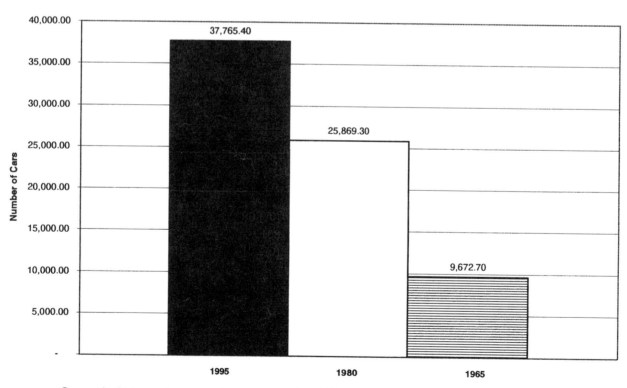

Germany's phenomenal economic rise out of the ashes of World War II has been likened to a "miracle." That miraculous rise can be seen in the explosive growth of private car ownership.

Labor Market

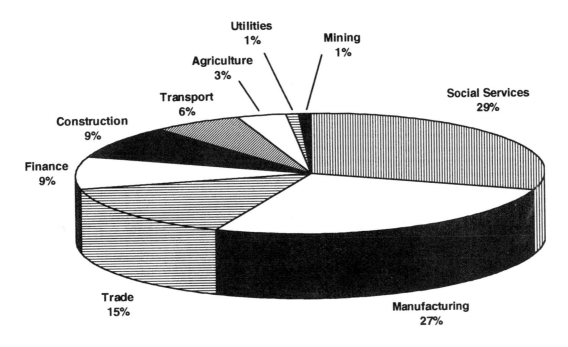

Utilities
1%

Mining
1%

Agriculture
3%

Transport
6%

Social Services
29%

Construction
9%

Finance
9%

Trade
15%

Manufacturing
27%

*Note: Finance includes insurance and real estate;
Transport includes communications;
Trade includes food and tourist industries.*

Like many other advanced economies, Germany's has seen a shift from a labor-force profile, in which manufacturing dominates, to one in which service-sector jobs predominate. Germany's current labor-force divisions reflect that transformation.

CHRONOLOGY

1961   Berlin Wall constructed, physically separating West Germany and East Germany.
1966   Long-time conservative Chancellor Konrad Adenauer loses office.
1969   Social Democrats under Willy Brandt win control of government.
1970   Brandt launches *ostpolitik*, calling for closer relations between Germany and socialist bloc.
1973   West Germany and East Germany join United Nations.
1975   Left-wing terrorism increases.
1982   Conservative Christian Democrat Helmut Kohl wins national elections in Germany, ending 13 years of Social Democrat rule.
1989   Berlin Wall comes down; communist government in East Germany falls.
1990   West Germany and East Germany formally united.
1998   Kohl government loses elections, ending 16 years of conservative rule.

	1995	1980[1]	1965[1]

GEOGRAPHY

AREA (square miles/kilometers)	137,803/356,910
LAND AREA (square miles/kilometers)	134,950/349,520
COASTLINE (miles/kilometers)	1,493/2,389

CITIES

CAPITAL	Berlin	3,472,009 (94)
MAJOR CITIES	Hamburg	1,705,872
	Munich	1,244,676
	Cologne	963,817
	Frankfurt am Main	652,412

POPULATION

	1995	1980[1]	1965[1]
TOTAL	83,536,115	n/a	75,278,231
DENSITY (per square mile/kilometer)	593/229		
ANNUAL GROWTH	0.7%		

AGE COHORTS

	1995	1980[1]	1965[1]
0–14	16%	n/a	23%
15–64	69%	n/a	65%
65 AND OVER	15%	n/a	12%

MALE	48%
FEMALE	52%

	1995	1980[1]	1965[1]
URBAN	87%	76.2%	n/a
RURAL	13%	23.8%	n/a

NET MIGRATION RATE	8.3

IDENTITY

ETHNICITY

GERMAN	95%
TURKISH	2%
ITALIAN	1%

LANGUAGE

GERMAN	n/a

	1995	1980[1]	1965[1]
RELIGION			
PROTESTANT	45%		
ROMAN CATHOLIC	37%		
MUSLIM	2%		

VITAL STATISTICS

	1995	1980[1]	1965[1]
BIRTHS			
BIRTH RATE	9.7		
INFANT MORTALITY RATE	5.6		
LIFE EXPECTANCY AT BIRTH	76		
MARRIAGES			
MARRIAGE RATE	5.4		
AVERAGE AGE AT MARRIAGE M/F	30.3/27.5		
DIVORCE RATE	1.9		
DEATHS			
DEATH RATE	12.2		

HOUSEHOLDS

	1995	1980[1]	1965[1]
NUMBER	n/a	6,218,438 (87)[2]	n/a
AVERAGE SIZE	n/a	2.3 (87)[2]	n/a
TYPE OF HOUSEHOLD			
SINGLE	19.6%		
MARRIED	57.9%		
WIDOWED	15.1%		
DIVORCED/SEPARATED	7.4%		
FEMALE HEADED	27.1%		

ECONOMICS AND LABOR

	1995	1980[1]	1965[1]
GDP PER CAPITA US$	$17,900		
LABOR FORCE M/F (thousands)	20,987.0/14,088.0 (94)		
AGRICULTURE	714.0/477		
MINING	234.0/32		
MANUFACTURING	6,877.0/2,765		
UTILITIES	295.0/79		
CONSTRUCTION	2,753.0/355		
TRADE/FOOD/TOURISM	2,273.6/3,111		

	1995	1980[1]	1965[1]
TRANSPORT/COMMUNICATIONS	1,555.0/614		
FINANCE/INSURANCE/REAL ESTATE	1,636.0/1,523		
SOCIAL AND PERSONAL SERVICES	4,651.0/6,133		
UNEMPLOYMENT M/F (official)	8.4/19.2%[3] (94)		
UNION DENSITY	29.6%		

TRANSPORT

	1995	1980[1]	1965[1]
JOURNEYS (by transport mode)			
RAILROAD PASSENGER TRIPS	38,329/61,327 (94)		
(millions of miles/kilometers)			
AIR PASSENGER TRIPS (thousands)	30,964.0 (94)		
VEHICLES (thousands)			
PRIVATE CARS	37,765.4	25,869.30	9,672.70
COMMERCIAL	3,150.7	2,200.60	1023.5

HEALTH AND HEALTH CARE

	1995	1980[1]	1965[1]
HEALTH CARE			
ACCESS TO SANITATION	100%		
MEASLES IMMUNIZATION	75%		
RATE OF PHYSICIANS	3.3	2.2	n/a
RATE OF HOSPITAL BEDS	9.7		
HEALTH INDICATORS			
SMOKING PREVALENCE M/F	37/22%		
TUBERCULOSIS INCIDENCE RATE	0.18		
AIDS/HIV CASES	14,423	11,552 (93)	
TOTAL DEATHS	875,071		

EDUCATION

	1995	1980[1]	1965[1]
SCHOOL AGE IN SCHOOL			
PRIMARY	102%	n/a	n/a
SECONDARY	103%	98%	n/a
HIGHER	43%	34%	n/a
FEMALES IN SCHOOL			
PRIMARY	100%	n/a	n/a
SECONDARY	103%	n/a	n/a
HIGHER	n/a	36.4% (70)	28.8% (70)

	1995	1980[1]	1965[1]

COMMUNICATIONS

RATE OF NEWSPAPERS	323	335/524[3]	n/a
RATE OF RADIOS	890	893/536[3]	351/323 (70)[3]
RATE OF TELEVISIONS	559	439/514[3]	275/264[3]

FOOTNOTES

1. Statistics for both West and East Germany unless otherwise noted.
2. West Germany only.
3. First statistic for the former West Germany; second statistic for former East Germany.

Source: CIA, The World Factbook, 1997; ILO, World Labour Report, 1997; UN, Demographic Yearbook, 1997; UN, Statistical Yearbook, 1996; World Bank, World Development Indicators, 1998.

GHANA

Ghana is located in West Africa on the Gulf of Guinea, an inlet of the Atlantic Ocean. Côte d'Ivoire borders the 92,100-square-mile (238,540-square-kilometer) country on the west, Burkina Faso on the north, and Togo on the east. Ghana gained independence from the United Kingdom in March 1957. Much of the formative years of Ghana's independence were marked by military intervention and economic and political instability. Jerry Rawlings, the current president, himself gained power in a military putsch. In recent years, however, the government has had relative political stability and economic growth. The country emerged from a painful privatization and market-reform process and is now expanding exports dramatically. Nevertheless, the majority of Ghana's exports are raw materials and agricultural commodities. In 1995 the country had a per capita gross domestic product (GDP) of $1,400. The population of 17.7 million in 1995 was growing at an annual rate of 2.3 percent, lower than preceding years, but still fairly high by international standards. Ghana has a life expectancy at birth of 56.2 years and an infant mortality rate of 81.1 infant deaths per 1,000 live births. The country has an ethnically diverse population.

	1995	**1980**	**1965**
GEOGRAPHY			
AREA (square miles/kilometers)	92,100/238,540		
LAND AREA (square miles/kilometers)	88,811/230,020		
COASTLINE (miles/kilometers)	337/539		
CITIES			
CAPITAL	Accra	n/a	n/a	564,194 (70)
MAJOR CITIES	Kumasi	n/a	n/a	260,286
	Sekondi-Takoradi	n/a	n/a	91,874
POPULATION			
TOTAL	17,698,271	12,205,574 (84)	6,726,815 (60)
DENSITY (per square mile/kilometer)	189/73	148/57	n/a
ANNUAL GROWTH	2.3%	3.3%	2.7%
AGE COHORTS			
0–14	43%		45%
15–64	54%		52%
65 AND OVER	3%		3%
MALE	49%		
FEMALE	51%		

	1995	1980	1965
URBAN	36%	31.3% (84)	n/a
RURAL	64%	68.7% (84)	n/a
NET MIGRATION	−0.9	n/a	0 (64)

IDENTITY

ETHNICITY

AKAN	44%
MOSHI-DAGOMBA	16%
EWE	13%

LANGUAGE

ENGLISH (official)	n/a
AKAN	n/a
MOSHI-DAGOMBA	n/a

RELIGION

ANIMIST	38%
MUSLIM	30%
CHRISTIAN	24%

VITAL STATISTICS

BIRTHS

	1995	1980	1965
BIRTH RATE	35	46.9	47.5
INFANT MORTALITY RATE	81.1	156	156
LIFE EXPECTANCY AT BIRTH	56.2	52	38.7

DEATHS

	1995	1980	1965
DEATH RATE	11.2	14.6	24

ECONOMICS AND LABOR

GDP PER CAPITA US$	$1,400

LABOR FORCE (thousands) 186.3 (91)

AGRICULTURE	14.7
MINING	17.1
MANUFACTURING	20.6
UTILITIES	1.7
CONSTRUCTION	7.8
TRADE/FOOD/TOURISM	7.5
TRANSPORT/COMMUNICATIONS	10.4

	1995	**1980**	**1965**
FINANCE/INSURANCE/REAL ESTATE	8.4		
SOCIAL AND PERSONAL SERVICES	98.1		
UNION DENSITY	25.9%		

TRANSPORT

	1995	**1980**	**1965**
JOURNEYS (by transport mode)			
RAILROAD PASSENGER TRIPS	199/318 (87)		
(millions of miles/kilometers)			
AIR PASSENGER TRIPS (thousands)	182 (94)		
VEHICLES			
PRIVATE CARS	90,000	75,200	30,000
COMMERCIAL	44,700	33,200	19,500

HEALTH AND HEALTH CARE

	1995	**1980**	**1965**
HEALTH CARE			
ACCESS TO SAFE WATER	56%		
ACCESS TO SANITATION	27%		
MEASLES IMMUNIZATION	54%		
RATE OF PHYSICIANS	n/a	n/a	0.1 (60)
RATE OF HOSPITAL BEDS	1.5	n/a	0.8 (60)
HEALTH INDICATORS			
LOW-BIRTH-WEIGHT BABIES	17%		
CHILD MALNUTRITION	27%		
TUBERCULOSIS INCIDENCE RATE	2.22		
AIDS/HIV CASES	17,564	12,656 (93)	

EDUCATION

	1995	**1980**	**1965**
SCHOOL AGE IN SCHOOL			
PRIMARY	76%	79%	97%
SECONDARY	37%	41%	15%
HIGHER	n/a	2%	0.60%
FEMALES IN SCHOOL			
PRIMARY	74%	76%	81%
SECONDARY	n/a	38%	9%
ADULT ILLITERACY M/F	24/47%	35.9/57.2% (85)	56.9/89.6% (70)

	1995	1980	1965
COMMUNICATIONS			
RATE OF NEWSPAPERS	18	47	29
RATE OF RADIOS	269	158	83
RATE OF TELEVISIONS	16	5	0.1

Source: CIA, *The World Factbook, 1997*; ILO, *World Labour Report, 1997*; UN, *Demographic Yearbook, 1997*; UN, *Statistical Yearbook, 1996*; World Bank, *World Development Indicators, 1998*.

GREECE

Greece is located in southeastern Europe on the Aegean Sea, Ionian Sea, and Mediterranean Sea. Turkey borders the 50,942-square-mile (131,940-square-kilometer) country on the east; Albania, the former Yugoslav Republic of Macedonia, and Bulgaria on the north. Greece, a member state of the European Union, has a diversified economy consisting of industry, agriculture, and services, including tourism. The Greek economy has a large and growing state-owned public sector. The Greek government's effort to conform to the spending restrictions for entry into the European Monetary Union by curbing spending has in-

creased unemployment. In 1995, the country's per capita gross domestic product (GDP) was $9,500. In the same year, due to a slowing of Greece's birth rate, the country's population of more than 10.5 million was growing at the fairly slow annual pace of 0.4 percent. The country has comprehensive social and economic protection, including universal health insurance and compulsory education. In 1995, Greece had a very high average life expectancy of 78.1 years and a low infant mortality rate of 7.9 infant deaths per 1,000 live births.

	1995	1980	1965
GEOGRAPHY			
AREA (square miles/kilometers)	50,942/131,940		
LAND AREA (square miles/kilometers)	50,502/130,800		
COASTLINE (miles/kilometers)	8,548/13,676		
CITIES			
CAPITAL	Athens	772,072 (91)	
MAJOR CITIES	Thessaloniki	383,967	
	Piraeus	182,671	
	Patras	153,344	
	Peristeri	137,288	
POPULATION			
TOTAL	10,538,594	9,740,151 (81)	8,387,201 (61)
DENSITY (per square mile/kilometer)	205/79	194/75	168/65
ANNUAL GROWTH	0.4%	0.6%	0.7%
AGE COHORTS			
0–14	16%	n/a	26%
15–64	68%	n/a	65%
65 AND OVER	16%	n/a	9%
MALE	49%		
FEMALE	51%		

	1995	1980	1965
URBAN	65%	58.1%	n/a
RURAL	35%	41.9%	n/a
NET MIGRATION RATE	4.0		

IDENTITY

ETHNICITY
GREEK	98%

LANGUAGE
GREEK	n/a

RELIGION
GREEK ORTHODOX	98%
MUSLIM	1%

VITAL STATISTICS

BIRTHS
	1995	1980	1965
BIRTH RATE	9.8	11.7 (85)	18.1
URBAN BIRTH RATE	11.2 (91)		
RURAL BIRTH RATE	8.2 (91)		
INFANT MORTALITY RATE	7.9	14 (85)	33.7
ABORTION RATE	115. 2 (92)		
LIFE EXPECTANCY AT BIRTH	78.1	72.4 (85)	69.1

MARRIAGES
	1995	1980	1965
MARRIAGE RATE	5.7	6.3 (85)	8.8
AVERAGE AGE AT MARRIAGE M/F	29.4/24.5		
DIVORCE RATE	0.7	0.6 (85)	0.4

DEATHS
	1995	1980	1965
DEATH RATE	9.5	9.3 (85)	7.9

HOUSEHOLDS

	1995	1980	1965
NUMBER	3,203,834 (91)	n/a	2,142,968 (61)
URBAN	1,945,097		
RURAL	1,258,737		

	1995	1980	1965
AVERAGE SIZE	3 (91)		
URBAN	2.9		
RURAL	3.1		
TYPE OF HOUSEHOLD			
SINGLE	8.9%		
MARRIED	76.4%		
WIDOWED	12.0%		
DIVORCED/SEPARATED	2.8%		
FEMALE HEADED	20.2%		

ECONOMICS AND LABOR

	1995	1980	1965
GDP PER CAPITA US$	$9,500		
LABOR FORCE M/F (thousands)	2,403.2/1,281.3 (92)		
AGRICULTURE	468.7/338.0		
MINING	17.6/0.7		
MANUFACTURING	487.3/211.4		
UTILITIES	30.9/5.8		
CONSTRUCTION	242.5/3.7		
TRADE/FOOD/TOURISM	423.9/263.4		
TRANSPORT/COMMUNICATIONS	220.7/29.5		
FINANCE/INSURANCE/REAL ESTATE	120.1/80.5		
SOCIAL AND PERSONAL SERVICES	391.5/348.1		
UNEMPLOYMENT (official)	9.7% (93)		
UNION DENSITY	15.4%		

TRANSPORT

	1995	1980	1965
JOURNEYS (by transport mode)			
RAILROAD PASSENGER TRIPS	874/1,399 (94)		
(millions of miles/kilometers)			
AIR PASSENGER TRIPS (thousands)	5,813 (94)		
VEHICLES (thousands)			
PRIVATE CARS	2,074.10	862.6	104.3
COMMERCIAL	849.1	425	73.4

	1995	1980	1965

HEALTH AND HEALTH CARE

HEALTH CARE

	1995	1980	1965
ACCESS TO SANITATION	96%		
MEASLES IMMUNIZATION	70%		
RATE OF PHYSICIANS	4	2.4	1.3 (60)
RATE OF HOSPITAL BEDS	5	6.2	5.8 (60)

HEALTH INDICATORS

	1995	1980	1965
LOW-BIRTH-WEIGHT BABIES	9%		
SMOKING PREVALENCE M/F	46/28%		
TUBERCULOSIS INCIDENCE RATE	12%		
AIDS/HIV CASES	1,314	953 (93)	
TOTAL DEATHS	98,000		

EDUCATION

SCHOOL AGE IN SCHOOL

	1995	1980	1965
PRIMARY	n/a	103%	111%
SECONDARY	95%	81%	54%
HIGHER	38%	17%	6.8%

FEMALES IN SCHOOL

	1995	1980	1965
PRIMARY	91%	99%	109%
SECONDARY	38%	81%	44%
HIGHER	n/a	14.2%	8.8% (70)

	1995	1980	1965
ADULT ILLITERACY M/F	n/a	3.9/15.7 (81)	n/a

COMMUNICATIONS

	1995	1980	1965
RATE OF NEWSPAPERS	135	120	80 (70)
RATE OF RADIOS	416	343	108
RATE OF TELEVISIONS	202	171	19 (70)

Source: CIA, *The World Factbook, 1997;* ILO, *World Labour Report, 1997;* UN, *Demographic Yearbook, 1997;* UN, *Statistical Yearbook, 1996;* World Bank, *World Development Indicators, 1998.*

GRENADA

Grenada is an island located in the Windward Islands Archipelago of the southeastern Caribbean Sea. The 340-square-mile (131-square-kilometer) island is located south of The Grenadines and north of Trinidad and Tobago, and the Venezuelan coast. Grenada gained independence from the United Kingdom in February 1974. In 1983, American armed forces and allies in the region invaded the country, ousted the government, and expelled Cuban nationals assisting with the country's economic development. The country had previously relied almost exclusively on the export of spices and plants to North American and Western European markets. Cuban assistance in constructing the airport greatly contributed to the development of a rapidly growing tourist industry. The country's population of 94,961 in 1995 was growing at the slow pace of 0.6 percent, primarily due to a net out-migration rate of 17.9 per 1,000 residents. Grenadans have an average life expectancy at birth of 70.9 years and an infant mortality rate of 15.4 deaths per 1,000 live births.

	1995	1965	1980
GEOGRAPHY			
AREA (square miles/kilometers)	340/131		
LAND AREA (square miles/kilometers)	340/131		
COASTLINE (miles/kilometers)	76/121		
CITIES			
CAPITAL Saint George's	n/a	4,788 (81)	n/a
POPULATION			
TOTAL	94,961	89,068 (81)	88,677 (60)
DENSITY (per square mile/kilometer)	692/267	844/326	733/283
CHANGE	0.6%	0.9%	1.2%
AGE COHORTS			
0–14	43%	n/a	36%
15–64	52%	n/a	59%
65 AND OVER	5%	n/a	5%
NET MIGRATION RATE	−17.9	n/a	−1.8
IDENTITY			
ETHNICITY			
BLACK	n/a		

	1995	1980	1965
LANGUAGE			
ENGLISH	n/a		
FRENCH PATOIS	n/a		
RELIGION			
ROMAN CATHOLIC	n/a		
ANGLICAN	n/a		

VITAL STATISTICS

	1995	1980	1965
BIRTHS			
BIRTH RATE	29.1	25.1	29
INFANT MORTALITY RATE	15.4	15.4	42.9
LIFE EXPECTANCY AT BIRTH	70.9	62.9	62.7
MARRIAGES			
MARRIAGE RATE	3.3	3.3	3.4
DIVORCE RATE	0.2	0.4	0.1
DEATHS			
DEATH RATE	5.7	7	8.8

HOUSEHOLDS

	1995	1980	1965
NUMBER	n/a	n/a	19,564 (60)
AVERAGE SIZE	n/a	n/a	4.5 (60)

ECONOMICS AND LABOR

	1995	1980	1965
GDP PER CAPITA US$	$3,000		

TRANSPORT

	1995	1980	1965
VEHICLES			
PRIVATE CARS	n/a	n/a	2,400
COMMERCIAL	n/a	n/a	600

HEALTH AND HEALTH CARE

	1995	1980	1965
HEALTH CARE			
RATE OF PHYSICIANS	n/a	n/a	0.2 (60)
RATE OF HOSPITAL BEDS	n/a	n/a	6.1 (60)

	1995	1980	1965
HEALTH INDICATORS			
AIDS/HIV CASES	76	56 (93)	

EDUCATION

	1995	1980	1965
SCHOOL AGE IN SCHOOL			
PRIMARY	n/a	n/a	156%
SECONDARY	n/a	n/a	21%
FEMALES IN SCHOOL			
PRIMARY	n/a	n/a	155%
SECONDARY	n/a	n/a	24%
ADULT ILLITERACY M/F	n/a	n/a	2.0/2.4% (70)

COMMUNICATIONS

	1995	1980	1965
RATE OF NEWSPAPERS	n/a	45	13
RATE OF RADIOS	594	393	79
RATE OF TELEVISIONS	332	n/a	0

Source: CIA, The World Factbook, 1997; ILO, World Labour Report, 1997; UN, Demographic Yearbook, 1997; UN, Statistical Yearbook, 1996; World Bank, World Development Indicators, 1998.

GUATEMALA

Guatemala is located in Central America, bordered by the Caribbean Sea on the northeast and the Pacific Ocean on the southwest. Mexico borders the 42,042-square-mile (108,890-square-kilometer) country on the northwest, Belize on the northeast, Honduras on the east, and El Salvador on the southeast. In 1954, the Guatemalan military overthrew a democratically elected government. The military was supported by the U.S. government, which subsequently supplied the country with arms to fight an internal guerrilla insurgency that continued through the mid-1990s. The Guatemalan economy is dominated by the production of coffee, bananas, and other agricultural commodities. Guatemala is one of the poorest countries in the Western Hemisphere. Though the country has a per capita gross domestic product (GDP) of $3,300, over 75 percent of the population survives on the equivalent of under $2 a day and over 53 percent survives on less than $1 a day. Guatemala's population of 11,277,614 in 1995 was growing at a rapid annual rate of 2.5 percent, even though the country had a net out-migration rate of 2 percent. Guatemala has a larger proportion of indigenous people than any other country in the Western Hemisphere (aside Bolivia). About 56 percent of the Guatemala's population is mestizo (mixture of indigenous Indian and white), and 44 percent is Indian. Though Spanish is the country's official language, 40 percent of the population speak indigenous Indian languages.

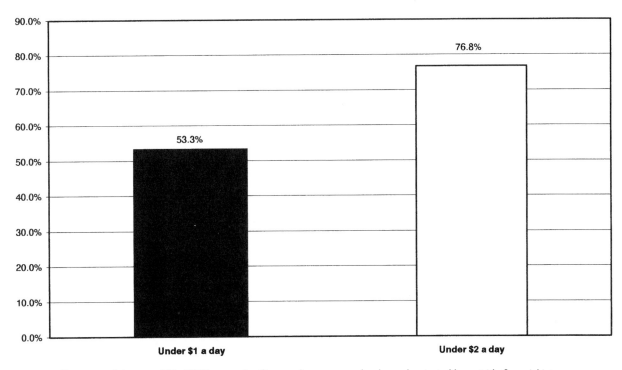

Poverty, 1989

For most of the post–World War era, the Guatemalan economy has been dominated by outside financial interests, especially the North American firm United Fruit. This domination, say many experts, is reflected in the high levels of poverty that have persisted throughout the era.

Urbanization

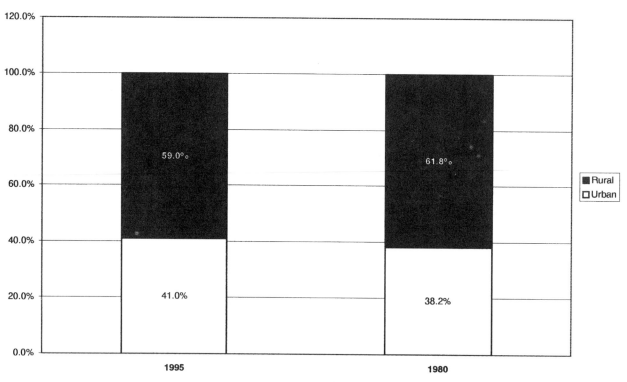

The need of United Fruit and other agricultural giants for a readily available labor force is one of the reasons Guatemala's population, which is dominated by Indians to an extent not seen in any other Latin American nation (with the exception of Bolivia), remains predominantly rural.

CHRONOLOGY

1966   Julio César Méndez Montenegro, a moderate, wins presidential elections over military candidate.

1970   Conservative Arana Osorio wins presidential elections, launches massive antiguerrilla campaign.

1974   Right-wing candidate wins suspicious election.

1981   Guatemala signs agreement with Britain, leading to independence of British Honduras (Belize), a territory claimed by Guatemala.

1982   Military officers, led by Efrem Rios Montt, seize power in coup.

1983   Montt overthrown.

1985   Election of centrist candidate sparks hope of end to vicious war against leftist guerrillas and massacre of civilians.

1991   Government begins negotiations with leftist guerrillas.

		1995	1980	1965

GEOGRAPHY

AREA (square miles/kilometers)	42,042/108,890	
LAND AREA (square miles/kilometers)	41,865/108,430	
COASTLINE (miles/kilometers)	250/400	

CITIES		
CAPITAL	Guatemala City	1,675,589 (90)
MAJOR CITY	Quetzaltenango	101,168

POPULATION

	1995	1980	1965
TOTAL	11,227,614	6,054,227 (81)	4,284,473 (64)
DENSITY (per square mile/kilometer)	254/98	189/73	n/a
ANNUAL GROWTH	2.5%	2.9%	3.1%
AGE COHORTS			
0–14	43%	n/a	46%
15–64	54%	n/a	51%
65 AND OVER	3%	n/a	3%
MALE	50%		
FEMALE	50%		
URBAN	41%	38.20%	n/a
RURAL	59%	61.80%	n/a
NET MIGRATION RATE	−2	n/a	−1.9

IDENTITY

ETHNICITY	
MESTIZO	56%
INDIAN	44%

LANGUAGE	
SPANISH	60%
INDIAN LANGUAGES	40%

RELIGION	
ROMAN CATHOLIC	n/a
PROTESTANT	n/a
MAYAN	n/a

	1995	1980	1965

VITAL STATISTICS

BIRTHS

	1995	1980	1965
BIRTH RATE	34	38.3 (83)	46.5
URBAN BIRTH RATE	35.5 (92)		
RURAL BIRTH RATE	38.5 (92)		
INFANT MORTALITY RATE	46.2	71.2 (83)	91.5
LIFE EXPECTANCY AT BIRTH	65.2	54.6 (83)	43.6

MARRIAGES

	1995	1980	1965
MARRIAGE RATE	4.7	4 (83)	3.5
AVERAGE AGE AT MARRIAGE M/F	23.8/21.3		
DIVORCE RATE	0.2	0.2 (83)	0.1

DEATHS

	1995	1980	1965
DEATH RATE	7.2	7.2 (83)	n/a

HOUSEHOLDS

	1995	1980	1965
NUMBER	n/a	n/a	804,940 (64)
AVERAGE SIZE	n/a	n/a	5.2 (64)

ECONOMICS AND LABOR

	1995
GDP PER CAPITA US$	$3,300

	1995
LABOR FORCE (thousands)	823.2 (93)
AGRICULTURE	214.6
MINING	2.4
MANUFACTURING	136.7
UTILITIES	11.1
CONSTRUCTION	26.4
TRADE/FOOD/TOURISM	102.6
TRANSPORT/COMMUNICATIONS	25.2
SOCIAL AND PERSONAL SERVICES	304.2

	1995
UNEMPLOYMENT (official)	1% (93)
UNION DENSITY	4.40%

POVERTY

	1995
UNDER $1/DAY	53.3% (89)
UNDER $2/DAY	76.8% (89)

	1995	1980	1965

TRANSPORT

JOURNEYS (by transport mode)

RAILROAD PASSENGER TRIPS	12,531.0 (91)		
(millions of miles/kilometers)			
AIR PASSENGER TRIPS (thousands)	252.0 (94)		

VEHICLES

PRIVATE CARS	102,000	n/a	29,000
COMMERCIAL	96,800	n/a	17,200

HEALTH AND HEALTH CARE

HEALTH CARE

ACCESS TO SAFE WATER	60%		
ACCESS TO SANITATION	66%		
MEASLES IMMUNIZATION	84%		
RATE OF PHYSICIANS	0.3	n/a	0.2 (60)
RATE OF HOSPITAL BEDS	1.1	n/a	2.7 (60)

HEALTH INDICATORS

PREGNANT WOMEN W/ANEMIA	39%		
LOW-BIRTH-WEIGHT BABIES	14%		
CHILD MALNUTRITION	33%		
SMOKING PREVALENCE M/F	38/25%		
TUBERCULOSIS INCIDENCE RATE	1.1		
AIDS/HIV CASES	711	497 (93)	
TOTAL DEATHS	73,870 (93)		

EDUCATION

SCHOOL AGE IN SCHOOL

PRIMARY	84%	71%	55%
SECONDARY	25%	18%	9%
HIGHER	8%	8%	1.7%

FEMALES IN SCHOOL

PRIMARY	76%	61%	55%
SECONDARY	n/a	11%	7%

ADULT ILLITERACY M/F	38/51%	37.4/52.% (85)	55.9/68.2%

	1995	1980	1965
COMMUNICATIONS			
RATE OF NEWSPAPERS	18	29	31
RATE OF RADIOS	68	51	n/a
RATE OF TELEVISIONS	53	25	13

Source: CIA, The World Factbook, 1997; ILO, World Labour Report, 1997; UN, Demographic Yearbook, 1997; UN, Statistical Yearbook, 1996; World Bank, World Development Indicators, 1998.

GUINEA

Guinea is located in West Africa, facing the Atlantic Ocean. Guinea-Bissau borders the 94,927-square-mile (245,860-square-kilometer) country on the northwest, Senegal and Mali on the north, Côte D'Ivoire on the southeast, and Liberia and Sierra Leone on the south. In October 1958 Guinea gained independence from France. For much of its formative years of independence, Guinea was ruled by a one-party state. In the early 1990s, the country adopted a multiparty democracy-style political system and held elections in June 1995. Though Guinea is endowed with abundant natural resources, the country is one of the least-developed countries in the world with a 1995 annual per capita gross domestic product

(GDP) of only $1,020. In 1995, the country's population of over 7.4 million was growing at an annual rate of 1.9 percent, lower than other countries in the region, but still high by international standards. In part because of the lack of economic opportunity, a growing number of residents are migrating out of the country to Western Europe. The three leading ethnic groups in the country are the Peuhl (40 percent), Malinke (30 percent), and Soussou (20 percent). Although the country has one of the lowest life expectancies at birth (45.1 percent) and highest infant mortality rates (134.2 per 1,000 live births), life expectancy and infant mortality have both shown improvement over the past three decades.

	1995	**1980**	**1965**
GEOGRAPHY			
AREA (square miles/kilometers)	94,927/245,860		
LAND AREA (square miles/kilometers)	94,927/245,860		
COASTLINE (miles/kilometers)	200/320		
CITIES			
CAPITAL	Conakry n/a	n/a	197,267 (67)
POPULATION			
TOTAL	7,411,981	5,781,014 (83)	2,570,219 (64)
DENSITY (per square mile/kilometer)	70/27	65/25	70/27
ANNUAL GROWTH	1.9%	2.4%	2.8%
AGE COHORTS			
0–14	44%	n/a	42%
15–64	53%	n/a	53% (64)[1]
65 AND OVER	3%	n/a	5.1% (64)[2]
URBAN	30%		
RURAL	70%		
NET MIGRATION RATE	−5.4		

	1995	1980	1965

IDENTITY

ETHNICITY
PEUHL   40%
MALINKE   30%
SOUSSOU   20%

LANGUAGE
FRENCH (official)   n/a

RELIGION
MUSLIM   85%
CHRISTIAN   8%
ANIMIST   7%

VITAL STATISTICS

BIRTHS
BIRTH RATE   42.6   46.8   62
INFANT MORTALITY RATE   134.2   216   216
LIFE EXPECTANCY AT BIRTH   45.1   40.2   27

DEATHS
DEATH RATE   18.7   23.5   40

ECONOMICS AND LABOR

GDP PER CAPITA US$ $1,020

LABOR FORCE M/F
AGRICULTURE M/F   83/92%
INDUSTRY M/F   2/1%
SERVICES M/F   15/7%

UNION DENSITY   2.5%

POVERTY
UNDER $1/DAY   26.3% (91)
UNDER $2/DAY   50.2% (91)

	1995	1980	1965

TRANSPORT

JOURNEYS (by transport mode)
AIR PASSENGER TRIPS (thousands)	45 (94)		

VEHICLES
PRIVATE CARS	23,100	23,000 (83)	9,300
COMMERCIAL	13,000	9,900	13,500

HEALTH AND HEALTH CARE

HEALTH CARE
ACCESS TO SAFE WATER	62%		
ACCESS TO SANITATION	70%		
MEASLES IMMUNIZATION (under 12)	69%		
RATE OF PHYSICIANS	0.2	negligible	negligible (60)
RATE OF HOSPITAL BEDS	0.6		0.8 (60)

HEALTH INDICATORS
PREGNANT WOMEN WITH ANEMIA			
LOW-BIRTH-WEIGHT BABIES	21%		
CHILD MALNUTRITION	24%		
SMOKING PREVALENCE M/F	40/2%		
TUBERCULOSIS INCIDENCE RATE	1.66		
AIDS/HIV CASES	2,158	1,005 (93)	

EDUCATION

SCHOOL AGE IN SCHOOL
PRIMARY	48%	36%	31%
SECONDARY	12%	17%	5%
HIGHER	n/a	5%	0.1%

FEMALES IN SCHOOL
PRIMARY	33%	33%	19%
SECONDARY	24%	28%	1%

ADULT ILLITERACY M/F	50/78%	60.3/82.8% (85)	n/a

	1995	1980	1965
COMMUNICATIONS			
RATE OF NEWSPAPERS	n/a	4 (79)	1 (70)
RATE OF RADIOS	43	30	29
RATE OF TELEVISIONS	8	1	0

FOOTNOTES
1. Ages 15–19.
2. Ages 60 and over.

Source: CIA, The World Factbook, 1997; ILO, World Labour Report, 1997; UN, Demographic Yearbook, 1997; UN, Statistical Yearbook, 1996; World Bank, World Development Indicators, 1998.

GUINEA-BISSAU

Guinea-Bissau is located in West Africa, facing the Atlantic Ocean. Senegal borders the 13,946-square-mile (36,120-square-kilometer) country on the north, and Guinea on the east and south. Formerly known as Portuguese Guinea, the country gained independence from Portugal in September 1974. In early 1991, Guinea-Bissau made the transition to multiparty democracy. Though the country exports agricultural commodities, the vast majority of the country's population resides in rural areas and engages in subsistence farming.

Guinea-Bissau has one of the world's highest poverty rates. In 1991, 96.7 percent of the population was subsisting on the equivalent of under $2 a day, and 88.2 percent were surviving on less than $1 a day. The country's population of 1,151,330 in 1995 was growing at 2.4 percent per year. Average life expectancy at birth in Guinea-Bissau is only 48.3 years, and the country has one of the highest infant mortality rates in the world. Portuguese is the official language, though much of the population speaks local languages.

	1995	1980	1965
GEOGRAPHY			
AREA (square miles/kilometers)	13,946/36,120		
LAND AREA (square miles/kilometers)	10,811/28,000		
COASTLINE (miles/kilometers)	219/350		
CITIES			
CAPITAL	Bissau	n/a	109,214 (79)	n/a
POPULATION			
TOTAL	1,151,330	767,739 (79)	n/a
DENSITY (per square mile/kilometer)	78/30	65/25	n/a
ANNUAL GROWTH	2.4%	1.9%	n/a
AGE COHORTS			
0–14	43%		
15–64	54%		
65 AND OVER	3%		
MALE	48%		
FEMALE	52%		
URBAN	22%		
RURAL	78%		
NET MIGRATION RATE	0	n/a	0

	1995	1980	1965
IDENTITY			
ETHNICITY			
BALANTA	30%		
FULA	20%		
MANJACA	14%		
LANGUAGE			
PORTUGUESE (official)	n/a		
CRIOLO	n/a		
RELIGION			
ANIMIST	65%		
MUSLIM	30%		
CHRISTIAN	5%		
VITAL STATISTICS			
BIRTHS			
BIRTH RATE	39.7	40.7	n/a
INFANT MORTALITY RATE	140	143	n/a
LIFE EXPECTANCY AT BIRTH	48.3	43	n/a
MARRIAGES			
MARRIAGE RATE	n/a	0.2	n/a
DEATHS			
DEATH RATE	16.2	21.7	n/a
ECONOMICS AND LABOR			
GDP PER CAPITA US$	$900		
LABOR FORCE M/F			
AGRICULTURE	78/96%		
INDUSTRY	3/1%		
SERVICES	19/3%		
POVERTY			
UNDER $1/DAY	88.2% (91)		
UNDER $2/DAY	96.7% (91)		

	1995	1980	1965

TRANSPORT

JOURNEYS (by transport mode)

	1995	1980	1965
AIR PASSENGER TRIPS (thousands)	21.0 (94)		
VEHICLES			
PRIVATE CARS	3,500 (92)		
COMMERCIAL	2,500		

HEALTH AND HEALTH CARE

	1995	1980	1965
HEALTH CARE			
ACCESS TO SAFE WATER	23%		
ACCESS TO SANITATION	20%		
MEASLES IMMUNIZATION	68%		
RATE OF PHYSICIANS	n/a	0.1	0.1 (60)
RATE OF HOSPITAL BEDS	1.5	1.8	1.7 (60)
HEALTH INDICATORS			
PREGNANT WOMEN WITH ANEMIA	74%		
LOW-BIRTH-WEIGHT BABIES	20%		
CHILD MALNUTRITION	23%		
TUBERCULOSIS INCIDENCE RATE	2.2		
AIDS/HIV CASES	786	453 (93)	

EDUCATION

	1995	1980	1965
SCHOOL AGE IN SCHOOL			
PRIMARY	64%	68%	39% (70)
SECONDARY	n/a	6%	8% (70)

Source: CIA, *The World Factbook, 1997;* ILO, *World Labour Report, 1997;* UN, *Demographic Yearbook, 1997;* UN, *Statistical Yearbook, 1996;* World Bank, *World Development Indicators, 1998.*

GUYANA

Guyana is located in north central South America, facing the Atlantic Ocean. Brazil borders the 83,000-square-mile (214,970-square-kilometers) country on the south, Suriname on the east, and Venezuela on the west. Guyana received its independence from the United Kingdom in May 1966. The country has a multiparty democracy. The primary industries in Guyana, one of the poorest countries in the Western Hemisphere, are mining, agriculture, and forestry. In the 1990s, to conform to structural adjustment demands made by Western lenders, Guyana implemented severe national austerity programs that reduced the value of the currency and led to rising unemployment. The country has a union density in excess of 25 percent, primarily due to the unionization of large segments of the mining industry. Guyana's small population of 712,091 was declining at a rate of nearly 1 percent in 1995, due mainly to the out-migration of residents seeking gainful employment. Guyana's population is divided racially between East Indians (constituting 51 percent of the country's population) and Africans (accounting for 43 percent of the population). Amer-Indians make up about 4 percent of the nation's residents. The ethnic divisions have frequently flared into conflict between the two major groups. The national life expectancy at birth in 1995 is 60.1 years, lower than the life expectancy in 1960. The infant mortality rate is 52.3 deaths per 1,000 live births.

	1995	1980	1965
GEOGRAPHY			
AREA (square miles/kilometers)	83,000/214,970		
LAND AREA (square miles/kilometers)	76,004/196,850		
COASTLINE (miles/kilometers)	287/459		
CITIES			
CAPITAL	Georgetown n/a	72,049 (76)	n/a
POPULATION			
TOTAL	712,091	758,619	560,330 (60)
DENSITY (per square mile/kilometer)	10.4/4	10.4/4	7.8/3
ANNUAL GROWTH	−0.9%	n/a	2.8%
AGE COHORTS			
0–14	33%	n/a	46%
15–64	63%	n/a	51%
65 AND OVER	4%	n/a	3%
MALE	50%		
FEMALE	50%		

	1995	1980	1965
URBAN	36%		
RURAL	64%		
NET MIGRATION RATE	−18.5	n/a	−0.6

IDENTITY

	1995	1980	1965
ETHNICITY			
EAST INDIAN	51%		
AFRICAN	43%		
AMER-INDIAN	4%		
LANGUAGE			
ENGLISH	n/a		
RELIGION			
CHRISTIAN	57%		
HINDU	33%		
MUSLIM	9%		

VITAL STATISTICS

	1995	1980	1965
BIRTHS			
BIRTH RATE	19	28.3 (78)	41 (60)
INFANT MORTALITY RATE	52.3	45.9 (78)	39.8 (60)
LIFE EXPECTANCY AT BIRTH	60.1	61 (78)	61 (60)
MARRIAGES			
MARRIAGE RATE	n/a	4 (78)	3.5 (60)
DIVORCE RATE	n/a	0.6 (78)	0.6 (60)
DEATHS			
DEATH RATE	9.6	7.3 (78)	10 (60)

HOUSEHOLDS

	1995	1980	1965
NUMBER	n/a	n/a	110,057 (61)

ECONOMICS AND LABOR

	1995	1980	1965
GDP PER CAPITA US$	$2,200		
UNION DENSITY	25.2%		

	1995	1980	1965
TRANSPORT			
JOURNEYS (by transport mode)			
AIR PASSENGER TRIPS (thousands)	115 (94)		
VEHICLES			
PRIVATE CARS	24,000	n/a	10,400
COMMERCIAL	9,000	n/a	3,600
HEALTH AND HEALTH CARE			
HEALTH CARE			
RATE OF PHYSICIANS	n/a	n/a	0.3 (60)
HEALTH INDICATORS			
AIDS/HIV CASES	698	497 (93)	
EDUCATION			
SCHOOL AGE IN SCHOOL			
PRIMARY	n/a	100%	117%
SECONDARY	n/a	60%	44%
HIGHER	n/a	2.6%	0.5%
FEMALES IN SCHOOL			
PRIMARY		99%	116%
SECONDARY	n/a	62%	43%
HIGHER	n/a	2.3%	0.8% (70)
ADULT ILLITERACY M/F	n/a	3.0/5.2% (85)	5.7/11.0% (70)
COMMUNICATIONS			
RATE OF NEWSPAPERS	99	76	93
RATE OF RADIOS	490	408	125
RATE OF TELEVISIONS	39	n/a	0

Source: CIA, The World Factbook, 1997; ILO, World Labour Report, 1997; UN, Demographic Yearbook, 1997; UN, Statistical Yearbook, 1996; World Bank, World Development Indicators, 1998.

HAITI

Haiti is located in the Caribbean Sea on the western one-third of the island of Hispaniola. Haiti shares the island with the Dominican Republic, which occupies the eastern two-thirds of the island. The Caribbean borders the 10,714-square-mile (27,750-square-kilometer) country on the south and the Atlantic Ocean on the north. The country is located about 50 miles east of Cuba. Under authoritarian rule for much of the post–World War II era, Haiti has endured a long history of political turmoil and economic despair. Even with the emergence of democratic rule in the early 1990s, the vast majority of Haiti's pop-

ulation continues to suffer economic hardship. In exchange for international aid, the country has had to conform to rigid economic conditions imposed by Western banks and lending agencies. In 1995, the country's per capita gross domestic product (GDP) was only $1,000. Even this low figure does not account for the country's unequal distribution of resources between an affluent minority and the poor majority. In 1995, the estimated unemployment rate was 60 percent. The country has a low life expectancy (under 50 years of age) and a high infant mortality rate of 86.2 deaths per 1,000 live births.

		1995	1980	1965
GEOGRAPHY				
AREA (square miles/kilometers)		10,714/27,750		
LAND AREA (square miles/kilometers)		10,641/27,560		
COASTLINE (miles/kilometers)		1,107/1,771		
CITIES				
CAPITAL	Port-au-Prince	690,168 (90)		
MAJOR CITIES	Carrefour	216,930		
	Delmas	178,990		
POPULATION				
TOTAL		6,731,539	5,053,792 (82)	4,450,900 (66)
DENSITY (per square mile/kilometer)		671/259	614/237 (82)	415/160
AGE COHORTS				
0–14		46%	n/a	38%
15–64		50%	n/a	59%
65 AND OVER		4%	n/a	3%
MALE		48%		
FEMALE		52%		

	1995	1980	1965
URBAN	32%	23.9%	n/a
RURAL	68%	76.1%	n/a
NET MIGRATION RATE	−4.5		

IDENTITY

ETHNICITY
BLACK	95%		
MULATTO	5%		

LANGUAGE
FRENCH (official)	10%		
CREOLE	90%		

RELIGION
ROMAN CATHOLIC AND VOODOO	80%		
PROTESTANT	16%		

VITAL STATISTICS

BIRTHS
	1995	1980	1965
BIRTH RATE	38.2	41.3	45.5
INFANT MORTALITY RATE	86.2	128	n/a
LIFE EXPECTANCY AT BIRTH	49.3	53	32.6

MARRIAGES
AVERAGE AGE AT MARRIAGE M/F	27.3/23.8		

DEATHS
	1995	1980	1965
DEATH RATE	16	14.2	20.2

ECONOMICS AND LABOR

GDP PER CAPITA US$
	$1,000		

LABOR FORCE M/F
AGRICULTURE	76/57%		
INDUSTRY	9/8%		
SERVICES	15/35%		

	1995	**1980**	**1965**

TRANSPORT

VEHICLES

PRIVATE CARS	32,000	21,800	4,800
COMMERCIAL	21,000	11,200	1,500

HEALTH AND HEALTH CARE

HEALTH CARE

ACCESS TO SAFE WATER	28%		
ACCESS TO SANITATION	24%		
MEASLES IMMUNIZATION	24%		
RATE OF PHYSICIANS	0.1	0.1	0.1 (60)
RATE OF HOSPITAL BEDS	0.8	0.7	0.6 (60)

HEALTH INDICATORS

PREGNANT WOMEN WITH ANEMIA	38%		
LOW-BIRTH-WEIGHT BABIES	15%		
CHILD MALNUTRITION	28%		
TUBERCULOSIS INCIDENCE RATE	3.33		
AIDS/HIV CASES	4,967	4,967 (93)	

EDUCATION

SCHOOL AGE IN SCHOOL

PRIMARY	n/a	76%	40%
SECONDARY	n/a	14%	4%
HIGHER	n/a	1%	0.4%

FEMALES IN SCHOOL

PRIMARY	n/a	46%	26%
SECONDARY	n/a	11%	3%

ADULT ILLITERACY M/F	n/a	52/58%	n/a

COMMUNICATIONS

RATE OF NEWSPAPERS	7	7	5
RATE OF RADIOS	48	20	1
RATE OF TELEVISIONS	5	3	0.1

Source: CIA, *The World Factbook, 1997*; ILO, *World Labour Report, 1997*; UN, *Demographic Yearbook, 1997*; UN, *Statistical Yearbook, 1996*; World Bank, *World Development Indicators, 1998*.

HONDURAS

Honduras, the largest country in Central America, is located between the Caribbean Sea and the Gulf of Fonseca, an inlet of the Pacific Ocean. Nicaragua borders the 43,278-square-mile (112,090-square-kilometer) country on the south, Guatemala on the west, and El Salvador on the southwest. Honduras has a democratic multiparty form of government. The economy is dominated by the production of cash crops and primary products for export, primarily to Western markets. The country's per capita gross domestic product (GDP) in 1995 was $1,980 per year. Because of the unequal distribution of land and resources, much of the country lives in poverty. In 1992, 75.7 percent of the population survived on the equivalent of less than $2 a day, and 46.9 percent lived on less than $1 a day. Mestizos make up the vast majority (90 percent) of the nation's population. Indigenous Indians (7 percent) and persons of African descent (2 percent) are the two leading minorities. Honduras's life expectancy at birth in 1995 was 68.4 years, and the infant mortality rate was 43 deaths per 1,000 live births.

	1995		1965	1980
GEOGRAPHY				
AREA (square miles/kilometers)	43,278/112,090			
LAND AREA (square miles/kilometers)	43,201/111,890			
COASTLINE (miles/kilometers)	513/820			
CITIES				
CAPITAL	Tegucigalpa	n/a	597,512 (86)	n/a
MAJOR CITIES	San Pedro Sula	n/a	397,201 (85)	n/a
	La Ceiba	n/a	103,600 (85)	n/a
POPULATION				
TOTAL	5,605,193		2,656,948 (74)	2,362,817 (66)
DENSITY (per square mile/kilometer)	137/53		61/24	55/21
ANNUAL GROWTH	n/a		3.4%	n/a
AGE COHORTS				
0–14	43%		n/a	40%
15–64	54%		n/a	58%
65 AND OVER	3%		n/a	2%
MALE	50%			
FEMALE	50%			

	1995	1980	1965
URBAN	44%	35.9%	n/a
RURAL	56%	64.1%	n/a
NET MIGRATION RATE	1.5	n/a	0.2 (63)

IDENTITY

ETHNICITY
MESTIZO	90%		
INDIAN	7%		
BLACK	2%		

LANGUAGE
SPANISH	n/a		

RELIGION
ROMAN CATHOLIC	97%		
PROTESTANT	3%		

VITAL STATISTICS

BIRTHS
	1995	1980	1965
BIRTH RATE	33.4	43.9	47.5
INFANT MORTALITY RATE	43	82	45.4
LIFE EXPECTANCY AT BIRTH	68.4	55.2	n/a

MARRIAGES
	1995	1980	1965
MARRIAGE RATE	4.9	4.9	3.3
DIVORCE RATE	0.4	0.4	0.2

DEATHS
	1995	1980	1965
DEATH RATE	5.8	10.1	n/a

HOUSEHOLDS

	1995	1980	1965
NUMBER	n/a	n/a	325,492 (61)
AVERAGE SIZE	n/a	n/a	5.7 (61)

ECONOMICS AND LABOR

GDP PER CAPITA US$	$1,980

	1995	1980	1965
LABOR FORCE M/F (thousands)	1,152.0/522.7 (92)		
AGRICULTURE	607.6/32.3		
MINING	5.4/358.0		
MANUFACTURING	125.4/125.0		
UTILITIES	6.8/1.1		
CONSTRUCTION	70.0/2.6		
TRADE/FOOD/TOURISM	130.8/151.1		
TRANSPORT/COMMUNICATIONS	45.7/6.3		
FINANCE/INSURANCE/REAL ESTATE	19.6/10.4		
SOCIAL AND PERSONAL SERVICES	140.1/193.5		
UNION DENSITY	4.5%		
POVERTY			
UNDER $1/DAY	46.9 (92)		
UNDER $2/DAY	75.7% (92)		

TRANSPORT

	1995	1980	1965
JOURNEYS (by transport mode)			
AIR PASSENGER TRIPS (thousands)	449 (94)		
VEHICLES			
PRIVATE CARS	68,500	25,600	9,000
COMMERCIAL	102,000	45,400	7,500

HEALTH AND HEALTH CARE

	1995	1980	1965
HEALTH CARE			
ACCESS TO SAFE WATER	65%		
ACCESS TO SANITATION	62%		
MEASLES IMMUNIZATION	90%		
RATE OF PHYSICIANS	0.4	0.3	0.1 (60)
RATE OF HOSPITAL BEDS	1	1.3	1.7 (60)
HEALTH INDICATORS			
PREGNANT WOMEN WITH ANEMIA	14%		
LOW-BIRTH-WEIGHT BABIES	9%		
CHILD MALNUTRITION	18%		
SMOKING PREVALENCE M/F	36/11%		
TUBERCULOSIS INCIDENCE RATE	1.33		
AIDS/HIV CASES	5,084	3,416 (93)	

	1995	1980	1965
EDUCATION			
SCHOOL AGE IN SCHOOL			
PRIMARY	111%	98%	73%
SECONDARY	30%	30%	8%
HIGHER	10%	8%	1.10%
FEMALES IN SCHOOL			
PRIMARY	111%	98%	73%
SECONDARY	n/a	30%	6%
ADULT ILLITERACY M/F	27/27%	39.3/41.6% (85)	n/a

COMMUNICATIONS			
RATE OF NEWSPAPERS	31	59	19
RATE OF RADIOS	408	140	57
RATE OF TELEVISIONS	78	18	3

Source: CIA, *The World Factbook, 1997;* ILO, *World Labour Report, 1997;* UN, *Demographic Yearbook, 1997;* UN, *Statistical Yearbook, 1996;* World Bank, *World Development Indicators, 1998.*

HUNGARY

Hungary is a landlocked country located in east central Europe. The 35,919-square-mile (93,030-square-kilometer) country is bordered by Romania on the east, Serbia and Croatia on the south, Slovenia on the southwest, Austria on the west, Slovakia on the north, and Ukraine on the northeast. After World War II, Hungary became part of the Soviet political and economic system, as a member state of the Warsaw Pact and the COMECON economic alliance. Following the collapse and breakup of the Soviet Union, Hungary sought to gain closer linkages with the West. In 1997, the country was admitted into the NATO military alliance and sought to gain entry into the European Union. Even before the breakup of the Soviet Union, Hungary had initiated market re-

forms. In the 1990s, the country implemented mass privatization of state-owned industry, and austerity programs were aimed at attracting foreign investors. Indeed, since the early 1990s, foreign investors have purchased large segments of Hungary's industry. By the late 1990s, however, many of the programs became politically unpopular. In 1995, the country's population of more than 10 million was declining at an annual rate of 0.7 percent, the result of a low birth rate and out-migration. In the 1990s, though infant mortality rates continued to decline, average life expectancy declined marginally from the levels in previous decades. Hungarians compose about 90 percent of the population; Gypsies and Germans are Hungary's two leading ethnic minorities.

	1995	**1980**	**1965**
GEOGRAPHY			
AREA (square miles/kilometers)	35,919/93,030		
LAND AREA (square miles/kilometers)	35,653/92,340		
COASTLINE	landlocked		
CITIES			
CAPITAL	Budapest	1,962,855 (94)	
MAJOR CITIES	Debrecen	214,245	
	Miskolc	185,877	
	Szeged	173,860	
	Pecs	167,772	
POPULATION			
TOTAL	10,002,541	10,709,463	9,961,044 (60)
DENSITY (per square mile/kilometer)	285/110	295/114	282/109
ANNUAL GROWTH	−0.7%	−0.1%	0.4%
AGE COHORTS			
0–14	18%	n/a	22%
15–64	68%	n/a	68%
65 AND OVER	14%	n/a	10%

	1995	1980	1965
MALE	48%		
FEMALE	52%		
URBAN	65%	53.2%	n/a
RURAL	35%	46.8%	n/a
NET MIGRATION RATE	−2.5	n/a	0

IDENTITY

ETHNICITY
HUNGARIAN	90%		
ROMANISH (Gypsy)	4%		
GERMAN	3%		

LANGUAGE
HUNGARIAN	98%		

RELIGION
ROMAN CATHOLIC	68%		
CALVINIST	20%		
LUTHERAN	5%		

VITAL STATISTICS

BIRTHS
	1995	1980	1965
BIRTH RATE	10.7	12.2 (85)	13.6
URBAN BIRTH RATE	10.6 (94)		
RURAL BIRTH RATE	12.2 (94)		
INFANT MORTALITY RATE	12.3	20.4 (85)	38.8
ABORTION RATE	647.7 (94)		
LIFE EXPECTANCY AT BIRTH	69	69.6	69.5

MARRIAGES
MARRIAGE RATE	5.3	6.9 (85)	9.1
AVERAGE AGE AT MARRIAGE M/F	27.1/23.8		
DIVORCE RATE	2.3	2.7 (85)	2

DEATHS
DEATH RATE	15.1	13.8 (85)	10

HOUSEHOLDS

NUMBER	3,889,532 (90)	n/a	3,309,900 (63)
AVERAGE SIZE	2.6 (90)	n/a	2.9 (63)

	1995	1980	1965
TYPE OF HOUSEHOLD			
SINGLE	8.5%		
MARRIED	64.3%		
WIDOWED	16.1%		
DIVORCED/SEPARATED	11.1%		
FEMALE HEADED	26.5%		

ECONOMICS AND LABOR

	1995	1980	1965
GDP PER CAPITA US$	$7,000		
LABOR FORCE M/F (thousands)	2,185.2/2,131.3 (92)		
AGRICULTURE	364.8/204.7		
MANUFACTURING	718.2/599.6		
CONSTRUCTION	211.2/60.1		
TRADE/FOOD/TOURISM	205.4/412.3		
TRANSPORT/COMMUNICATIONS	250.4/123.6		
SOCIAL AND PERSONAL SERVICES	435.2/791.0		
UNEMPLOYMENT (official)	10.9% (94)		
UNION DENSITY	52.5%		
POVERTY			
UNDER $1/DAY	1%		
UNDER $2/DAY	10.7%		

TRANSPORT

	1995	1980	1965
JOURNEYS (by transport mode)			
RAILROAD PASSENGER TRIPS	8,508.0 (94)		
(millions of miles/kilometers)			
AIR PASSENGER TRIPS (thousands)	1,325.0 (94)		
VEHICLES (thousands)			
PRIVATE CARS	2,176.9	1,013.4	99.4
COMMERCIAL	297.1	162.8	n/a

HEALTH AND HEALTH CARE

	1995	1980	1965
HEALTH CARE			
ACCESS TO SANITATION	94%		
MEASLES IMMUNIZATION	100%		

	1995	1980	1965
RATE OF PHYSICIANS	3.6	2.5	1.4 (60)
RATE OF HOSPITAL BEDS	9.6	9.1	6.9 (60)
HEALTH INDICATORS			
LOW-BIRTH-WEIGHT BABIES	9%		
SMOKING PREVALENCE M/F	40/27%		
TUBERCULOSIS INCIDENCE RATE	0.5		
AIDS/HIV CASES	202	148 (93)	
TOTAL DEATHS	144,000		

EDUCATION

	1995	1980	1965
SCHOOL AGE IN SCHOOL			
PRIMARY	97%	96%	101%
SECONDARY	81%	70%	35%
HIGHER	19%	14%	5%
FEMALES IN SCHOOL			
PRIMARY	96%	94%	100%
SECONDARY	63%	65%	41%
HIGHER	n/a	13.1%	8.8% (70)
ADULT ILLITERACY	n/a	0.7/1.5%	2.1/3.1% (63)

COMMUNICATIONS

	1995	1980	1965
RATE OF NEWSPAPERS	282	178	247
RATE OF RADIOS	617	249	499
RATE OF TELEVISIONS	427	83	310

Source: CIA, *The World Factbook, 1997*; ILO, *World Labour Report, 1997*; UN, *Demographic Yearbook, 1997*; UN, *Statistical Yearbook, 1996*; World Bank, *World Development Indicators, 1998*.

ICELAND

Iceland is an island located in Northern Europe in the Atlantic Ocean, northwest of the British Isles. The mountainous 39,768-square-mile (103,000-square-kilometer) island is located southeast of Greenland. In June 1944, Iceland gained independence from Denmark. The country has a democratic multiparty political system. The country has an advanced economy dominated by the commercial fishing industry. In 1995, Iceland had an average annual per capita gross domestic product of $18,800. The country has a high standard of living, due in part to the result of an extensive system of social protection provided by the Icelandic government. The country's 1995 population of 270,292 was declining by 0.8 percent. The country's decline in population reflects a net out-migration trend. Iceland has among the world's highest life expectancies that reached over 80 years in 1995. The country's infant mortality rate of 4.3 deaths per 1,000 live births is also among the lowest in the world. Nearly all of the country's population are descendants of Norwegians and Celtics, and Icelandic is the country's official language.

	1995	1980	1965
GEOGRAPHY			
AREA (square miles/kilometers)	39,768/103,000		
LAND AREA (square miles/kilometers)	38,707/100,250		
COASTLINE (miles/kilometers)	3,118/4,988		
CITIES			
CAPITAL	Reykjavik	101,418 (93)	
POPULATION			
TOTAL	270,292	204,930 (70)	175,680 (60)
DENSITY (per square mile/kilometer)	7.8/3	5.2/2	5.2/2
ANNUAL GROWTH	−0.8%	1.1%	1.8%
AGE COHORTS			
0–14	24%	n/a	35%
15–64	64%	n/a	57%
65 AND OVER	12%	n/a	8%
MALE	51%		
FEMALE	49%		
URBAN	92%	88.2	n/a
RURAL	8%	10.8%	n/a
NET MIGRATION RATE	−2.5	n/a	0

	1995	1980	1965

IDENTITY

ETHNICITY
NORWEGIAN AND CELT

| | 100% | | |

LANGUAGE
ICELANDIC

| | 100% | | |

RELIGION
EVANGELICAL LUTHERAN

| | 96% | | |

OTHER PROTESTANT AND ROMAN
  CATHOLIC

| | 3% | | |

NO RELIGION

| | 1% | | |

VITAL STATISTICS

BIRTHS

	1995	1980	1965
BIRTH RATE	16.9	n/a	24.7
URBAN BIRTH RATE	17.7 (93)		
RURAL BIRTH RATE	15.2 (93)		
INFANT MORTALITY RATE	4.3	n/a	15
ABORTION RATE	161.5 (92)		
LIFE EXPECTANCY AT BIRTH	80.8	n/a	72.9

MARRIAGES

	1995	1980	1965
MARRIAGE RATE	4.6	n/a	8.1
AVERAGE AGE AT MARRIAGE M/F	31.7/30.2		
DIVORCE RATE	1.8	n/a	1

DEATHS

	1995	1980	1965
DEATH RATE	9.6	n/a	6.7

HOUSEHOLDS

	1995	1980	1965
NUMBER			35,869 (50)
AVERAGE SIZE			3.9 (50)

ECONOMICS AND LABOR

	1995	1980	1965
GDP PER CAPITA US$	$18,800		
LABOR FORCE (thousands)	124.6 (90)		
AGRICULTURE	13.1		

	1995	1980	1965
MANUFACTURING	23.3		
UTILITIES	1.1		
CONSTRUCTION	12.4		
TRADE/FOOD/TOURISM	18.1		
TRANSPORT/COMMUNICATIONS	8.4		
FINANCE/INSURANCE/REAL ESTATE	10		
SOCIAL AND PERSONAL SERVICES	38.2		
UNEMPLOYMENT (official)	5.3% (94)		
UNION DENSITY	70.7%		

TRANSPORT

JOURNEYS (by transport mode)

	1995	1980	1965
AIR PASSENGER TRIPS (thousands)	1,031.0 (94)		
VEHICLES			
PRIVATE CARS	116,200	86,000	28,300
COMMERCIAL	15,600	9,700	6,600

HEALTH AND HEALTH CARE

HEALTH CARE

	1995	1980	1965
RATE OF PHYSICIANS	n/a	n/a	1.3 (60)
RATE OF HOSPITAL BEDS	n/a	n/a	10.6 (60)
HEALTH INDICATORS			
AIDS/HIV CASES	38	32 (93)	
TOTAL DEATHS	1,720 (94)		

EDUCATION

SCHOOL AGE IN SCHOOL

	1995	1980	1965
PRIMARY	n/a	97.0%	101.0%
SECONDARY	n/a	70.0%	68.0%
HIGHER	n/a	12.8%	5.8%
FEMALES IN SCHOOL			
PRIMARY	n/a	n/a	100% (70)
SECONDARY	n/a	83.0%	71.0%
HIGHER	n/a	18.7%	5.3%

	1995	1980	1965
COMMUNICATIONS			
RATE OF NEWSPAPERS	519	548	435
RATE OF RADIOS	791	711	330
RATE OF TELEVISIONS	335	285	201 (70)

Source: CIA, *The World Factbook, 1997;* ILO, *World Labour Report, 1997;* UN, *Demographic Yearbook, 1997;* UN, *Statistical Yearbook, 1996;* World Bank, *World Development Indicators, 1998.*

INDIA

India is located in southern Asia on the Arabian Sea, Bay of Bengal, and Indian Ocean. Pakistan borders the 1,269,397-square-mile (3,287,590-square-kilometer) country on the west; Bhutan, China, and Nepal on the north; and Bangladesh and Myanmar (Burma) on the east. India gained independence from the United Kingdom in 1947. Until the 1990s, India had a multiparty democracy dominated by the Congress Party. In 1997, the Bharatiya Janata Party, a Hindu-dominated group, gained enough votes to lead the government. Though India is undergoing industrial development and modernization, nearly 75 percent of the population continues to live in rural areas, and poverty remains a significant problem. Nearly 90 percent of the country's population subsists on less than the equivalent of $2 a day,

and over 50 percent survives on less than $1 a day. The country's population of more than 950 million is the second largest in the world. Though growth rates have declined from 2.4 percent in 1961 to 1.6 percent in 1995, India's population is still increasing faster than the country can accommodate. Religious differences are the country's major source of internal political conflict. Hindus are the religious majority (80 percent), followed by Muslims (14 percent), Christians (2.4 percent), Sikhs (2 percent), and Buddhists (1 percent). In the 1990s, conflicts between Hindus and Muslims have been accompanied by violence. In recent decades, as a result of improvements in health care and sanitation, life expectancy has increased and infant mortality has declined.

Annual Growth

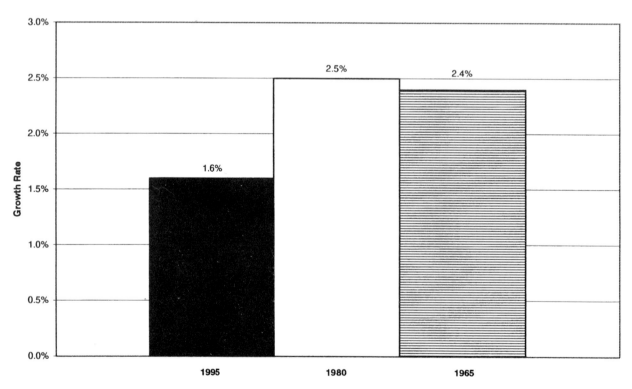

Unlike China, its giant neighbor to the north, India never imposed draconian birth-control programs. Not surprisingly, its annual growth rate has fallen, but not to the degree necessary to stop the huge growth in population.

Population

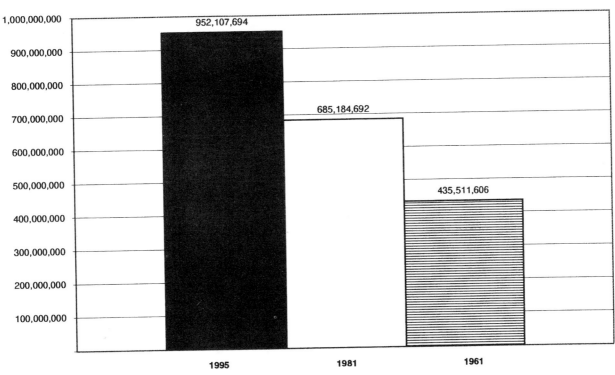

The country's continuing high birth rates, versus China's falling ones, make it almost inevitable that India will replace its East Asian counterpart as the most populous nation on earth sometime in the first half of the twenty-first century.

CHRONOLOGY

1965   India and Pakistan go to war for second time, over disputed territory in Kashmir.

1966   Indira Gandhi, daughter of Indian founding father Jawaharlal Nehru, becomes prime minister.

1971   India defeats Pakistan in third war, leading to independence of Bangladesh.

1974   India tests first nuclear bomb.

1977   Harsh policies lead to Gandhi's ouster from power and expulsion from parliament.

1980   Gandhi returns to power.

1984   Gandhi sends troops into Punjab to end Sikh separatist uprising there, and thousands are killed; Gandhi assassinated by Sikh bodyguards and succeeded by son, Rajiv.

1989   Congress Party loses power for first time since independence.

1991   Rajiv Gandhi assassinated by Tamil terrorists.

1998   Right-wing Hindu Nationalist Party wins power in parliament and launches renewed nuclear testing.

	1995	1980	1965

GEOGRAPHY

AREA (square miles/kilometers)	1,269,397/3,287,590	
LAND AREA (square miles/kilometers)	1,147,950/2,973,190	
COASTLINE (miles/kilometers)	4,375/7,000	

CITIES

CAPITAL	New Delhi	301,297 (91)
MAJOR CITIES	Bombay	9,925,891
	Delhi	7,206,704
	Calcutta	4,399,819
	Madras	3,841,396

POPULATION

	1995	1980	1965
TOTAL	952,107,694	685,184,692 (81)	435,511,606 (61)
DENSITY (per square mile/kilometer)	738/285	591/228	422/163
ANNUAL GROWTH	1.6%	2.5%	2.4%

AGE COHORTS

	1995	1980	1965
0–14	34%	n/a	41%
15–64	62%	n/a	56%
65 AND OVER	4%	n/a	3%
MALE	52%		
FEMALE	48%		
URBAN	27%	21.9%	n/a
RURAL	73%	78.1%	n/a
NET MIGRATION RATE	0.04		

IDENTITY

ETHNICITY

INDO-ARYAN	72%
DRAVIDIAN	25%
MONGOLOID/OTHER	3%

LANGUAGE

ENGLISH	n/a
HINDI	30%
BENGALI	n/a

	1995	1980	1965
RELIGION			
HINDU	80%		
MUSLIM	14%		
CHRISTIAN	2.4%		
SIKH	2%		
BUDDHIST	1%		

VITAL STATISTICS

	1995	1980	1965
BIRTHS			
BIRTH RATE	25.9	33.7 (83)	38.4 (61)
URBAN BIRTH RATE	24.3 (91)		
RURAL BIRTH RATE	30.9 (91)		
INFANT MORTALITY RATE	71.1	110.4 (83)	139 (61)
LIFE EXPECTANCY AT BIRTH	59.7	45.1 (83)	41.2 (61)
DEATHS			
DEATH RATE	9.6	11.9 (83)	12.9 (61)

HOUSEHOLDS

	1995	1980	1965
NUMBER	152,009,467 (91)	n/a	83,523,895 (60)
URBAN	40,418,141		
RURAL	111,591,326		
AVERAGE SIZE	5.5 (91)	n/a	5.2 (60)
URBAN	5.3		
RURAL	5.6		

ECONOMICS AND LABOR

	1995	1980	1965
GDP PER CAPITA US$	$1,500		
LABOR FORCE M/F (thousands)	22,417.0/3,545 (89)		
AGRICULTURE	953/467		
MINING	975/78		
MANUFACTURING	5,670/575		
UTILITIES	880/28		
CONSTRUCTION	1,157/58		
TRADE/FOOD/TOURISM	404/31		
TRANSPORT/COMMUNICATIONS	2,895/130		
FINANCE/INSURANCE/REAL ESTATE	1,204/152		
SOCIAL AND PERSONAL SERVICES	8,280/2,025		

	1995	1980	1965
UNION DENSITY	5.4%		
POVERTY			
UNDER $1/DAY	52.5%		
UNDER $2/DAY	88.8%		

TRANSPORT

	1995	1980	1965
JOURNEYS (by transport mode)			
RAILROAD PASSENGER TRIPS	314,564.0 (91)		
(millions of miles/kilometers)			
AIR PASSENGER TRIPS (thousands)	11,518.0 (94)		
VEHICLES (thousands)			
PRIVATE CARS	3,205	1,054.4	415.7
COMMERCIAL	2,396.7	1,002.7	314.5

HEALTH AND HEALTH CARE

	1995	1980	1965
HEALTH CARE			
ACCESS TO SAFE WATER	81%		
ACCESS TO SANITATION	29%		
MEASLES IMMUNIZATION	84%		
RATE OF PHYSICIANS	0.4	0.4	0.2 (60)
RATE OF HOSPITAL BEDS	0.8	0.8	0.5 (60)
HEALTH INDICATORS			
PREGNANT WOMEN WITH ANEMIA	88%		
LOW-BIRTH-WEIGHT BABIES	33%		
CHILD MALNUTRITION	66%		
SMOKING PREVALENCE M/F	40/3%		
TUBERCULOSIS INCIDENCE RATE	2.2		
AIDS/HIV CASES	2,095	494 (93)	

EDUCATION

	1995	1980	1965
SCHOOL AGE IN SCHOOL			
PRIMARY	100%	83%	56%
SECONDARY	49%	30%	15%
HIGHER	6%	5%	2.2%
FEMALES IN SCHOOL			
PRIMARY	93%	72%	46%
SECONDARY	38%	32%	7%

	1995	1980	1965
ADULT ILLITERACY M/F	35/62%	45.2/74.3% (81)	n/a

COMMUNICATIONS

RATE OF NEWSPAPERS	31	21	12
RATE OF RADIOS	80	38	10
RATE OF TELEVISIONS	40	4	0

Source: CIA, The World Factbook, 1997; ILO, World Labour Report, 1997; UN, Demographic Yearbook, 1997; UN, Statistical Yearbook, 1996; World Bank, World Development Indicators, 1998.

INDONESIA

Indonesia is an island archipelago located in Southeast Asia between the Indian Ocean and the Pacific Ocean. Australia is southeast of the 741,097-square-mile (1,919,440-square-kilometer) country, Papua New Guinea is east, and Malaysia and the Philippines are to the country's north. Indonesia gained independence from the Netherlands in August 1945. Following the collapse of Indonesia's economy in May 1998, President Suharto, who came to power in a military coup in March 1968, was forced to resign by a mass opposition movement. Although Indonesia was considered a model for economic development by Western economists in the mid-1990s, nearly 60 percent of the population was subsisting on under $2 a day. In the late 1990s, the Indonesian government was forced by Western lending agencies and banks to conform to severe austerity measures. The government collapsed under popular pressure following the plummeting of the currency and spiraling unemployment. In 1995, Indonesia's population of nearly 207 million was growing at an annual rate of 1.5 percent. The Javanese are the most populous ethnic group in Indonesia (45 percent), followed by the Sundanese (14 percent), Madurese (7.5 percent), and Malays (7.5 percent). Muslims constitute about 87 percent of the country's population. Indonesia's average life expectancy at birth in 1995 was 61.6 years, and the country had an infant mortality rate of 63.1 deaths per 1,000 live births.

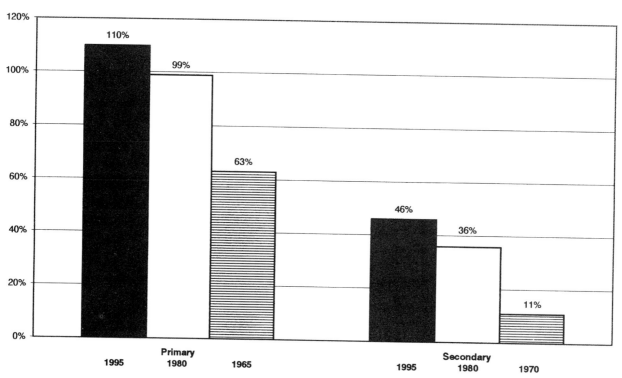

Females in School

Unlike the more orthodox Muslim nations of the Persian Gulf, Indonesia has always emphasized equal educational opportunities for its girls, a fact reflected in the number of male and female students attending secondary school.

Rate of Televisions per 1,000 Persons

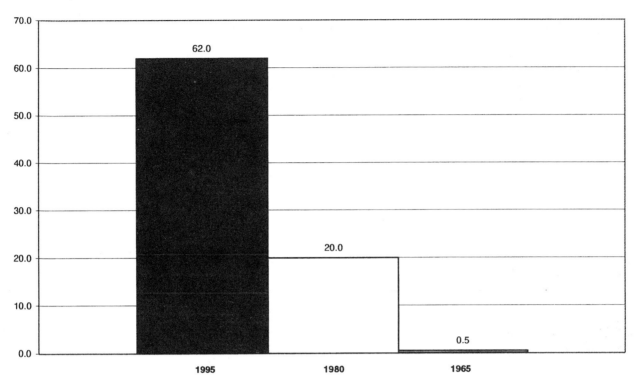

With its population of more than 200 million spread out over hundreds of islands across thousands of miles of ocean, Indonesia has found that television offers one of the best media for promoting a common nationalism.

CHRONOLOGY

1965   Leftist prime minister Sukarno overthrown in military coup by Suharto; 200,000 leftists massacred.
1968   Suharto declared Indonesian president.
1974   Portugal vacates East Timor; Indonesia invades.
1975   Economic boom in country begins.
1997   Economic crisis hits Indonesia; forest fires burn out of control.
1998   Popular uprising leads to overthrow of Suharto.

	1995	1980	1965

GEOGRAPHY

AREA (square miles/kilometers)   741,097/1,919,440
LAND AREA (square miles/kilometers)   705,189/1,826,440
COASTLINE (miles/kilometers)   34,198/54,716

CITIES

		1995		
CAPITAL	Jakarta	9,160,500		
MAJOR CITIES	Surabaya	2,701,300		
	Bandung	2,368,200		
	Medan	1,909,700		
	Semarang	1,366,500		

POPULATION

	1995	1980	1965
TOTAL	206,611,600	147,490,298	96,318,829 (61)
DENSITY (per square mile/kilometer)	264/102	223/86	186/72
ANNUAL GROWTH	1.5%	2.2%	2.3%
AGE COHORTS			
0–14	32%	n/a	42%
15–64	64%	n/a	55%
65 AND OVER	4%	n/a	3%
URBAN	35%	22.4%	n/a
RURAL	65%	77.6%	n/a
NET MIGRATION RATE	0	n/a	0 (62)

IDENTITY

ETHNICITY	
JAVANESE	45%
SUNDANESE	14%
MADURESE	7.5%
MALAYS	7.5%

LANGUAGE	
BAHASA INDONESIA	n/a
ENGLISH	n/a
DUTCH	n/a

	1995	1980	1965
RELIGION			
MUSLIM	87%		
PROTESTANT	6%		
ROMAN CATHOLIC	3%		
HINDU	2%		
BUDDHIST	1%		

VITAL STATISTICS

	1995	1980	1965
BIRTHS			
BIRTH RATE	23.7	32.1	43 (61)
INFANT MORTALITY RATE	63.1	125	125 (61)
LIFE EXPECTANCY AT BIRTH	61.6	47.5	n/a
MARRIAGES			
MARRIAGE RATE	7.4	10.6	10.6 (61)
AVERAGE AGE AT MARRIAGE M/F	25.2/21.6		
DIVORCE RATE	0.8		
DEATHS			
DEATH RATE	8.4	12.6	21.4 (61)

HOUSEHOLDS

	1995
NUMBER	39,695,158 (90)
URBAN	11,692,856
RURAL	28,002,302
AVERAGE SIZE	4.5 (90)
URBAN	4.7
RURAL	4.4

ECONOMICS AND LABOR

	1995
GDP PER CAPITA US$	$3,500
LABOR FORCE M/F (thousands)	47,644.6/30,459.5 (92)
AGRICULTURE	25,629.5/17,224.0
MINING	489.9/104.9
MANUFACTURING	4,187.1/3,660.5
UTILITIES	157.5/15.8
CONSTRUCTION	2,259.4/104.0
TRADE/FOOD/TOURISM	5,604.6/5,495.7
TRANSPORT/COMMUNICATIONS	2,439.7/72.5

	1995	1980	1965
FINANCE/INSURANCE/REAL ESTATE	376.9/184.9		
SOCIAL AND PERSONAL SERVICES	6,447.5/3,525.5		
UNEMPLOYMENT (official)	2.8% (92)		
UNION DENSITY	2.6%		
POVERTY			
UNDER $1/DAY	11.8% (92)		
UNDER $2/DAY	58.7% (92)		

TRANSPORT

	1995	1980	1965
JOURNEYS (by transport mode)			
RAILROAD PASSENGER TRIPS	13,610.0 (94)		
(millions of miles/kilometers)			
AIR PASSENGER TRIPS (thousands)	12,290 (94)		
VEHICLES (thousands)			
PRIVATE CARS	1,890.3	639.5	151
COMMERCIAL	1,903.6	560.1	108.4

HEALTH AND HEALTH CARE

	1995	1980	1965
HEALTH CARE			
ACCESS TO SAFE WATER	62%		
ACCESS TO SANITATION	51%		
MEASLES IMMUNIZATION	89%		
RATE OF PHYSICIANS	0.2	0.1	negligible (60)
RATE OF HOSPITAL BEDS	0.7	n/a	0.7 (60)
HEALTH INDICATORS			
PREGNANT WOMEN WITH ANEMIA	64%		
LOW-BIRTH-WEIGHT BABIES	14%		
CHILD MALNUTRITION	40%		
SMOKING PREVALENCE M/F	53/4%		
TUBERCULOSIS INCIDENCE RATE	2.2		
AIDS/HIV CASES	87	51 (93)	

EDUCATION

	1995	1980	1965
SCHOOL AGE IN SCHOOL			
PRIMARY	114%	107%	69%
SECONDARY	48%	29%	11%
HIGHER	11%	4%	1.8%

	1995	1980	1965
FEMALES IN SCHOOL			
PRIMARY	110%	99%	63%
SECONDARY	46%	36%	11% (70)
ADULT ILLITERACY M/F	22/10%	22.5/42.3%	47.2/73.9% (61)

COMMUNICATIONS

RATE OF NEWSPAPERS	24	15	7
RATE OF RADIOS	148	99	2 (48)
RATE OF TELEVISIONS	62	20	0.5

Source: CIA, *The World Factbook, 1997;* ILO, *World Labour Report, 1997;* UN, *Demographic Yearbook, 1997;* UN, *Statistical Yearbook, 1996;* World Bank, *World Development Indicators, 1998.*

IRAN

Iran is located in Southwest Asia on the Persian Gulf. Pakistan and Afghanistan border the 636,293-square-mile (1,648,000-square-kilometer) country on the east, the former Soviet Republic of Turkmenistan on the northeast, Armenia and Azerbaijan on the northwest, and Iraq on the west. Across the Persian Gulf lie Saudi Arabia and the Gulf States of Bahrain, Kuwait, Oman, and the United Arab Emirates. In 1979, amid the the Iranian Revolution, the autocratic government of Shah Pahlevi was ousted and replaced by an Islamic government. During much of the 1980s, Iran was embroiled in a major border war with Iraq. Though Iran had tremendous wealth, the shah had squandered most of the earnings and had failed to modernize the economy equitably. Following the revolution, as a result of relative international isolation, the Iranian economy continued to contract. In 1997, after nearly two decades of strict Islamic rule, a moderate government was elected to office. In 1995, Iran's population of more than 66 million was growing at a rapid annual rate of 2.2 percent. The country has a life expectancy at birth of 67.4 years, and an infant mortality rate of 52.7 deaths per 1,000 live births. The leading ethnic groups in Iran are Persian (51 percent) and Azerbaijani (24 percent).

Age Distribution

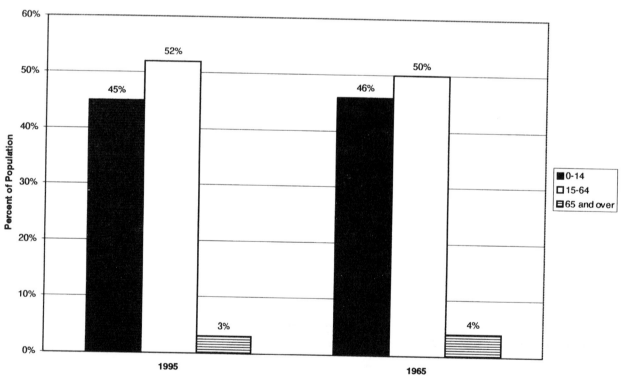

Like many Islamic countries, Iran has an extremely young population, a factor, many observers say, in the volatile politics of the country.

Divorce Rate per 1,000 Residents

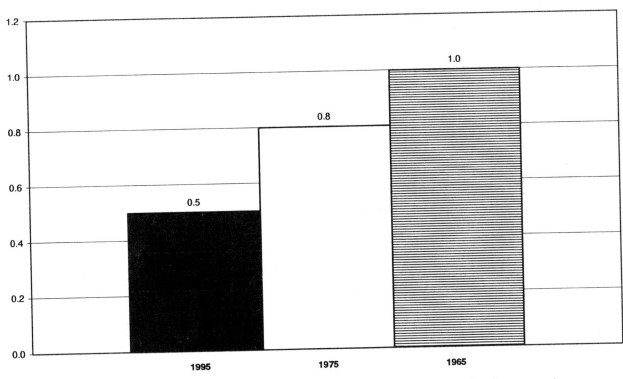

The impact of the socially conservative Islamic revolution is reflected in the country's falling divorce rate since 1979; it contrasts with most other countries in the region and world, where the divorce rates have climbed.

CHRONOLOGY

1962 Shah Reza Pahlevi launches economic "White Revolution."
1974 Quadrupling of oil prices leads to vast increase in government revenues.
1978 Unrest against Shah's regime increases.
1979 Shah overthrown and exiled from country as Ayatollah Khomeini takes power; national referendum approves Islamic government.
1980 Iraq invades Iran, leading to eight-year civil war.
1981 American embassy hostages freed after 444-day captivity.
1988 Iran-Iraq War ends largely in a draw.
1989 Khomeini dies.
1996 Liberal reformist prime minister wins power, leading to struggle with hard-liners.

		1995	1980	1966
GEOGRAPHY				
AREA (square miles/kilometers)		636,293/1,648,000		
LAND AREA (square miles/kilometers)		631,660/1,636,000		
COASTLINE (miles/kilometers)		1,525/2,440		
CITIES				
CAPITAL	Teheran	6,750,043 (94)		
MAJOR CITIES	Mashhad	1,964,489		
	Esfahan	1,220,595		
	Tabriz	1,166,203		
	Shiraz	1,042,801		
POPULATION				
TOTAL		66,094,264	33,708,744 (76)	25,781,090
DENSITY (per square mile/kilometer)		106/41	70/27	39/15
ANNUAL GROWTH		2.2%	2.9%	2.8%
AGE COHORTS				
0–14		45%	n/a	46%
15–64		52%	n/a	50%
65 AND OVER		3%	n/a	4%
MALE		52%		
FEMALE		48%		
URBAN		59%	49%	n/a
RURAL		41%	51%	n/a
NET MIGRATION RATE		−0.5		
IDENTITY				
ETHNICITY				
PERSIAN		51%		
AZERBAIJANI		24%		
GILAKI AND MAZANDURANI		8%		
KURD		7%		
ARAB		3%		

	1995	1980	1965
LANGUAGE			
PERSIAN	58%		
TURKIC	26%		
KURDISH	9%		
LURI	2%		
RELIGION			
SHI'A MUSLIM	89%		
SUNNI MUSLIM	10%		
ZOROASTRIAN, JEWISH, CHRISTIAN, BAHA'I	1%		

VITAL STATISTICS

	1995	1980	1965
BIRTHS			
BIRTH RATE	33.7	42.5 (75)	48
INFANT MORTALITY RATE	52.7	108.1 (75)	n/a
LIFE EXPECTANCY AT BIRTH	67.4	55.4 (75)	n/a
MARRIAGES			
MARRIAGE RATE	7.9	8.9 (75)	6
AVERAGE AGE AT MARRIAGE M/F	24.5/21.1		
DIVORCE RATE	0.5	0.8 (75)	1
DEATHS			
DEATH RATE	6.6	11.5 (75)	24.5

HOUSEHOLDS

	1995		
NUMBER	10,785,221 (91)		
AVERAGE SIZE	5.2 (91)		
FEMALE HEADED	5.9%		

ECONOMICS AND LABOR

	1995		
GDP PER CAPITA US$	$4,700		
LABOR FORCE M/F (thousands)			
AGRICULTURE	30/73		
INDUSTRY	26/9		
SERVICES	44/18		

	1995	1980	1965

TRANSPORT

JOURNEYS (by transport mode)

	1995	1980	1965
RAILROAD PASSENGER TRIPS (millions of miles/kilometers)	6,422.0 (93)		
AIR PASSENGER TRIPS (thousands)	5,803.0 (94)		

VEHICLES (thousands)

	1995	1980	1965
PRIVATE CARS	1,557	958	105.9
COMMERCIAL	588.9	132	44.1

HEALTH AND HEALTH CARE

HEALTH CARE

	1995	1980	1965
ACCESS TO SAFE WATER	n/a	50%	n/a
ACCESS TO SANITATION	n/a	60%	n/a
MEASLES IMMUNIZATION	88%		
RATE OF PHYSICIANS	0.3		0.3 (60)
RATE OF HOSPITAL BEDS	1.4	1.5 (70)	0.9 (60)

HEALTH INDICATORS

	1995	1980	1965
LOW-BIRTH-WEIGHT BABIES	12%		
CHILD MALNUTRITION	16%		
TUBERCULOSIS INCIDENCE RATE	0.5		
AIDS/HIV CASES	118	92 (93)	
TOTAL DEATHS	461,443 (91)		

EDUCATION

SCHOOL AGE IN SCHOOL

	1995	1980	1965
PRIMARY	99%	87%	53%
SECONDARY	69%	42%	17%
HIGHER	15%	n/a	1.2%

FEMALES IN SCHOOL

	1995	1980	1965
PRIMARY	47%	40%	36%
SECONDARY	46%	36%	11%

	1995	1980	1965
ADULT ILLITERACY M/F	22/34%	51.8/75.6% (76)	67.2/87.8%

	1995	1980	1965
COMMUNICATIONS			
RATE OF NEWSPAPERS	20	25	15 (61)
RATE OF RADIOS	230	163	62
RATE OF TELEVISIONS	63	51	4

Source: CIA, The World Factbook, 1997; ILO, World Labour Report, 1997; UN, Demographic Yearbook, 1997; UN, Statistical Yearbook, 1996; World Bank, World Development Indicators, 1998.

IRAQ

Iraq is located in Southwest Asia, northwest of the Persian Gulf. The 168,754-square-mile (437,072-square-kilometer) country is bordered by Iran on the east, Turkey on the north, Jordan and Syria on the west, and Kuwait and Saudi Arabia on the south. In the early 1970s, the Iraqi Ba'th Party came to power and dramatically expanded central planning. Since 1975, under the leadership of President Saddam Hussein, Iraq has come into conflict with neighboring countries. In the 1980s, the government was embroiled in a costly eight-year border war with Iran. After invading Kuwait in 1990, Iraqi troops were expelled by an alliance of international forces. The border hostilities have severely interfered with industrial growth and economic development. An international embargo against Iraqi oil exports has further limited the country's ability to earn foreign exchange for essential goods and has impoverished the population. Iraq's 1995 population of 21.4 million was growing at a rapid annual rate of 3.7 percent, due in part to a high birth rate. In the same year, Iraq had a life expectancy at birth of 67 years and an infant mortality rate of 60 deaths per 1,000 live births. Iraq is an ethnically and religiously divided nation. Just over 75 percent of the country's population is Arab and 18 percent is Kurdish. The three leading religious denominations are Shi'a Muslim (62 percent), Sunni Muslim (35 percent) and Christian (3 percent).

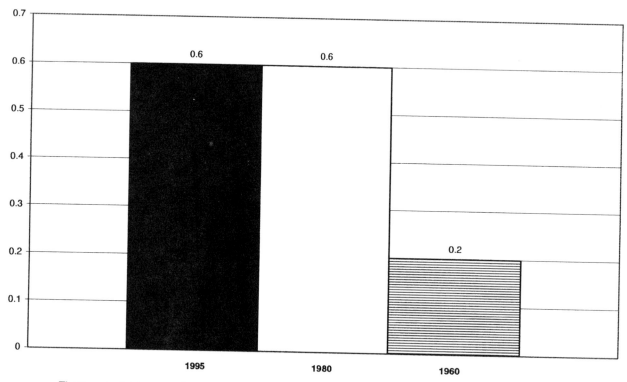

Rate of Physicians per 1,000 Persons

The impact of eight years of war with Iran (from 1980 to 1988), the Gulf War (1991), and international sanctions (1991–present) can be seen in stagnant or falling social indices, like the number of physicians per resident.

Secondary School Students

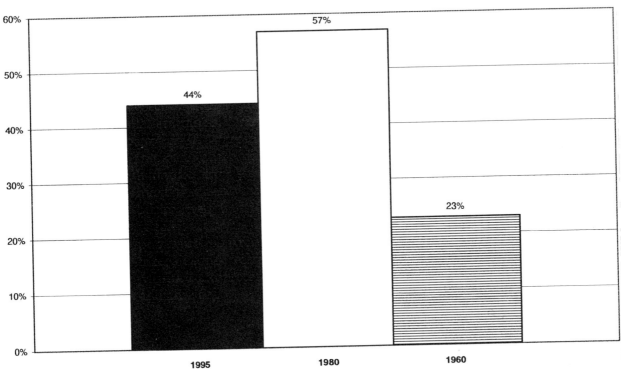

Another measure of the internationally perilous position of Iraq—and its impact on domestic social measures—can be seen in the continuing lack of educational opportunities.

CHRONOLOGY

1963	Baathist Party takes and loses power in a series of coups.
1968	Baathist Party, led by Saddam Hussein, retakes power.
1975	Government signs treaty with Iran, ceding territory in exchange for a halt in Iranian aid to Iraqi Kurd separatists.
1980	Iraq launches invasion of Iran, beginning eight-year war.
1987	Hussein government uses chemical weapons against Iranian troops and Kurdish civilians.
1988	Government signs truce with Iran, ending war with no discernible gains by either side.
1990	Hussein invades Kuwait.
1991	Allied coalition, led by United States, defeats Hussein, ousting Iraq from Kuwait; Kurds lead failed uprising; Allies establish economic sanctions againt Iraq and safe haven for Kurds.
1998	Obstruction of UN weapons inspectors leads to confrontation with United States; UN secretary-general defuses crisis.

	1995	1980	1965
GEOGRAPHY			
AREA (square miles/kilometers)	168,754/437,072		
LAND AREA (square miles/kilometers)	166,858/432,162		
COASTLINE (miles/kilometers)	36/58		

CITIES

		1995	1980	1965
CAPITAL				
MAJOR CITIES	Baghdad	n/a	3,841,268 (87)	n/a
	Diyala	n/a	961,073	n/a
	Al-Sulaimaniya	n/a	951,723	n/a
	Arbil	n/a	770,439	n/a
	Mosul	n/a	664,221	n/a

POPULATION

	1995	1980	1965
TOTAL	21,422,292	12,000,497 (77)	8,261,527
DENSITY (per square mile/kilometer)	122/47	96/37	49/19
ANNUAL GROWTH	3.7%	3.7%	3.1%
AGE COHORTS			
0–14	48%	n/a	45.5% (57)
15–64	49%	n/a	49% (57)
65 AND OVER	3%	n/a	5.1% (57)
MALE	51%		
FEMALE	49%		
URBAN	75%	68%	n/a
RURAL	25%	32%	n/a
NET MIGRATION RATE	0.4	n/a	0.3 (64)

IDENTITY

	1995	1980	1965
ETHNICITY			
ARAB	77%		
KURDISH	18%		
TURKOMAN, ASSYRIAN, OTHER	5%		
LANGUAGE			
ARABIC	n/a		
KURDISH	n/a		
ASSYRIAN	n/a		
ARMENIAN	n/a		

	1995	1980	1965
RELIGION			
SHI'A MUSLIM	62%		
SUNNI MUSLIM	35%		
CHRISTIAN, OTHER	3%		

VITAL STATISTICS

	1995	1980	1965
BIRTHS			
BIRTH RATE	43.1	44.4	n/a
INFANT MORTALITY RATE	60	77	n/a
LIFE EXPECTANCY AT BIRTH	67	62.4	n/a
MARRIAGES			
MARRIAGE RATE	8.6	8.5	n/a
AVERAGE AGE AT MARRIAGE M/F	n/a	26.3/22.3	n/a
DIVORCE RATE	0.1	0.1	n/a
DEATHS			
DEATH RATE	6.6	8.7	n/a

ECONOMICS AND LABOR

	1995	1980	1965
GDP PER CAPITA US$	2,000		
LABOR FORCE M/F			
AGRICULTURE	12/1%		
INDUSTRY	19/9%		
SERVICES	69/52%		

TRANSPORT

	1995	1980	1965
JOURNEYS (by transport mode)			
RAILROAD PASSENGER TRIPS (millions of miles/kilometers)	1,570 (88)		
AIR PASSENGER TRIPS (thousands)	53 (92)		
VEHICLES (thousands)			
PRIVATE CARS	672.4	237.1	62.9
COMMERCIAL	309.3	145.2	26

	1995	1980	1965

HEALTH AND HEALTH CARE

HEALTH CARE

	1995	1980	1965
ACCESS TO SAFE WATER	44%		
ACCESS TO SANITATION	87%		
MEASLES IMMUNIZATION	88%		
RATE OF PHYSICIANS	0.6	0.6	0.2 (60)
RATE OF HOSPITAL BEDS	1.7	1.9	1.8 (60)

HEALTH INDICATORS

	1995	1980	1965
PREGNANT WOMEN WITH ANEMIA	18%		
LOW-BIRTH-WEIGHT BABIES	15%		
CHILD MALNUTRITION	12%		
SMOKING PREVALENCE M/F	40/5%		
TUBERCULOSIS INCIDENCE RATE	1.5		
AIDS/HIV CASES	42	24 (93)	

EDUCATION

SCHOOL AGE IN SCHOOL

	1995	1980	1965
PRIMARY	90%	113%	72%
SECONDARY	44%	57%	23%
HIGHER	n/a	9%	3.5%

FEMALES IN SCHOOL

	1995	1980	1965
PRIMARY	85%	109%	65%
SECONDARY	39%	32%	11%
HIGHER	n/a	6.1%	2.4% (70)

ADULT ILLITERACY M/F	n/a	9.8/12.5% (85)	n/a

COMMUNICATIONS

	1995	1980	1965
RATE OF NEWSPAPERS	35	26	12 (63)
RATE OF RADIOS	217	161	85
RATE OF TELEVISIONS	75	50	18

Source: CIA, *The World Factbook, 1997;* ILO, *World Labour Report, 1997;* UN, *Demographic Yearbook, 1997;* UN, *Statistical Yearbook, 1996;* World Bank, *World Development Indicators, 1998.*

IRELAND

Ireland occupies about 85 percent of the island of Ireland between the Atlantic Ocean and the Irish Sea. Northern Ireland is located to the northeast of the 27,135-square-mile (70,280-square-kilometer) country. The United Kingdom is located to Ireland's east, across the Irish Sea. Ireland gained independence from the United Kingdom in December 1921. The country is a competitive multiparty democracy with a wide range of parties competing in a bicameral parliamentary system. Ireland has a modern, diversified, export-oriented economy dominated by manufacturing and agriculture. Though Ireland has one of the fastest-growing economies in the world, the country suffers from persistent unemployment. In 1995, the country's per capita gross domestic product (GDP) was $15,400. Because of a rapidly declining birth rate and a high rate of out-migration, the country's population of nearly 3.6 million is growing at a slow rate of 0.4 percent. Ireland has a life expectancy at birth of 75.6 years and an infant mortality rate of 6.4 deaths per 1,000 live births.

	1995	1980	1965
GEOGRAPHY			
AREA (square miles/kilometers)	27,135/70,280		
LAND AREA (square miles/kilometers)	26,598/68,890		
COASTLINE (miles/kilometers)	905/1,448		
CITIES			
CAPITAL	Dublin	533,929 (91)	
MAJOR CITY	Cork	127,253	
POPULATION			
TOTAL	3,566,833	3,443,405 (81)	2,880,752 (66)
DENSITY (per square mile/kilometer)	132/51	127/49	106/41
ANNUAL GROWTH	0.4%	0.9%	0.1%
AGE COHORTS			
0–14	23%	n/a	31.1% (61)
15–64	65%	n/a	61% (61)
65 AND OVER	12%	n/a	8.2% (61)
MALE	50%		
FEMALE	50%		

	1995	1980	1965
URBAN	58%	55.6%	
RURAL	42%	44.4%	
NET MIGRATION RATE	−6.5		

IDENTITY

ETHNICITY
CELTIC	n/a		
ENGLISH	n/a		

LANGUAGE
ENGLISH	n/a		
IRISH (Gaelic)	n/a		

RELIGION
ROMAN CATHOLIC	93%		
ANGLICAN	3%		
NONE	1%		

VITAL STATISTICS

BIRTHS
	1995	1980	1965
BIRTH RATE	13.2	18.2 (84)	21.6
URBAN BIRTH RATE	12.2 (91)		
RURAL BIRTH RATE	18.6 (91)		
INFANT MORTALITY RATE	6.4	10.1 (84)	24.9
LIFE EXPECTANCY AT BIRTH	75.6	72.7 (84)	70

MARRIAGES
	1995	1980	1965
MARRIAGE RATE	4.4	5.2 (84)	5.8
AVERAGE AGE AT MARRIAGE M/F	29.2/28		

DEATHS
	1995	1980	1965
DEATH RATE	8.9 (94)	9.1	12.1

HOUSEHOLDS

	1995	1980	1965
NUMBER	1,029,080 (91)	n/a	676,402 (61)
AVERAGE SIZE	3.3 (91)	n/a	4 (61)

TYPE OF HOUSEHOLD
SINGLE	19.2%		
MARRIED	63.0%		

	1995	1980	1965
WIDOWED	13.7%		
DIVORCED/SEPARATED	4.1%		
FEMALE HEADED	26.3%		

ECONOMICS AND LABOR

	1995	1980	1965
GDP PER CAPITA US$	$15,400		
LABOR FORCE M/F (thousands)	748.1/377.0 (91)		
AGRICULTURE	141.9/12.3		
MINING	6.1/0.5		
MANUFACTURING	157.8/63.4		
UTILITIES	12.5/1.5		
CONSTRUCTION	76.3/3.5		
TRADE/FOOD/TOURISM	113.9/85.7		
TRANSPORT/COMMUNICATIONS	52.3/12.9		
FINANCE/INSURANCE/REAL ESTATE	51.0/43.5		
SOCIAL AND PERSONAL SERVICES	133.7/151.3		
UNEMPLOYMENT (official)	19% (91)		
UNION DENSITY	36%		

TRANSPORT

	1995	1980	1965
JOURNEYS (by transport mode)			
RAILROAD PASSENGER TRIPS	1,102 (94)		
(millions of miles/kilometers)			
AIR PASSENGER TRIPS (thousands)	4,826 (94)		
VEHICLES (thousands)			
PRIVATE CARS	947.2	738.1	284.9
COMMERCIAL	143.9	70.1	51.1

HEALTH AND HEALTH CARE

	1995	1980	1965
HEALTH CARE			
ACCESS TO SANITATION	100%		
RATE OF PHYSICIANS	2	1.3	1 (60)
RATE OF HOSPITAL BEDS	5	9.7	15.2 (60)
HEALTH INDICATORS			
LOW-BIRTH-WEIGHT BABIES	4%		
SMOKING PREVALENCE M/F	29/28%		

	1995	1980	1965
TUBERCULOSIS INCIDENCE RATE	0.18		
AIDS/HIV CASES	511	418 (43)	
TOTAL DEATHS	31,494		

EDUCATION

SCHOOL AGE IN SCHOOL

	1995	1980	1965
PRIMARY	104%	100%	105%
SECONDARY	114%	90%	40%
HIGHER	37%	18%	7.6%

FEMALES IN SCHOOL

	1995	1980	1965
PRIMARY	103%	99%	106%
SECONDARY	114%	91%	44%
HIGHER	n/a	17.20%	9.4% (70)

COMMUNICATIONS

	1995	1980	1965
RATE OF NEWSPAPERS	186	229	246
RATE OF RADIOS	636	375	212
RATE OF TELEVISIONS	301	231	114

Source: CIA, *The World Factbook, 1997;* ILO, *World Labour Report, 1997;* UN, *Demographic Yearbook, 1997;* UN, *Statistical Yearbook, 1996;* World Bank, *World Development Indicators, 1998.*

ISRAEL

Israel is located in Southwest Asia on the Mediterranean Sea within borders disputed by regional states and the international community. In 1948, the country gained independence from the United Kingdom. Israel has occupied the territory of bordering states following the 1967 Arab-Israeli war, including most of the West Bank and part of the Gaza Strip (claimed by the Palestine Authority) and the Golan Heights (claimed by Syria). In 1979, Israel withdrew from the Sinai Peninsula, captured from Egypt in 1967. The country's internationally recognized boundaries encompass a 8,019-square-mile (20,770-square kilometer) area that extends from Lebanon on the north to the Gulf of Aqaba on the south. Although the status of the West Bank is under negotiation with the Palestine Authority, the Israeli government continues to sanction the expansion of Jewish settlement of the territory. The country is the most economically and technologically advanced in the region, with a 1995 per capita gross domestic product (GDP) of $15,500. Despite Israel's modernity (which tends to produce population stabilization) the country's population of more than 5.4 million is growing faster than Egypt, in part due to a high rate of in-migration and a high birth rate by Western standards. Jews represent a population majority of 82 percent, but only but 50 percent of the Jewish population is native born. Arabs account for 18 percent of the population. Millions of Palestinian refugees from within Israel's 1948 boundaries and the Occupied Territories are scattered throughout the region. The country has an average life expectancy at birth of 78 years and an infant mortality rate of 8.5 deaths per 1,000 live births.

Urban Population

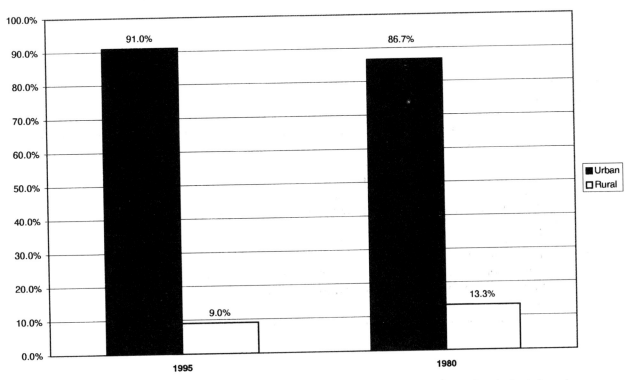

Although many of Israel's Zionist founders hoped that the new society would be rooted in the land, through farming and rural living, most citizens have always lived in urban areas.

Percentage of Students in Higher Education

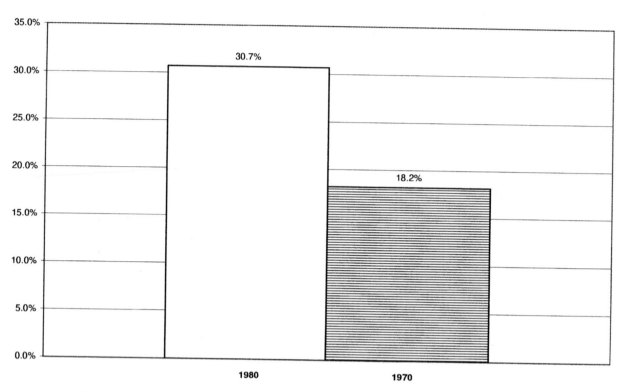

Israel has increasingly become one of the high-tech hubs of the world, a development that has much to do with the country's extensive system of higher education and large number of university students and graduates.

CHRONOLOGY

1967 Israel decisively defeats Arab countries in war; occupies Sinai, West Bank, East Jerusalem, and Gaza.
1973 Israel fights Arab countries to draw.
1977 Conservative Likud Party takes power for first time.
1978 Prime Minister Menachem Begin signs peace treaty with Egypt.
1982 Israel launches second invasion of Lebanon in effort to destroy Palestine Liberation Organization.
1987 Palestinian uprising, known as *intifada,* begins.
1992 Labor Party returns to power.
1993 Labor government signs accords with PLO, recognizing it for first time.
1996 Likud Party returns to power under Binyamin Netanyahu, vowing to go slower on peace process.

	1995[1]	1980[1]	1965

GEOGRAPHY

AREA (square miles/kilometers)	8,019/20,770		
LAND AREA (square miles/kilometers)	7,849/20,330		
COASTLINE (miles/kilometers)	171/273		

CITIES

CAPITAL	Jerusalem	573,000 (94)
MAJOR CITIES	Tel Aviv-Yafo	356,300
	Haifa	246,600
	Holon	163,300
	Rishon Leziyyon	157,200

POPULATION

	1995[1]	1980[1]	1965
TOTAL	5,421,995	4,037,620 (83)	2,183,332 (61)
DENSITY (per square mile/kilometer)	681/263	528/204	329/127
ANNUAL GROWTH	2.1%	1.8%	3.5%
AGE COHORTS			
0–14	29%	n/a	35%
15–64	62%	n/a	59%
65 AND OVER	9%	n/a	6%
MALE	50%		
FEMALE	50%		
URBAN	91%	86.7%	n/a
RURAL	9%	13.3%	n/a
NET MIGRATION RATE	7.0	n/a	8.4 (64)

IDENTITY

	1995[1]		
ETHNICITY			
JEWISH	82%		
ARAB	18%		
LANGUAGE			
HEBREW	n/a		
ARAB	n/a		
ENGLISH	n/a		

	1995¹	1980¹	1965
RELIGION			
JUDAISM	82%		
ISLAM	14%		
CHRISTIAN	2%		
DRUZE, OTHER	2%		

VITAL STATISTICS

	1995¹	1980¹	1965
BIRTHS			
BIRTH RATE	20.3	23.7 (84)	22.6
URBAN BIRTH RATE	20.9 (94)		
RURAL BIRTH RATE	23.9 (94)		
INFANT MORTALITY RATE	8.5	12.8 (84)	22.7
ABORTION RATE	153.3 (93)		
LIFE EXPECTANCY AT BIRTH	78	74.8 (84)	71.3
MARRIAGES			
MARRIAGE RATE	6.5	7.2 (84)	8
AVERAGE AGE AT MARRIAGE M/F	27.5/24.3		
DIVORCE RATE	1.4	1.2 (84)	1
DEATHS			
DEATH RATE	6.3	6.7 (84)	6.4

HOUSEHOLDS

	1995¹	1980¹	1965
NUMBER	n/a	n/a	594,800 (63)
AVERAGE SIZE	n/a	n/a	3.8 (63)

ECONOMICS AND LABOR

	1995¹
GDP PER CAPITA US$	15,500
LABOR FORCE (M/F) (thousands)	1,090.3/781.1 (94)
AGRICULTURE	48.3/14.0
MINING	
MANUFACTURING	285.4/110.7
UTILITIES	17.1/3.2
CONSTRUCTION	111.5/6.5
TRADE/FOOD/TOURISM	162.2/118.6
TRANSPORT/COMMUNICATIONS	83.8/25.2
FINANCE/INSURANCE/REAL ESTATE	111.2/95.2
SOCIAL AND PERSONAL SERVICES	262.3/405.0

	1995[1]	1980[1]	1965
UNEMPLOYMENT (official)	7.8% (94)		
UNION DENSITY	23.1%		

TRANSPORT

JOURNEYS (by transport mode)			
RAILROAD PASSENGER TRIPS	238.0 (94)		
(millions of miles/kilometers)			
AIR PASSENGER TRIPS (thousands)	2,980.0 (94)		
VEHICLES (thousands)			
PRIVATE CARS	1,057	409.5	75.7
COMMERCIAL	251.7	89	40

HEALTH AND HEALTH CARE

HEALTH CARE			
ACCESS TO SAFE WATER	99%		
ACCESS TO SANITATION	70%		
MEASLES IMMUNIZATION	94%		
RATE OF PHYSICIANS	n/a	2.5	2.5 (60)
RATE OF HOSPITAL BEDS	6	5.1	6.8 (60)
HEALTH INDICATORS			
SMOKING PREVALENCE M/F	45/30%		
TUBERCULOSIS INCIDENCE RATE	0.12		
AIDS/HIV CASES	372	293 (93)	
TOTAL DEATHS	35,117		

EDUCATION

SCHOOL AGE IN SCHOOL			
PRIMARY	99%	95%	96%
SECONDARY	89%	73%	48%
HIGHER	41%	29%	14%
FEMALES IN SCHOOL			
PRIMARY	98%	94%	95%
SECONDARY	53%	56%	51%
HIGHER	n/a	30.70%	18.2% (70)
ADULT ILLITERACY M/F	n/a	5.0/11.3% (83)	n/a

	1995[1]	1980[1]	1965
COMMUNICATIONS			
RATE OF NEWSPAPERS	246	260	202 (70)
RATE OF RADIOS	478	245	273
RATE OF TELEVISIONS	272	232	7

FOOTNOTE

1. Statistics are for Israel proper only; they do not include the Occupied Territories.

Source: CIA, The World Factbook, 1997; ILO, World Labour Report, 1997; UN, Demographic Yearbook, 1997; UN, Statistical Yearbook, 1996; World Bank, World Development Indicators, 1998.

ITALY

Italy is located in southern Europe on a peninsula bordering the Adriatic Sea, Ionian Sea, Mediterranean Sea, and Tyrrhenian Sea. The country also includes Sicily and Sardinia, two large adjacent islands. Austria and Slovenia border the 116,305-square-mile (301,230-square-kilometer) country on the northeast, and France and Switzerland on the northwest. Tunisia, on the North African coast, lies across the Mediterranean from Sicily. The country is a multiparty democracy that, since World War II, has endured extensive political instability. In 1996, Italians elected the first left-leaning government under a coalition known as the Olive Tree. Since taking office, however, the new government has imposed an economic austerity program and reduced social benefits to conform to the demands for integration in the European Monetary Union. Though Italy as a whole has a high standard of living, the country is divided between a highly industrial north and a less-developed south. The country's 1995 population of nearly 57.5 million was growing at a very slow pace of 0.1 percent, owing to a declining birth rate. The country has a life expectancy at birth of 78.1 years and an infant mortality rate of 6.9 deaths per 1,000 live births.

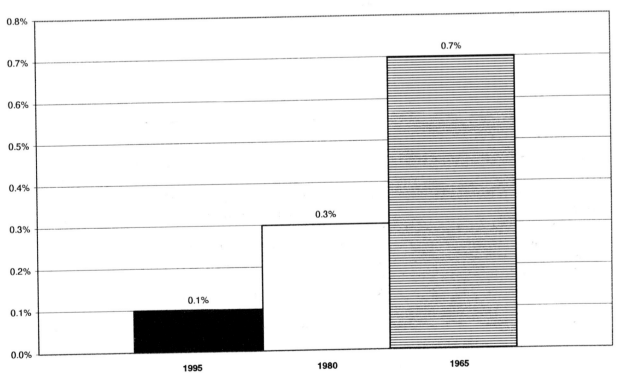

Annual Population Growth Rate

Like many Western European countries, Italy has seen its annual growth rate drop to near zero. Indeed, deaths now outnumber births, and the population's slight growth is due entirely to immigration.

Age Distribution

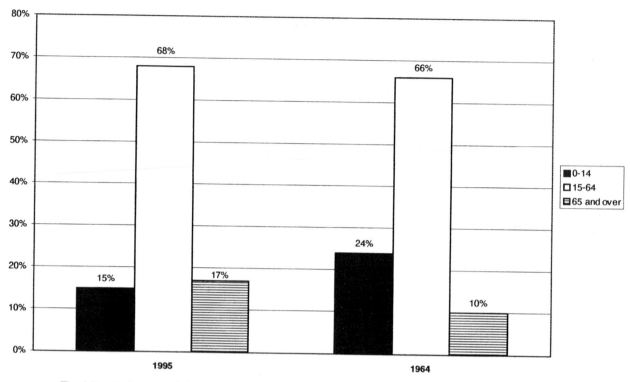

The falling birth rate in Italy can be reflected in the population's age profile. Like most other industrialized countries, Italy is becoming increasingly elderly, a trend that concerns many economists, who wonder how a large population of retired persons will be supported by a shrinking number of working-age people.

CHRONOLOGY

1966   Italy hurt by worst floods in centuries; hundreds die; precious artworks destroyed.

1971   Worst recession since World War II sets off nationwide strikes.

1978   Former prime minister Aldo Moro kidnapped and assassinated by left-wing terrorists.

1981   Corruption scandal leads to overthrow of Christian Democrats; Benito Craxi becomes first Socialist prime minister in Italy's postwar history.

1986   Major government campaign against Mafia in southern Italy begins.

1989   Major banking scandal rocks Italian government and business community.

1994   Silvio Berlusconi, a media mogul, leads his Forza Italia Party to victory in elections, as voters grow disgusted with corruption in government; personal corruption leads to his fall at end of year.

	1995	1980	1965

GEOGRAPHY

AREA (square miles/kilometers)	116,305/301,230		
LAND AREA (square miles/kilometers)	113,521/294,020		
COASTLINE (miles/kilometers)	4,750/7,600		

CITIES				
CAPITAL	Rome	2,693,383 (91)		
MAJOR CITIES	Milan	1,371,008		
	Naples	1,054,601		
	Turin	961,916		
	Palermo	697,162		

POPULATION

	1995	1980	1965
TOTAL	57,460,274	56,556,911 (81)	49,903,878 (61)
DENSITY (per square mile/kilometer)	492/190	483/186	445/172
ANNUAL GROWTH	0.1%	0.3%	0.7%

AGE COHORTS			
0–14	15%	n/a	23.8% (64)
15–64	68%	n/a	66% (64)
65 AND OVER	17%	n/a	9.7% (64)

URBAN	67%		
RURAL	33%		

NET MIGRATION RATE	1.25	n/a	−0.1

IDENTITY

ETHNICITY			
ITALIAN	n/a		
SICILIAN	n/a		
SARDINIAN	n/a		

LANGUAGE			
ITALIAN	n/a		
GERMAN	n/a		
FRENCH	n/a		
SLOVENE	n/a		

	1995	1980	1965
RELIGION			
ROMAN CATHOLIC	98%		
OTHER	2%		

VITAL STATISTICS

BIRTHS			
BIRTH RATE	9.9	10.1 (85)	18.9
INFANT MORTALITY RATE	6.9	10.9 (85)	35.6
LIFE EXPECTANCY AT BIRTH	78.1	73.9 (85)	69.7
MARRIAGES			
MARRIAGE RATE	5	5.2	7.4
DIVORCE RATE	0.4	0.3	n/a
DEATHS			
DEATH RATE	9.8	9.5	9.5

HOUSEHOLDS

NUMBER	13,681,568 (61)
AVERAGE SIZE	3.6 (61)

ECONOMICS AND LABOR

GDP PER CAPITA US$	$18,700
LABOR FORCE M/F (thousands)	12,972.0/7,030 (94)
AGRICULTURE	998/574
MINING	267/27
MANUFACTURING	3,120/1,421
UTILITIES	
CONSTRUCTION	1,554/88
TRADE/FOOD/TOURISM	2,663/1,557
TRANSPORT/COMMUNICATIONS	914/168
FINANCE/INSURANCE/REAL ESTATE	959/557
SOCIAL AND PERSONAL SERVICES	2,496/2,638
UNEMPLOYMENT (official)	11.3% (94)
UNION DENSITY	30.6%

	1995	1980	1965

TRANSPORT

JOURNEYS (by transport mode)
RAILROAD PASSENGER TRIPS — 47,101.0 (93)
  (millions of miles/kilometers)
AIR PASSENGER TRIPS (thousands) — 22,933.0 (94)

VEHICLES (thousands)

	1995	1980	1965
PRIVATE CARS	29,600	17,686.2	5,469
COMMERCIAL	2,745.5	1,691.2	665.8

HEALTH AND HEALTH CARE

HEALTH CARE

	1995	1980	1965
ACCESS TO SAFE WATER	n/a	99%	n/a
ACCESS TO SANITATION	100%		
MEASLES IMMUNIZATION	50%		
RATE OF PHYSICIANS	1.7	1.3	1.6 (60)
RATE OF HOSPITAL BEDS	6.5	n/a	9.1 (60)

HEALTH INDICATORS

	1995	1980
LOW-BIRTH-WEIGHT BABIES	7%	
SMOKING PREVALENCE M/F	38/26%	
TUBERCULOSIS INCIDENCE RATE	0.25	
AIDS/HIV CASES	32,624	21,928 (93)
TOTAL DEATHS	548,081 (94)	

EDUCATION

SCHOOL AGE IN SCHOOL

	1995	1980	1965
PRIMARY	98%	100%	109%
SECONDARY	74%	72%	47%
HIGHER	41%	27%	5.8%

FEMALES IN SCHOOL

	1995	1980	1965
PRIMARY	97%	99%	107%
SECONDARY	74%	70%	42%

	1995	1980	1965
ADULT ILLITERACY M/F	n/a	n/a	7.3/11.2% (61)

	1995	1980	1965
COMMUNICATIONS			
RATE OF NEWSPAPERS	106	85	113
RATE OF RADIOS	802	602	215
RATE OF TELEVISIONS	429	390	121

Source: CIA, The World Factbook, 1997; ILO, World Labour Report, 1997; UN, Demographic Yearbook, 1997; UN, Statistical Yearbook, 1996; World Bank, World Development Indicators, 1998.